Peach Girl™
Change of Heart

by Miwa Ueda

7

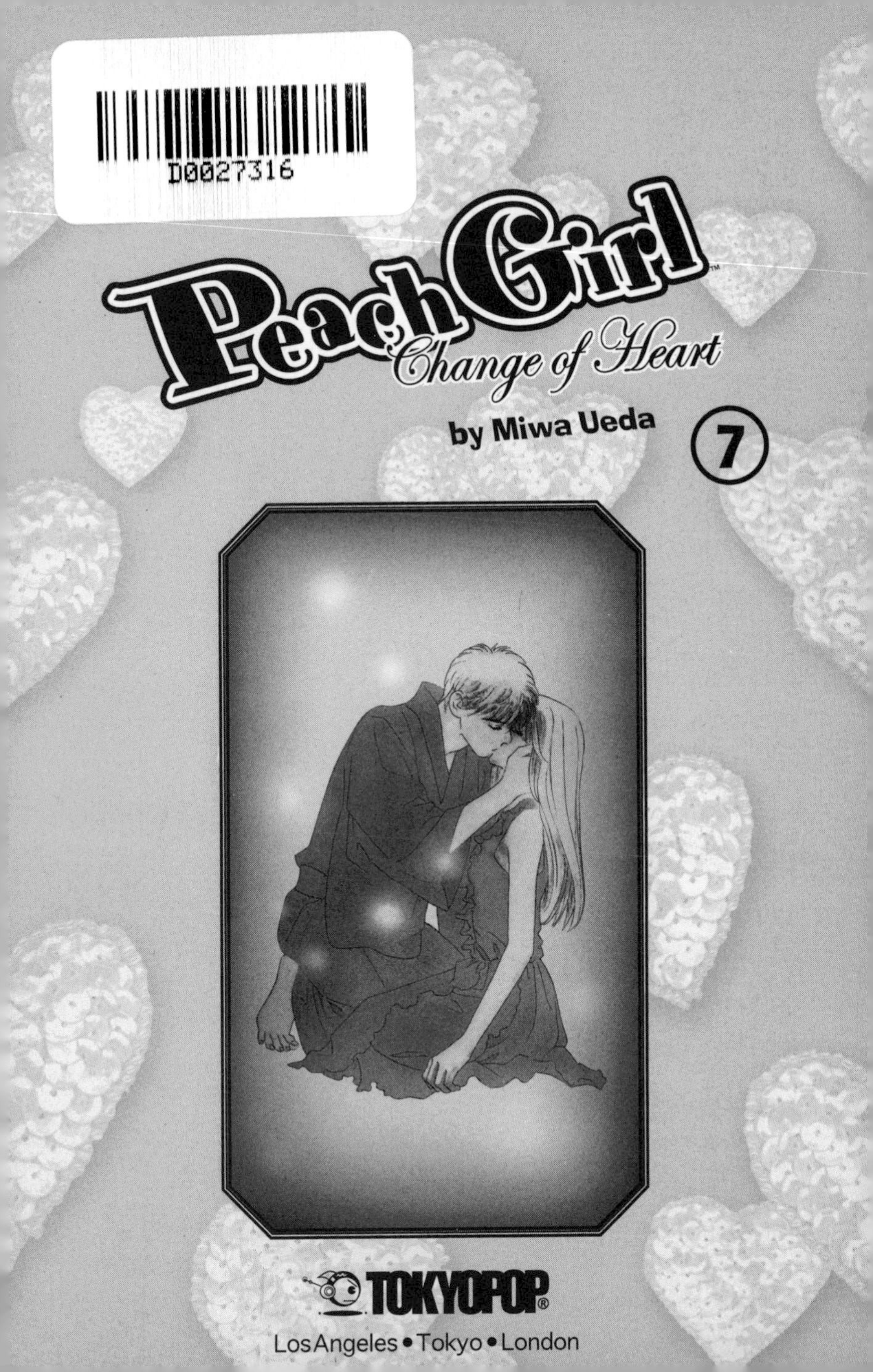

TOKYOPOP®

Los Angeles • Tokyo • London

ALSO AVAILABLE FROM 🔵 TOKYOPOP®

REBIRTH
REBOUND
REMOTE
RISING STARS OF MANGA
SABER MARIONETTE J
SAILOR MOON
SAINT TAIL
SAMURAI DEEPER KYO
SAMURAI GIRL REAL BOUT HIGH SCHOOL
SCRYED
SEIKAI TRILOGY, THE CREST OF THE STARS
SGT. FROG
SHAOLIN SISTERS
SHIRAHIME-SYO: SNOW GODDESS TALES
SHUTTERBOX
SKULL MAN, THE
SNOW DROP
SORCERER HUNTERS
STONE
SUIKODEN III
SUKI
TOKYO BABYLON
TOKYO MEW MEW
UNDER THE GLASS MOON
VAMPIRE GAME
VISION OF ESCAFLOWNE, THE
WILD ACT
WISH
WORLD OF HARTZ
X-DAY
ZODIAC P.I.

NOVELS
KARMA CLUB
SAILOR MOON

ART BOOKS
CARDCAPTOR SAKURA
CLAMP NORTHSIDE
CLAMP SOUTHSIDE
MAGIC KNIGHT RAYEARTH
PEACH: MIWA UEDA ILLUSTRATIONS

ANIME GUIDES
COWBOY BEBOP ANIME GUIDES
GUNDAM TECHNICAL MANUALS
SAILOR MOON SCOUT GUIDES

TOKYOPOP KIDS
STRAY SHEEP

CINE-MANGA™

ASTRO BOY
CARDCAPTORS
DUEL MASTERS
FAIRLY ODDPARENTS, THE
FINDING NEMO
G.I. JOE SPY TROOPS
JACKIE CHAN ADVENTURES
JIMMY NEUTRON BOY GENIUS, THE ADVENTURES OF
KIM POSSIBLE
LILO & STITCH
LIZZIE MCGUIRE
LIZZIE MCGUIRE: THE MOVIE
MALCOLM IN THE MIDDLE
POWER RANGERS: NINJA STORM
SHREK 2
SPONGEBOB SQUAREPANTS
SPY KIDS 2
SPY KIDS 3-D: GAME OVER
TEENAGE MUTANT NINJA TURTLES
THAT'S SO RAVEN
TRANSFORMERS: ARMADA
TRANSFORMERS: ENERGON

**For more
information visit
www.TOKYOPOP.com**

12.20.03T

ALSO AVAILABLE FROM 🐱 TOKYOPOP®

MANGA

.HACK//LEGEND OF THE TWILIGHT
@LARGE
ABENOBASHI
A.I. LOVE YOU
AI YORI AOSHI
ANGELIC LAYER
ARM OF KANNON
BABY BIRTH
BATTLE ROYALE
BATTLE VIXENS
BRAIN POWERED
BRIGADOON
B'TX
CANDIDATE FOR GODDESS, THE
CARDCAPTOR SAKURA
CARDCAPTOR SAKURA - MASTER OF THE CLOW

CHOBITS
CHRONICLES OF THE CURSED SWORD
CLAMP SCHOOL DETECTIVES
CLOVER
COMIC PARTY
CONFIDENTIAL CONFESSIONS
CORRECTOR YUI
COWBOY BEBOP
COWBOY BEBOP: SHOOTING STAR
CRESCENT MOON
CULDCEPT
CYBORG 009
D.N. ANGEL
DEMON DIARY
DEMON ORORON, THE
DEUS VITAE
DIGIMON
DIGIMON ZERO TWO
DIGIMON TAMERS
DOLL
DRAGON HUNTER
DRAGON KNIGHTS
DREAM SAGA
DUKLYON: CLAMP SCHOOL DEFENDERS
ERICA SAKURAZAWA COLLECTED WORKS
EERIE QUEERIE!
ET CETERA
ETERNITY
EVIL'S RETURN
FAERIES' LANDING
FAKE
FLCL
FORBIDDEN DANCE
FRUITS BASKET
G GUNDAM

GATE KEEPERS
GETBACKERS
GIRL GOT GAME
GRAVITATION
GTO
GUNDAM SEED ASTRAY
GUNDAM WING
GUNDAM WING: BATTLEFIELD OF PACIFISTS
GUNDAM WING: ENDLESS WALTZ
GUNDAM WING: THE LAST OUTPOST (G-UNIT)
HAPPY MANIA
HARLEM BEAT
I.N.V.U.
IMMORTAL RAIN
INITIAL D
ISLAND
JING: KING OF BANDITS
JULINE
KARE KANO
KILL ME, KISS ME
KINDAICHI CASE FILES, THE
KING OF HELL
KODOCHA: SANA'S STAGE
LAMENT OF THE LAMB
LES BIJOUX
LEGEND OF CHUN HYANG, THE
LOVE HINA
LUPIN III
MAGIC KNIGHT RAYEARTH I
MAGIC KNIGHT RAYEARTH II
MAHOROMATIC: AUTOMATIC MAIDEN
MAN OF MANY FACES
MARMALADE BOY
MARS
MINK
MIRACLE GIRLS
MIYUKI-CHAN IN WONDERLAND
MODEL
ONE
PARADISE KISS
PARASYTE
PEACH GIRL
PEACH GIRL: CHANGE OF HEART
PET SHOP OF HORRORS
PITA-TEN
PLANET LADDER
PLANETES
PRIEST
PRINCESS AI
PSYCHIC ACADEMY
RAGNAROK
RAVE MASTER
REALITY CHECK

12.20.03T

Translator - Ray Yoshimoto
English Adaptation - Jodi Bryson
Retouch and Lettering - Jennifer Nunn-Iwai
Cover Layout - Anna Kernbaum

Editor - Nora Wong
Managing Editor - Jill Freshney
Production Coordinator - Antonio DePietro
Production Managers - Jennifer Miller, Mutsumi Miyazaki
Art Director - Matt Alford
Editorial Director - Jeremy Ross
VP of Production - Ron Klamert
President & C.O.O. - John Parker
Publisher & C.E.O. - Stuart Levy

E-mail: editor@TOKYOPOP.com

Come visit us online at www.TOKYOPOP.com

A  TOKYOPOP® Manga

TOKYOPOP Inc.
5900 Wilshire Blvd. Suite 2000
Los Angeles, CA 90036

PEACH GIRL: CHANGE OF HEART VOL. 7

ISBN: 1-59182-496-6

First TOKYOPOP printing: March 2004

10 9 8 7 6 5 4 3 2 1

Printed in the USA

ピーチガール

15

HEY PEACH GIRL FANS!

Keep those fan art and letters coming 'cause we might just publish 'em! We love hearing from you so write me, okay?

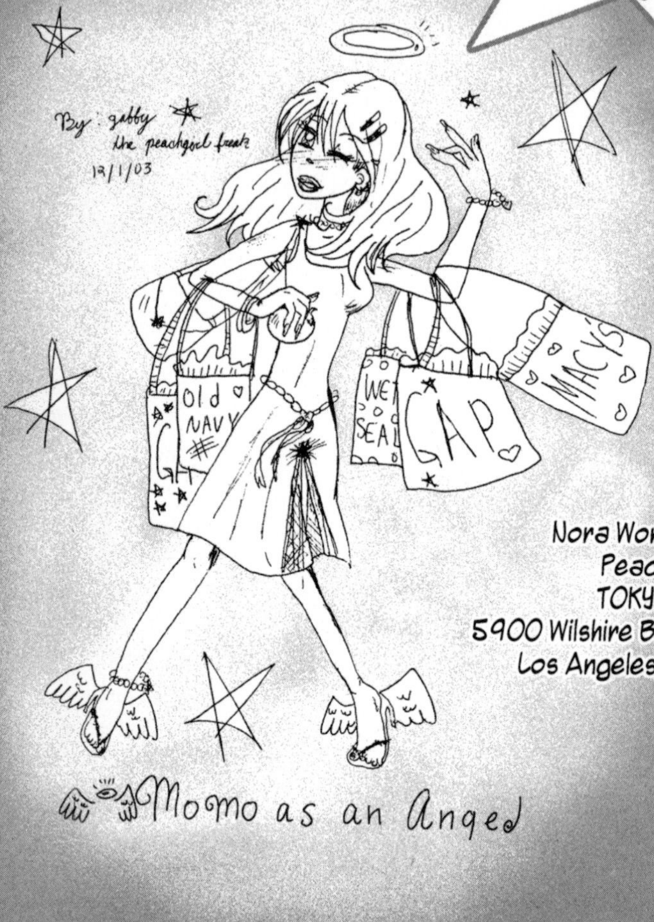

By: gabby
the peachgirl freak
12/1/03
Old
NAVY
WET
SEAL
GAP
MACY'S
Momo as an Angel

Nora Wong, Editor
Peach Girl
TOKYOPOP
5900 Wilshire Blvd., Suite 2000
Los Angeles, CA 90036

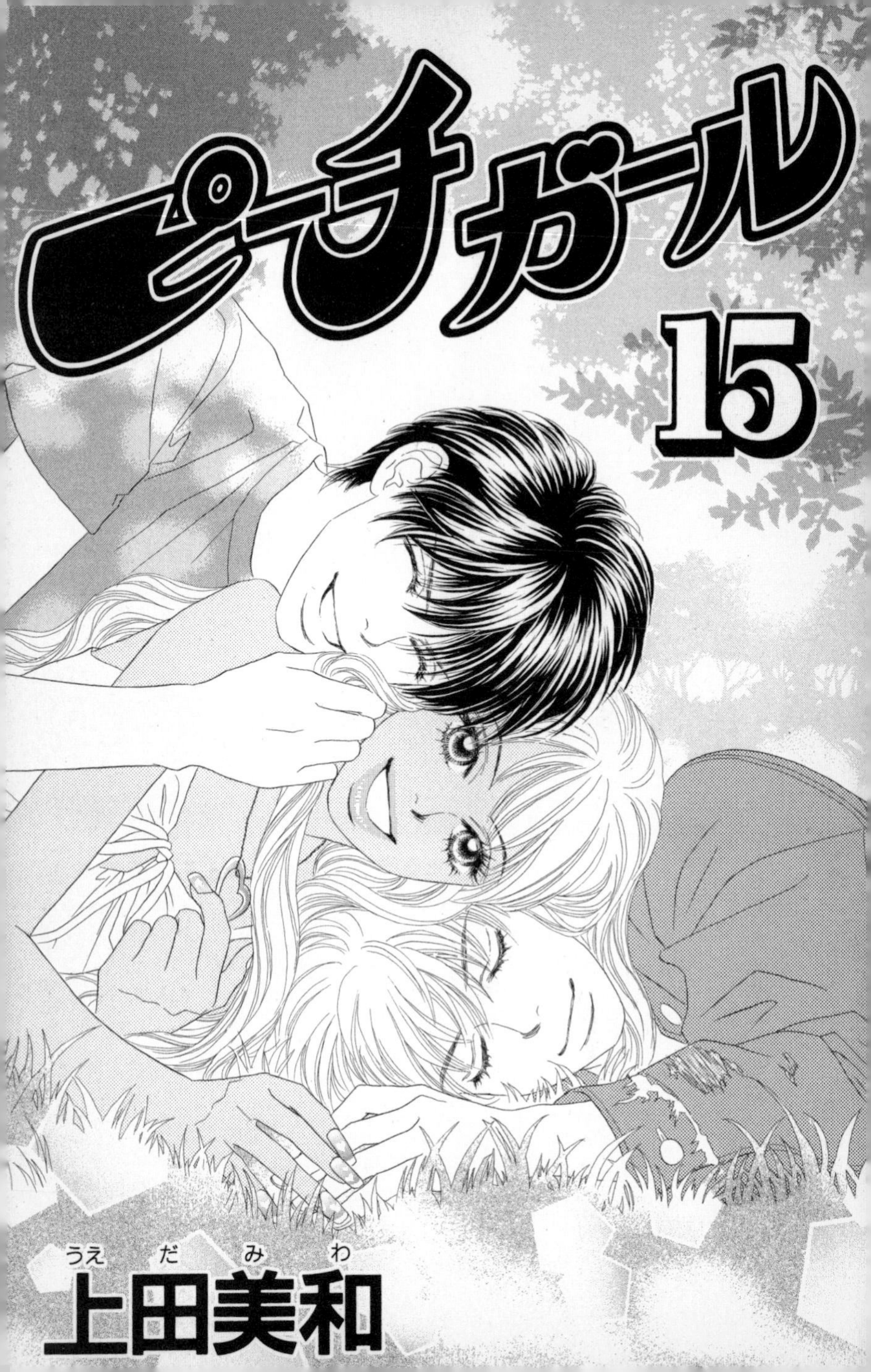
ピーチガール
15
うえだみわ
上田美和

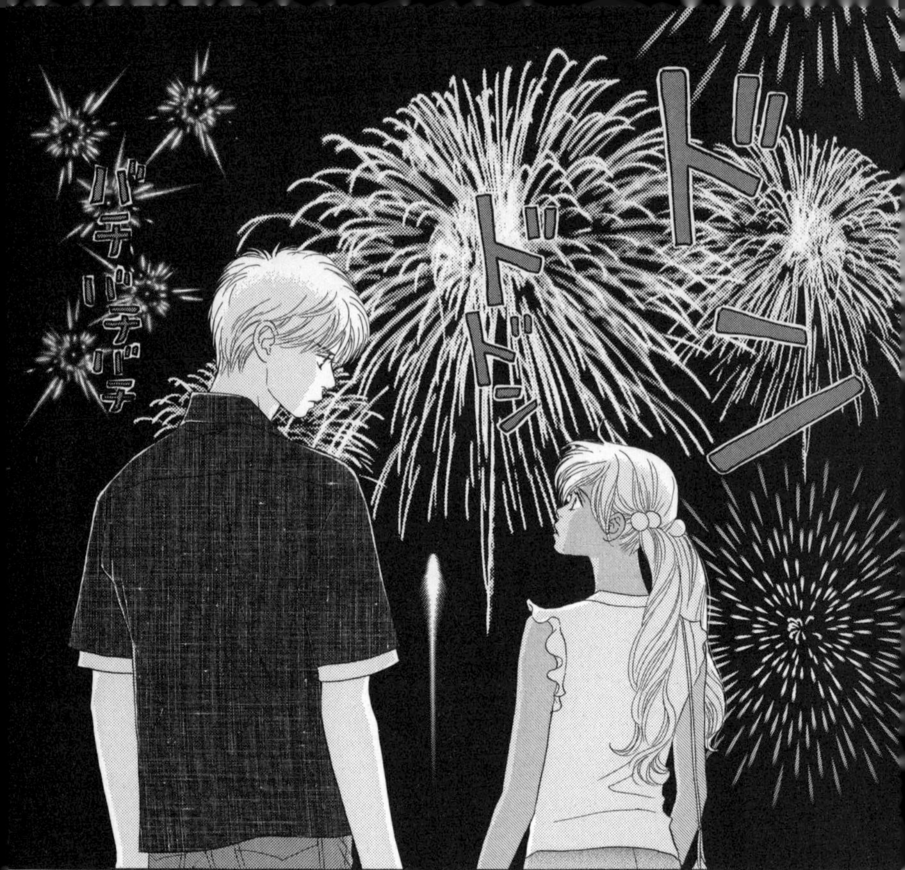
ドーン
ドドーン
バチバチバチ

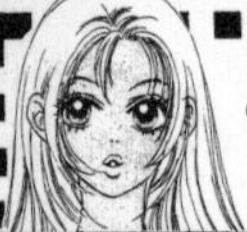

MOMO ADACHI: Currently dating Kiley. But now realizes Kiley's true love is Misao?!

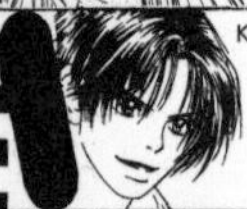

KILEY OKAYASU: Momo's boyfriend. He declares his love for Misao, but is rejected. Currently bunking down in a soba restaurant during his trip.

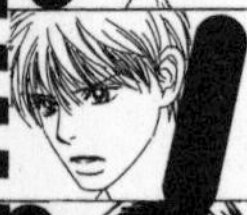

TOJI TOJIKAMORI: Momo's ex-boyfriend. Sae blackmailed him into dumping Momo for her.

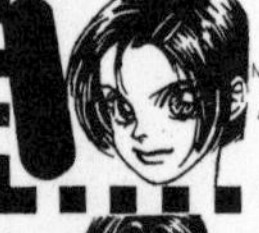

SAE KASHIWAGI: Momo's sworn enemy. Obsessed with Ryo and currently trying to break up Momo and Kiley.

MOMO vs. SAE

The Death Match and the Aftermath...

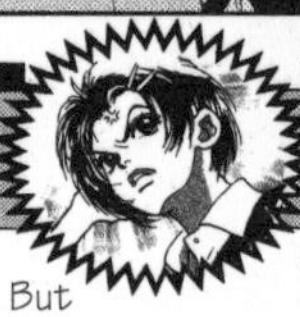

Momo and Toji were happily in love. But Sae, who always covets what Momo has, engineers their breakup. Momo eventually bounces back when she falls in love with Kiley, only to discover that his one true love is actually Misao!! But Misao sadly rejects Kiley after he tries to settle the issue by admitting his feelings for her. In desperate need of some soul searching, Kiley takes some time off and goes on the road. Meanwhile, Toji ends up working at the convenience store with Momo (talk about an awkward situation!). Sparks fly during the fireworks festival when Toji asks Momo if things don't work out between her and Kiley, is there any chance of getting back together again?!

Everything you need to know.

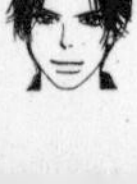

RYO: Kiley's older brother. Game designer. Has conquered Sae and mooching off her.

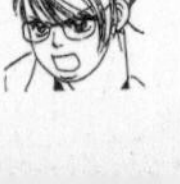

MISAO: The school nurse. Formerly Kiley's tutor, now in love with Ryo.

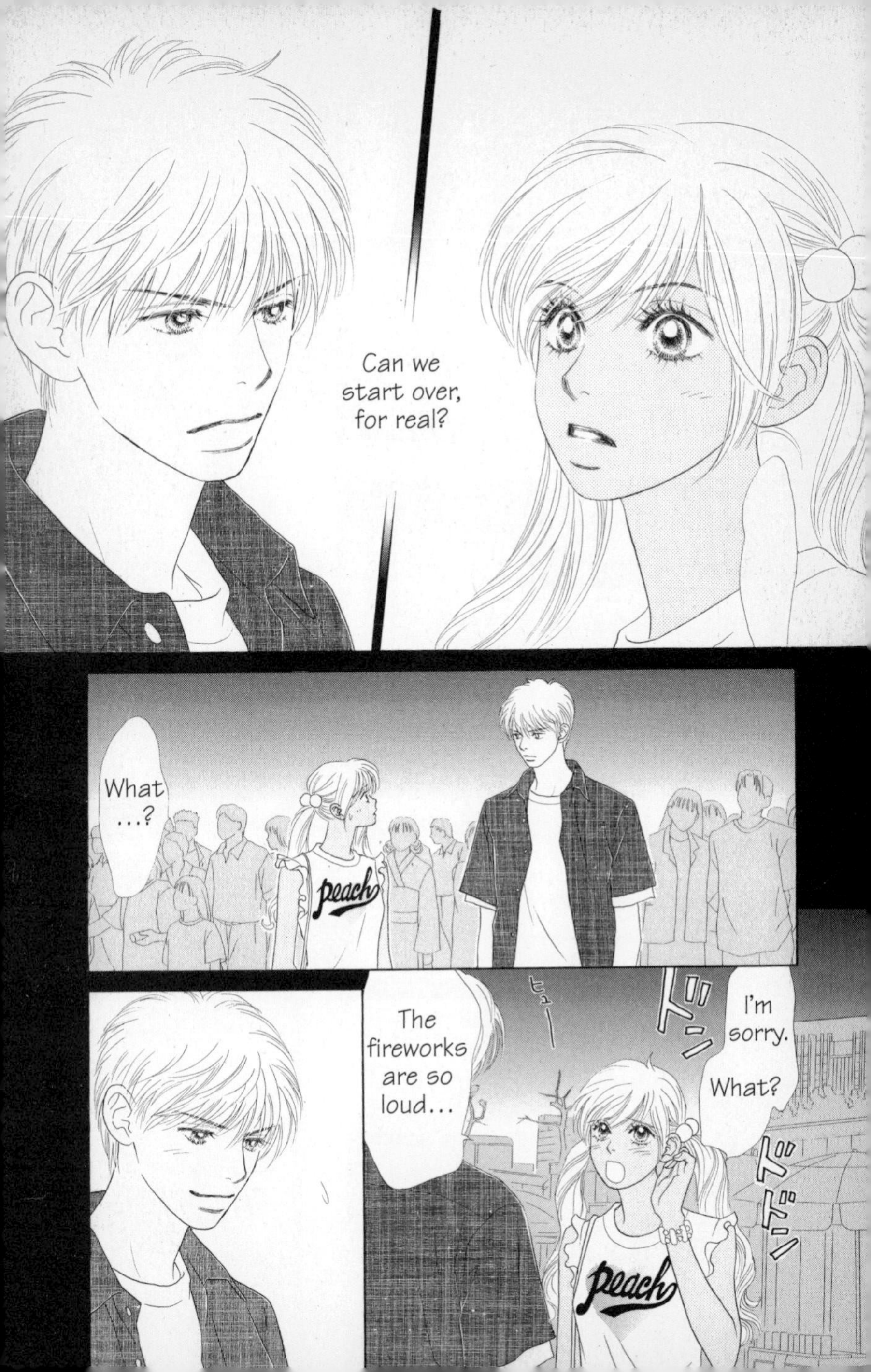
Can we start over, for real?
What ...?
ヒュー
ドン
I'm sorry.
What?
ドン ドン
The fireworks are so loud...

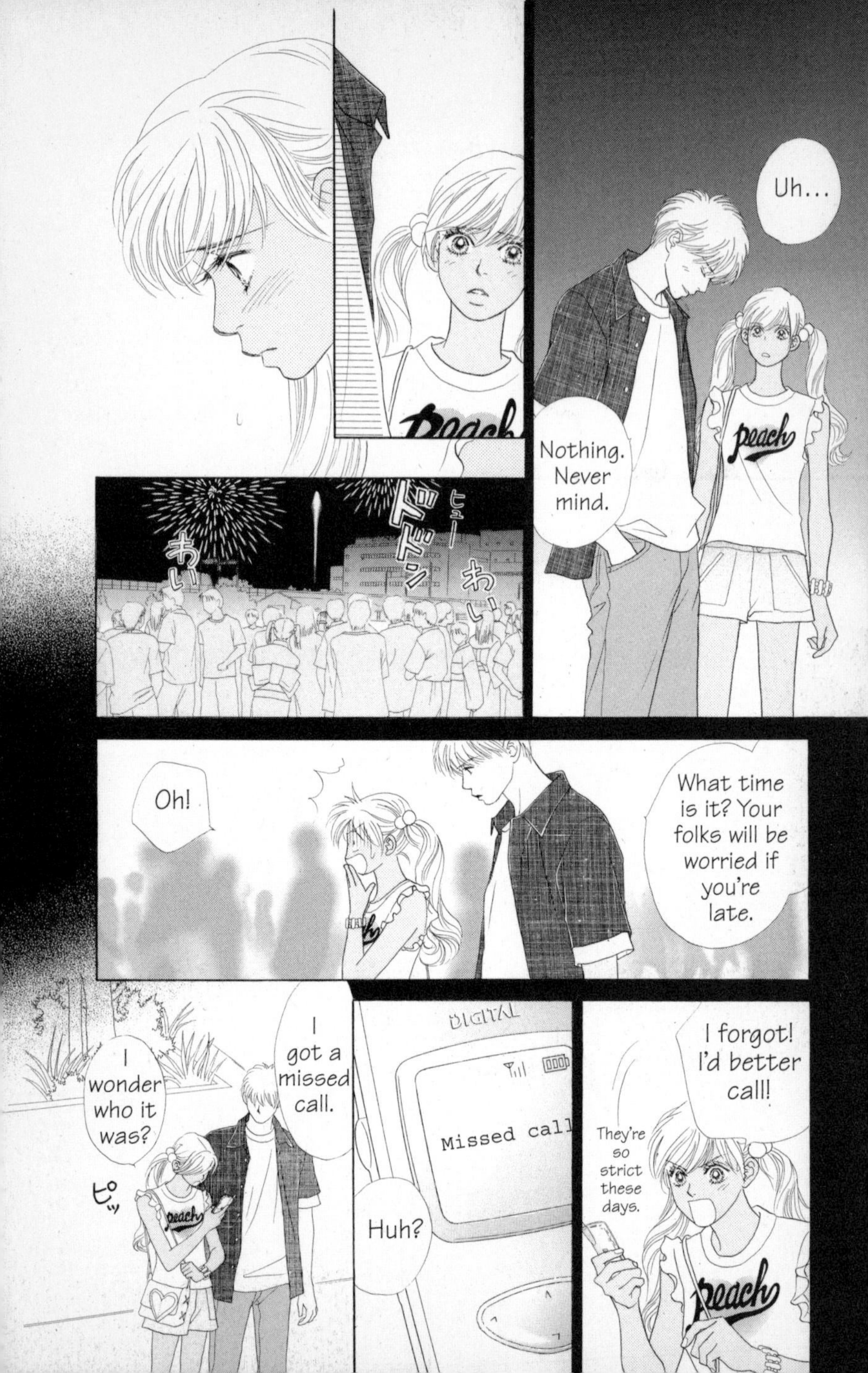
Uh...
Nothing. Never mind.
ヒュー
ドドン
わい
わい
What time is it? Your folks will be worried if you're late.
Oh!
I forgot! I'd better call!
They're so strict these days.
DIGITAL
Missed call
Huh?
I got a missed call.
I wonder who it was?
ピッ

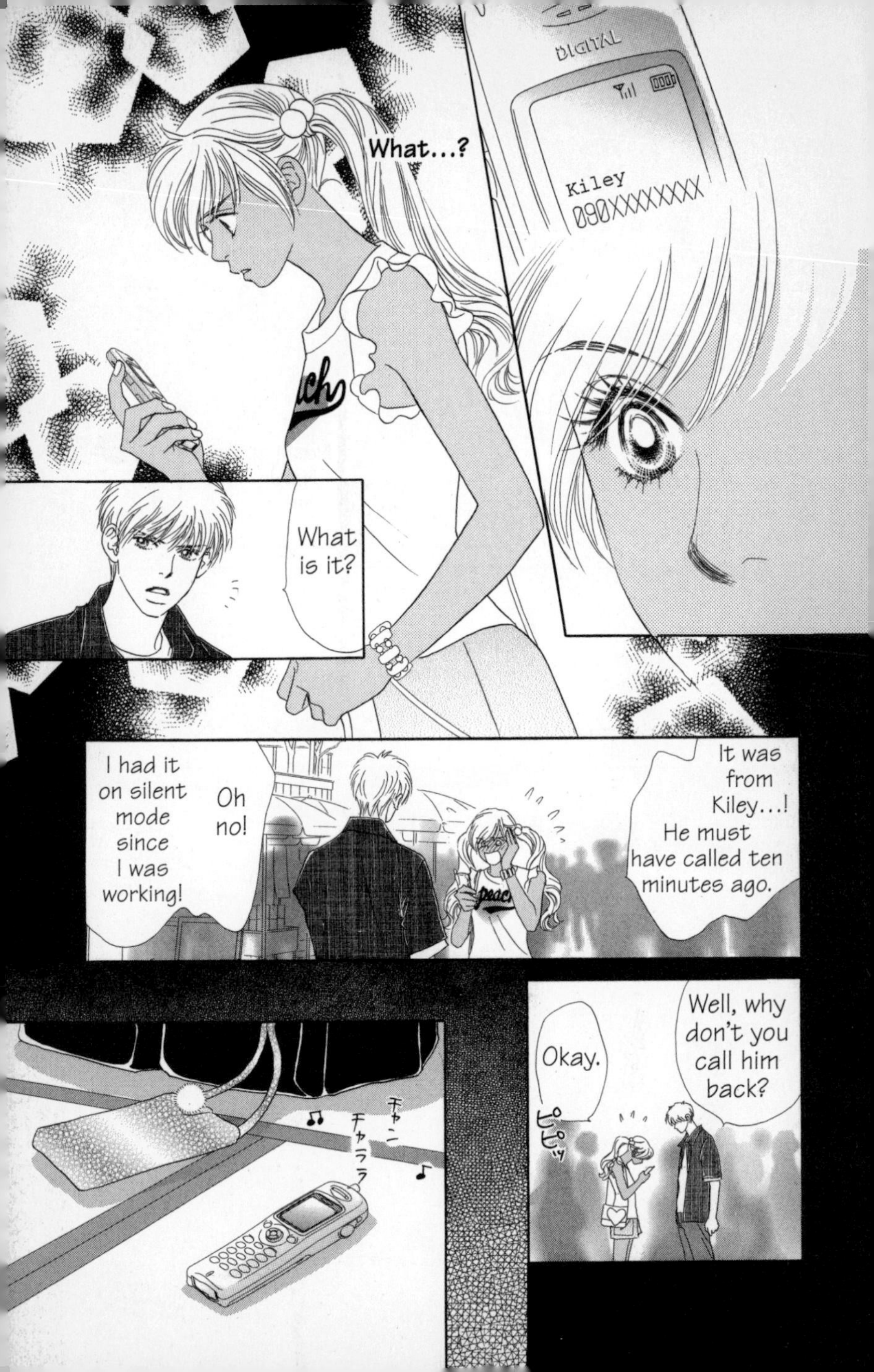
DIGITAL
Kiley
090XXXXXXXX
What...?
What is it?
It was from Kiley...! He must have called ten minutes ago.
Oh no!
I had it on silent mode since I was working!
Well, why don't you call him back?
Okay.
ピピッ
チャーン
チャララ

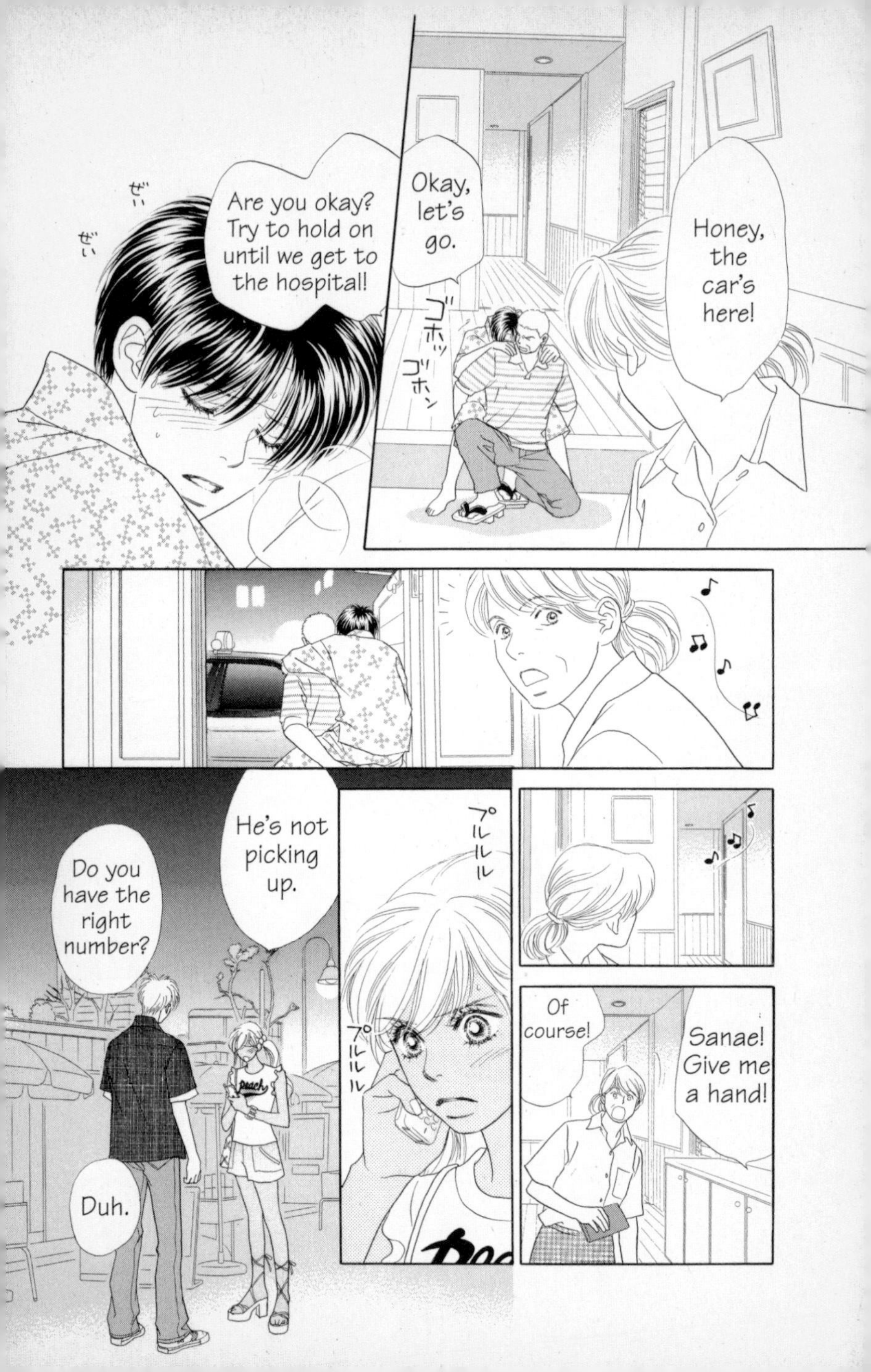

Honey, the car's here!
ゴホッ
ゴホン
Okay, let's go.
Are you okay? Try to hold on until we get to the hospital!
ぜい
ぜい
Sanae! Give me a hand!
Of course!
プルルル
プルルル
He's not picking up.
Do you have the right number?
Duh.

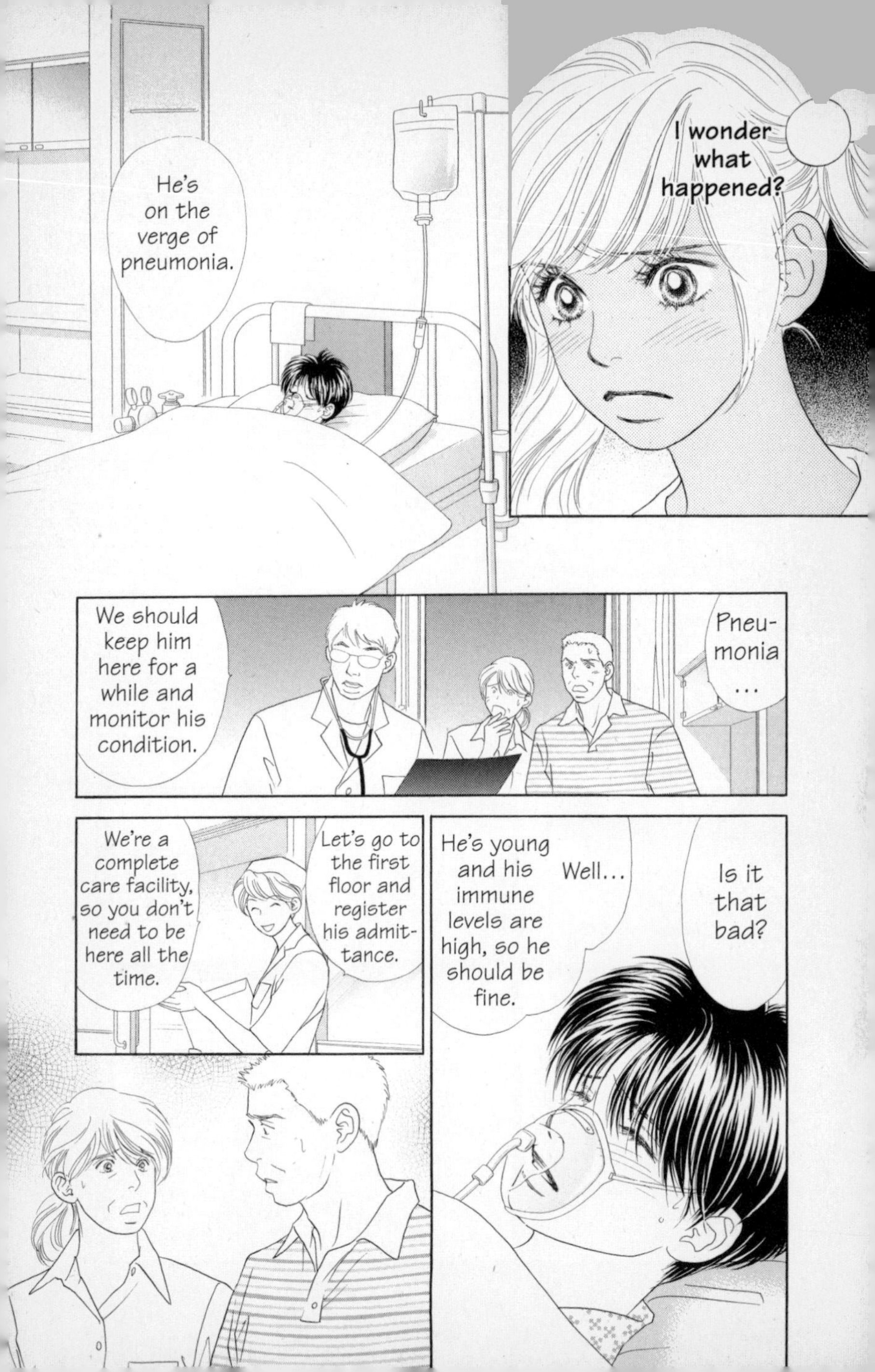
I wonder what happened?
He's on the verge of pneumonia.
Pneu-monia...
We should keep him here for a while and monitor his condition.
Is it that bad?
Well...
He's young and his immune levels are high, so he should be fine.
Let's go to the first floor and register his admit-tance.
We're a complete care facility, so you don't need to be here all the time.

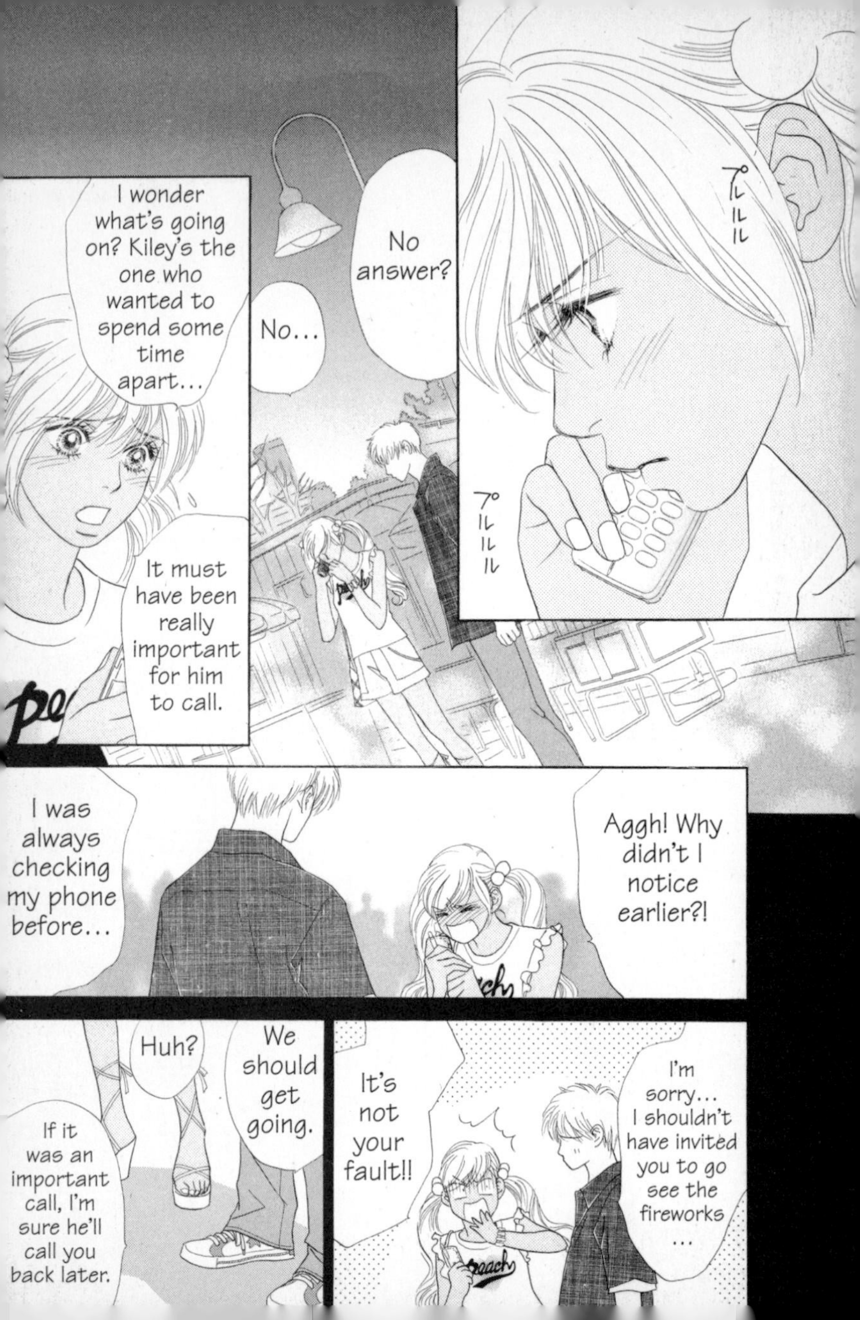
プルルル
プルルル
No answer?
No…
I wonder what's going on? Kiley's the one who wanted to spend some time apart…
It must have been really important for him to call.
Aggh! Why didn't I notice earlier?!
I was always checking my phone before…
I'm sorry… I shouldn't have invited you to go see the fireworks …
It's not your fault!!
We should get going.
Huh?
If it was an important call, I'm sure he'll call you back later.

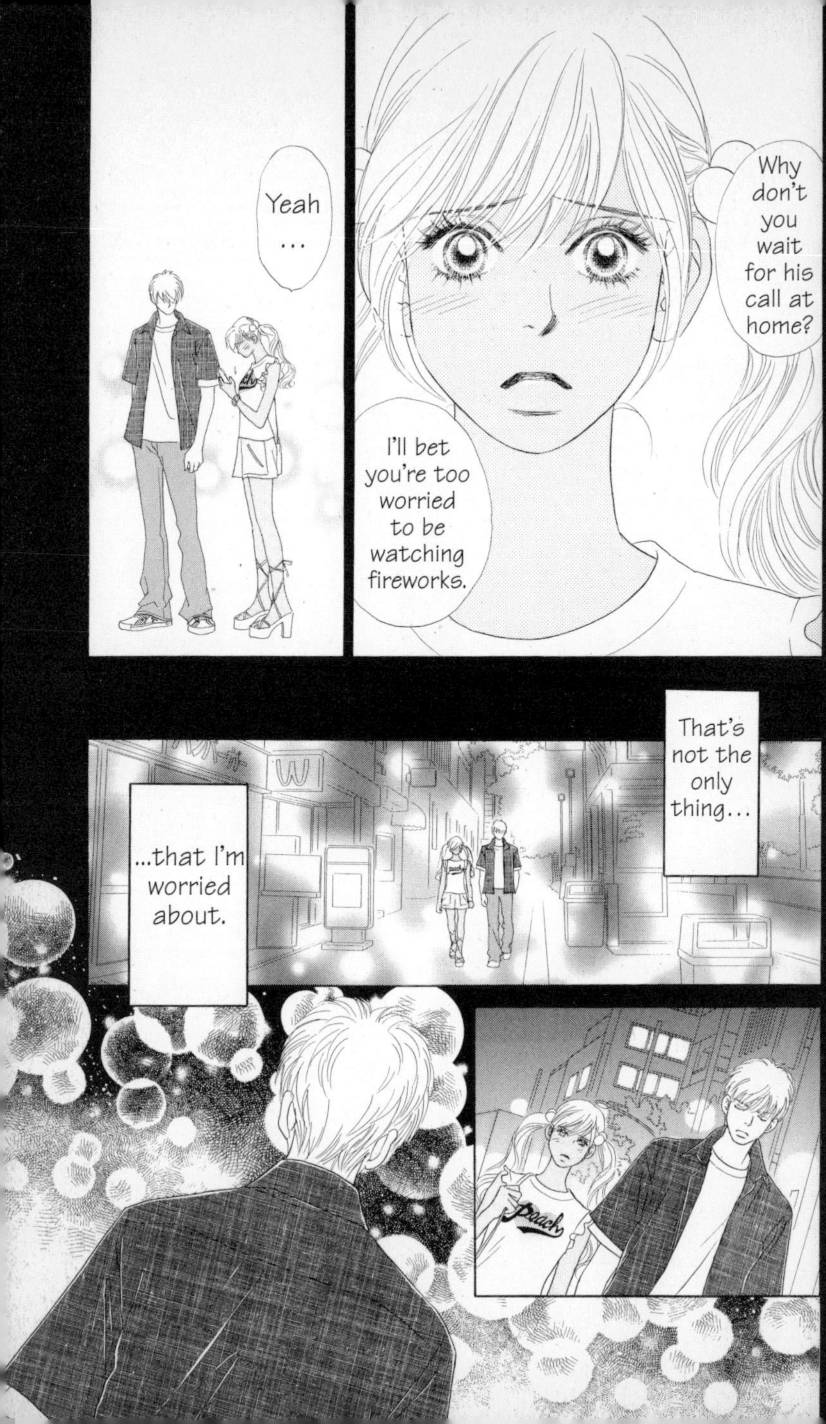
Why don't you wait for his call at home?
I'll bet you're too worried to be watching fireworks.
Yeah...
That's not the only thing...
...that I'm worried about.

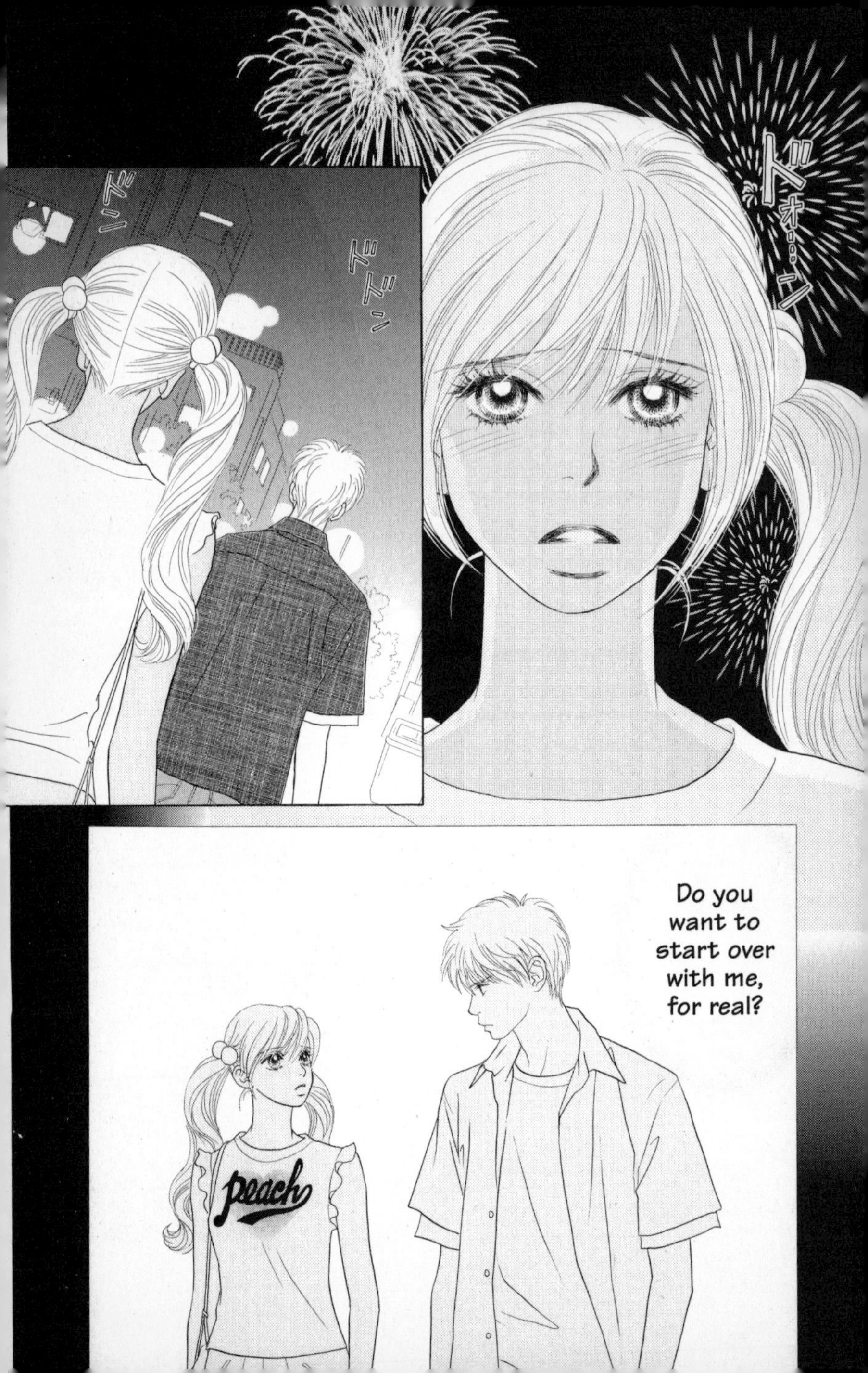
ドオ…ン
ドドン
ドン
Do you want to start over with me, for real?

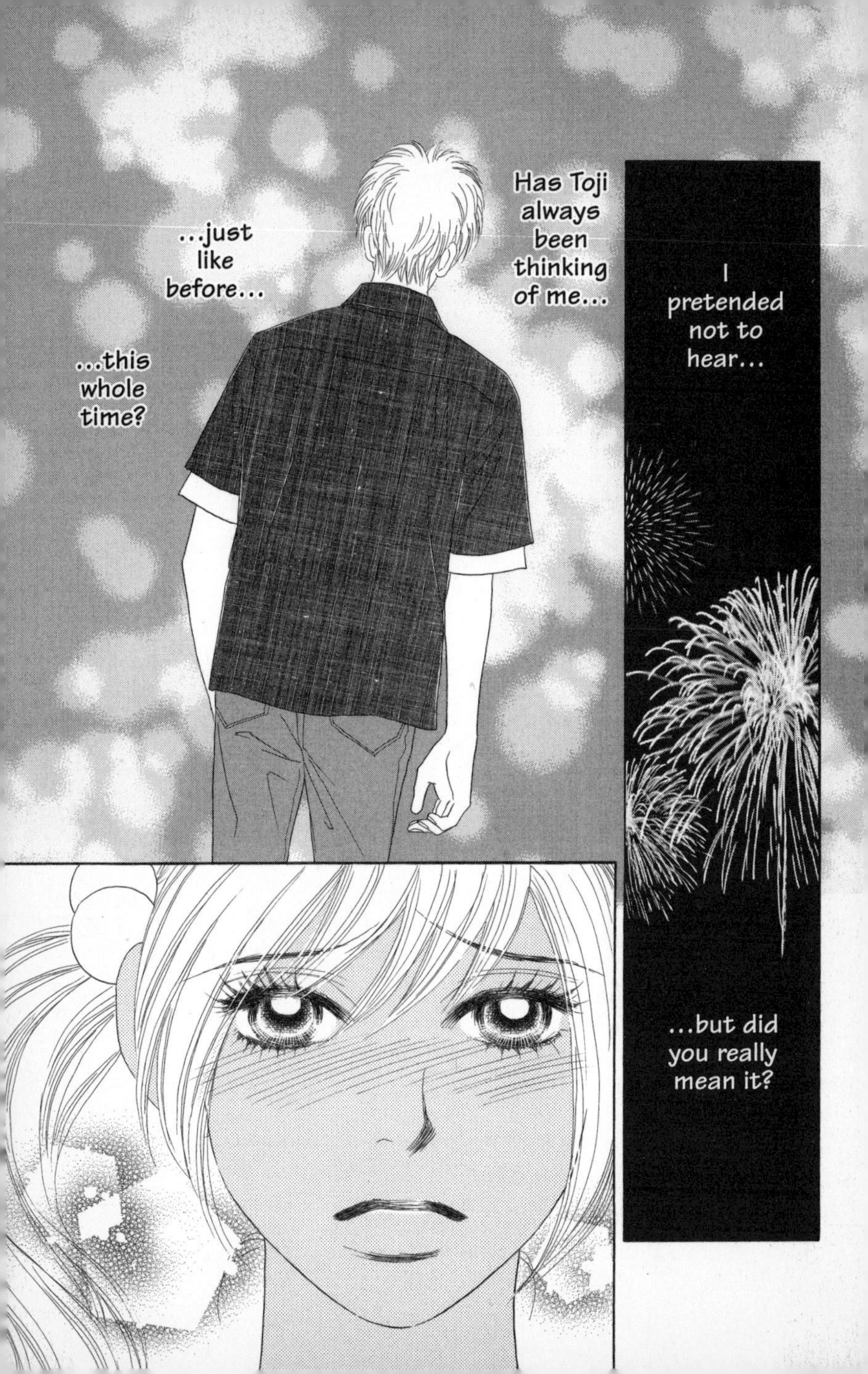
I pretended not to hear...
...but did you really mean it?
Has Toji always been thinking of me...
...just like before...
...this whole time?

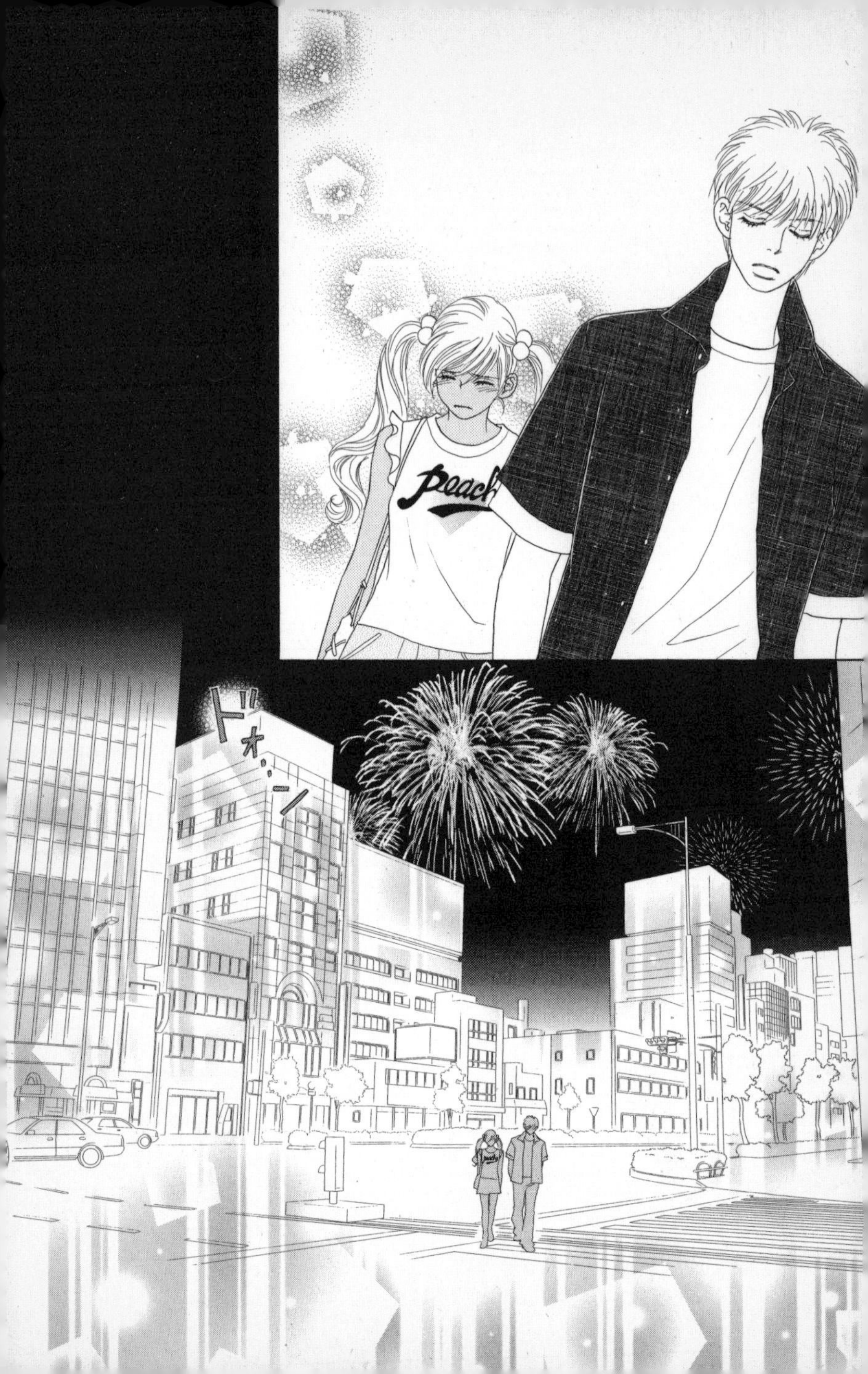
peach
ドォーン

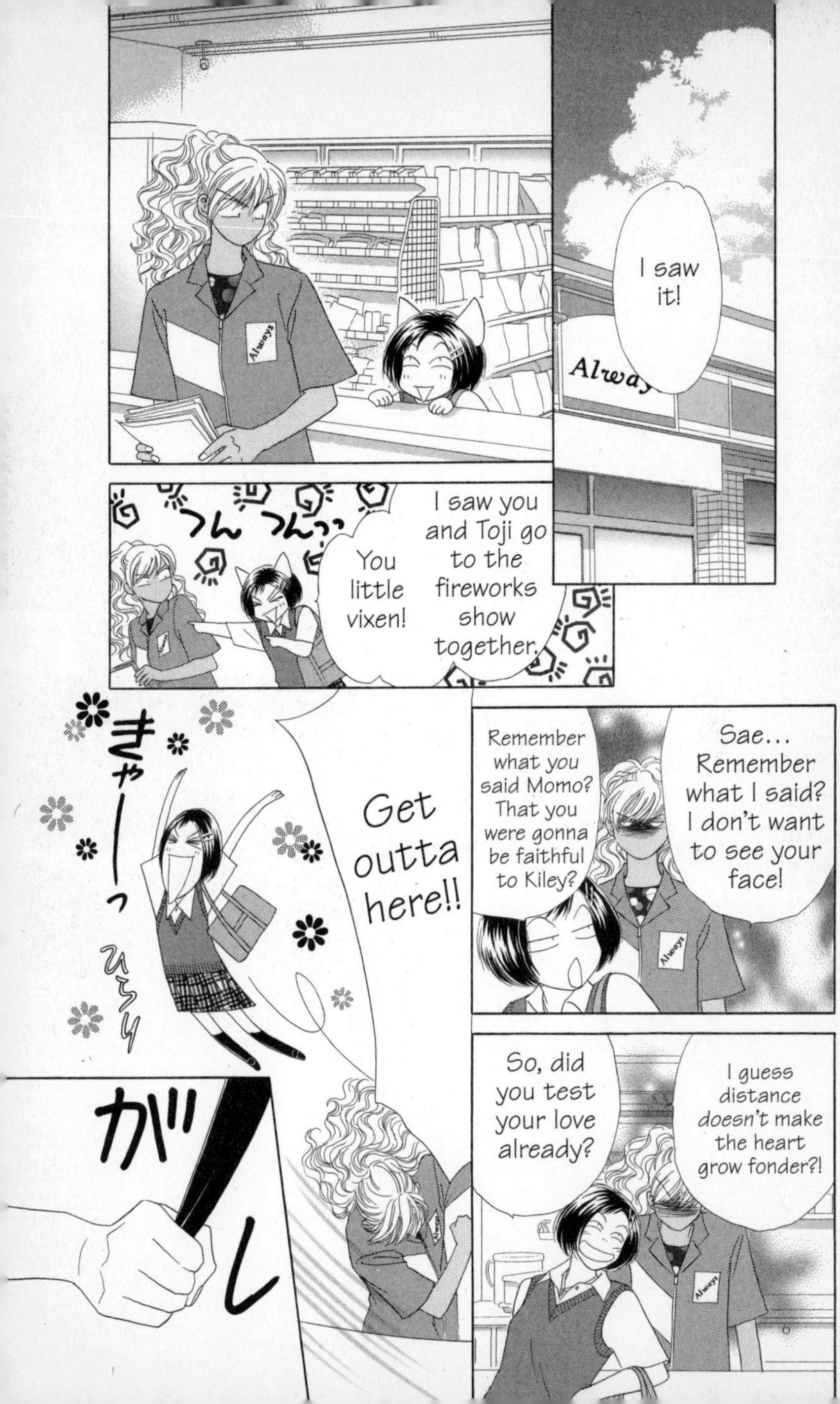
I saw it!
つん つんっ
I saw you and Toji go to the fireworks show together.
You little vixen!
Sae… Remember what I said? I don't want to see your face!
Remember what you said Momo? That you were gonna be faithful to Kiley?
I guess distance doesn't make the heart grow fonder?!
So, did you test your love already?
Get outta here!!
きゃーっ
ひらり
がし

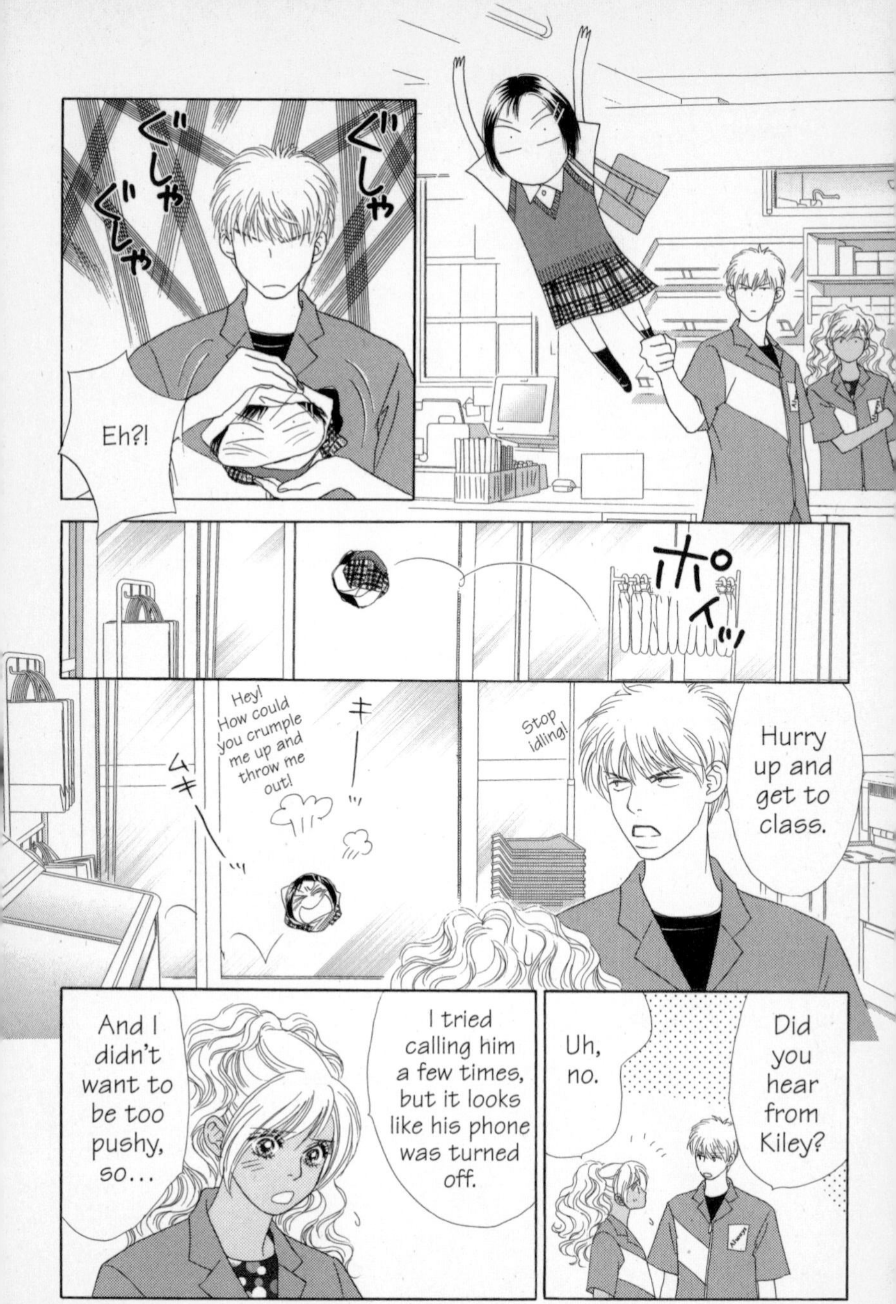
ぐしゃ ぐしゃ ぐしゃ
Eh?!
ポイッ
Hurry up and get to class.
Stop idling!
Hey! How could you crumple me up and throw me out!
キー…
ムキー…
Did you hear from Kiley?
Uh, no.
I tried calling him a few times, but it looks like his phone was turned off.
And I didn't want to be too pushy, so…

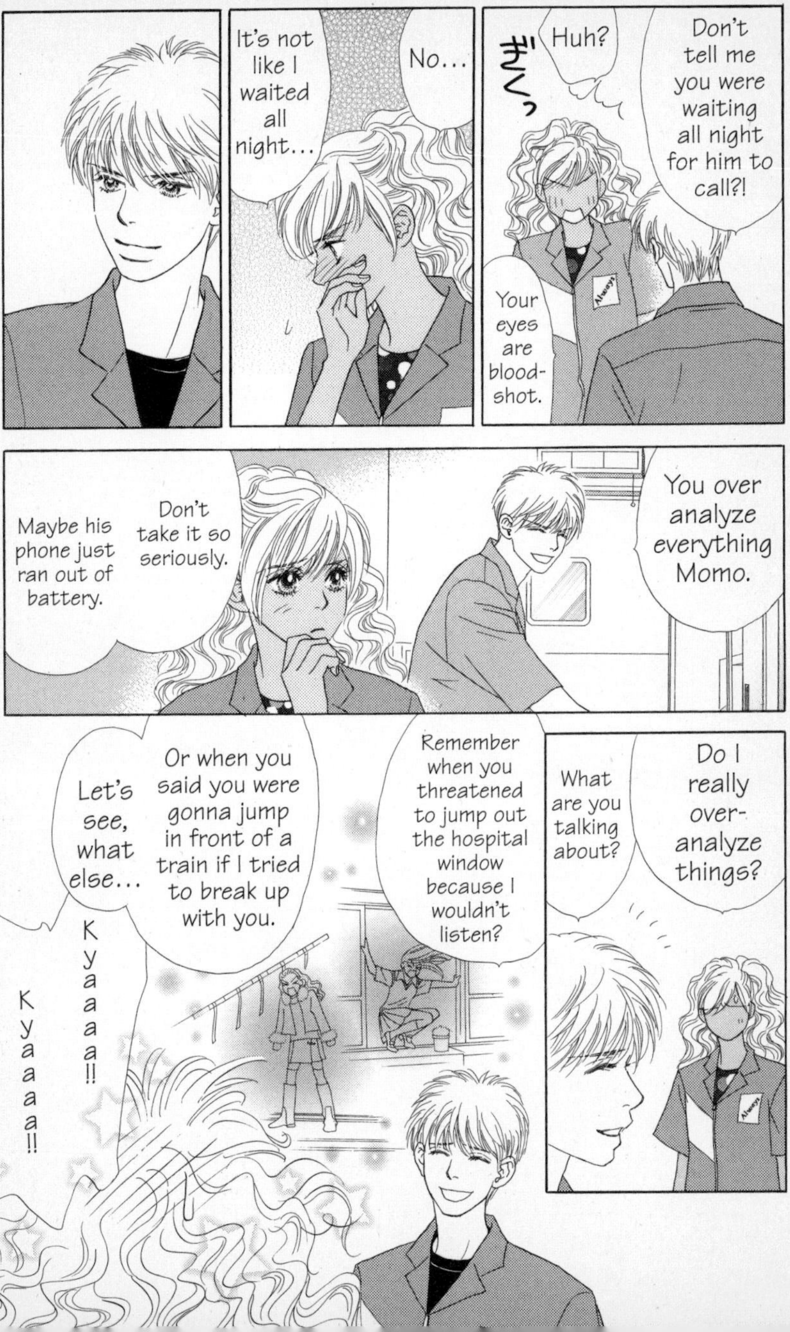
Don't tell me you were waiting all night for him to call?!
Huh?
ぎくっ
Your eyes are bloodshot.
No...
It's not like I waited all night...
You over analyze everything Momo.
Don't take it so seriously.
Maybe his phone just ran out of battery.
Do I really over-analyze things?
What are you talking about?
Remember when you threatened to jump out the hospital window because I wouldn't listen?
Or when you said you were gonna jump in front of a train if I tried to break up with you.
Let's see, what else...
Kyaaaaa!!
Kyaaaaa!!

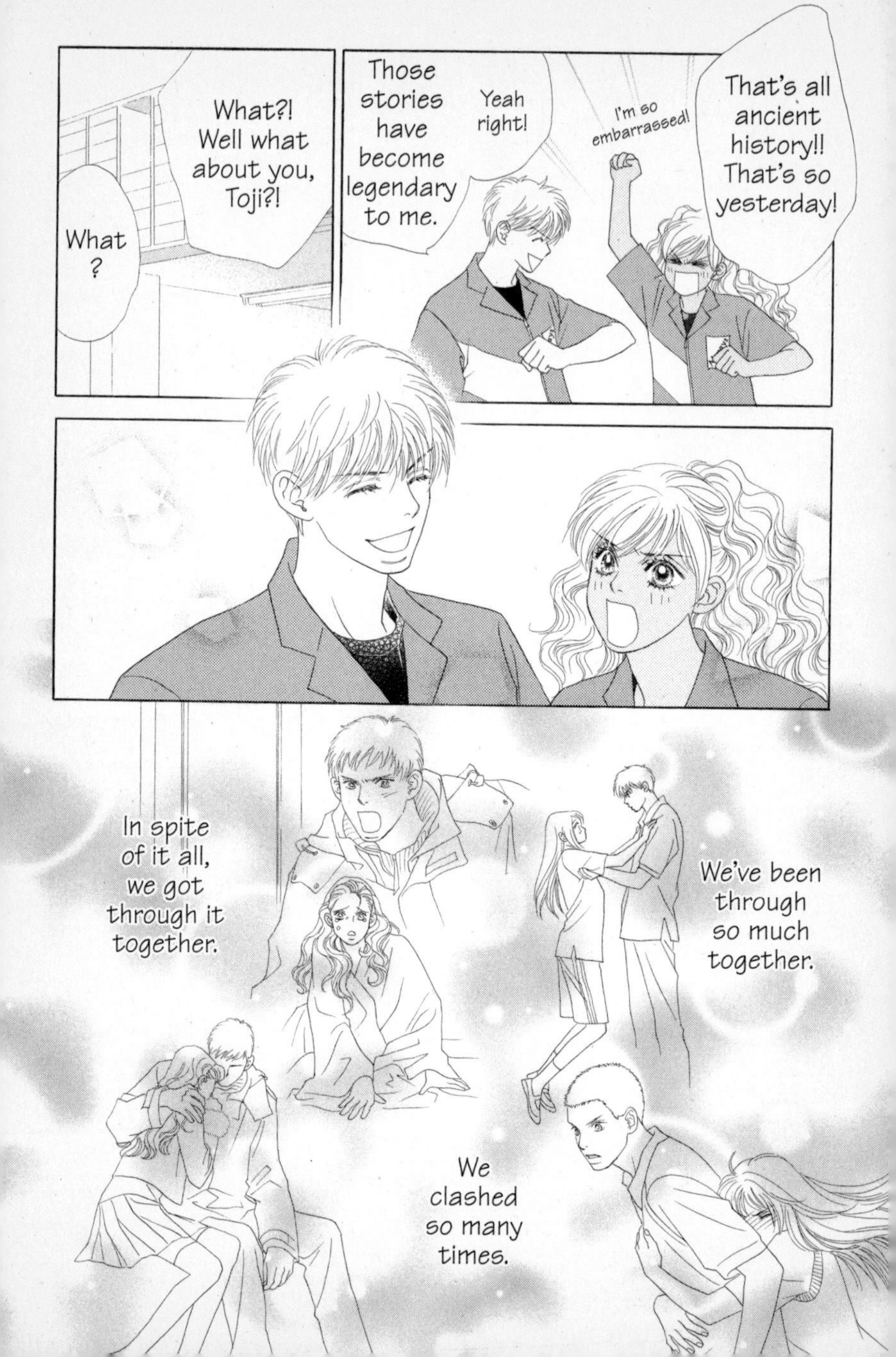
That's all ancient history!! That's so yesterday!
I'm so embarrassed!
Yeah right!
Those stories have become legendary to me.
What?! Well what about you, Toji?!
What?
We've been through so much together.
In spite of it all, we got through it together.
We clashed so many times.

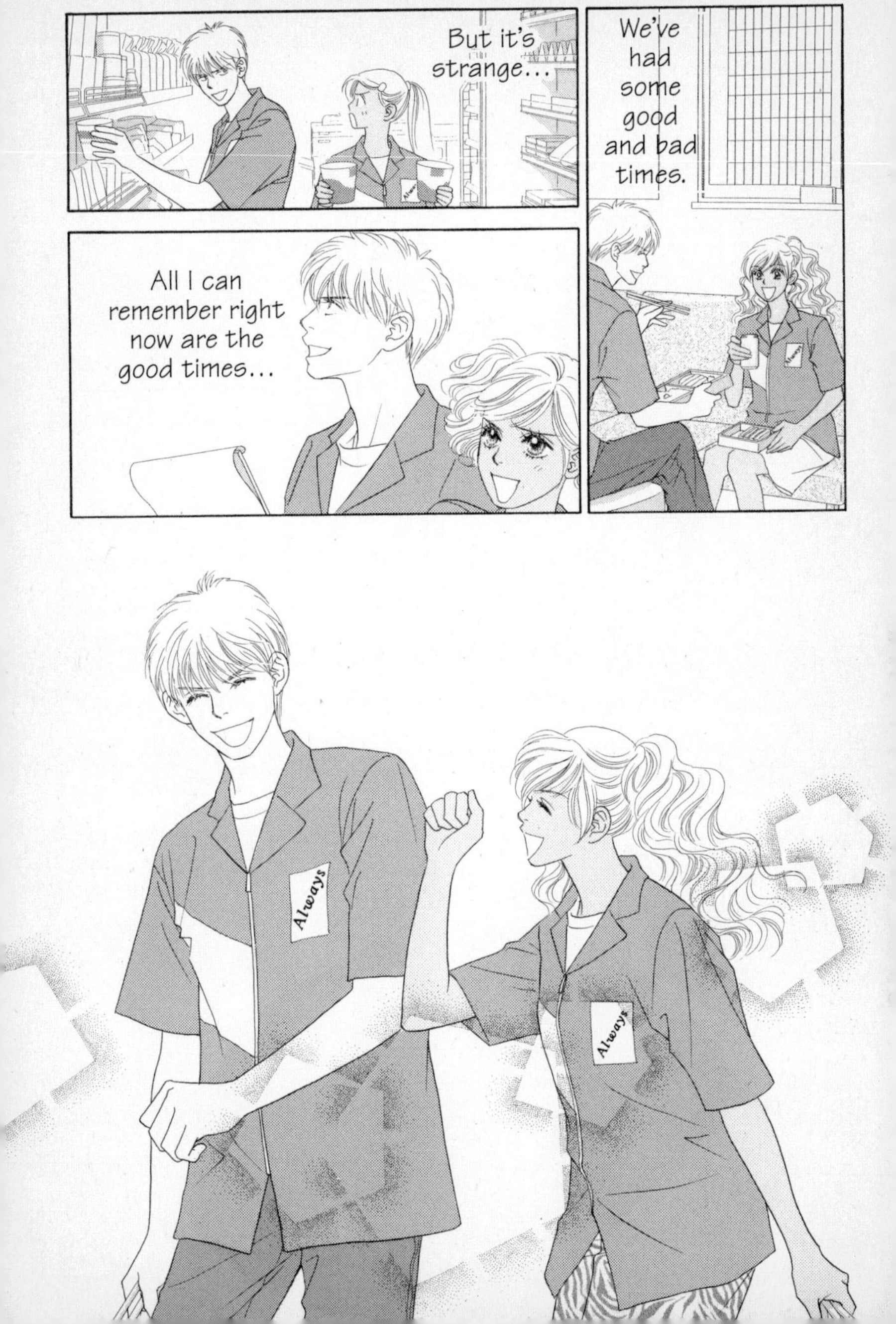
We've had some good and bad times.
But it's strange...
All I can remember right now are the good times...
Always
Always

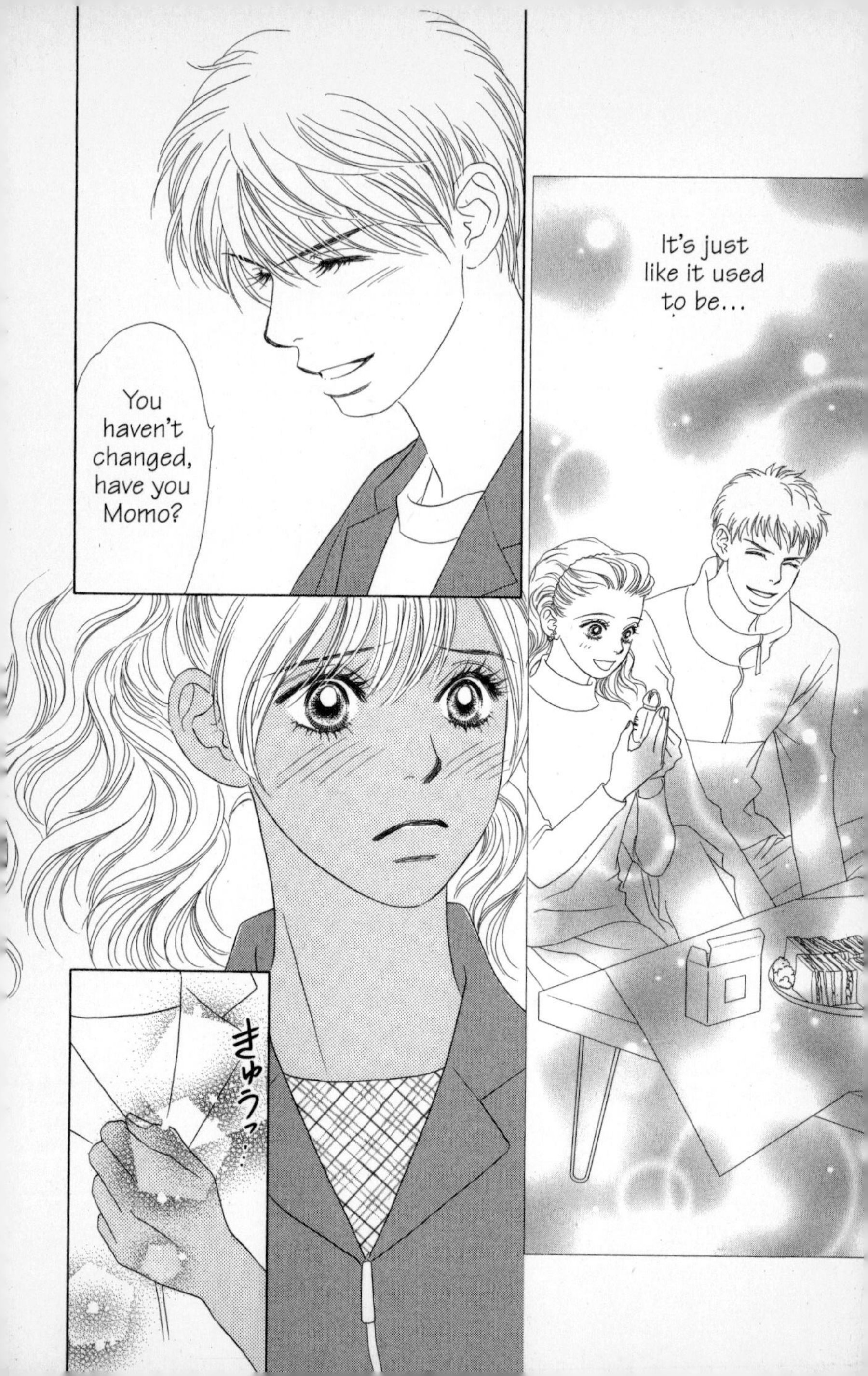
You haven't changed, have you Momo?
It's just like it used to be…
きゅうっ…

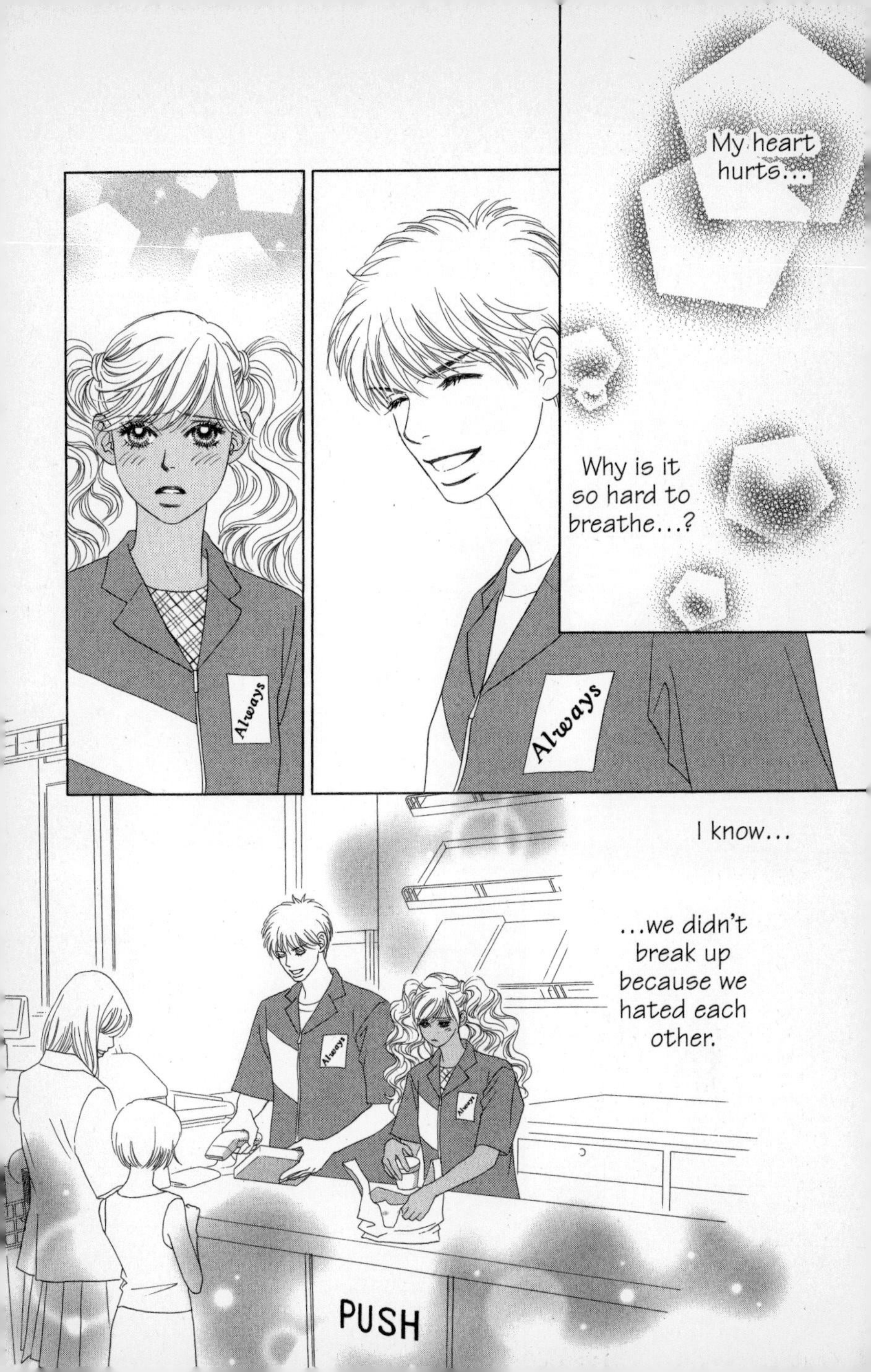
My heart hurts...
Why is it so hard to breathe...?
Always
Always
I know...
...we didn't break up because we hated each other.
Always
Always
PUSH

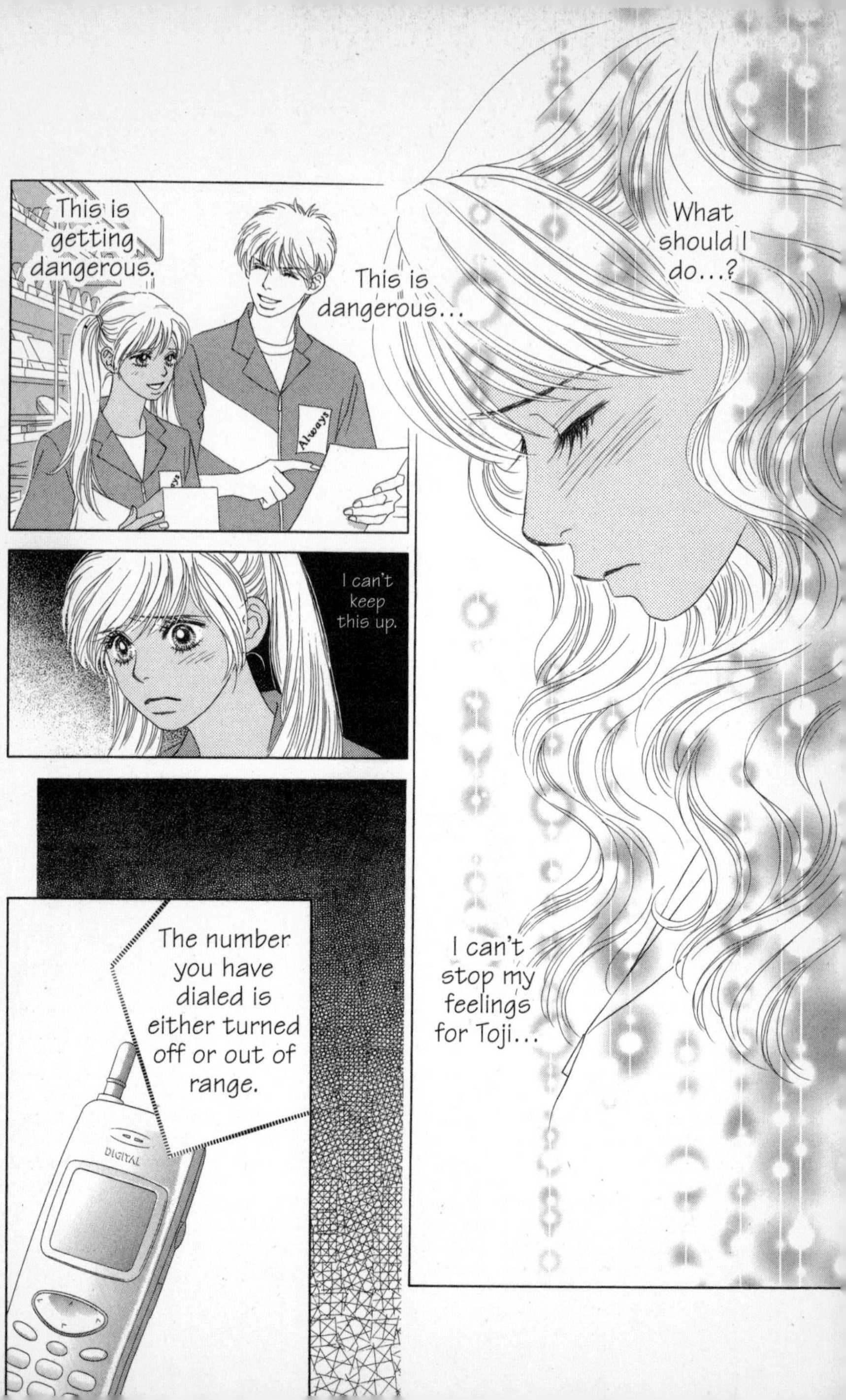

What should I do...?
This is dangerous...
I can't stop my feelings for Toji...
This is getting dangerous.
Always
I can't keep this up.
The number you have dialed is either turned off or out of range.
DIGITAL

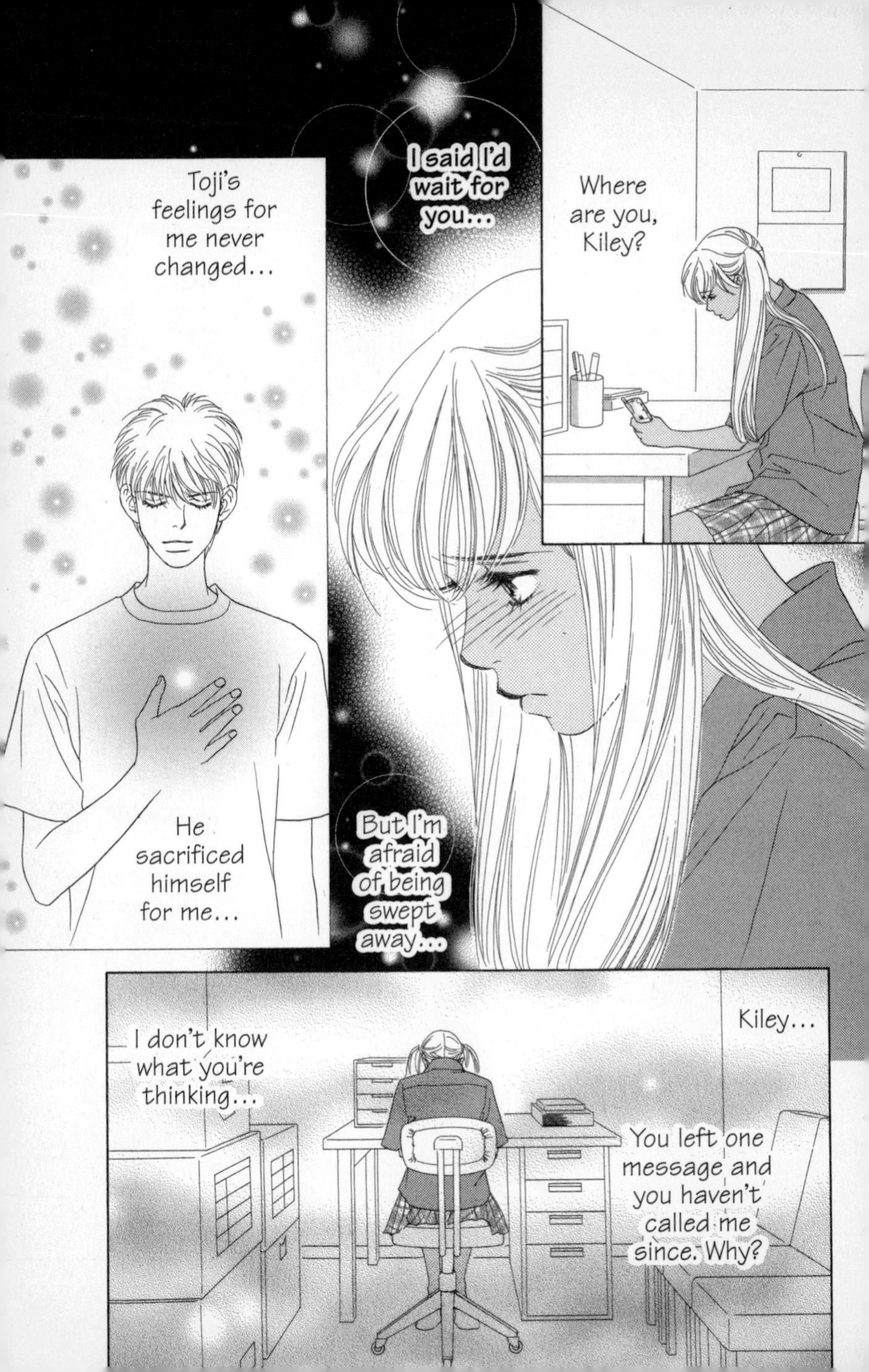
Where are you, Kiley?
I said I'd wait for you...
But I'm afraid of being swept away...
Toji's feelings for me never changed...
He sacrificed himself for me...
Kiley...
You left one message and you haven't called me since. Why?
I don't know what you're thinking...

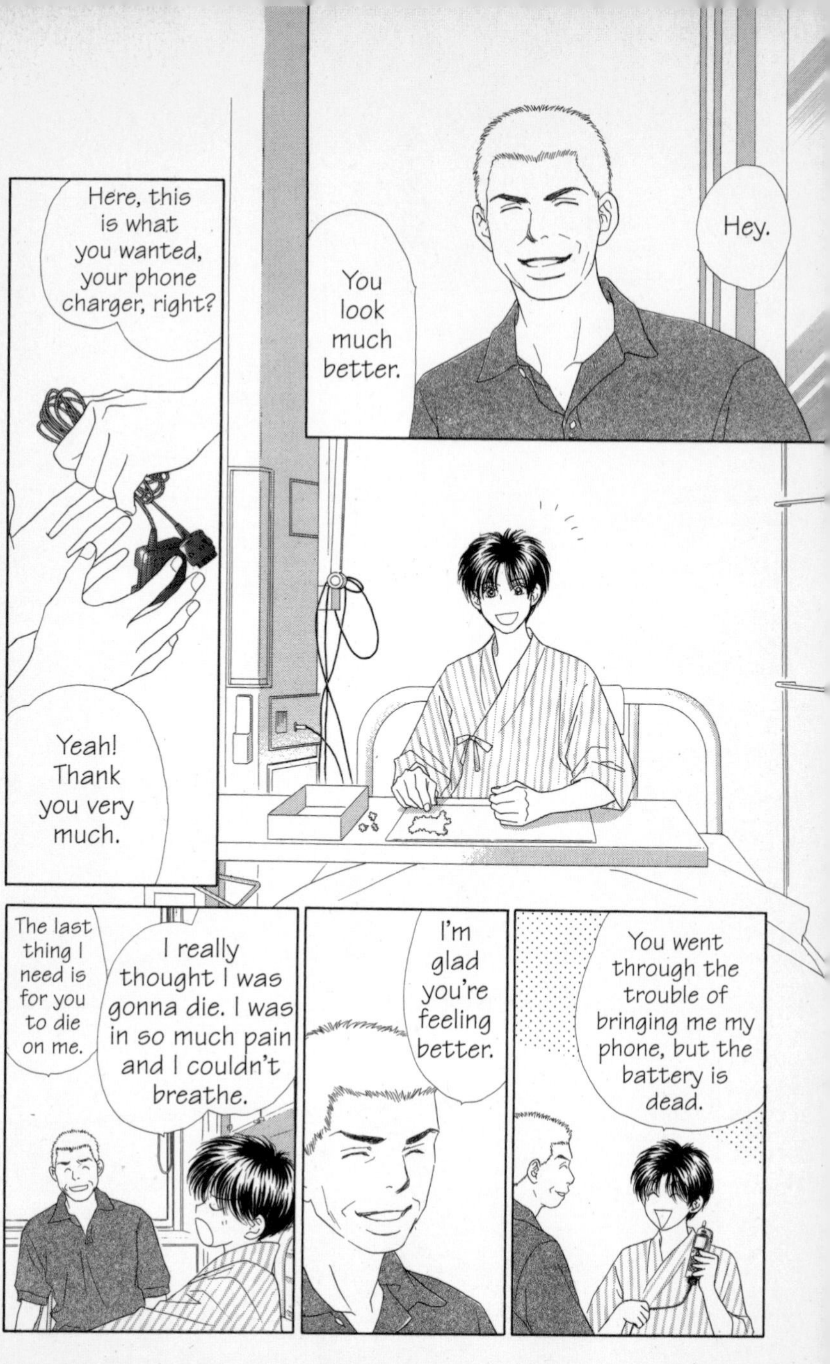
Hey.
You look much better.
Here, this is what you wanted, your phone charger, right?
Yeah! Thank you very much.
You went through the trouble of bringing me my phone, but the battery is dead.
I'm glad you're feeling better.
I really thought I was gonna die. I was in so much pain and I couldn't breathe.
The last thing I need is for you to die on me.

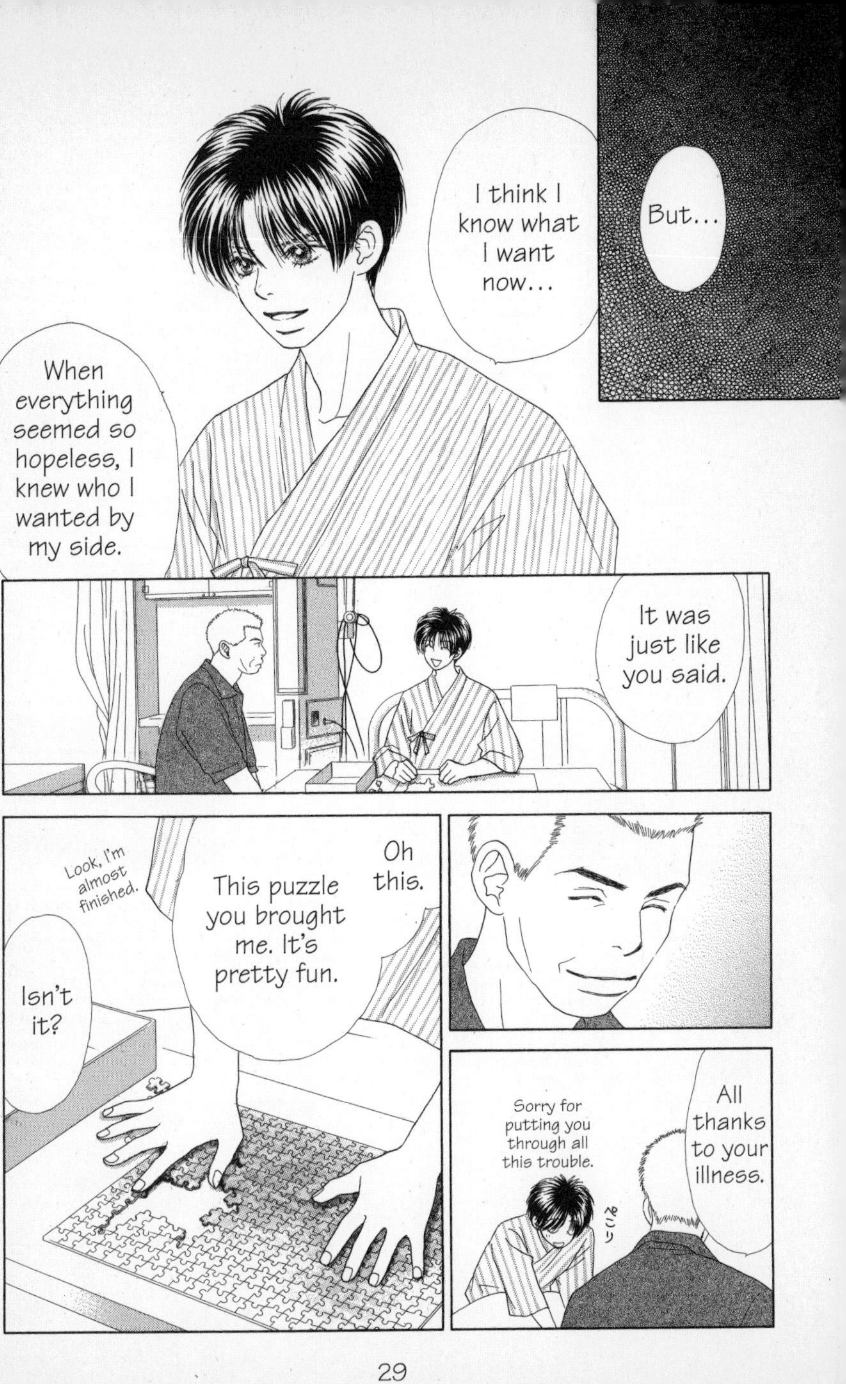
But…
I think I know what I want now…
When everything seemed so hopeless, I knew who I wanted by my side.
It was just like you said.
All thanks to your illness.
Sorry for putting you through all this trouble.
ぺこり
Oh this.
This puzzle you brought me. It's pretty fun.
Look, I'm almost finished.
Isn't it?

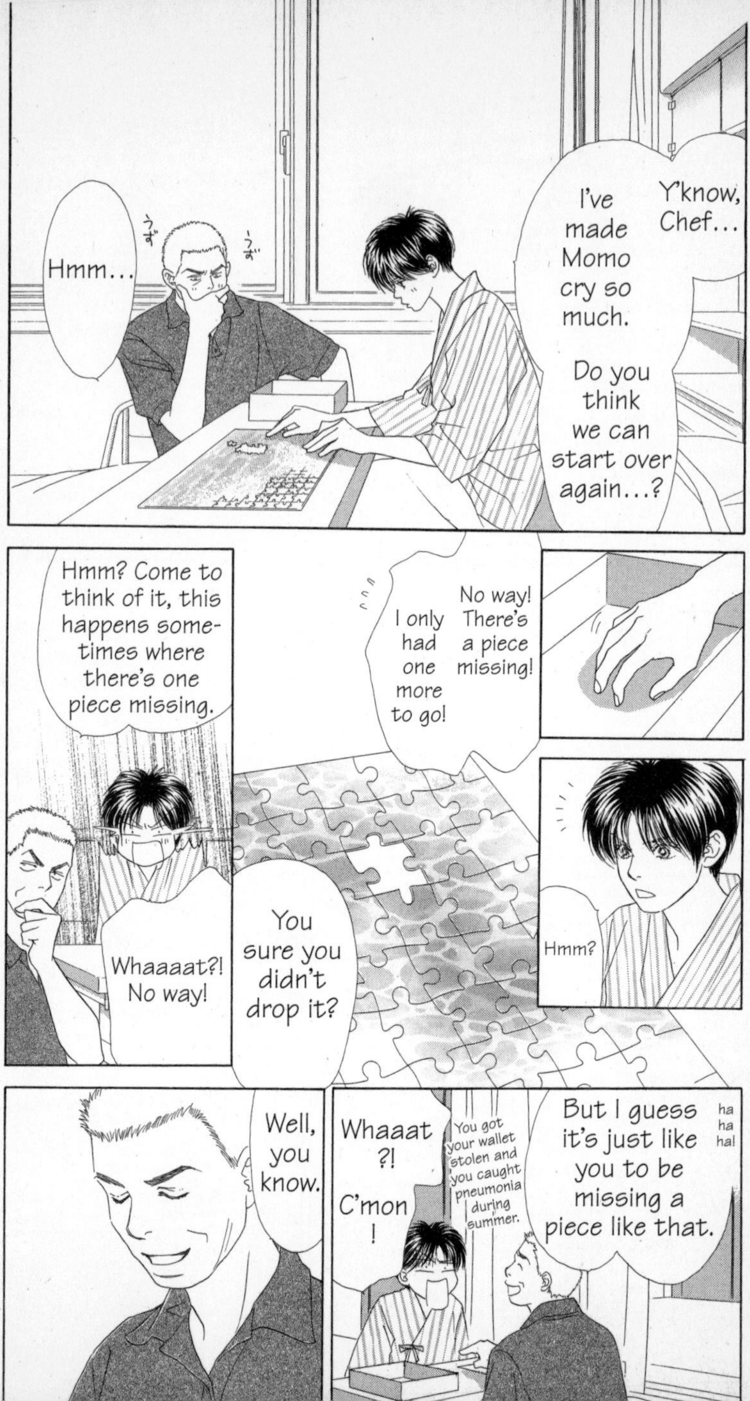

Y'know, Chef... I've made Momo cry so much.
Do you think we can start over again...?
うず うず
Hmm...
Hmm?
No way! There's a piece missing!
I only had one more to go!
You sure you didn't drop it?
Hmm? Come to think of it, this happens some-times where there's one piece missing.
Whaaaat?! No way!
But I guess it's just like you to be missing a piece like that.
ha ha ha!
You got your wallet stolen and you caught pneumonia during summer.
Whaaat?!
C'mon!
Well, you know.

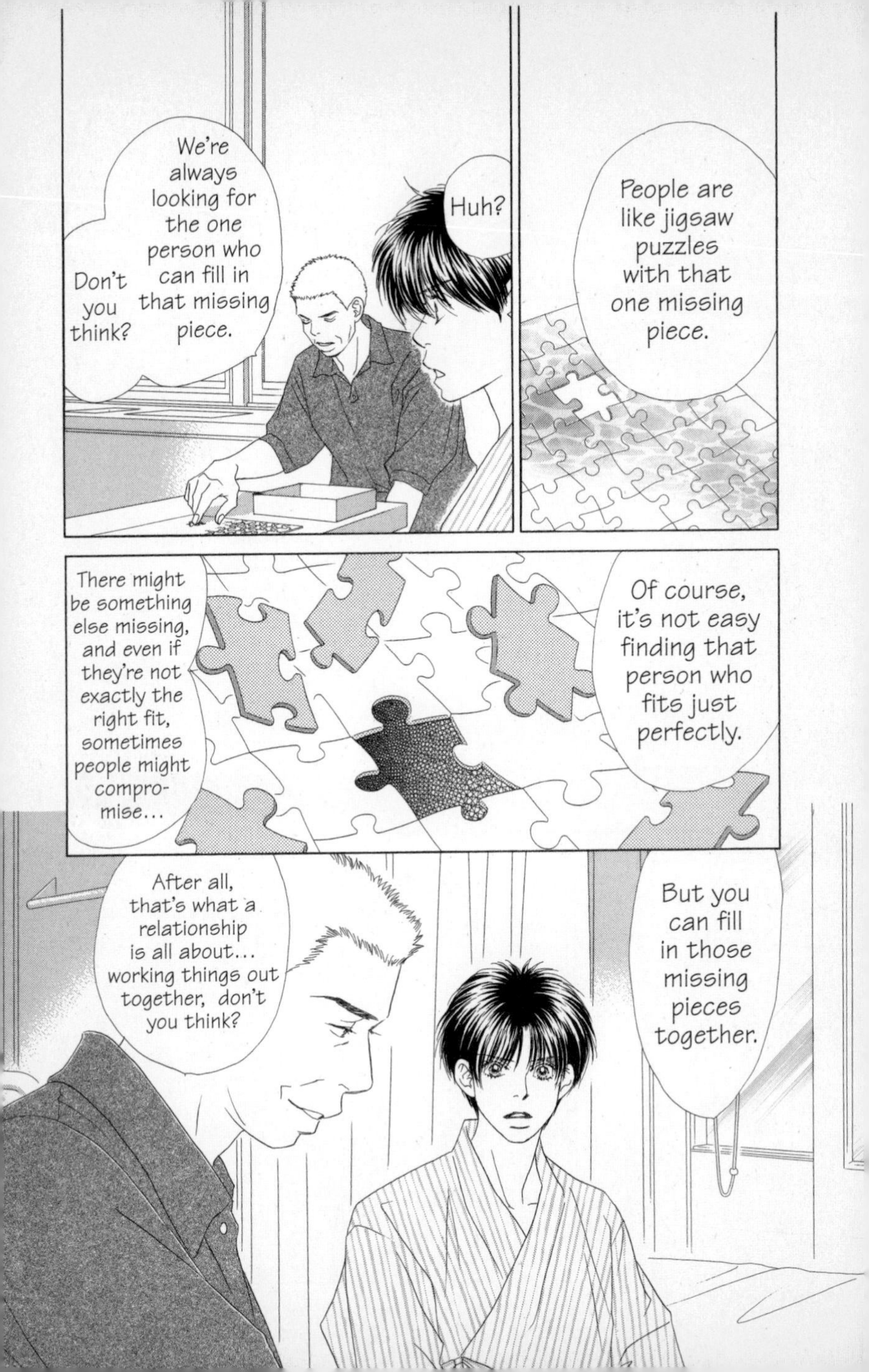
People are like jigsaw puzzles with that one missing piece.
Huh?
We're always looking for the one person who can fill in that missing piece.
Don't you think?
Of course, it's not easy finding that person who fits just perfectly.
There might be something else missing, and even if they're not exactly the right fit, sometimes people might compro-mise…
But you can fill in those missing pieces together.
After all, that's what a relationship is all about… working things out together, don't you think?

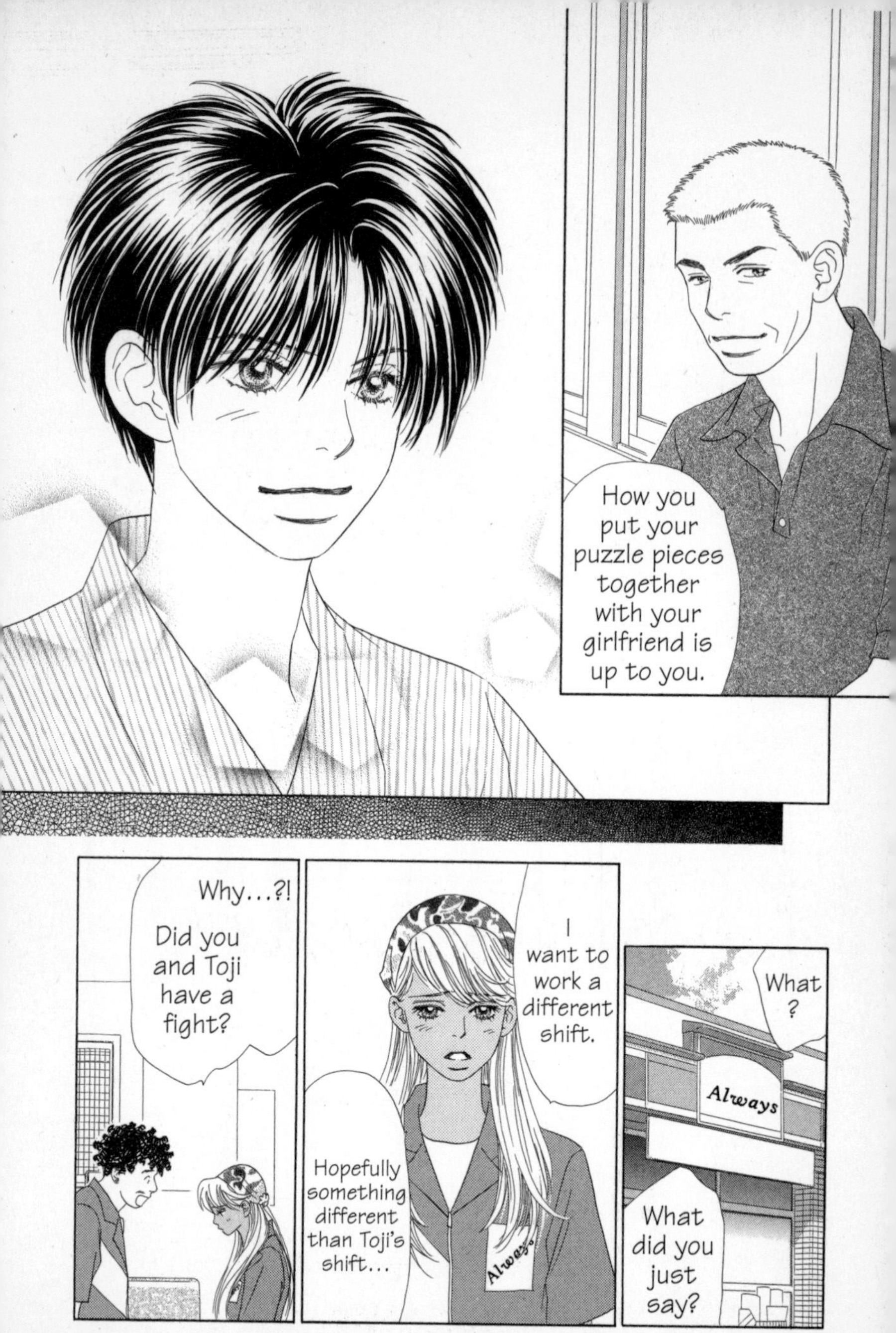
How you put your puzzle pieces together with your girlfriend is up to you.
What?
Always
What did you just say?
I want to work a different shift.
Hopefully something different than Toji's shift…
Always
Why…?!
Did you and Toji have a fight?

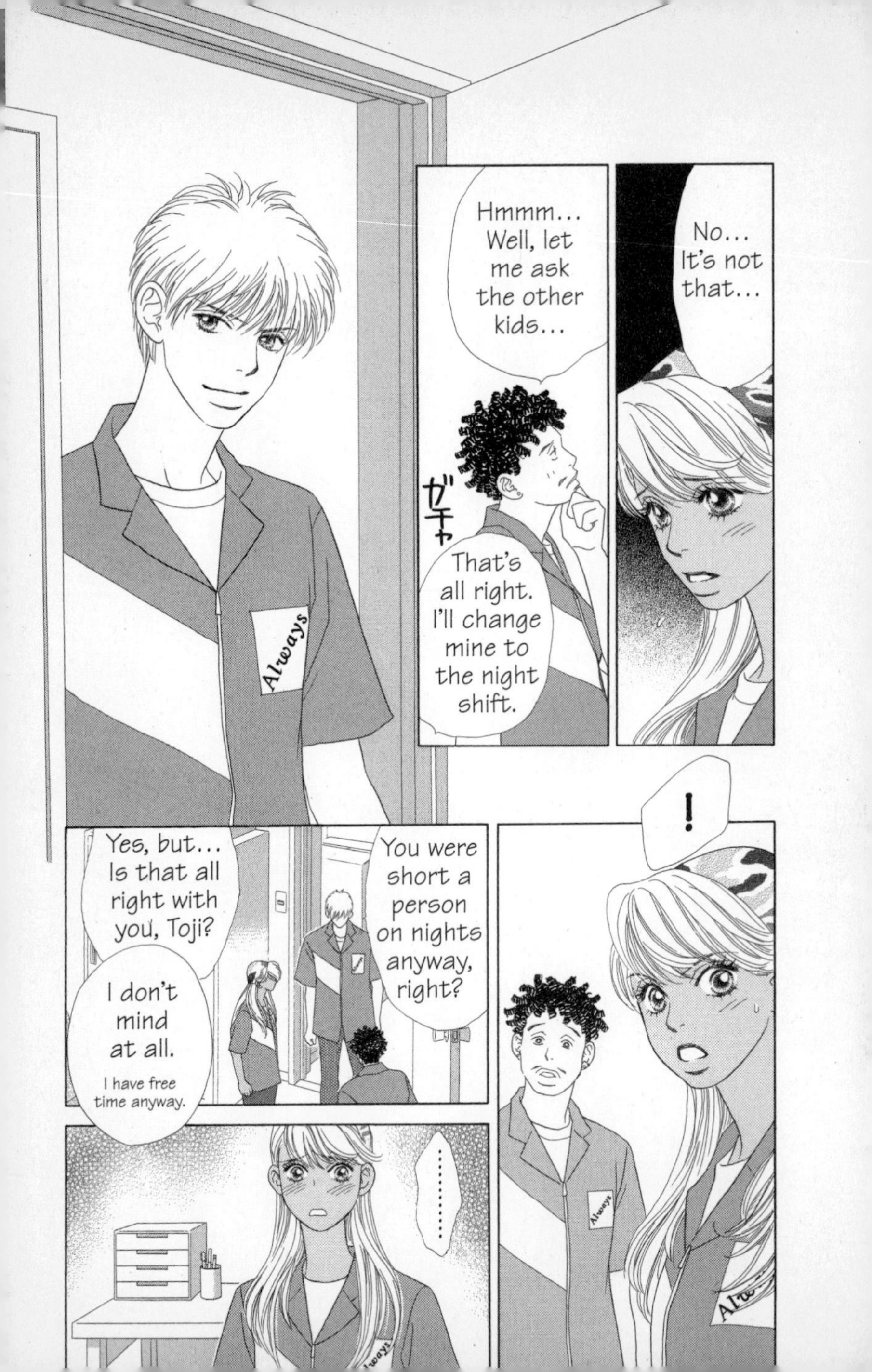
No… It's not that…
Hmmm… Well, let me ask the other kids…
ガチャ
That's all right. I'll change mine to the night shift.
Always
!
You were short a person on nights anyway, right?
Yes, but… Is that all right with you, Toji?
I don't mind at all.
I have free time anyway.
……

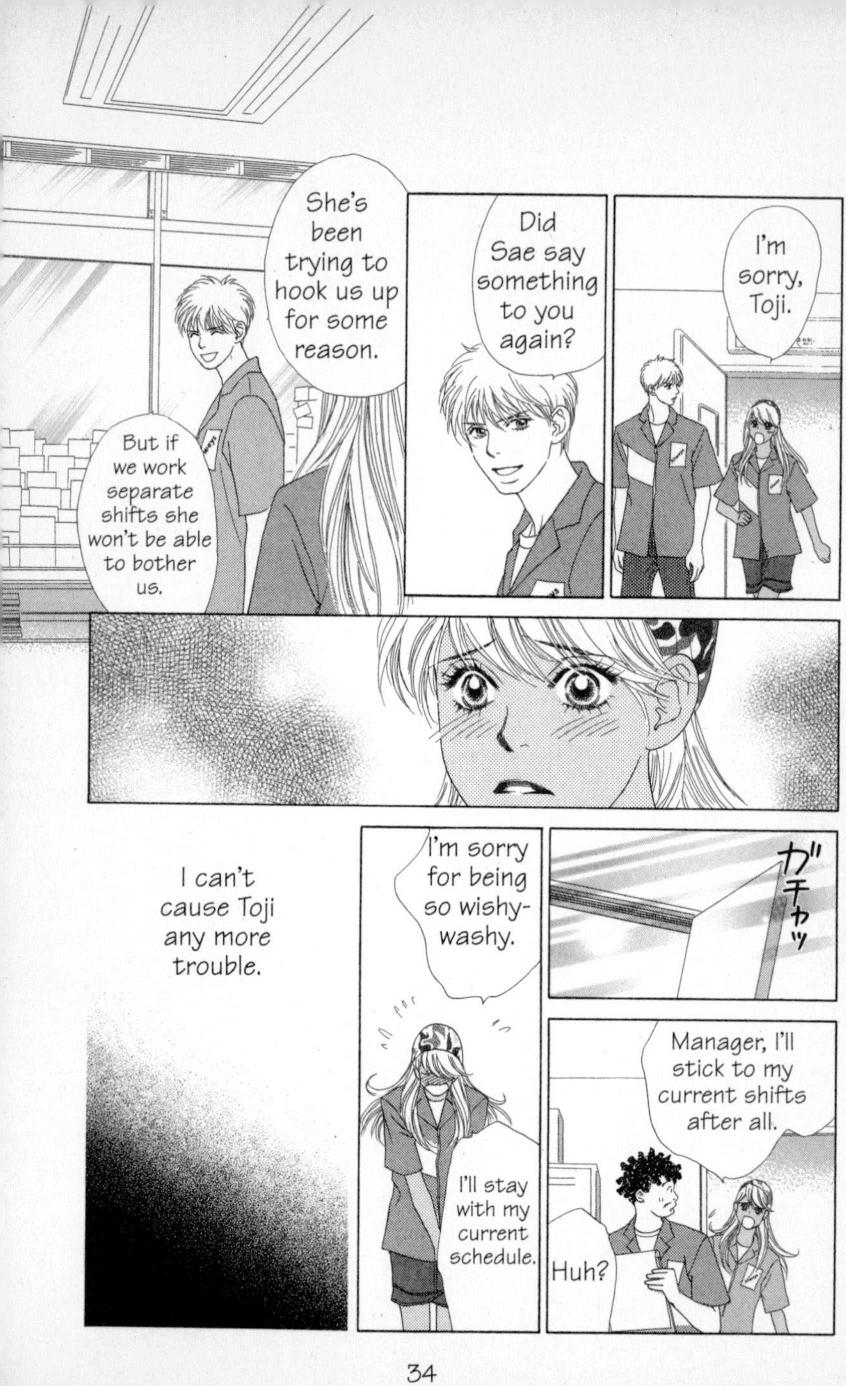
I'm sorry, Toji.
Did Sae say something to you again?
She's been trying to hook us up for some reason.
But if we work separate shifts she won't be able to bother us.
ガチャッ
Manager, I'll stick to my current shifts after all.
Huh?
I'm sorry for being so wishy-washy.
I'll stay with my current schedule.
I can't cause Toji any more trouble.

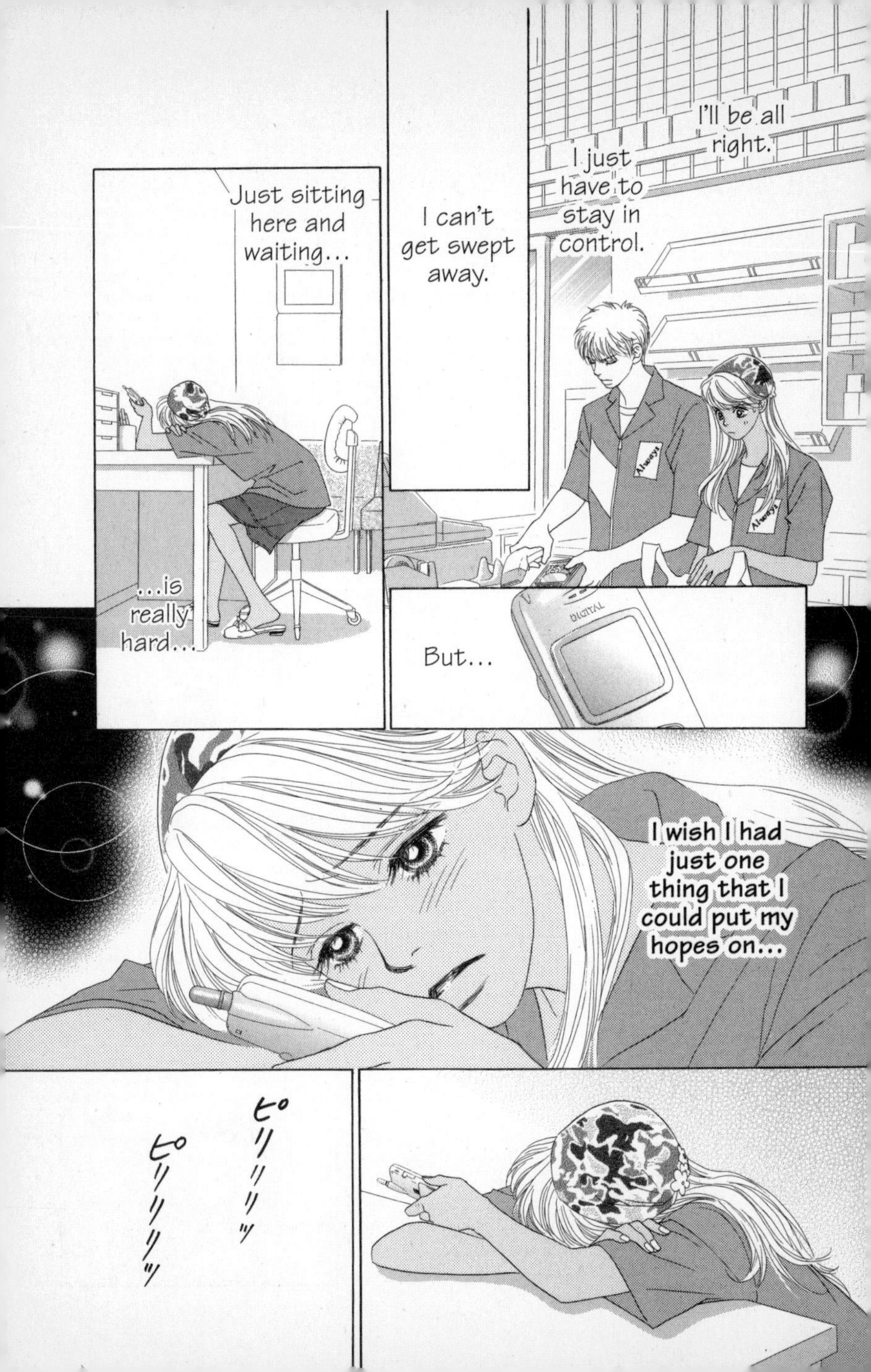

I'll be all right.
I just have to stay in control.
I can't get swept away.
But…
Just sitting here and waiting…
…is really hard…
I wish I had just one thing that I could put my hopes on…
ピリリリッ
ピリリリリッ

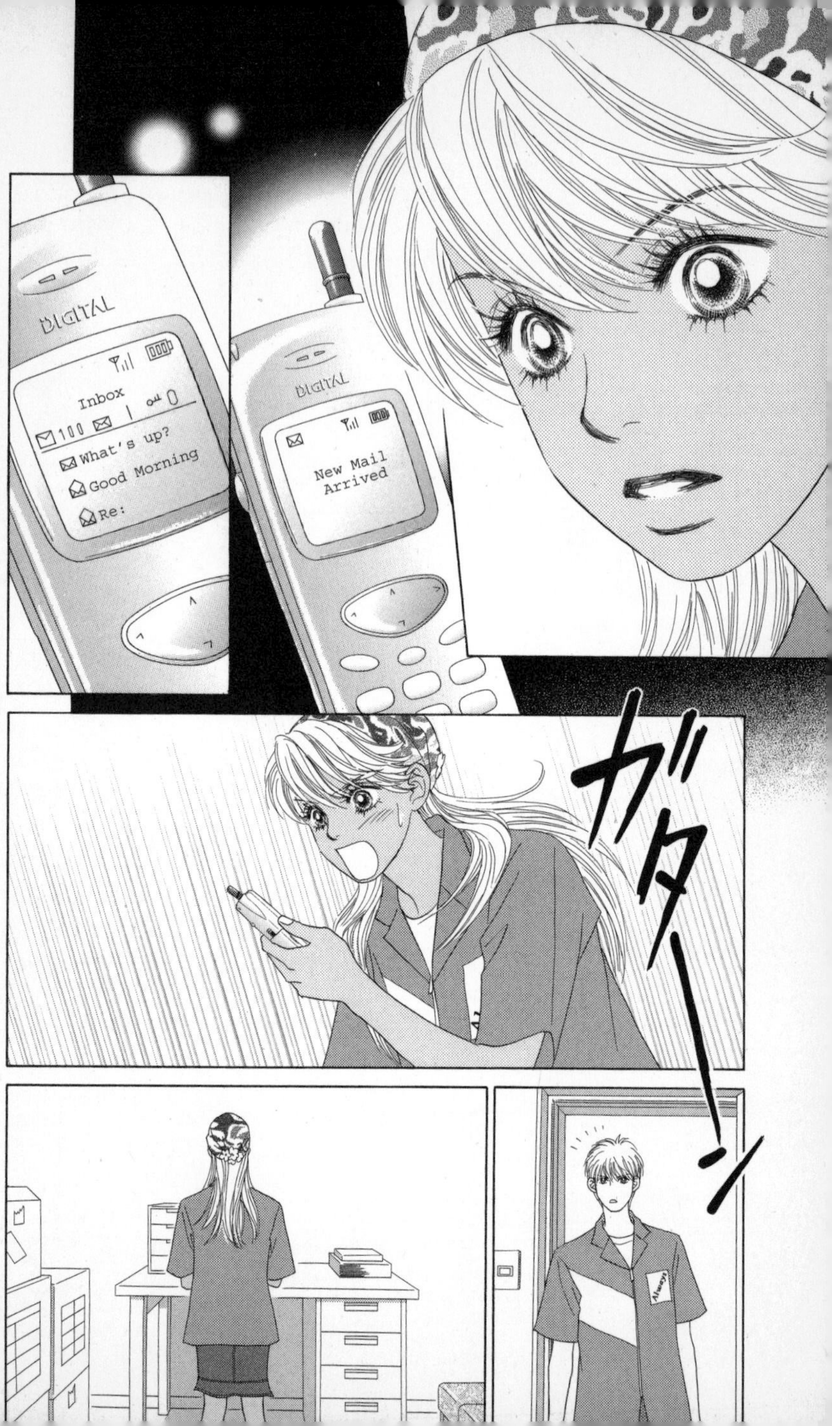
DIGITAL
New Mail
Arrived
DIGITAL
Inbox
100
What's up?
Good Morning
Re:
ガターン
Always

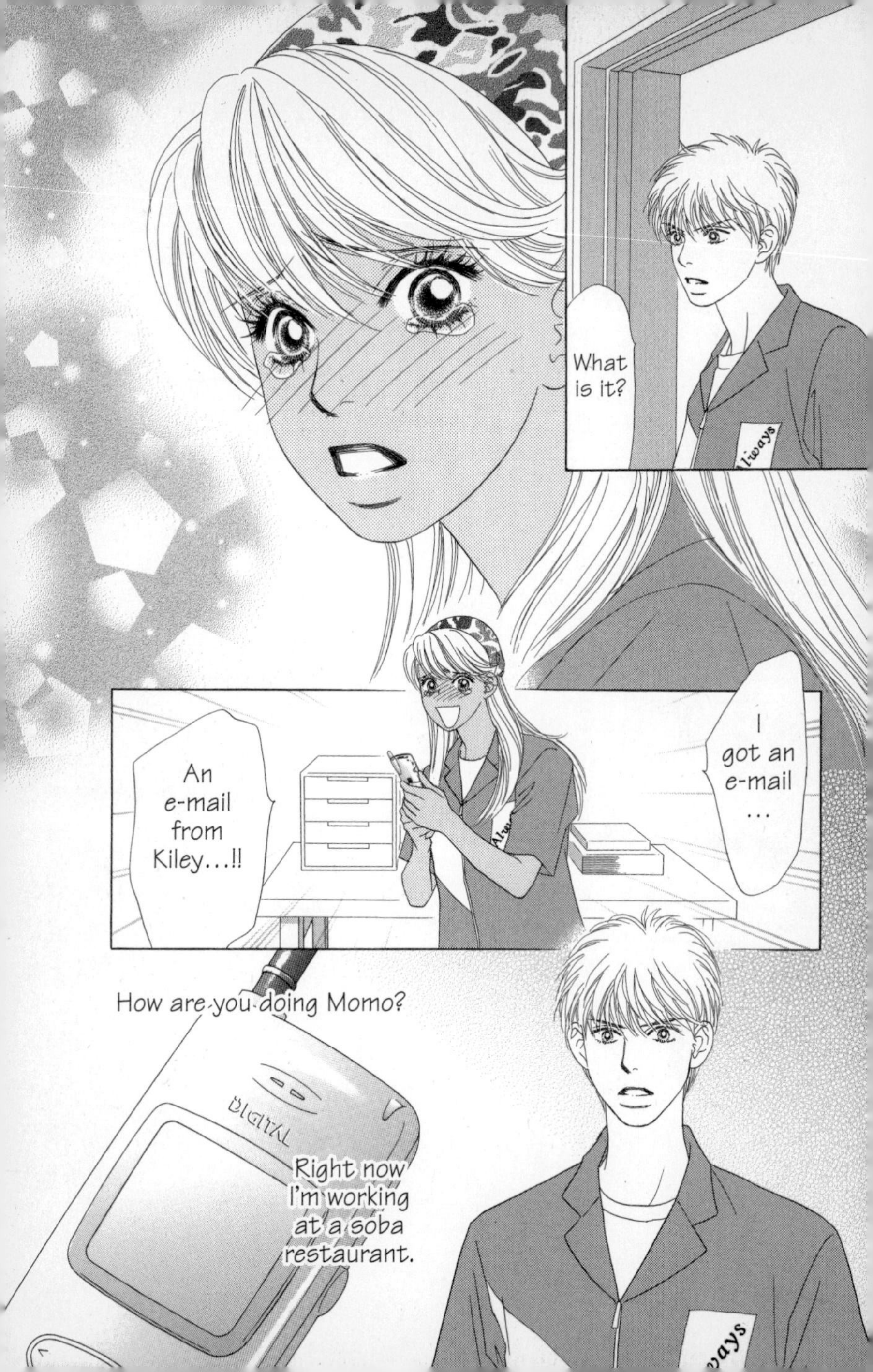
What is it?
I got an e-mail…
An e-mail from Kiley…!!
How are you doing Momo?
Right now I'm working at a soba restaurant.

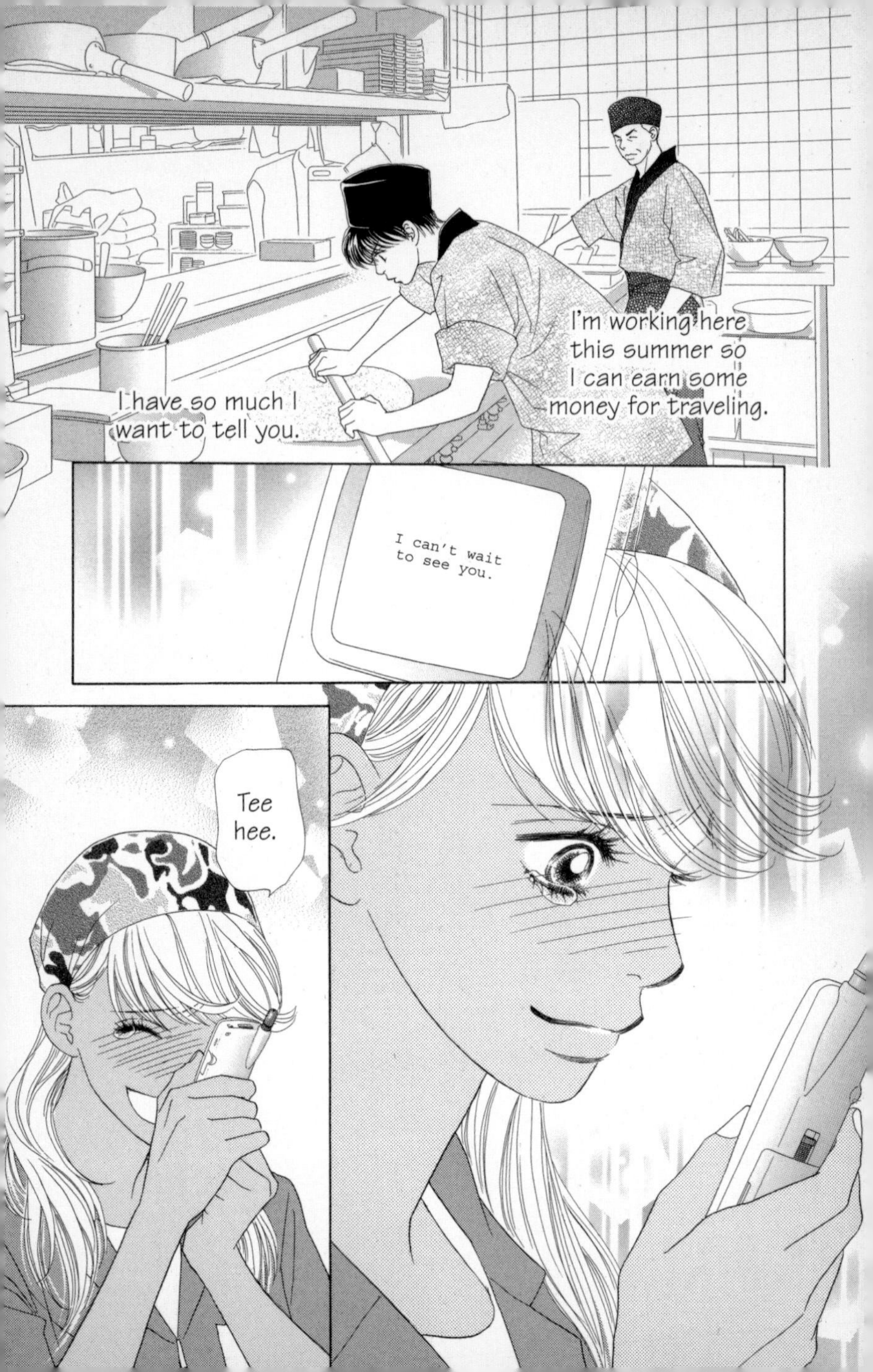
I'm working here this summer so I can earn some money for traveling.
I have so much I want to tell you.
I can't wait to see you.
Tee hee.

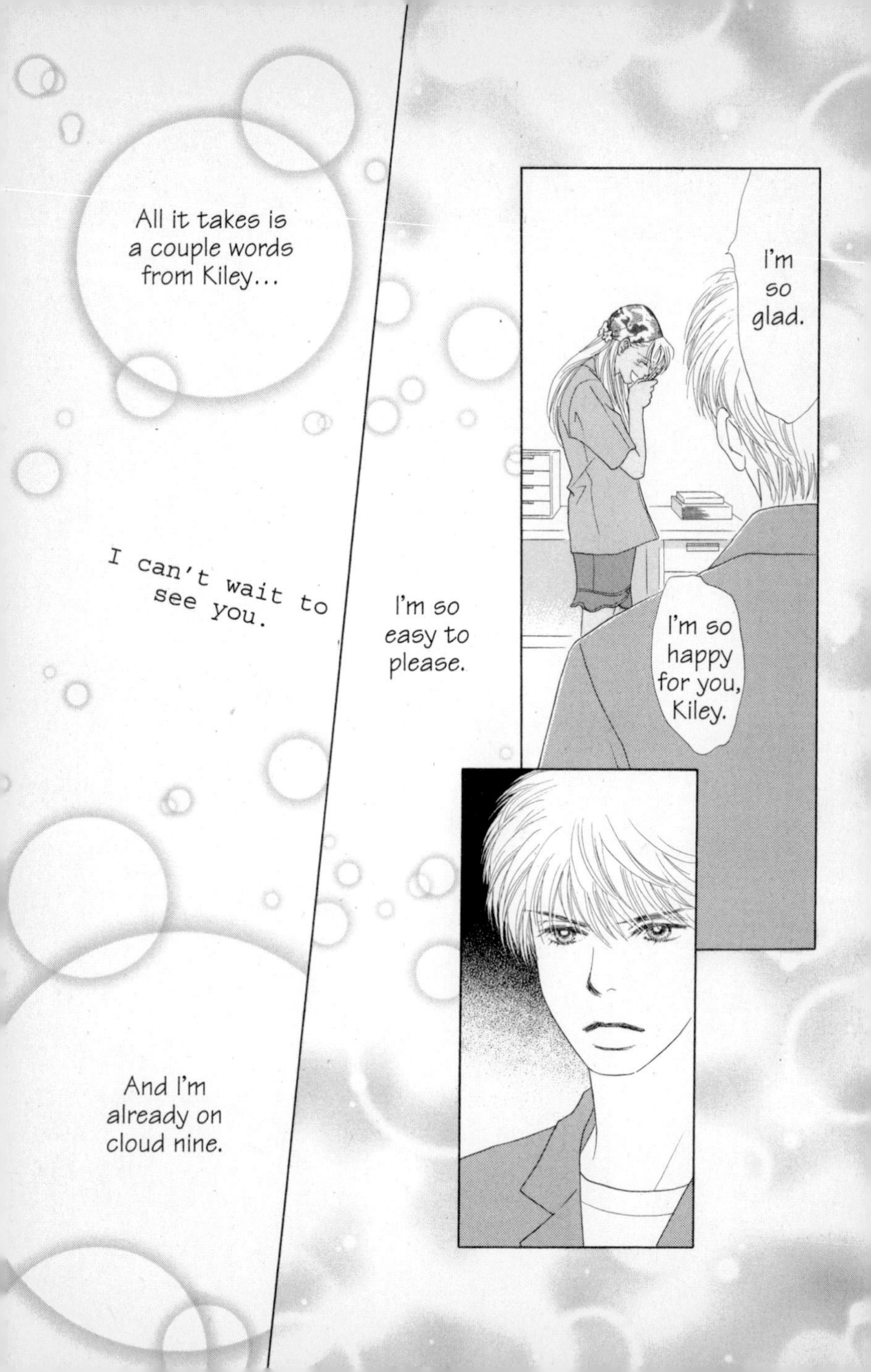
I'm so glad.
I'm so happy for you, Kiley.
I'm so easy to please.
All it takes is a couple words from Kiley…
I can't wait to see you.
And I'm already on cloud nine.

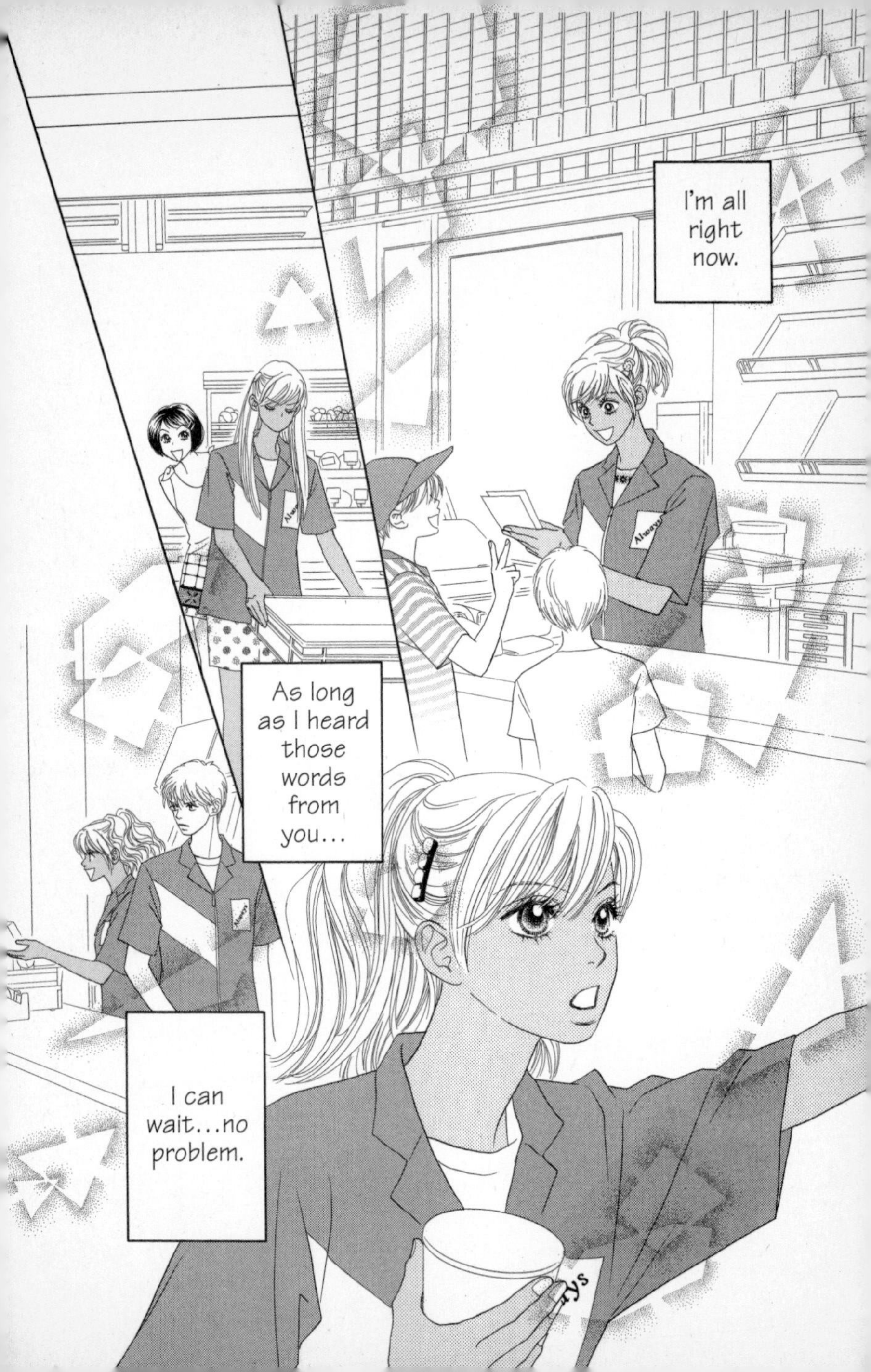
I'm all right now.
As long as I heard those words from you…
I can wait…no problem.

I love
Kiley
after
all.

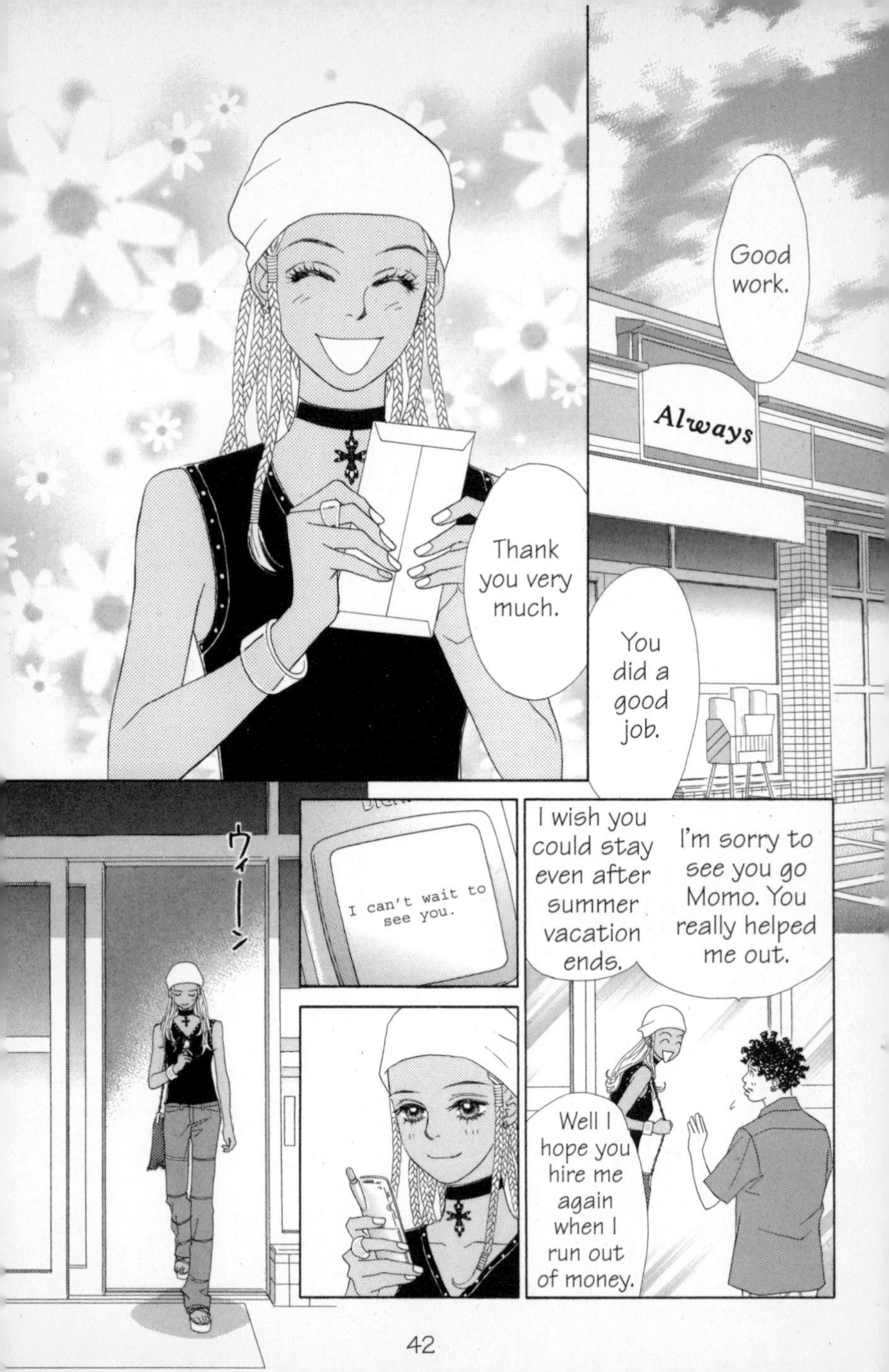
Good work.
Always
You did a good job.
Thank you very much.
I'm sorry to see you go Momo. You really helped me out.
I wish you could stay even after summer vacation ends.
Well I hope you hire me again when I run out of money.
I can't wait to see you.
ウィーン

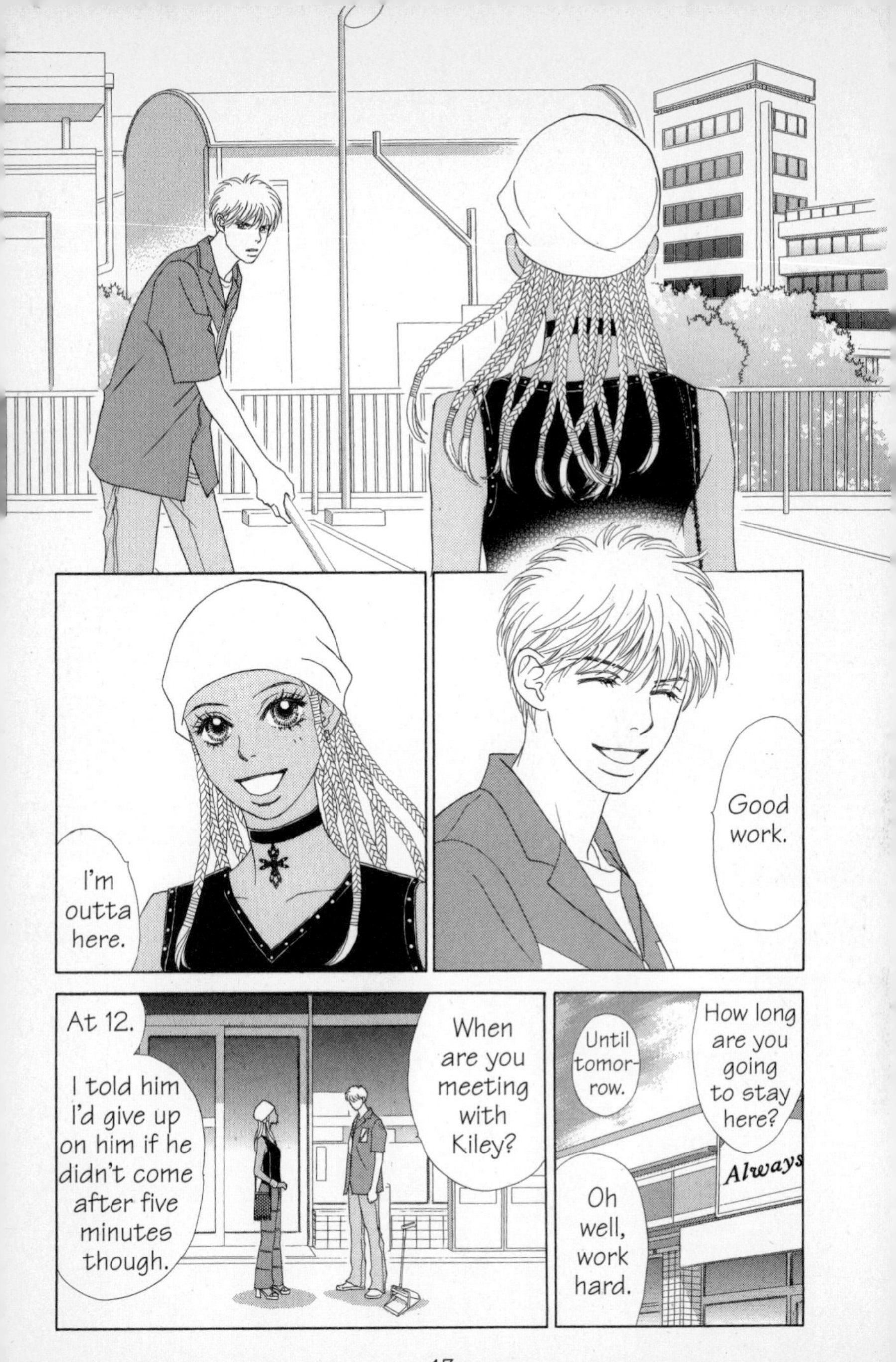
Good work.
I'm outta here.
How long are you going to stay here?
Until tomorrow.
Always
Oh well, work hard.
When are you meeting with Kiley?
At 12.
I told him I'd give up on him if he didn't come after five minutes though.

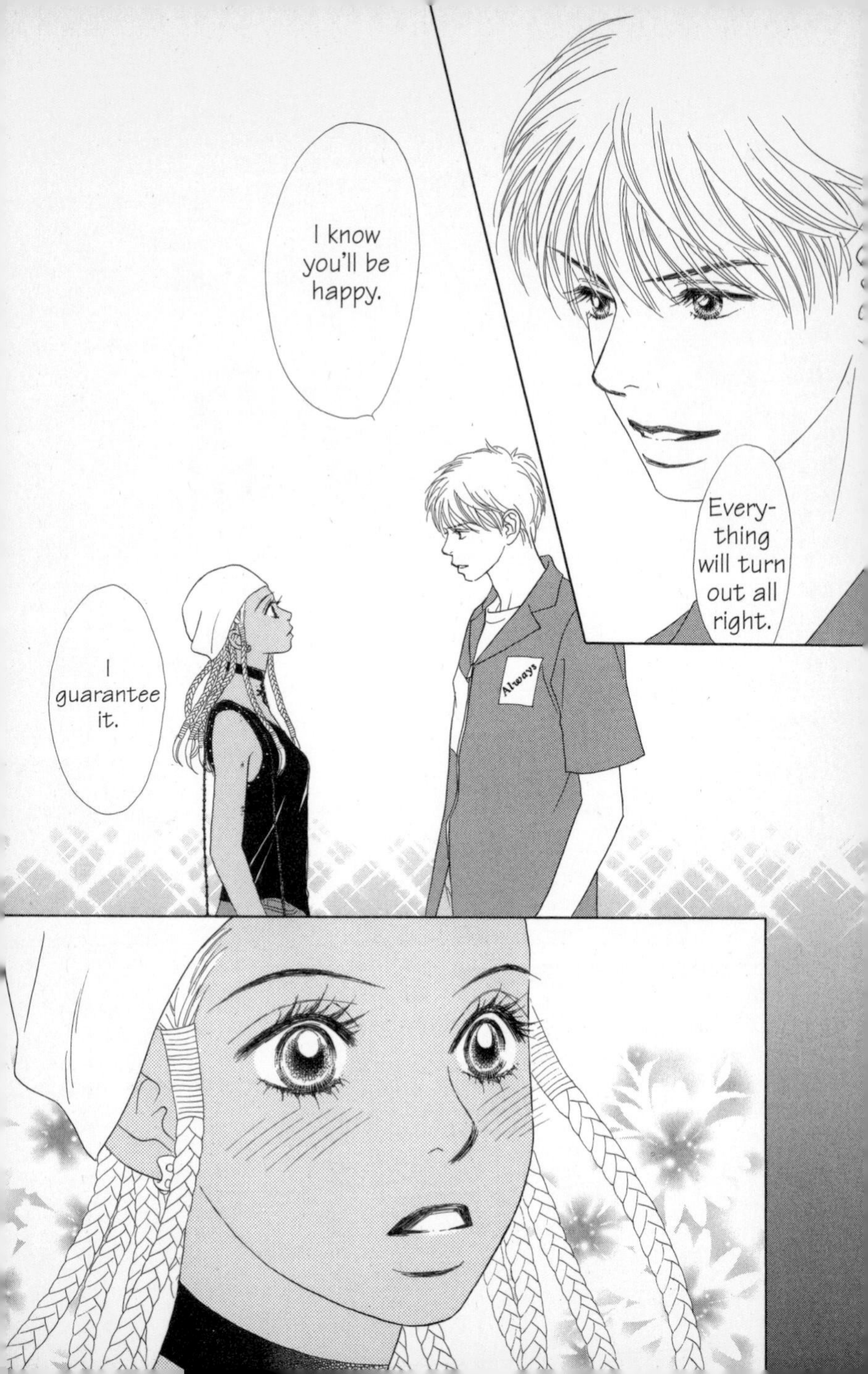
Every-thing will turn out all right.
I know you'll be happy.
Always
I guarantee it.

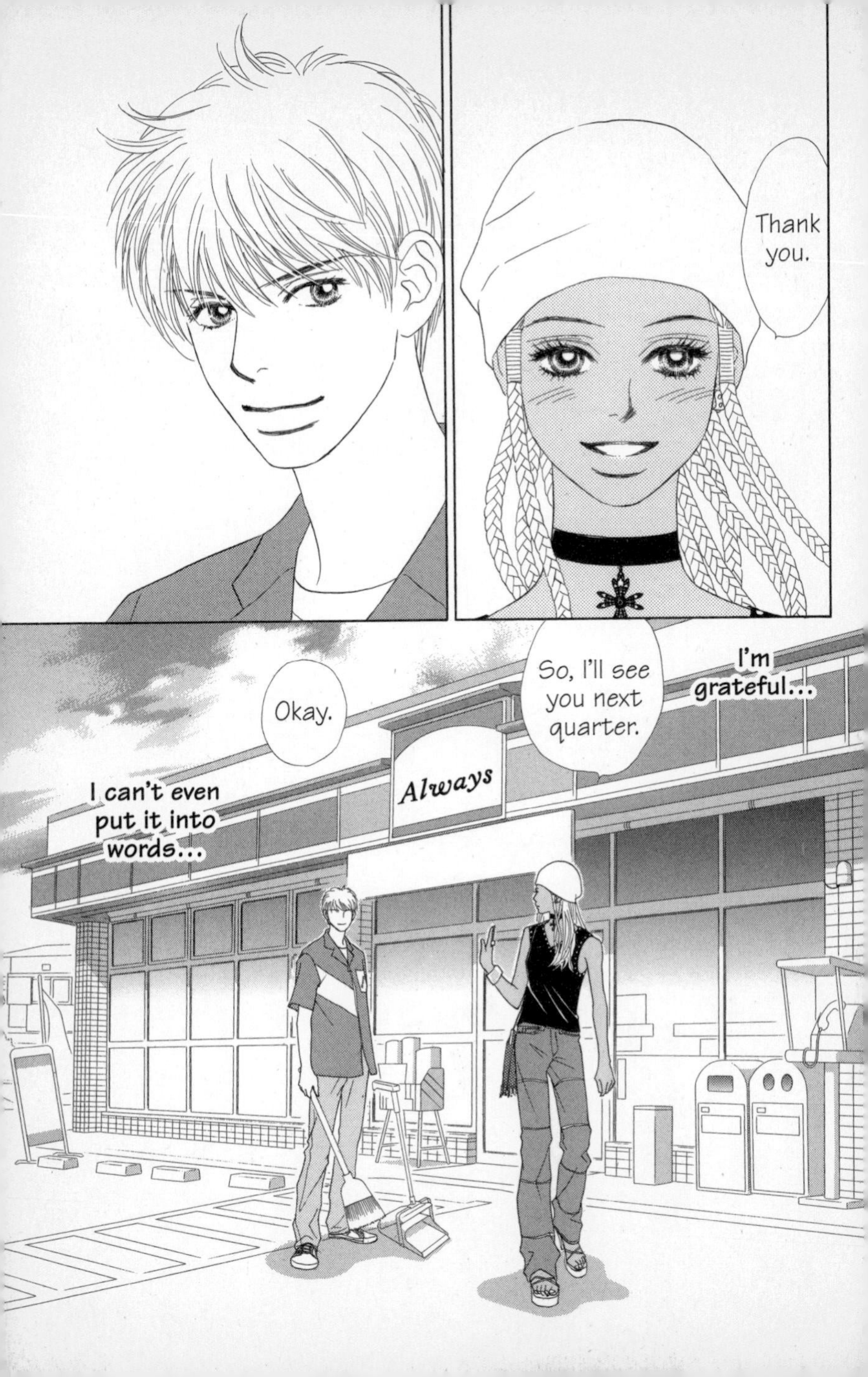
Thank you.
I'm grateful...
So, I'll see you next quarter.
Okay.
Always
I can't even put it into words...

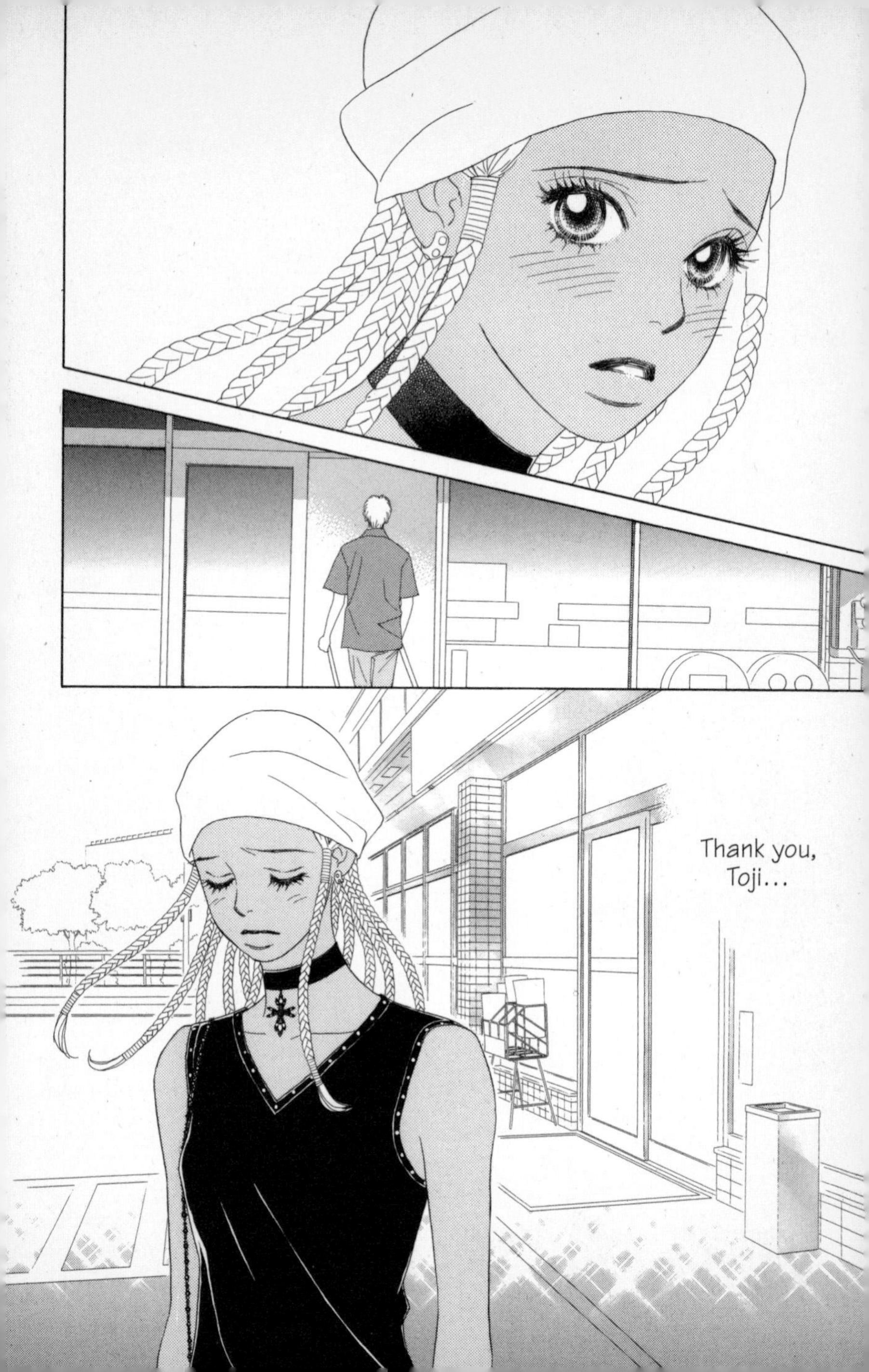
Thank you, Toji…

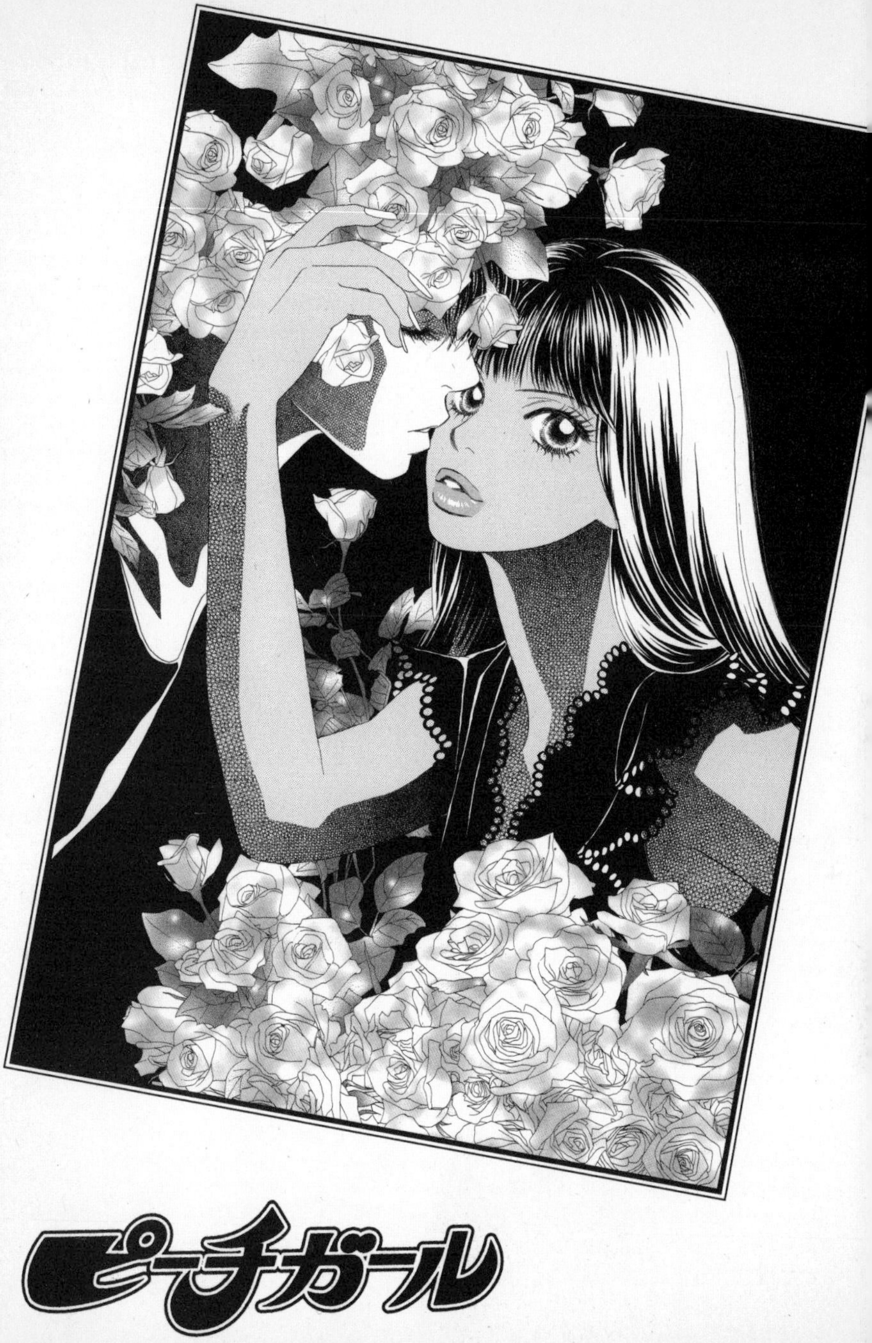

ピーチガール

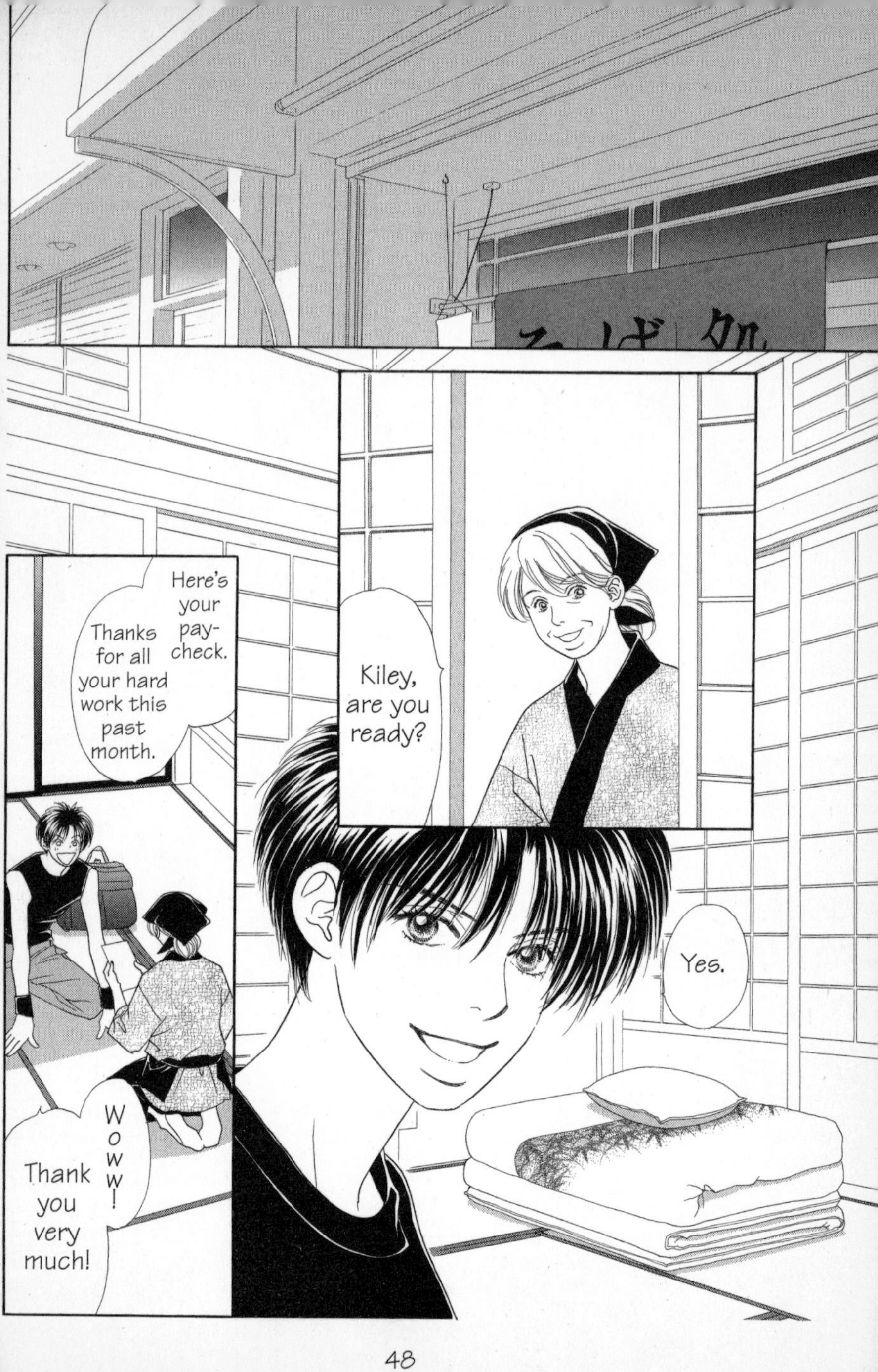
Kiley, are you ready?
Yes.
Here's your pay-check.
Thanks for all your hard work this past month.
Woww!
Thank you very much!

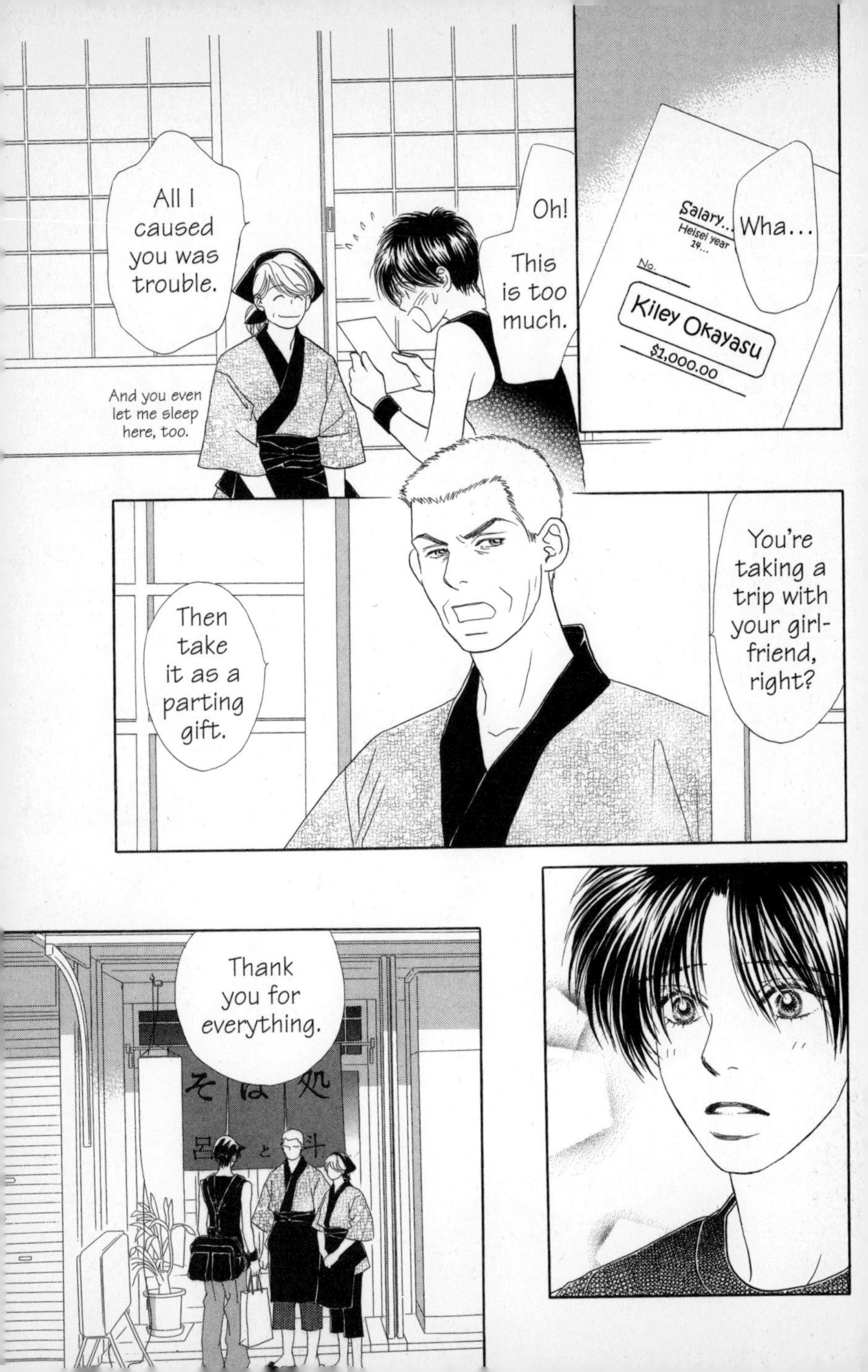
Salary...
Heisei year 14...
No.
Kiley Okayasu
$1,000.00
Wha...
Oh!
This is too much.
All I caused you was trouble.
And you even let me sleep here, too.
You're taking a trip with your girl-friend, right?
Then take it as a parting gift.
Thank you for everything.
そば処

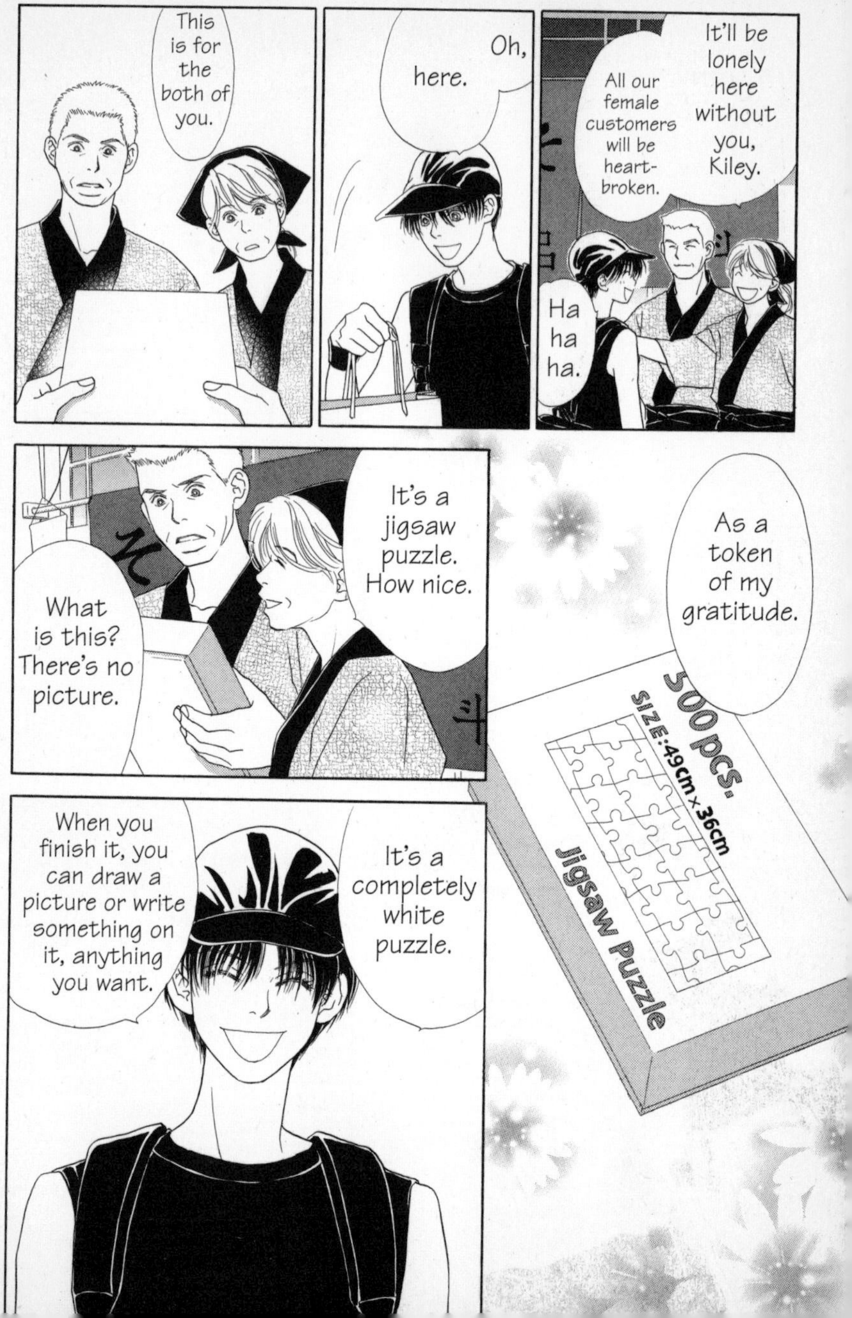
It'll be lonely here without you, Kiley.
All our female customers will be heart-broken.
Ha ha ha.
Oh, here.
This is for the both of you.
As a token of my gratitude.
500 pcs.
SIZE:49cm×36cm
Jigsaw Puzzle
It's a jigsaw puzzle. How nice.
What is this? There's no picture.
It's a completely white puzzle.
When you finish it, you can draw a picture or write something on it, anything you want.

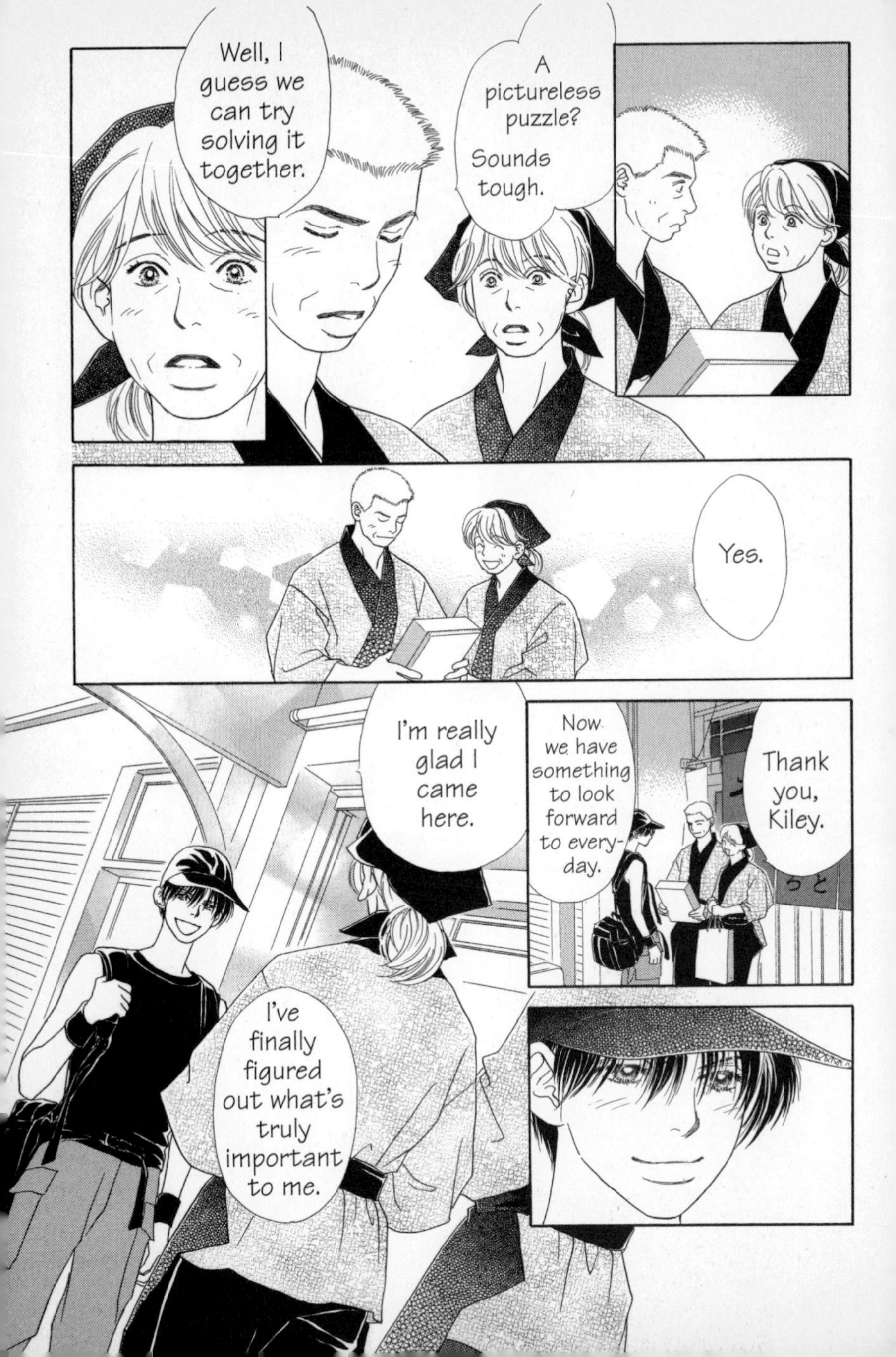
A pictureless puzzle? Sounds tough.
Well, I guess we can try solving it together.
Yes.
Thank you, Kiley.
Now we have something to look forward to every-day.
I'm really glad I came here.
I've finally figured out what's truly important to me.

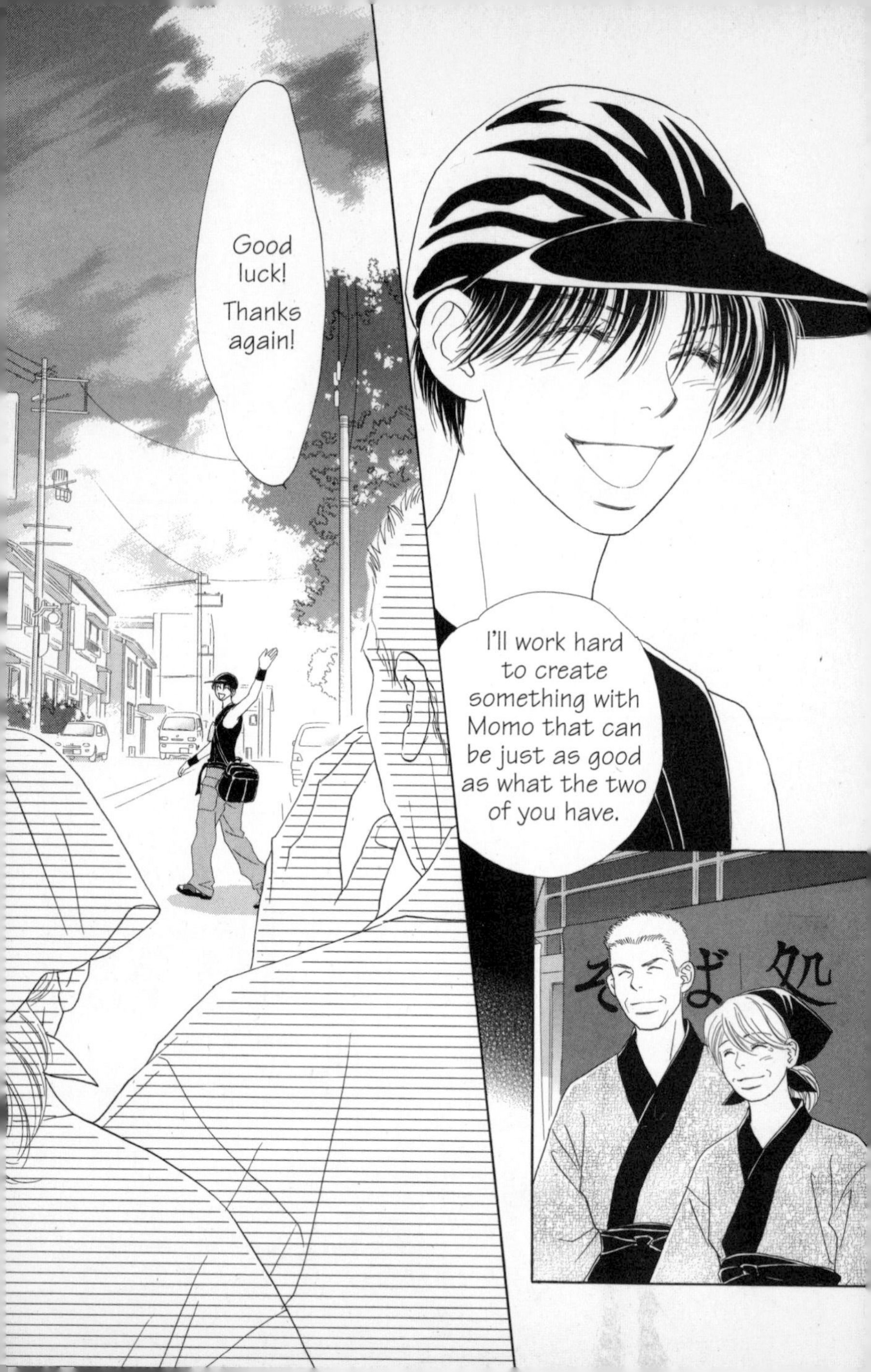
I'll work hard to create something with Momo that can be just as good as what the two of you have.
そば処
Good luck!
Thanks again!

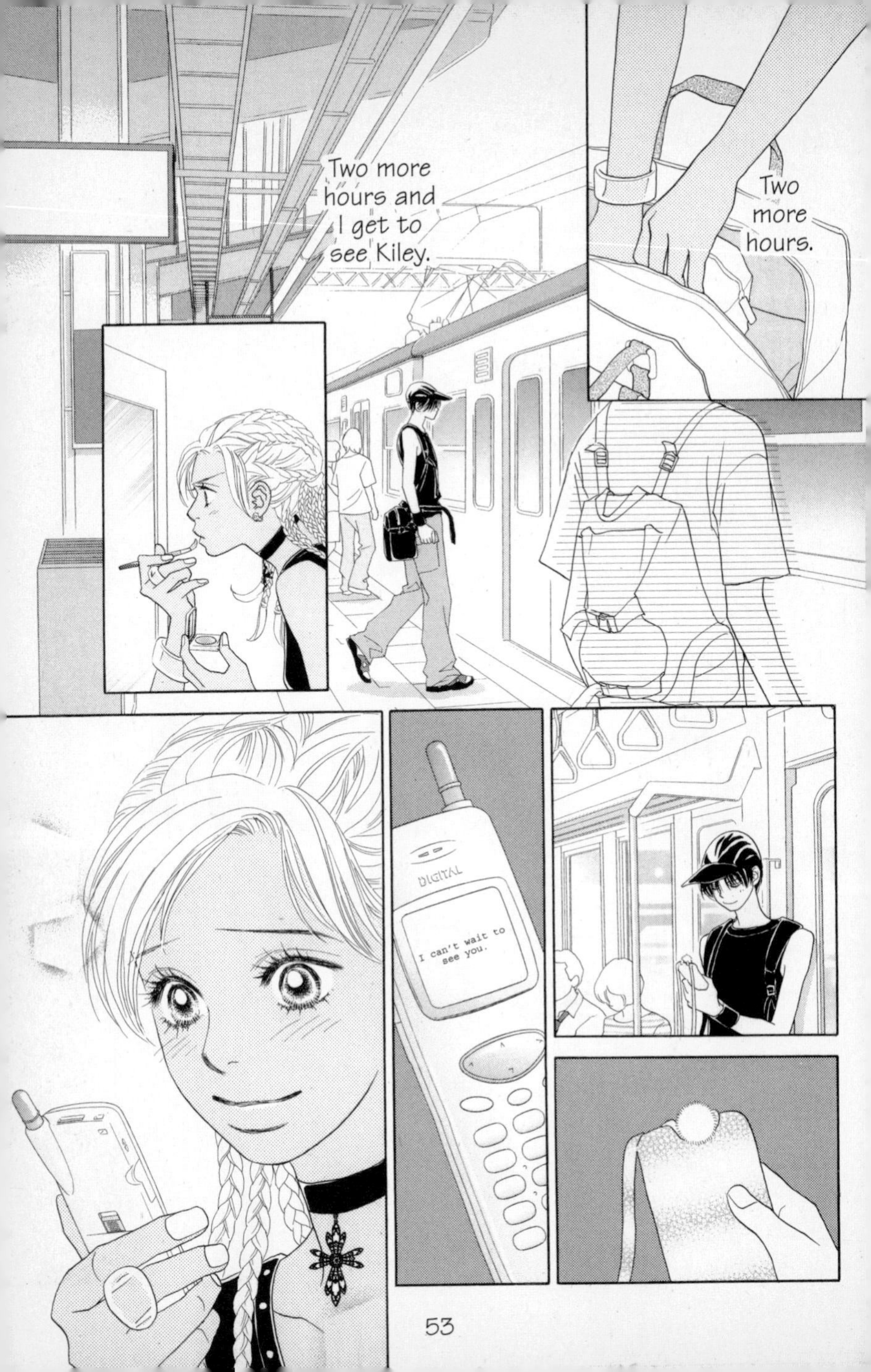
Two more hours.
Two more hours and I get to see Kiley.
I can't wait to see you.
DIGITAL

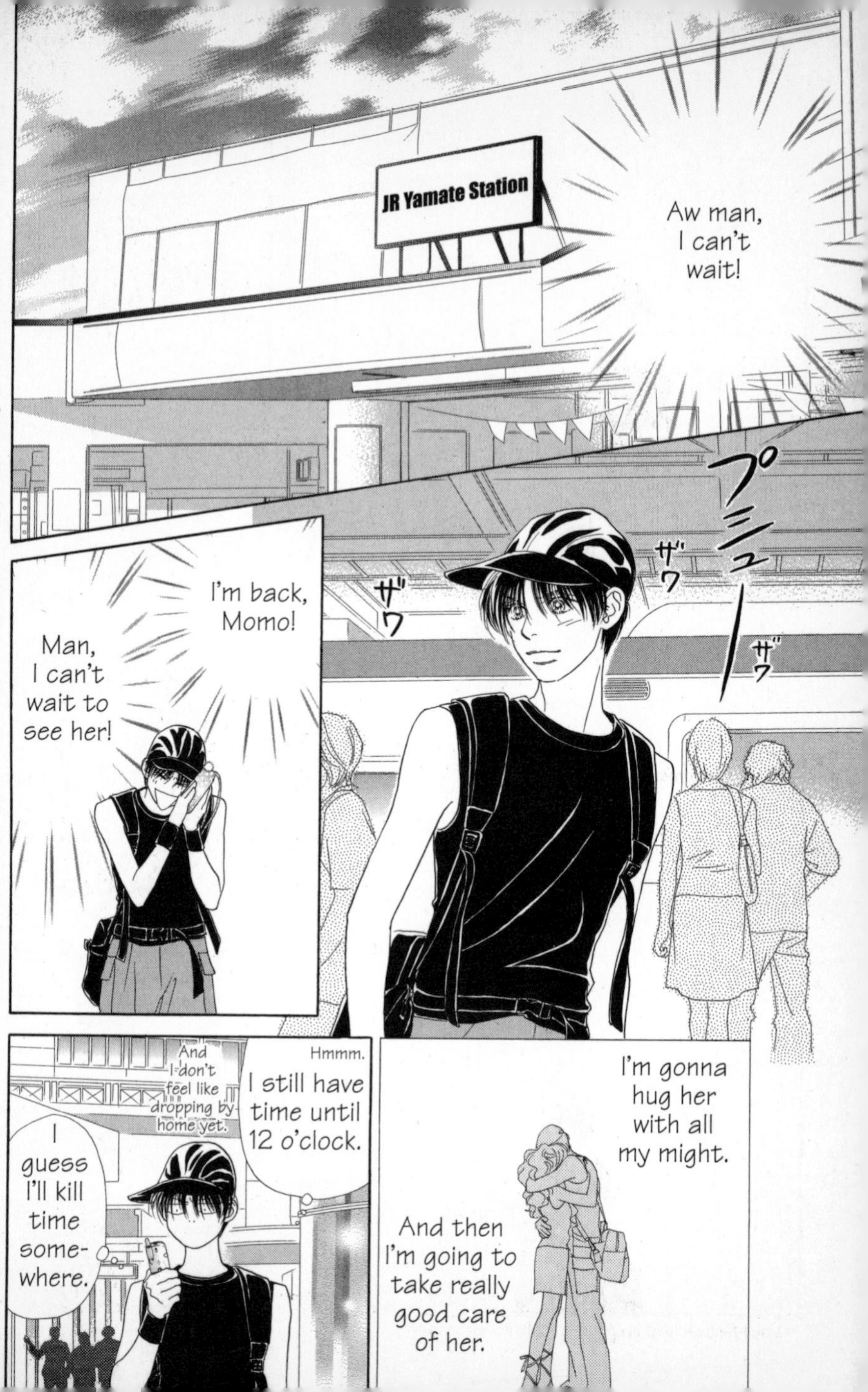
JR Yamate Station
Aw man, I can't wait!
プシュー
ザワ
ザワ
ザワ
I'm back, Momo!
Man, I can't wait to see her!
I'm gonna hug her with all my might.
And then I'm going to take really good care of her.
Hmmm.
I still have time until 12 o'clock.
And I don't feel like dropping by home yet.
I guess I'll kill time somewhere.

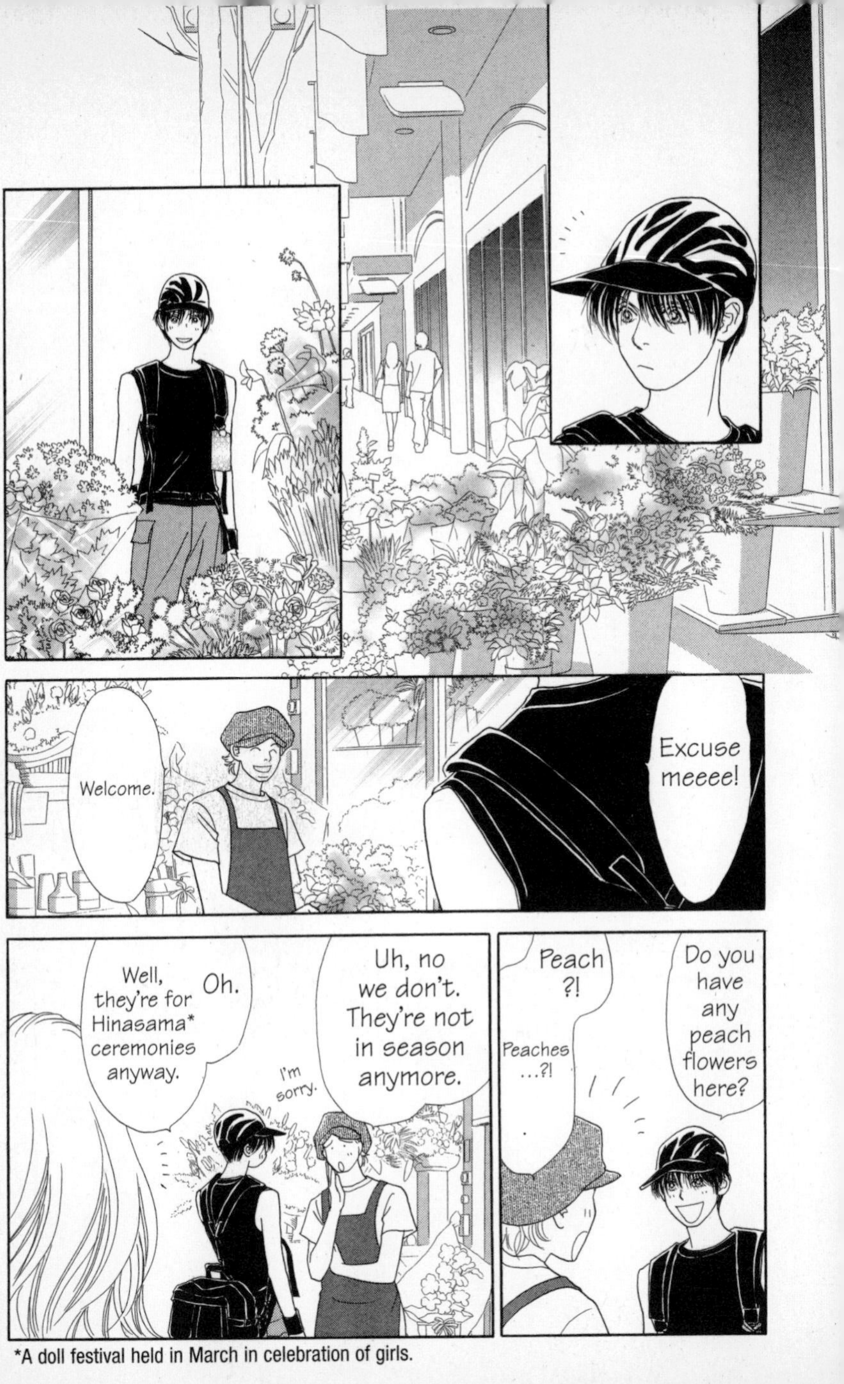
Excuse meeee!
Welcome.
Do you have any peach flowers here?
Peach ?!
Peaches ...?!
Uh, no we don't. They're not in season anymore.
I'm sorry.
Oh.
Well, they're for Hinasama* ceremonies anyway.

*A doll festival held in March in celebration of girls.

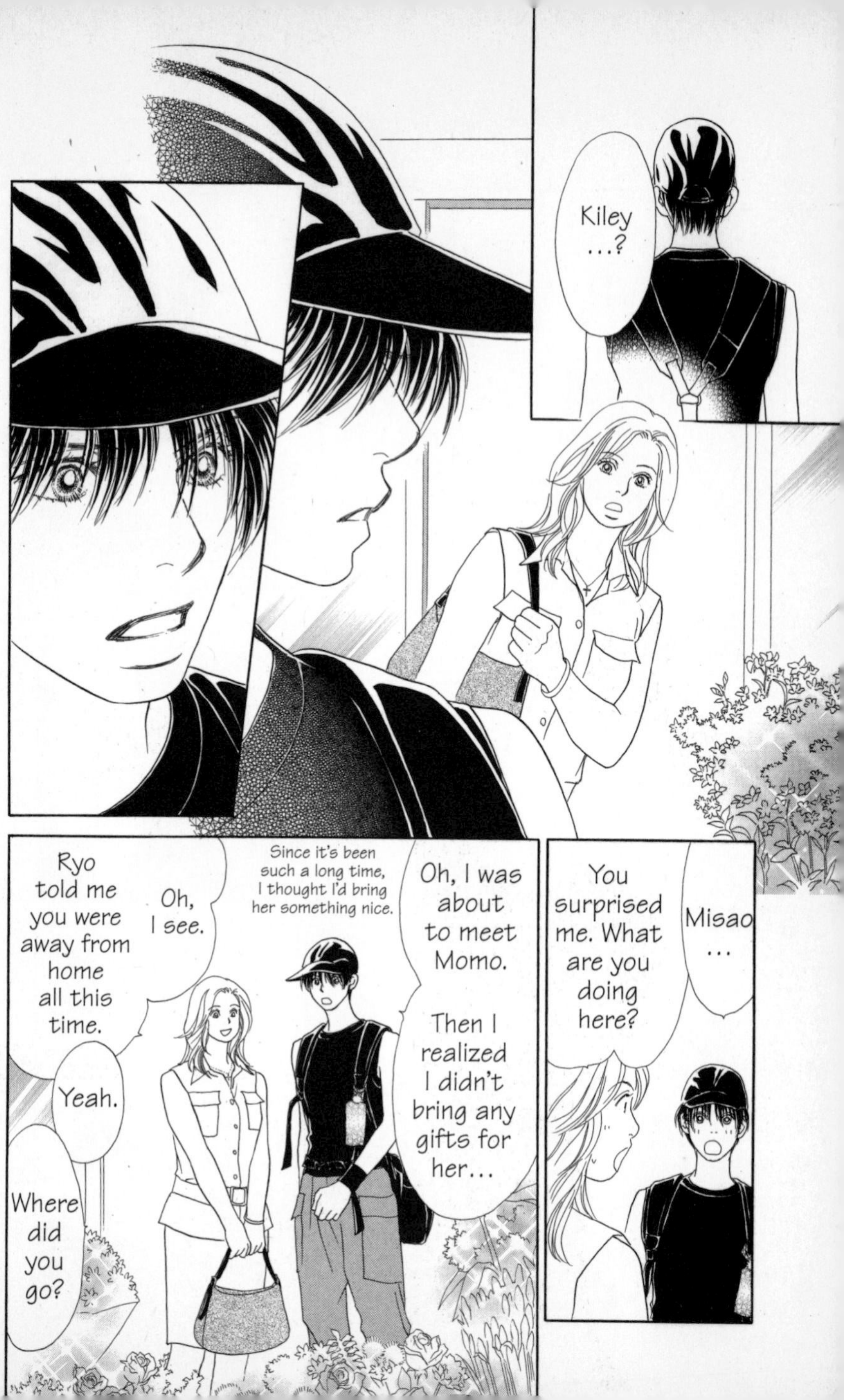
Kiley ...?
Misao ...
You surprised me. What are you doing here?
Oh, I was about to meet Momo.
Then I realized I didn't bring any gifts for her...
Since it's been such a long time, I thought I'd bring her something nice.
Oh, I see.
Ryo told me you were away from home all this time.
Yeah.
Where did you go?

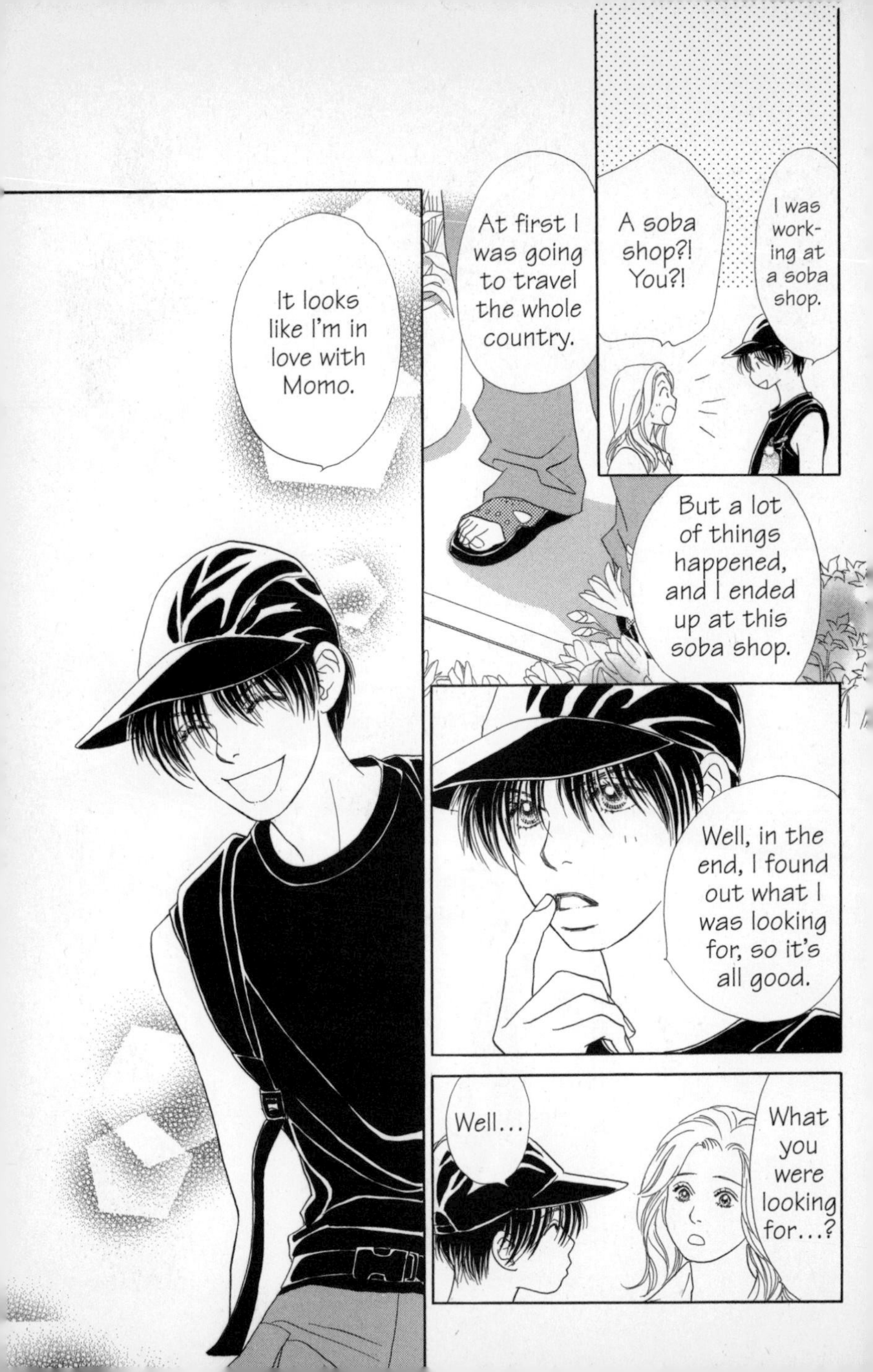
I was work-ing at a soba shop.
A soba shop?! You?!
At first I was going to travel the whole country.
But a lot of things happened, and I ended up at this soba shop.
Well, in the end, I found out what I was looking for, so it's all good.
What you were looking for...?
Well...
It looks like I'm in love with Momo.

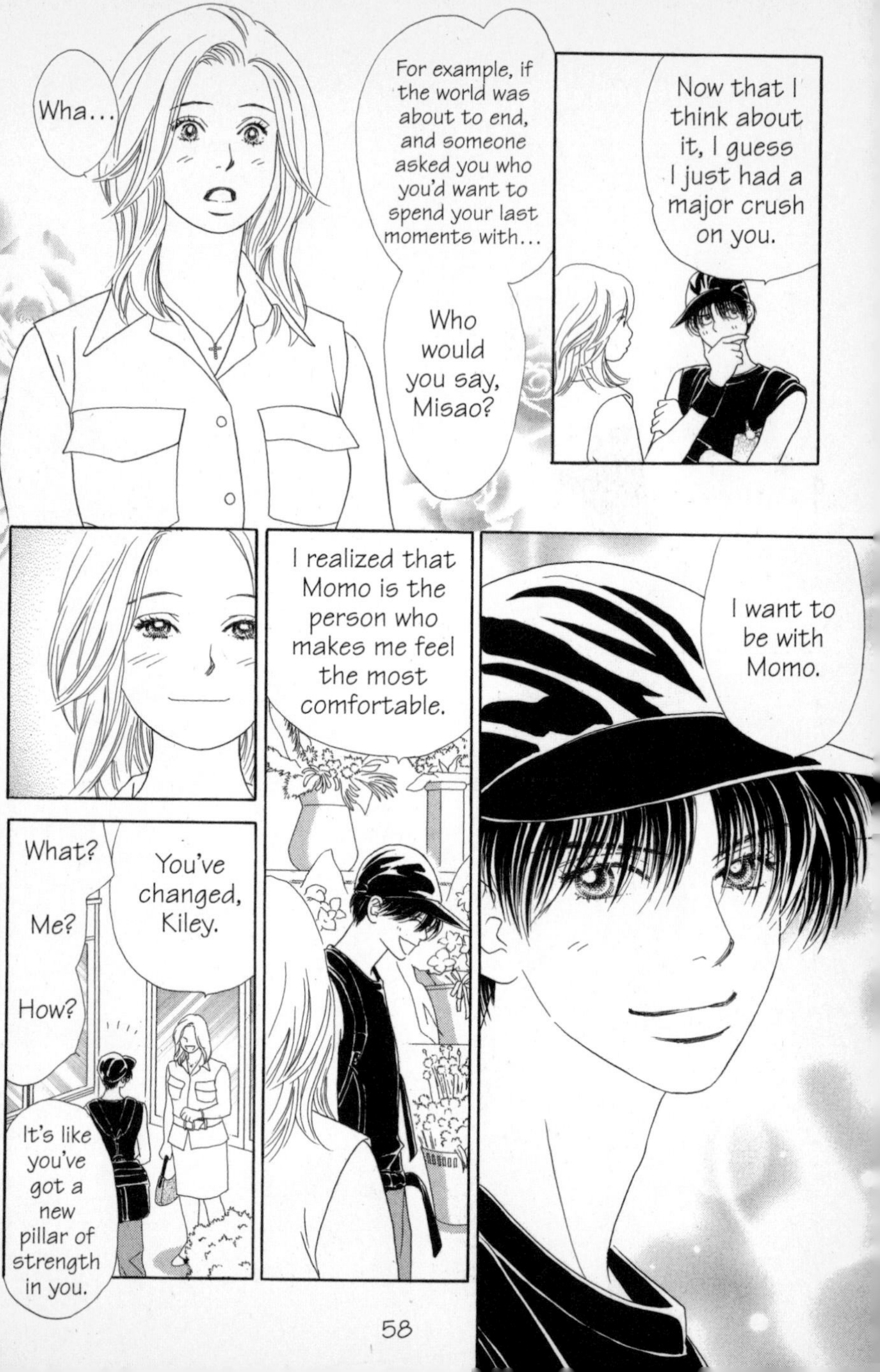

Now that I think about it, I guess I just had a major crush on you.
For example, if the world was about to end, and someone asked you who you'd want to spend your last moments with…
Who would you say, Misao?
Wha…
I want to be with Momo.
I realized that Momo is the person who makes me feel the most comfortable.
You've changed, Kiley.
What?
Me?
How?
It's like you've got a new pillar of strength in you.

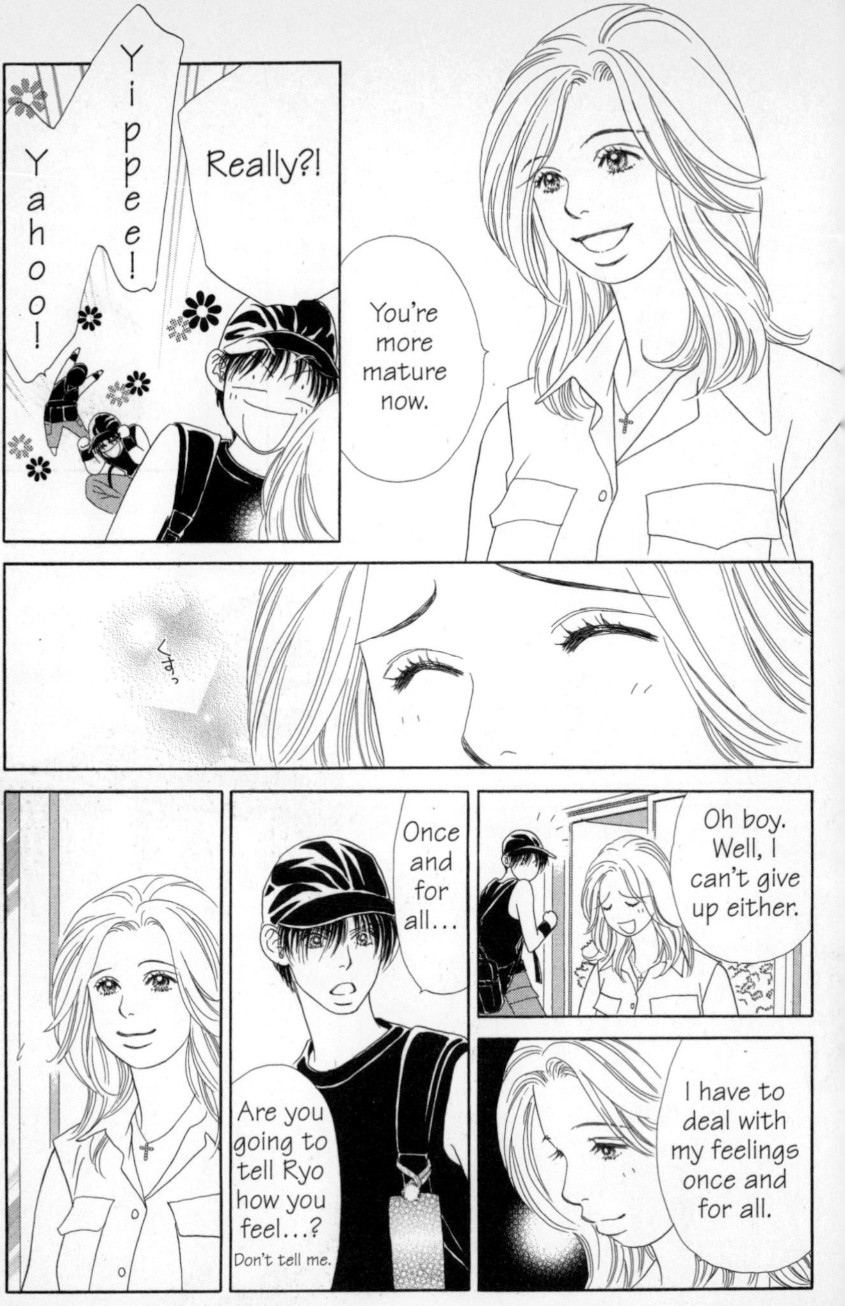

You're more mature now.
Really?!
Yippee!
Yahoo!
くすっ
Oh boy. Well, I can't give up either.
I have to deal with my feelings once and for all.
Once and for all…
Are you going to tell Ryo how you feel…?
Don't tell me.

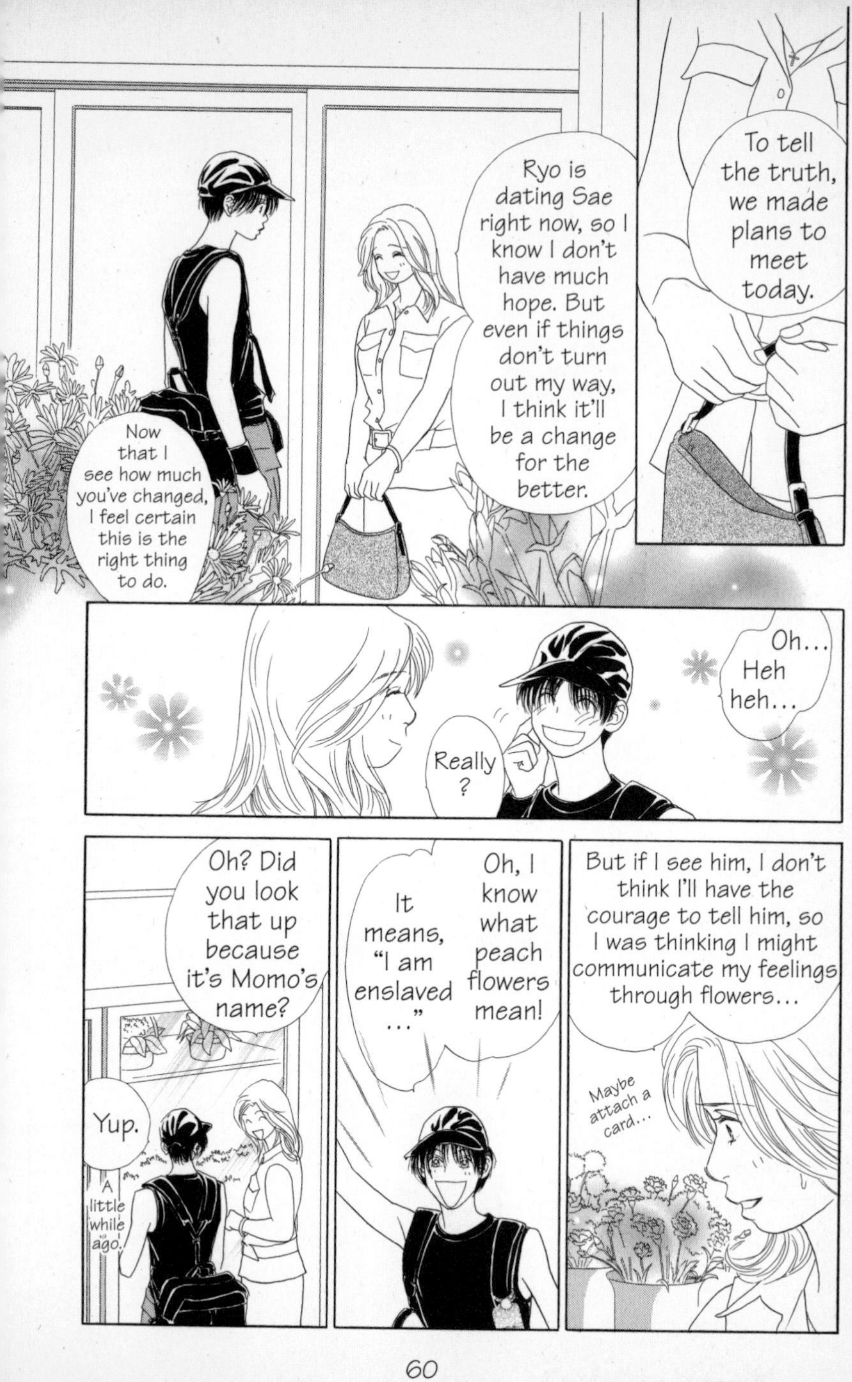
To tell the truth, we made plans to meet today.
Ryo is dating Sae right now, so I know I don't have much hope. But even if things don't turn out my way, I think it'll be a change for the better.
Now that I see how much you've changed, I feel certain this is the right thing to do.
Oh... Heh heh...
Really?
But if I see him, I don't think I'll have the courage to tell him, so I was thinking I might communicate my feelings through flowers...
Maybe attach a card...
Oh, I know what peach flowers mean!
It means, "I am enslaved..."
Oh? Did you look that up because it's Momo's name?
Yup.
A little while ago.

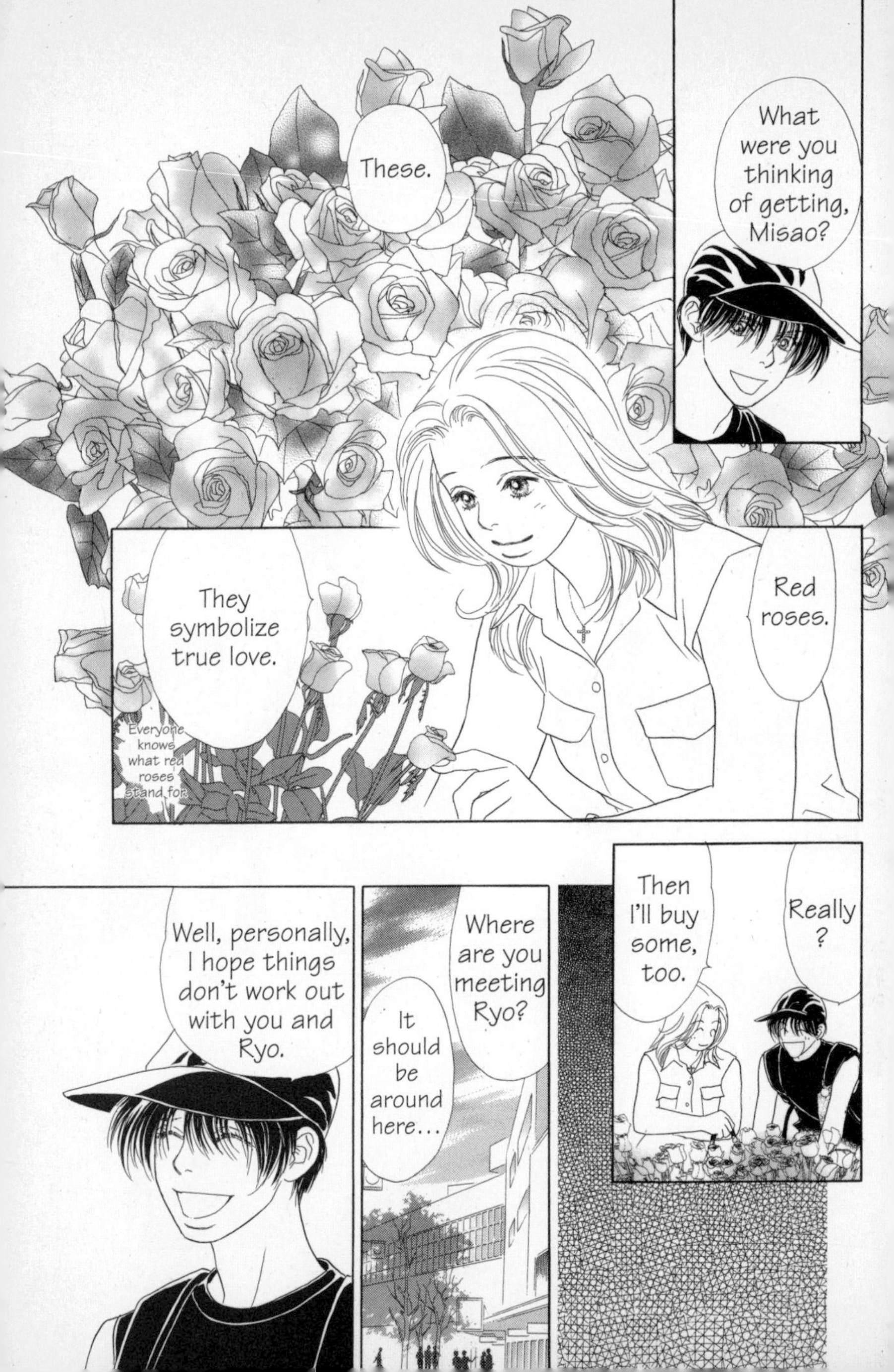
What were you thinking of getting, Misao?
These.
Red roses.
They symbolize true love.
Everyone knows what red roses stand for.
Really?
Then I'll buy some, too.
Where are you meeting Ryo?
It should be around here…
Well, personally, I hope things don't work out with you and Ryo.

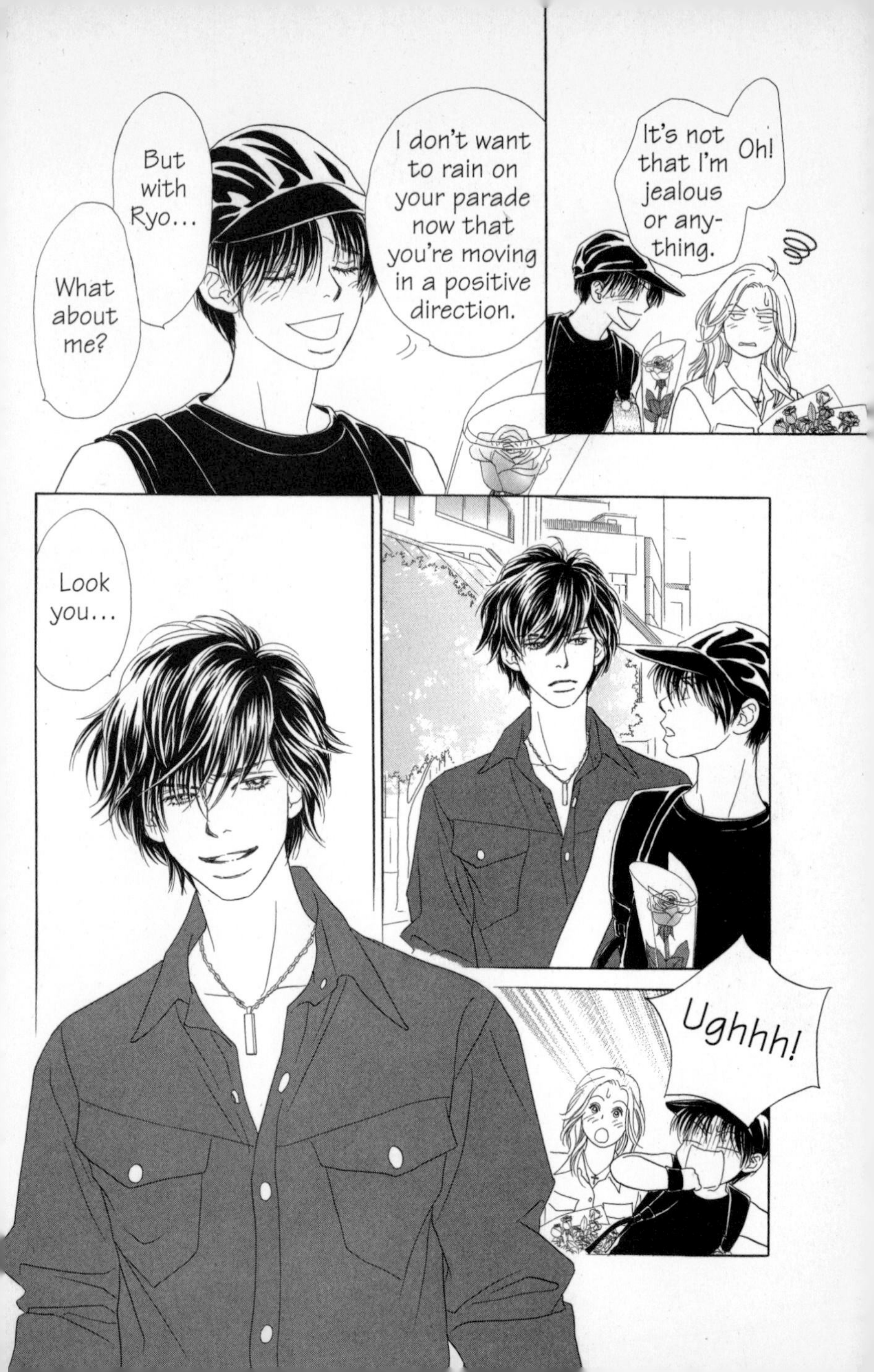
It's not that I'm jealous or anything.
Oh!
I don't want to rain on your parade now that you're moving in a positive direction.
But with Ryo...
What about me?
Ughhh!
Look you...

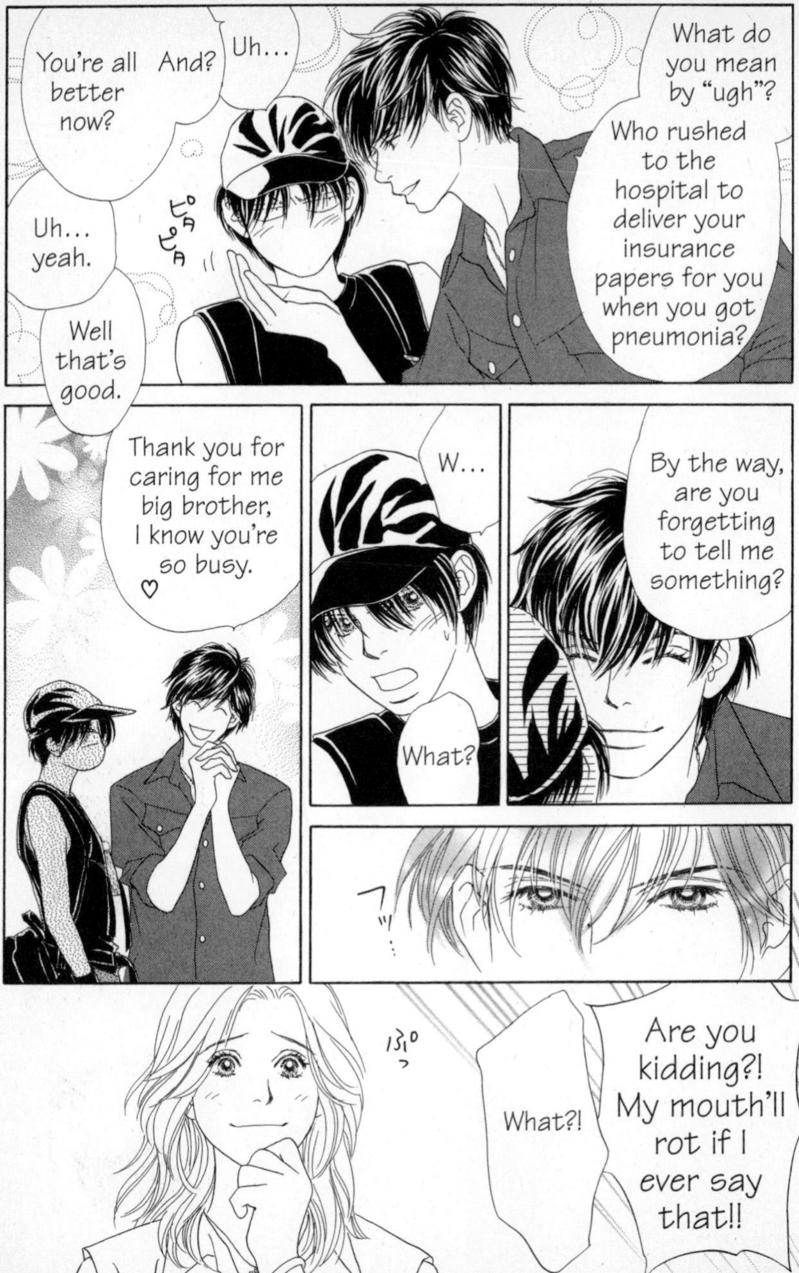
What do you mean by "ugh"?
Who rushed to the hospital to deliver your insurance papers for you when you got pneumonia?
Uh...
And?
You're all better now?
ピタ ピタ
Uh... yeah.
Well that's good.
By the way, are you forgetting to tell me something?
W...
What?
Thank you for caring for me big brother, I know you're so busy. ♡
Are you kidding?! My mouth'll rot if I ever say that!!
What?!

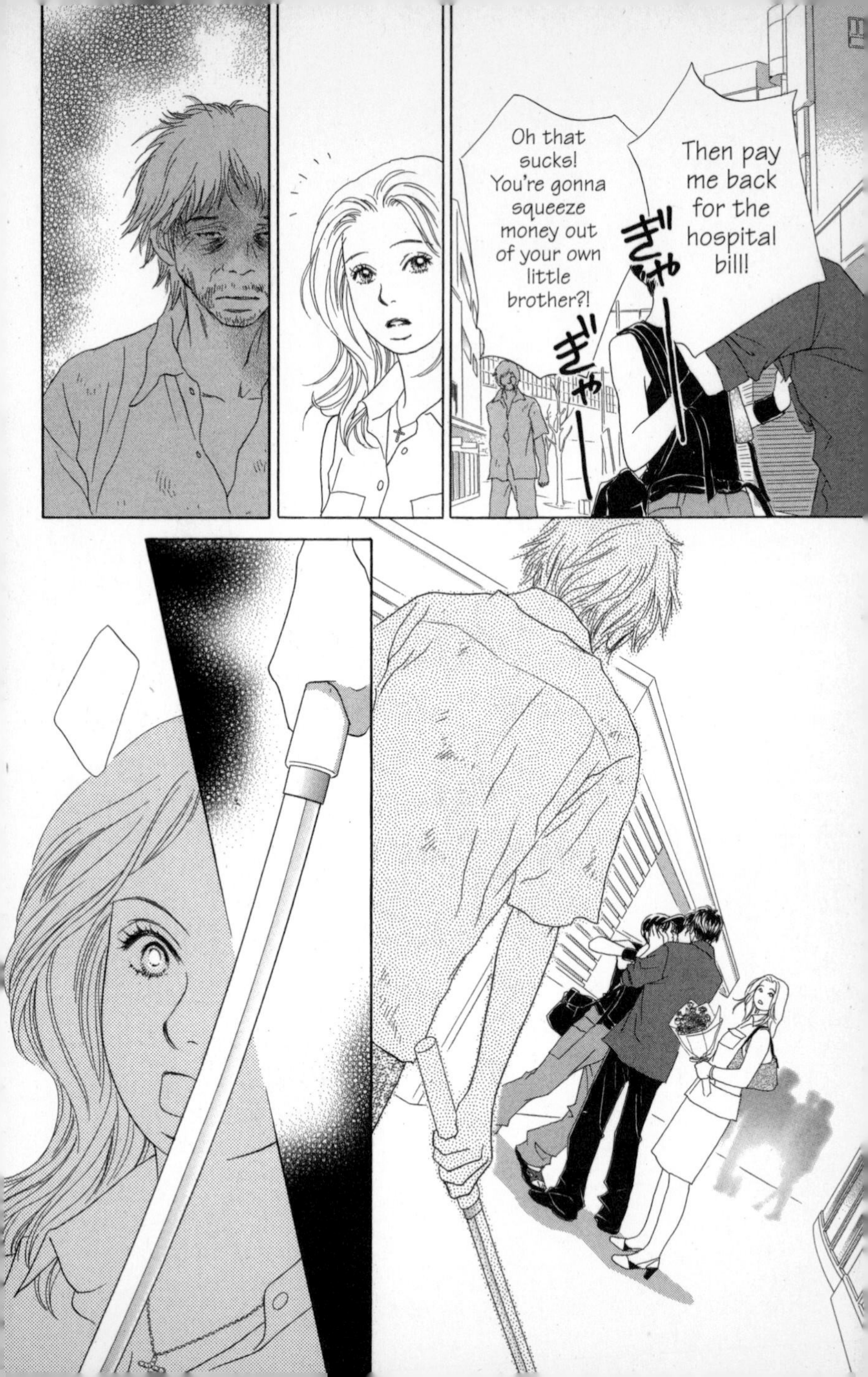
Then pay me back for the hospital bill!
ぎゃーぎゃー
Oh that sucks! You're gonna squeeze money out of your own little brother?!

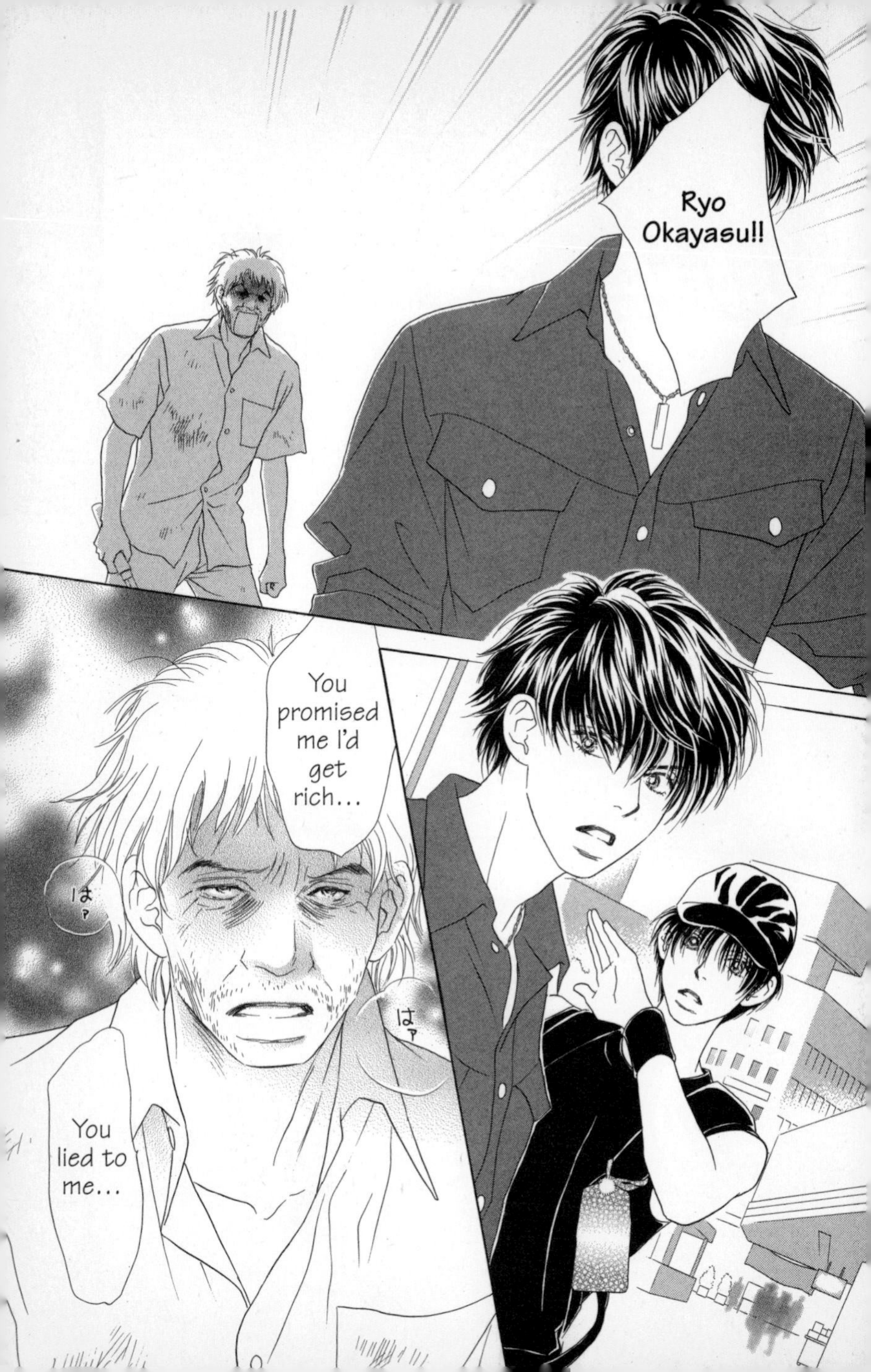
Ryo Okayasu!!
You promised me I'd get rich...
はァ
はァ
You lied to me...

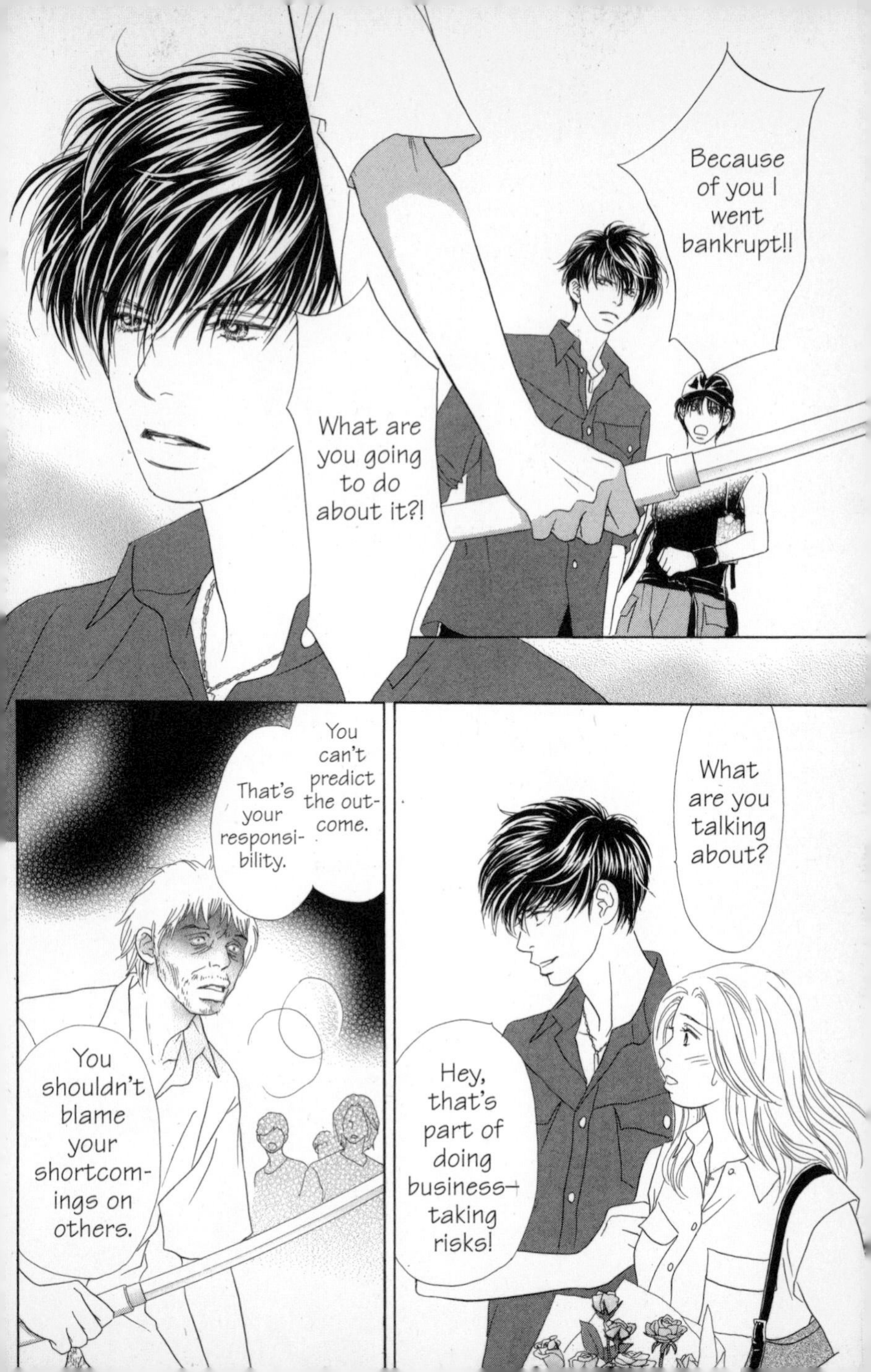
Because of you I went bankrupt!!
What are you going to do about it?!
What are you talking about?
Hey, that's part of doing business—taking risks!
You can't predict the outcome. That's your responsibility.
You shouldn't blame your shortcomings on others.

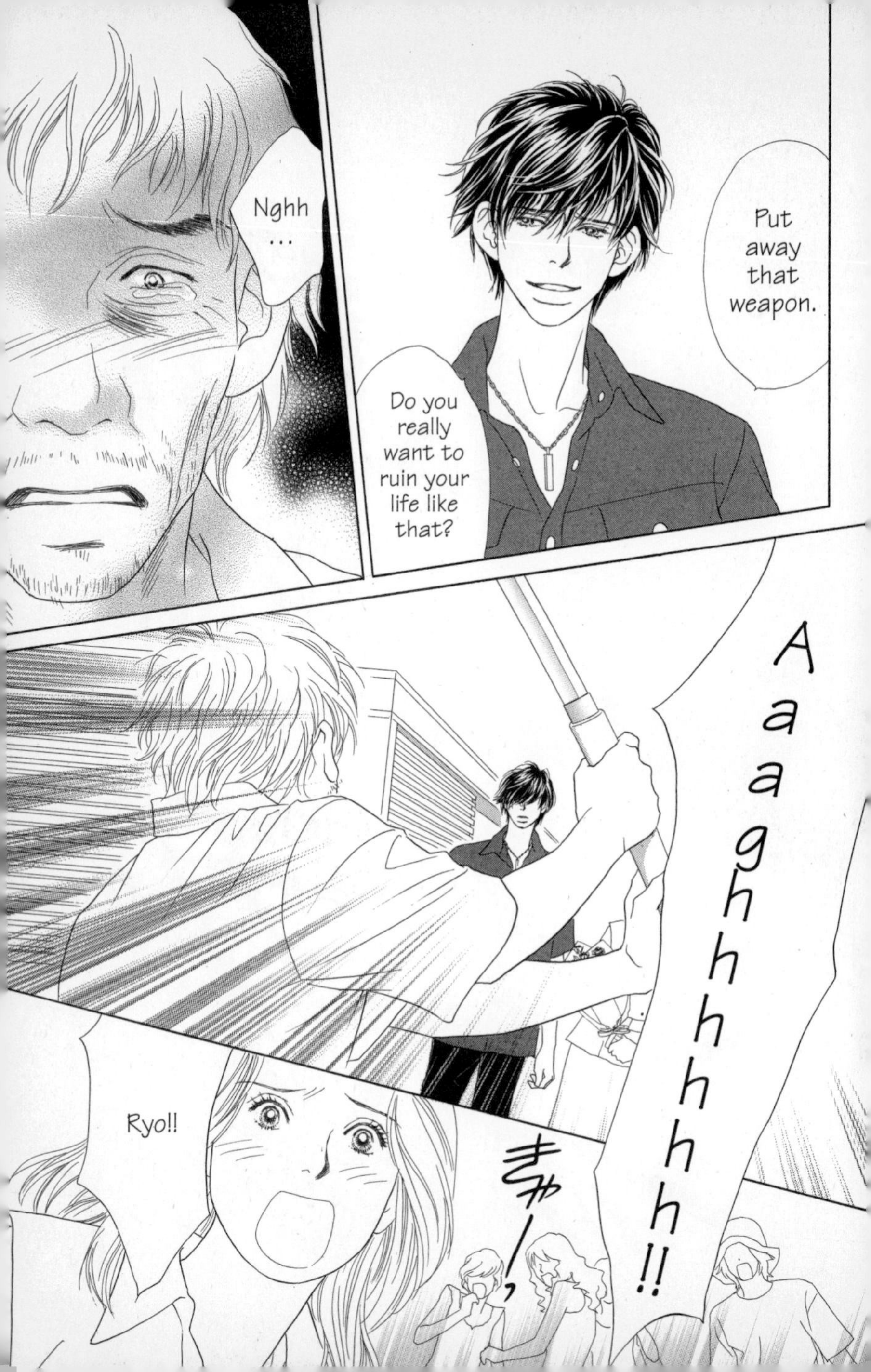
Put away that weapon.
Do you really want to ruin your life like that?
Nghh ...
Aaaghhhhhhhh!!
きゃー!
Ryo!!

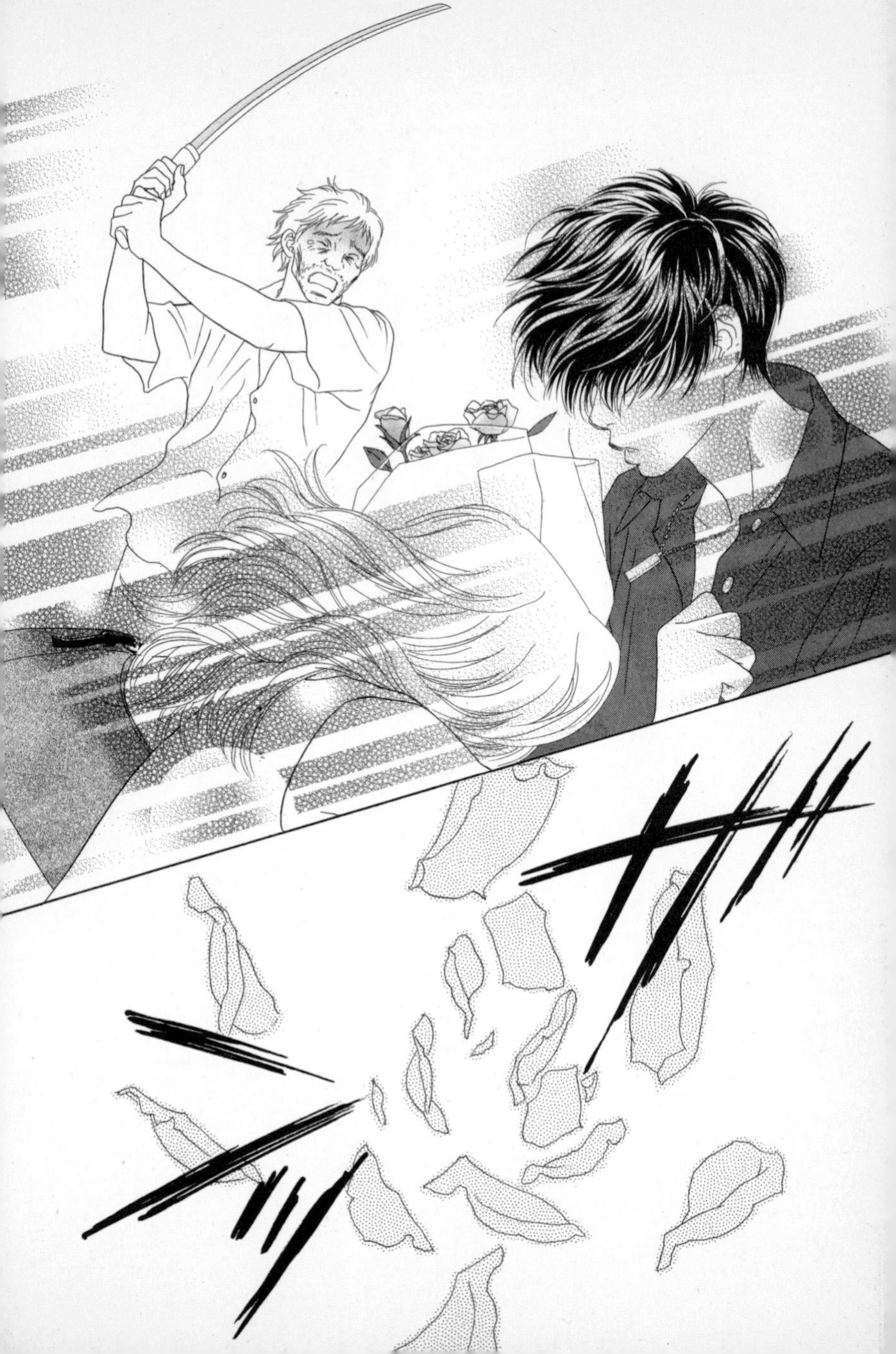

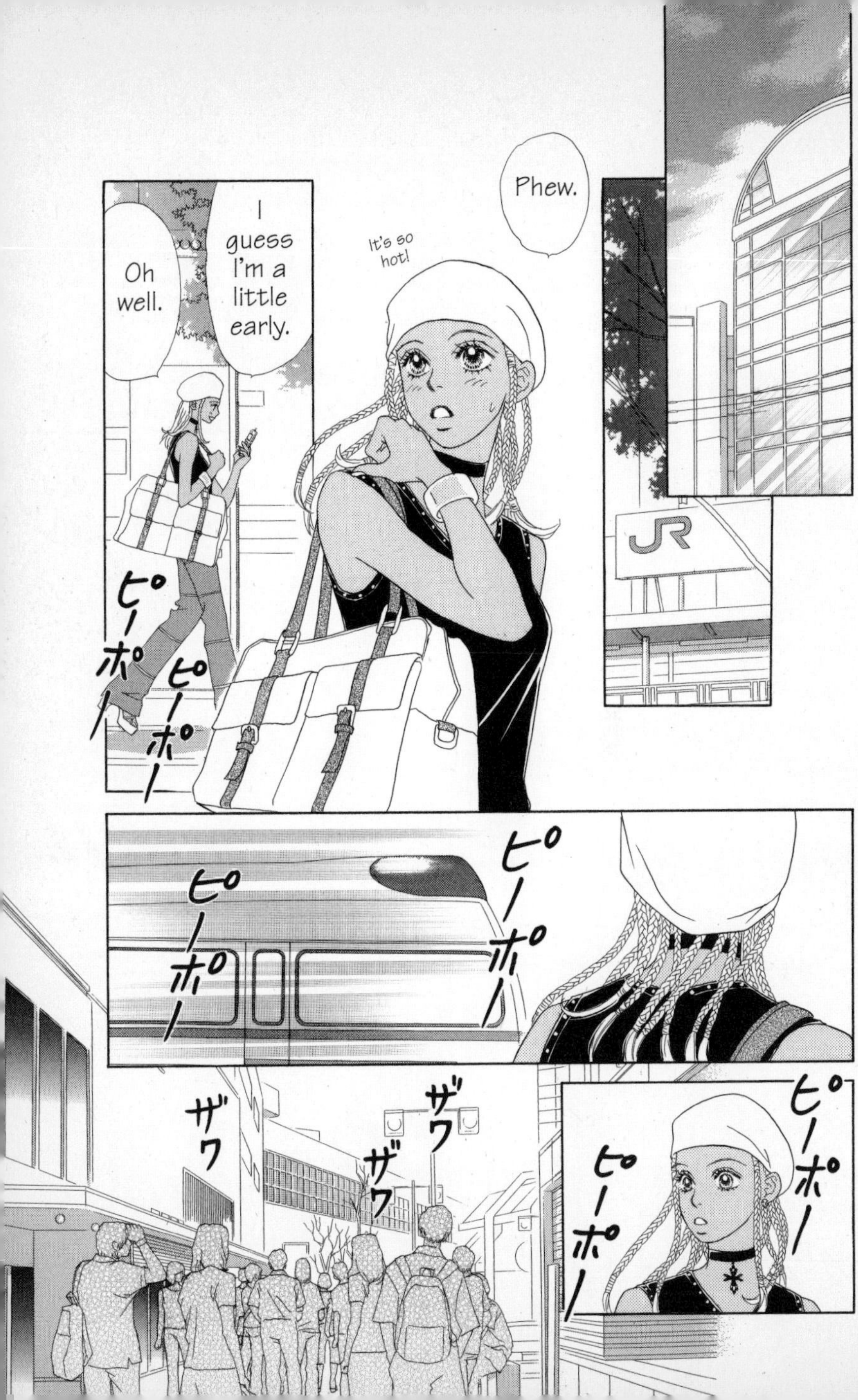
Phew.
It's so hot!
I guess I'm a little early.
Oh well.
ピーポー
ピーポー
ピーポー
ピーポー
ピーポー
ピーポー
ザワ
ザワ
ザワ
ザワ

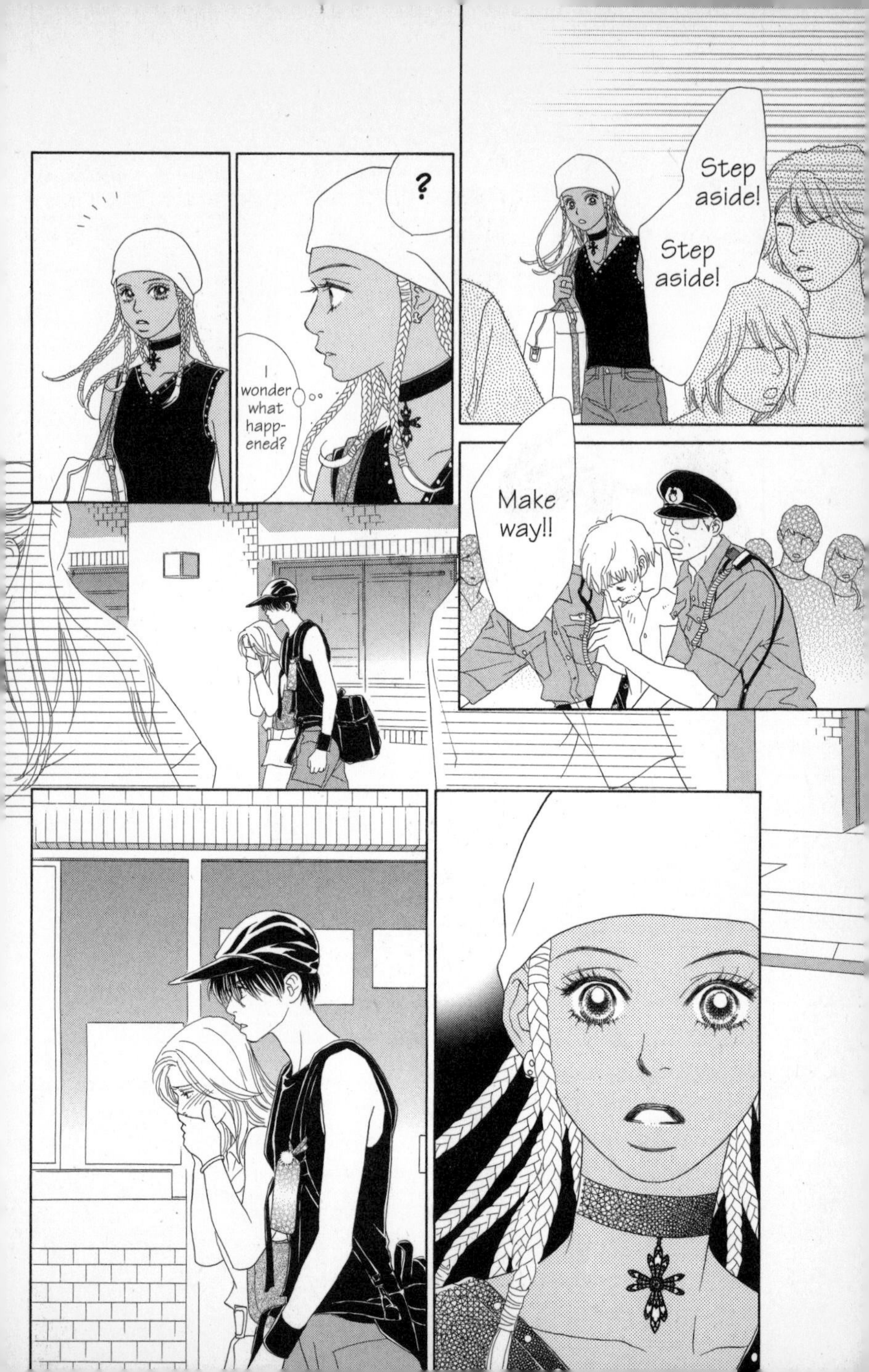
Step aside!
Step aside!
?
I wonder what happ-ened?
Make way!!

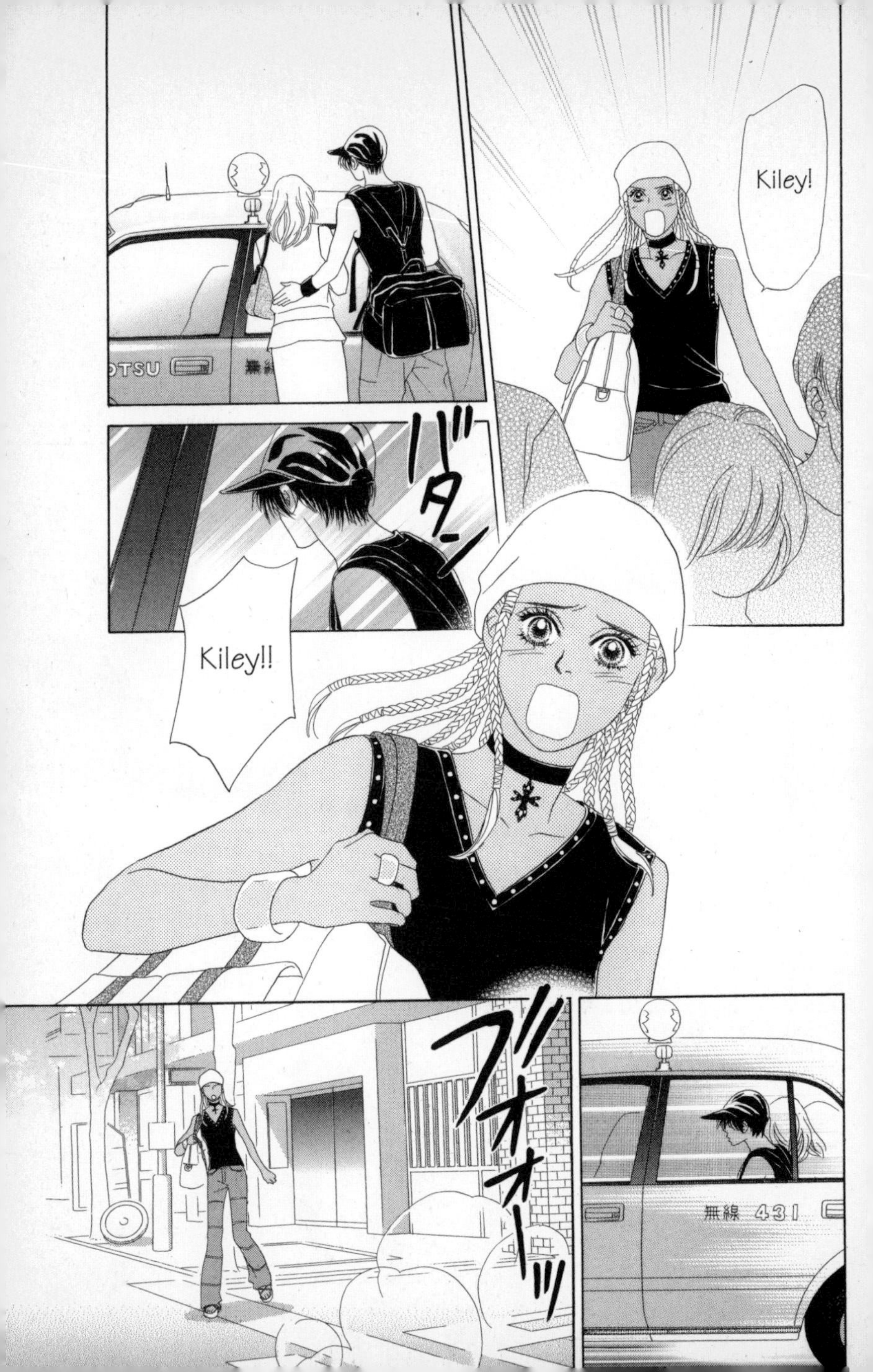
Kiley!
バタン
Kiley!!
無線 431
ブオオーッ

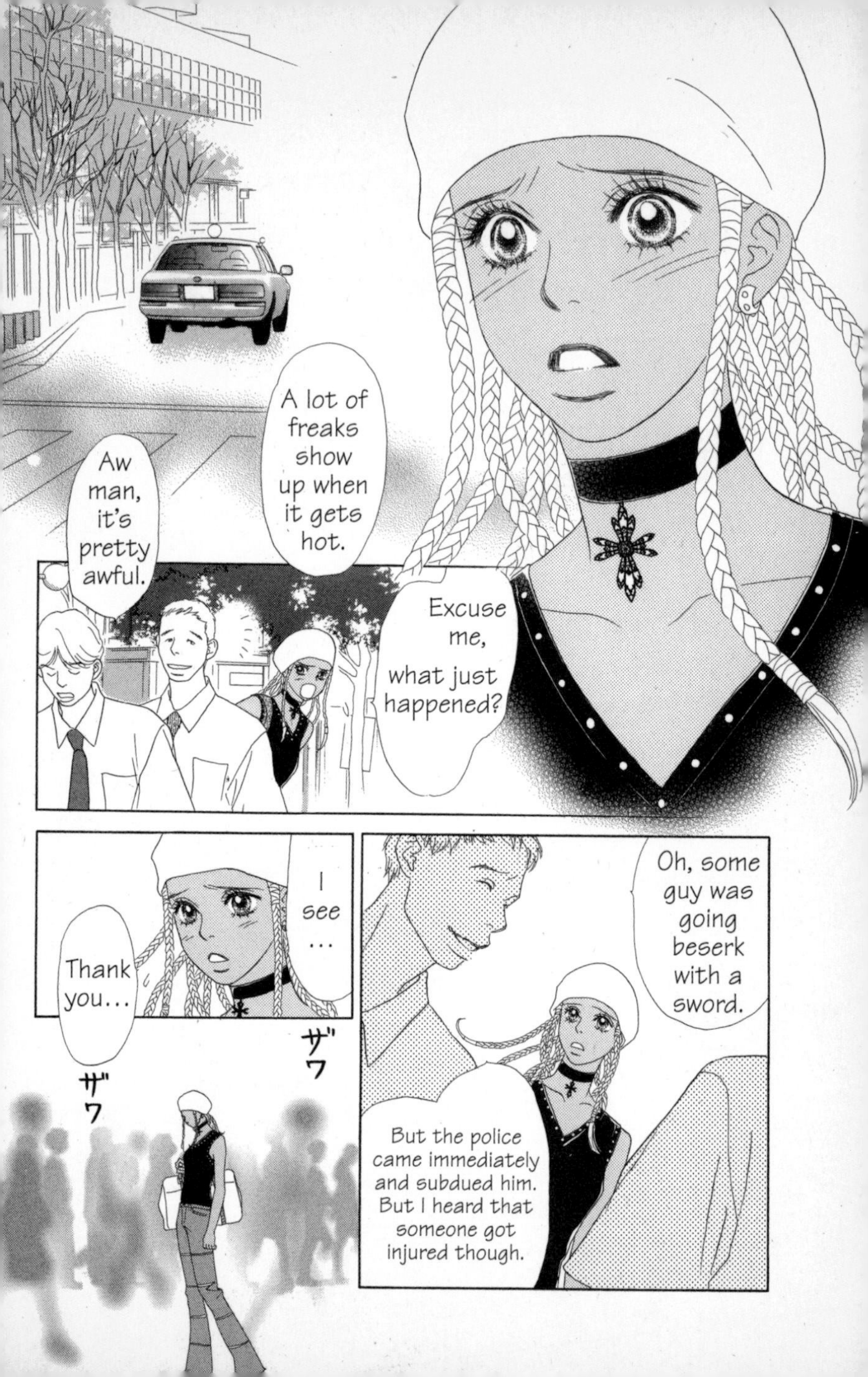
A lot of freaks show up when it gets hot.
Aw man, it's pretty awful.
Excuse me, what just happened?
Oh, some guy was going beserk with a sword.
But the police came immediately and subdued him. But I heard that someone got injured though.
I see...
Thank you...
ザワ
ザワ

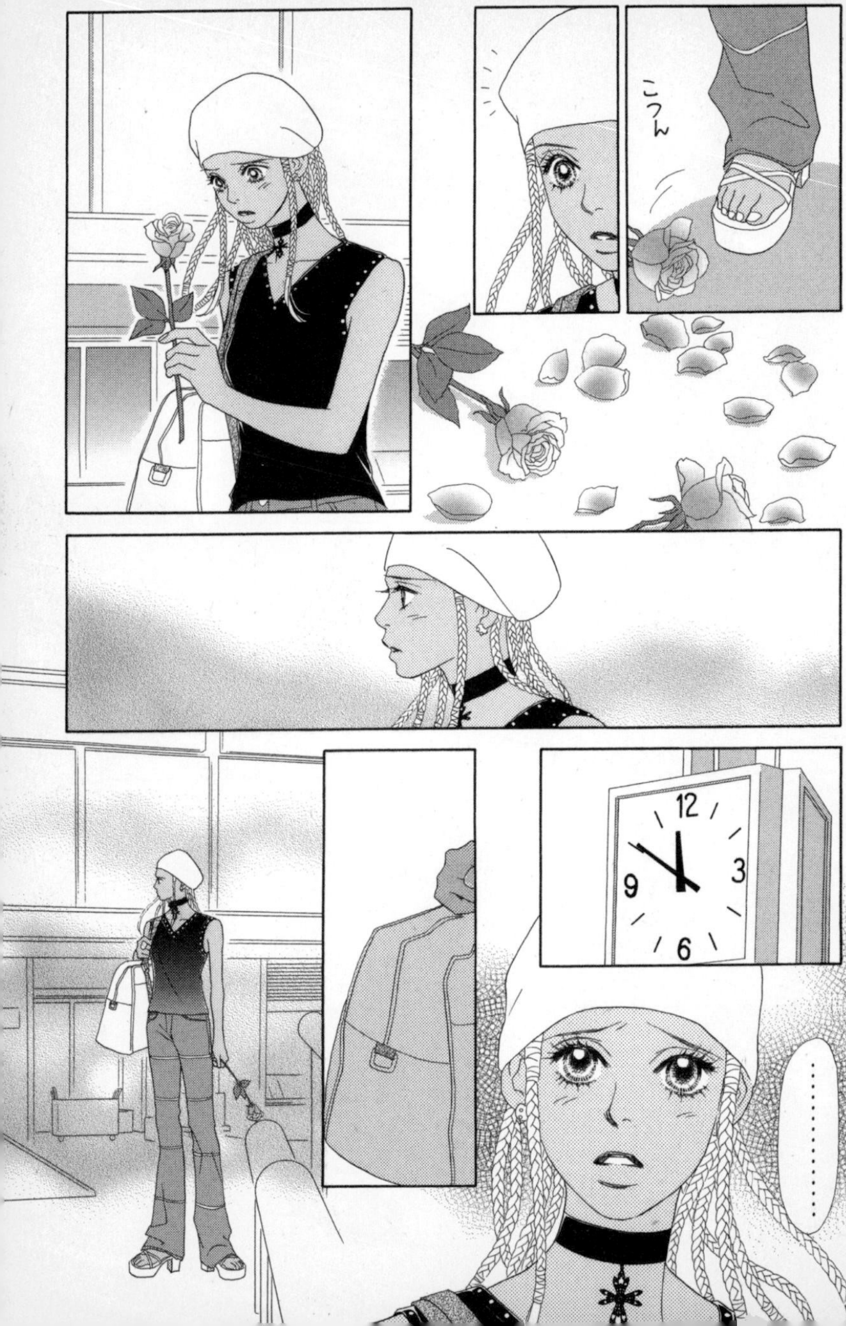
こつん
12
9
3
6
……

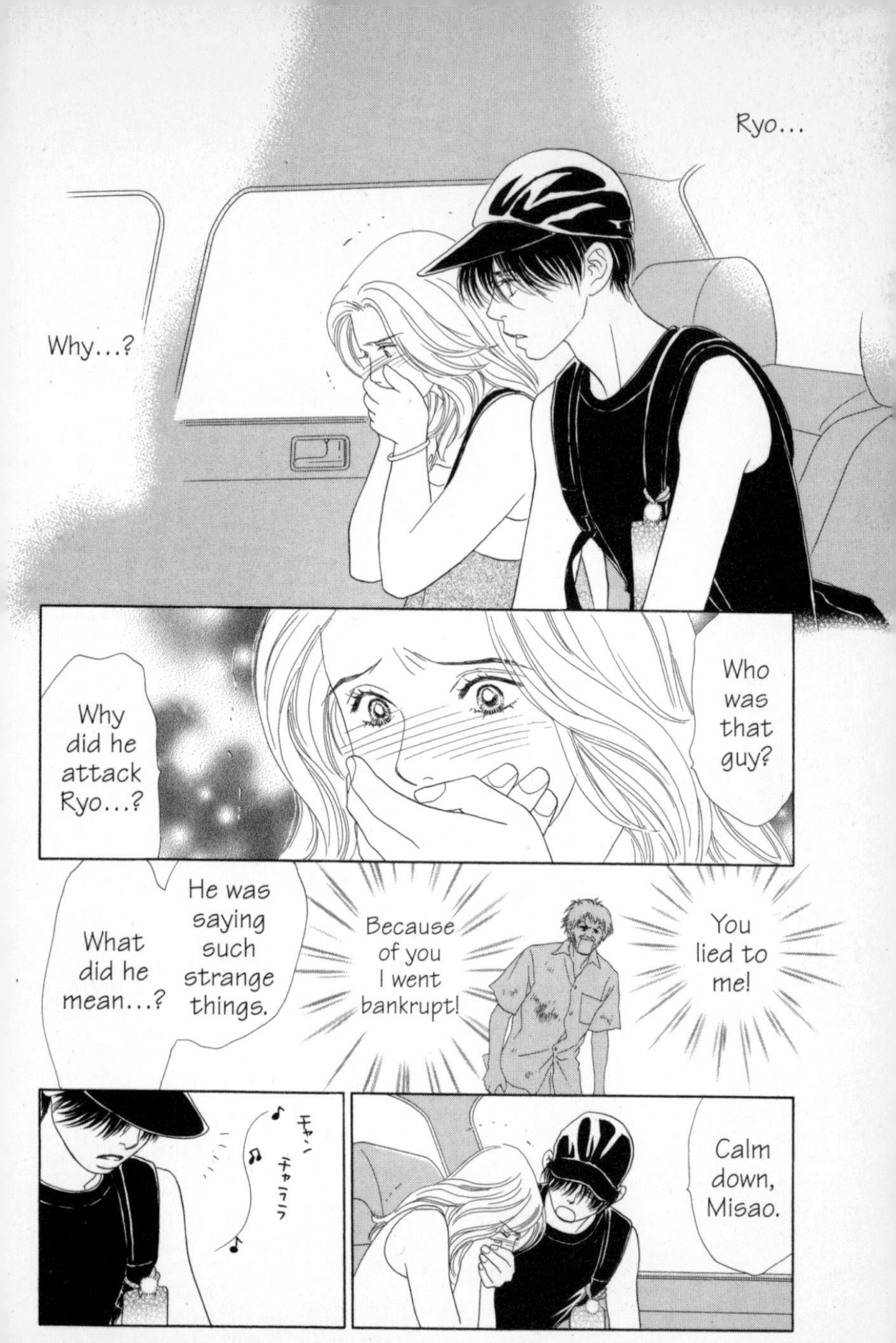
Ryo...
Why...?
Who was that guy?
Why did he attack Ryo...?
You lied to me!
Because of you I went bankrupt!
He was saying such strange things.
What did he mean...?
Calm down, Misao.

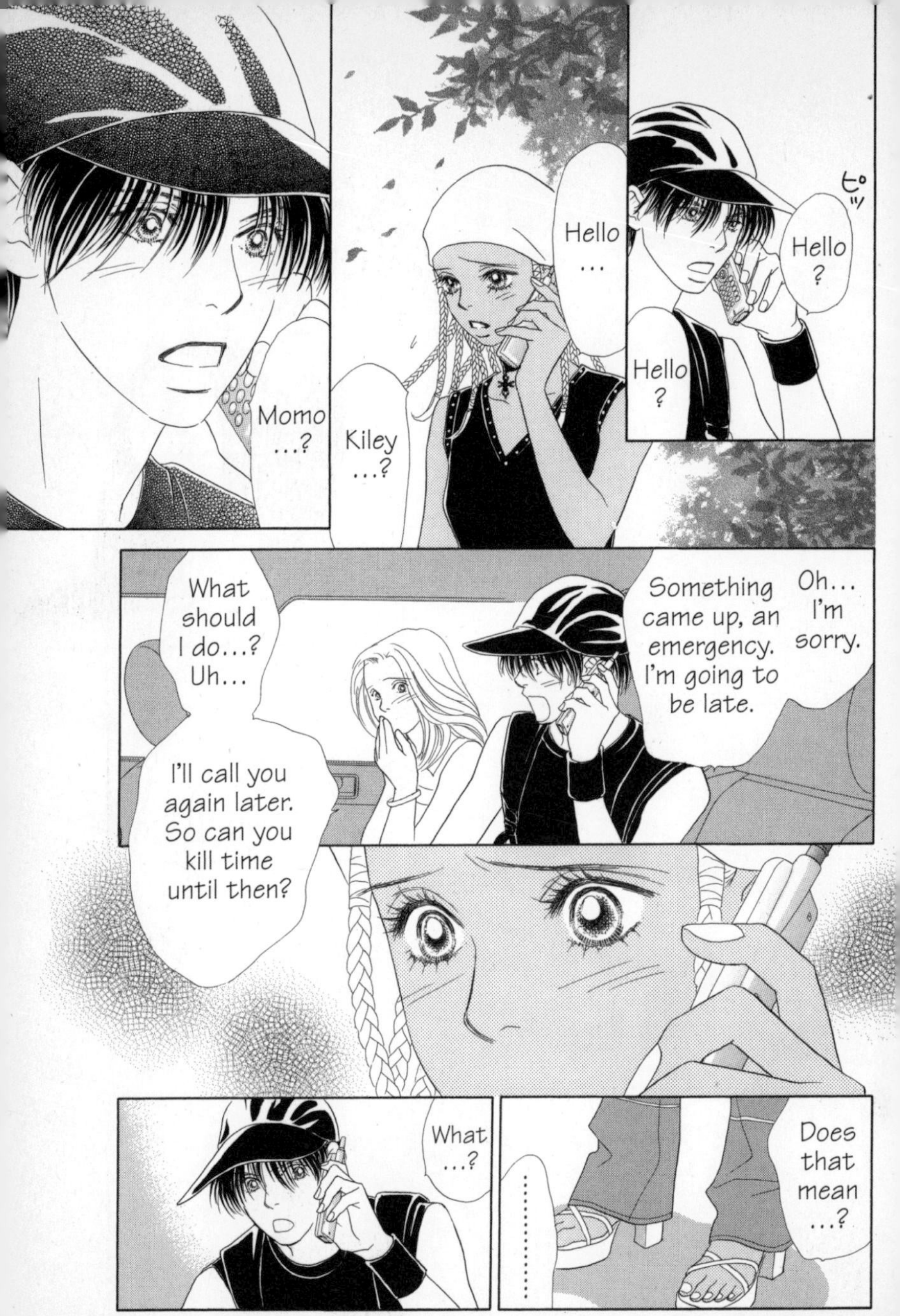
ピッ
Hello ?
Hello ?
Hello ...
Kiley ...?
Momo ...?
Oh... I'm sorry.
Something came up, an emergency. I'm going to be late.
What should I do...? Uh...
I'll call you again later. So can you kill time until then?
Does that mean ...?
......
What ...?

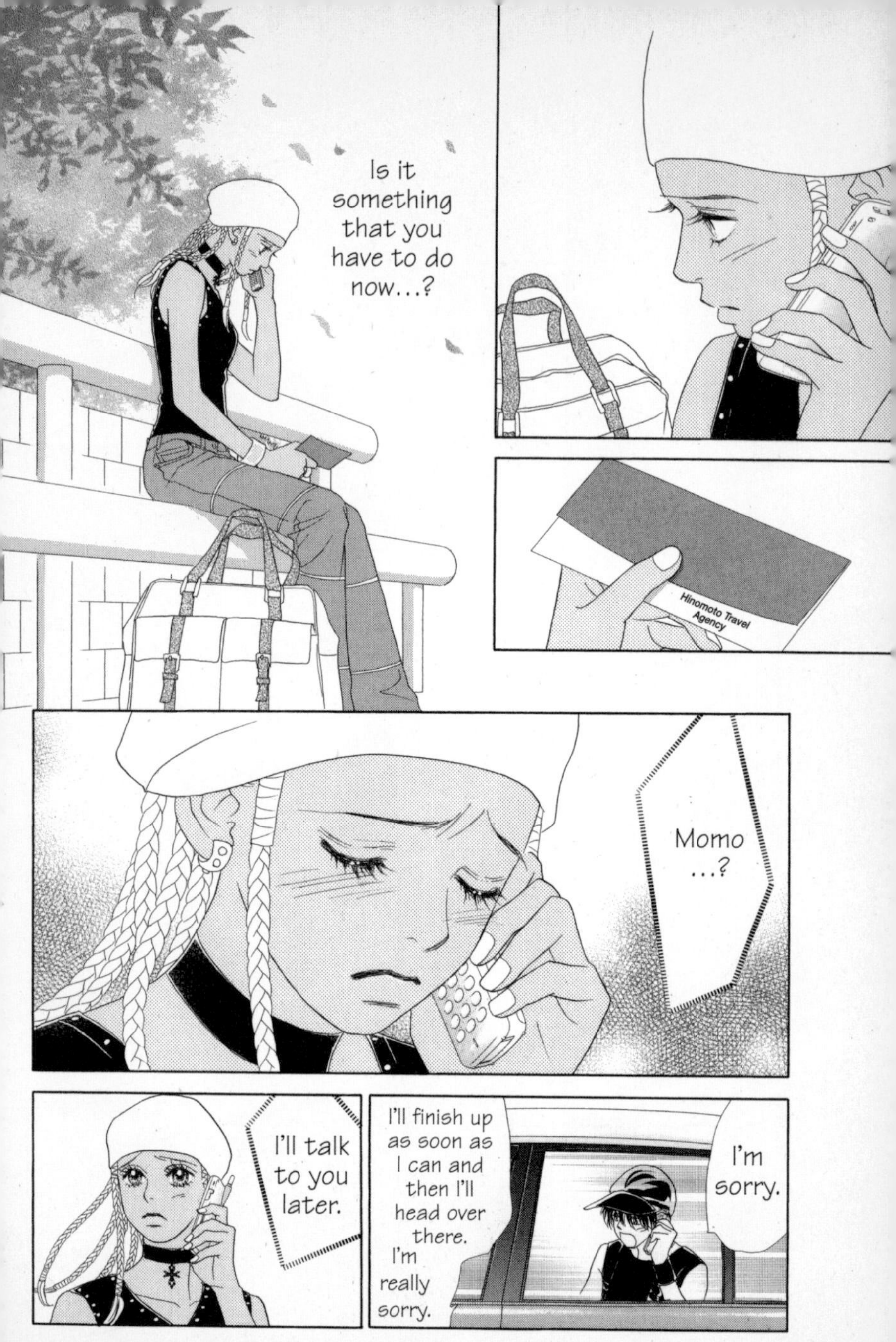
Hinomoto Travel Agency
Is it something that you have to do now...?
Momo ...?
I'm sorry.
I'll finish up as soon as I can and then I'll head over there.
I'm really sorry.
I'll talk to you later.

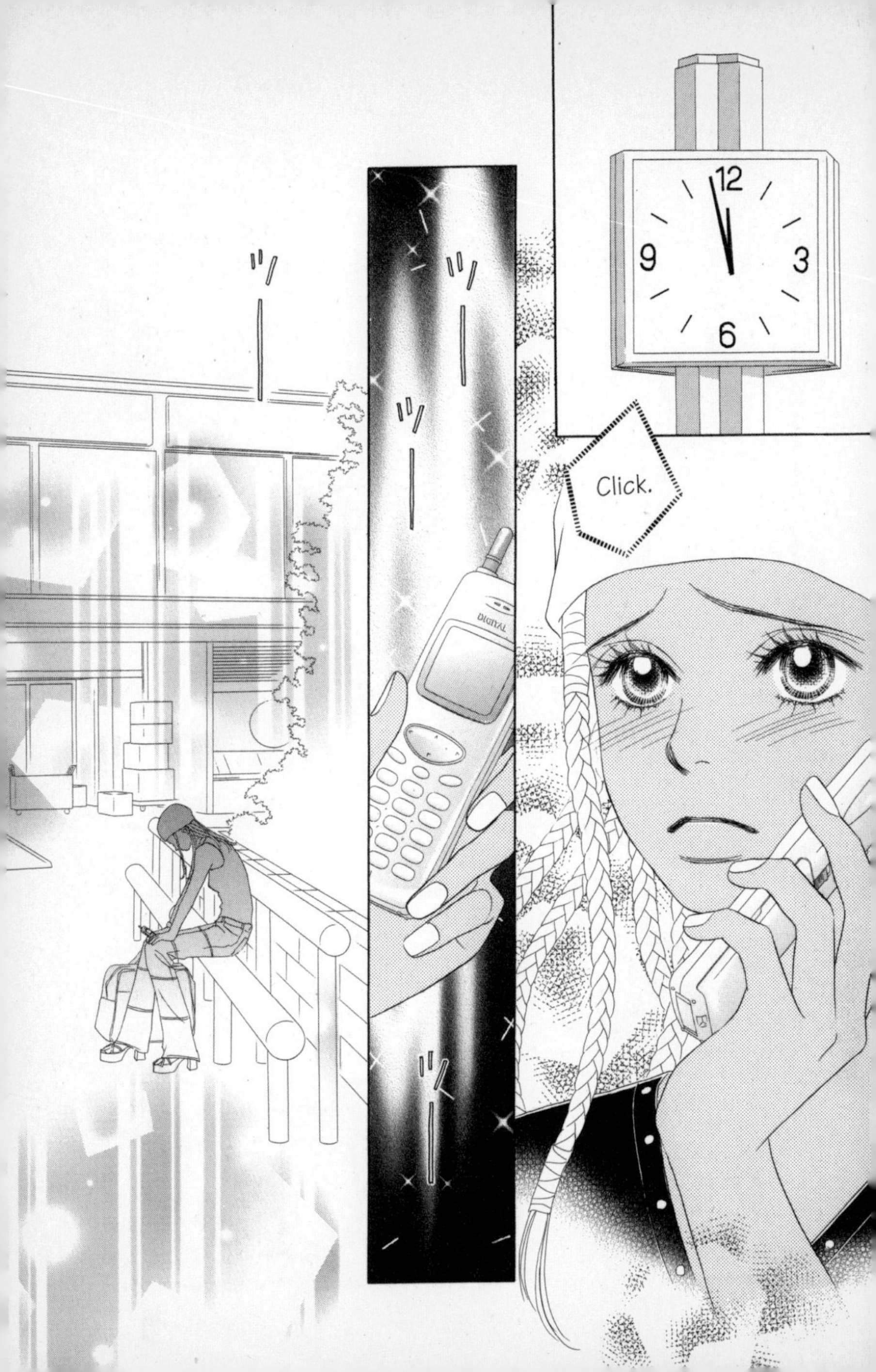
Click.

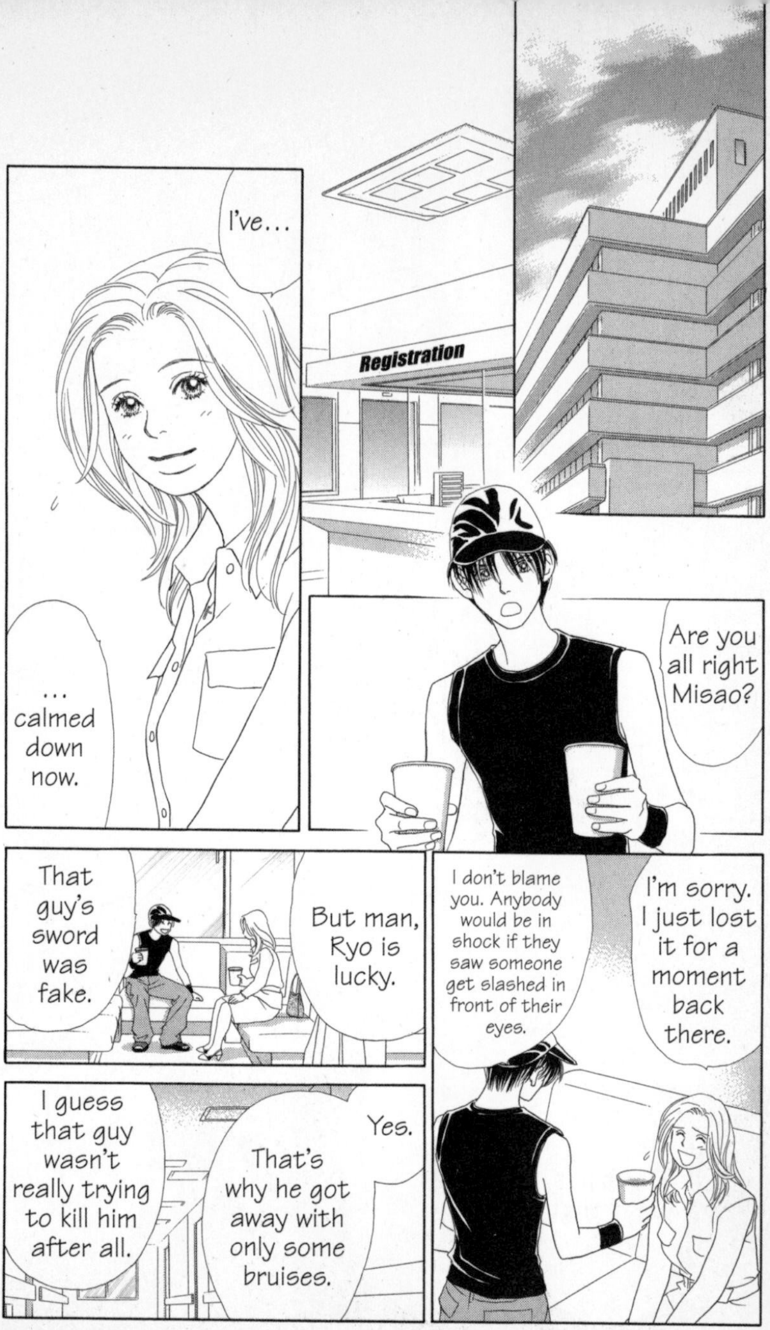
Registration
Are you all right Misao?
I've...
... calmed down now.
I'm sorry. I just lost it for a moment back there.
I don't blame you. Anybody would be in shock if they saw someone get slashed in front of their eyes.
But man, Ryo is lucky.
That guy's sword was fake.
Yes.
That's why he got away with only some bruises.
I guess that guy wasn't really trying to kill him after all.

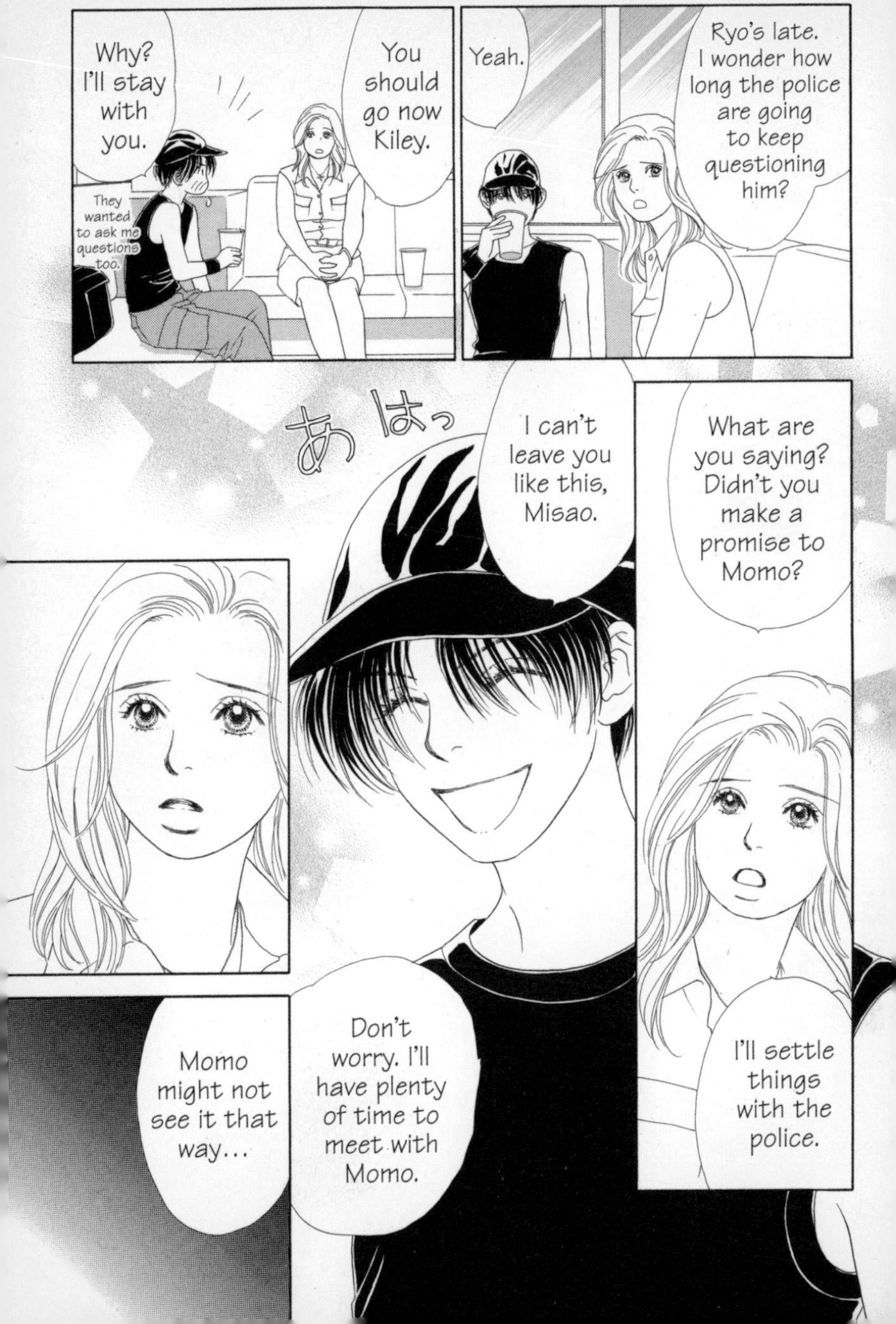
Ryo's late. I wonder how long the police are going to keep questioning him?
Yeah.
You should go now Kiley.
Why? I'll stay with you.
They wanted to ask me questions too.
What are you saying? Didn't you make a promise to Momo?
あはっ
I can't leave you like this, Misao.
I'll settle things with the police.
Don't worry. I'll have plenty of time to meet with Momo.
Momo might not see it that way…

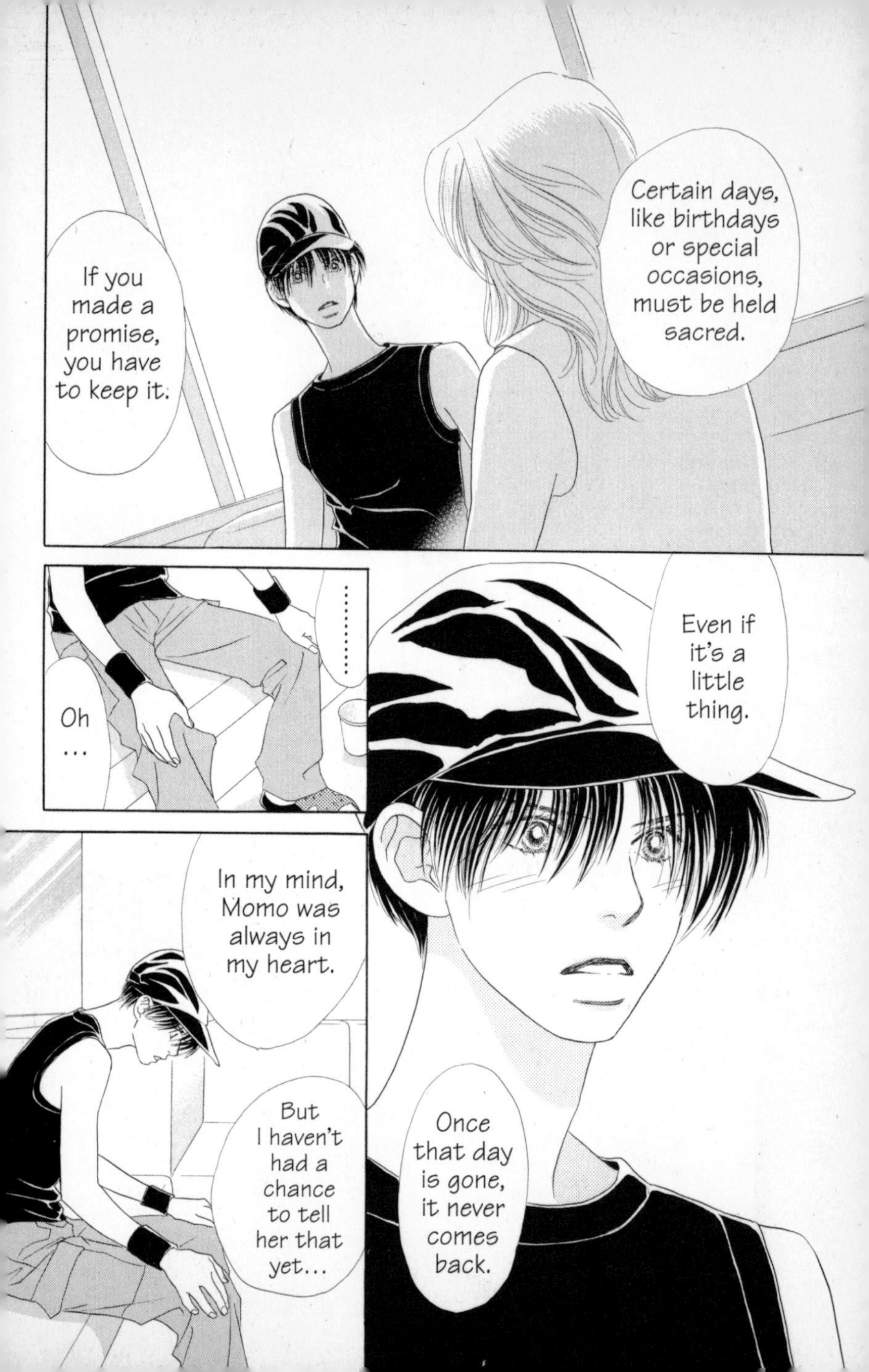
Certain days, like birthdays or special occasions, must be held sacred.
If you made a promise, you have to keep it.
Even if it's a little thing.
Once that day is gone, it never comes back.
......
Oh ...
In my mind, Momo was always in my heart.
But I haven't had a chance to tell her that yet...

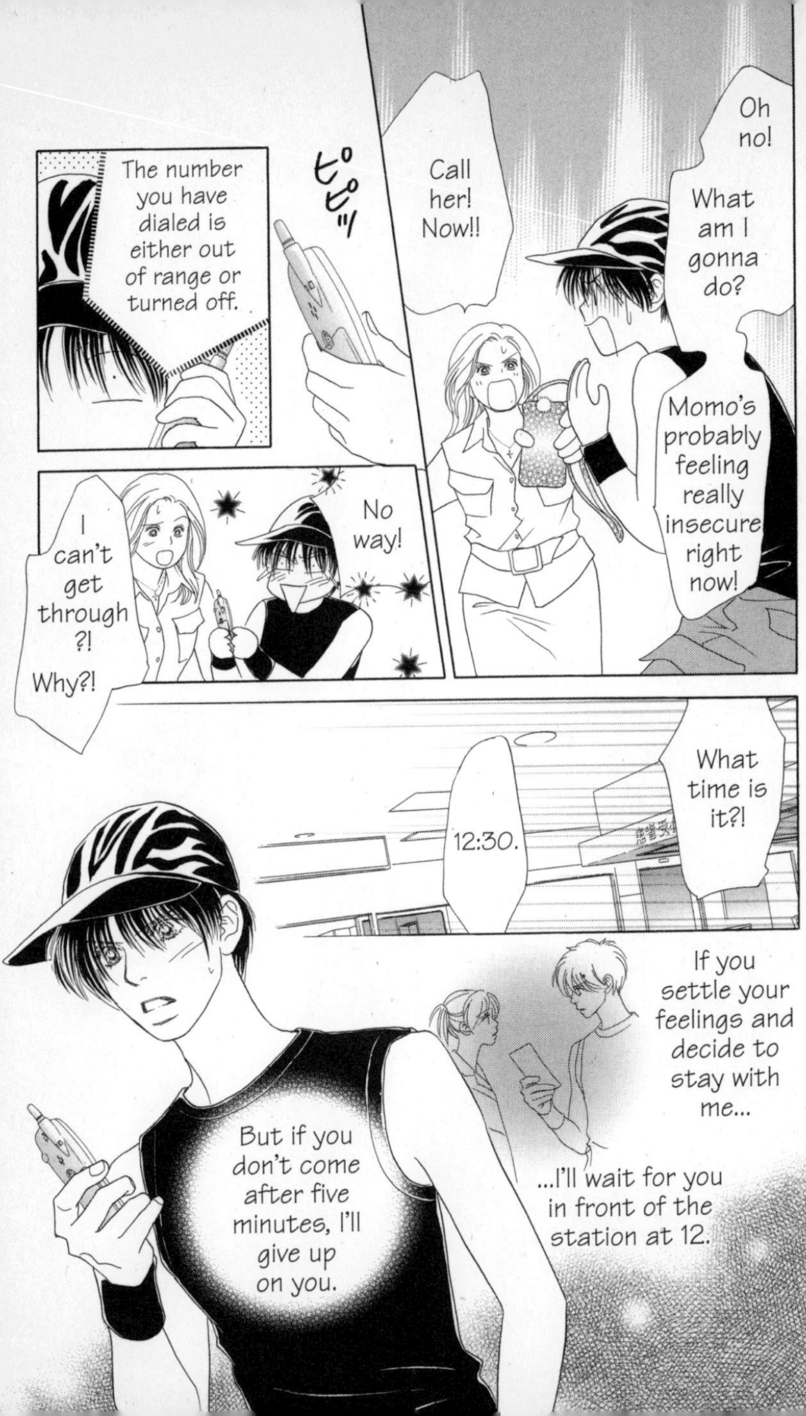
Oh no!
What am I gonna do?
Call her! Now!!
Momo's probably feeling really insecure right now!
ピピッ
The number you have dialed is either out of range or turned off.
No way!
I can't get through?!
Why?!
What time is it?!
12:30.
If you settle your feelings and decide to stay with me...
...I'll wait for you in front of the station at 12.
But if you don't come after five minutes, I'll give up on you.

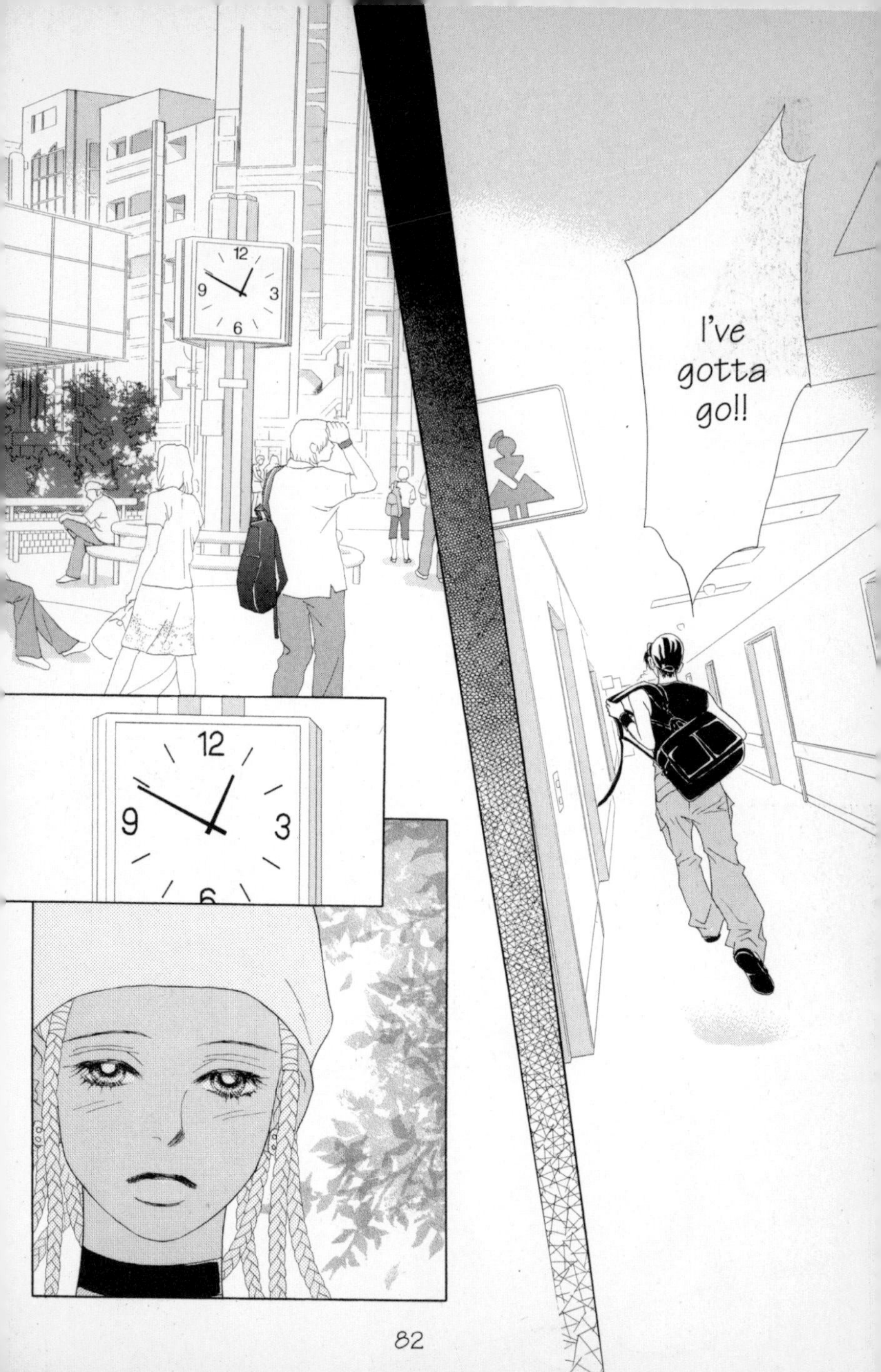
I've gotta go!!

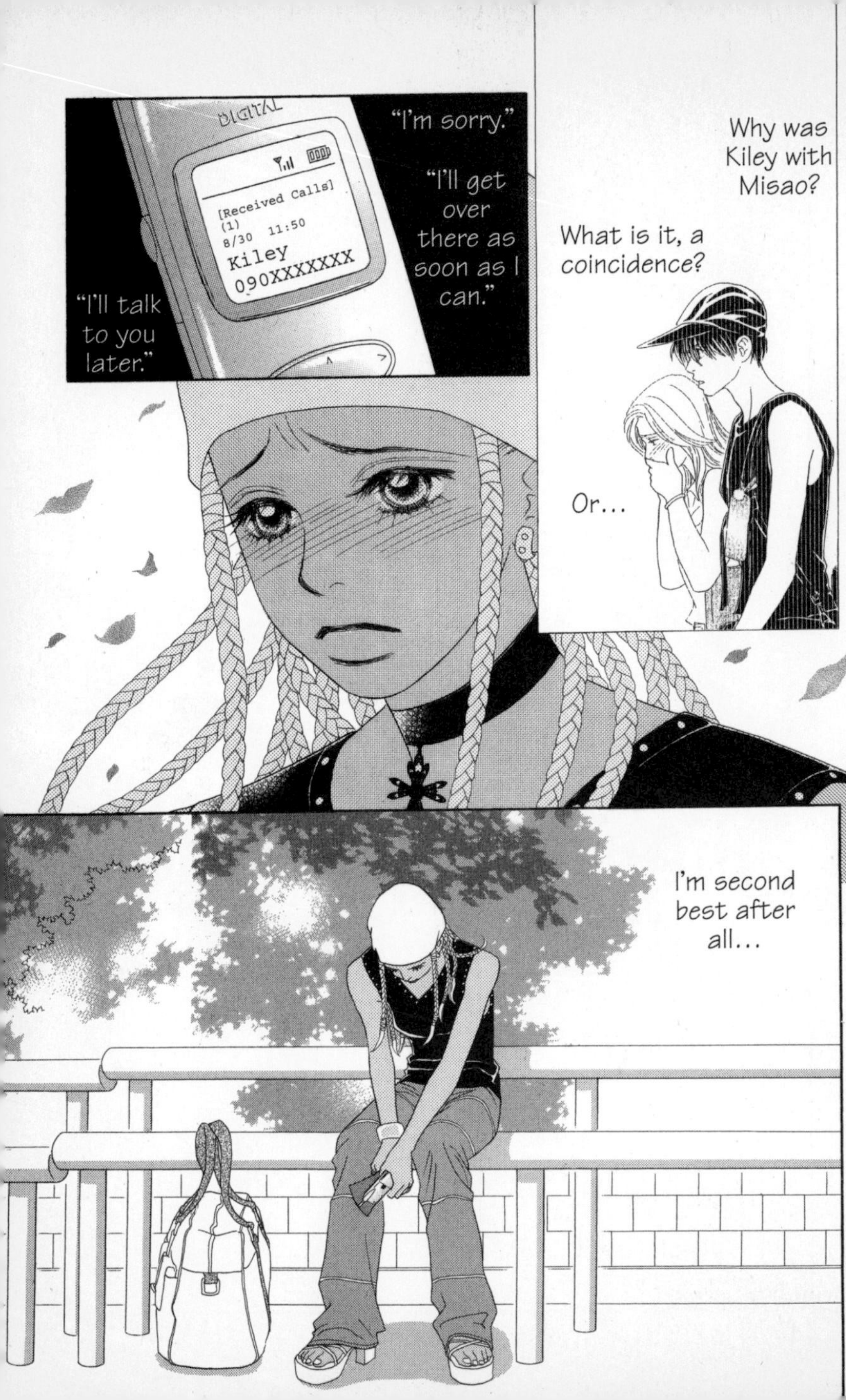
Why was Kiley with Misao?
What is it, a coincidence?
Or...
DIGITAL
[Received Calls]
(1)
8/30 11:50
Kiley
090XXXXXXX
"I'm sorry."
"I'll get over there as soon as I can."
"I'll talk to you later."
I'm second best after all...

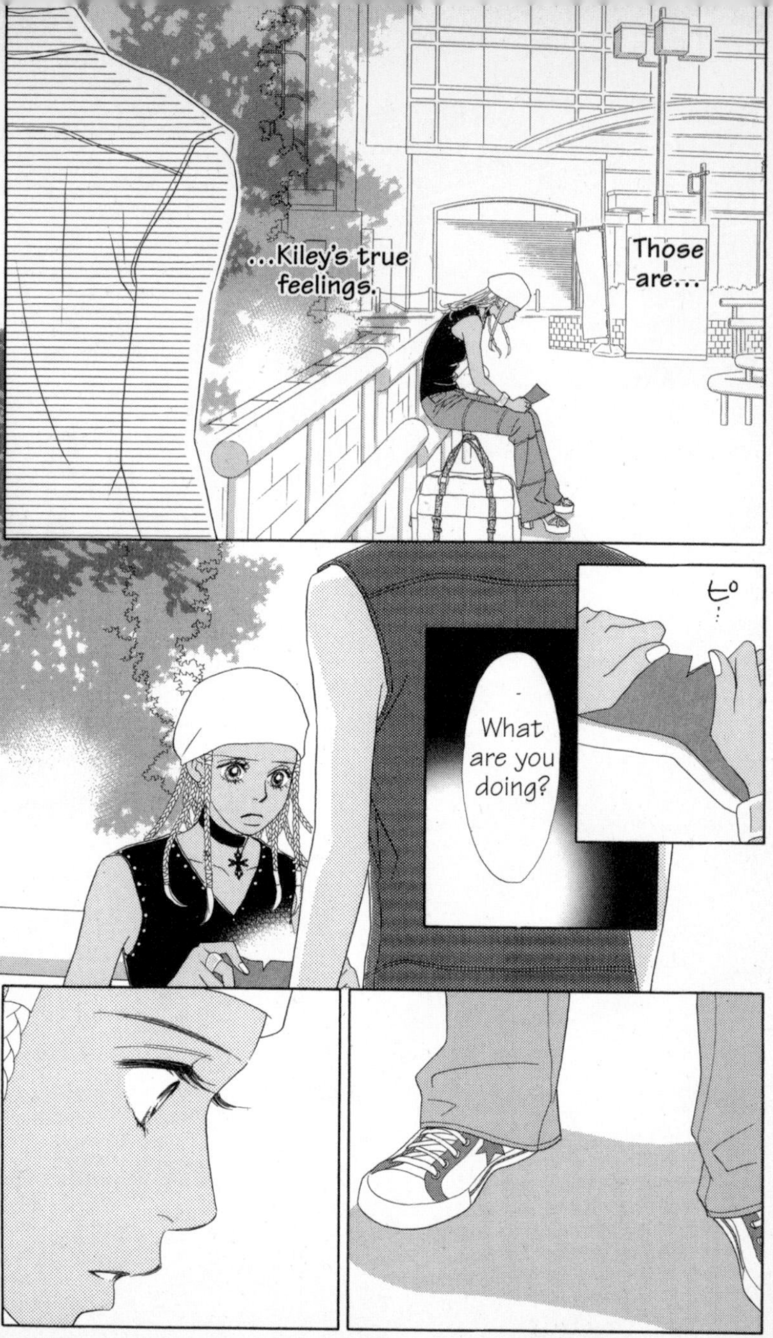
Those are...
...Kiley's true feelings.
ピ…
What are you doing?

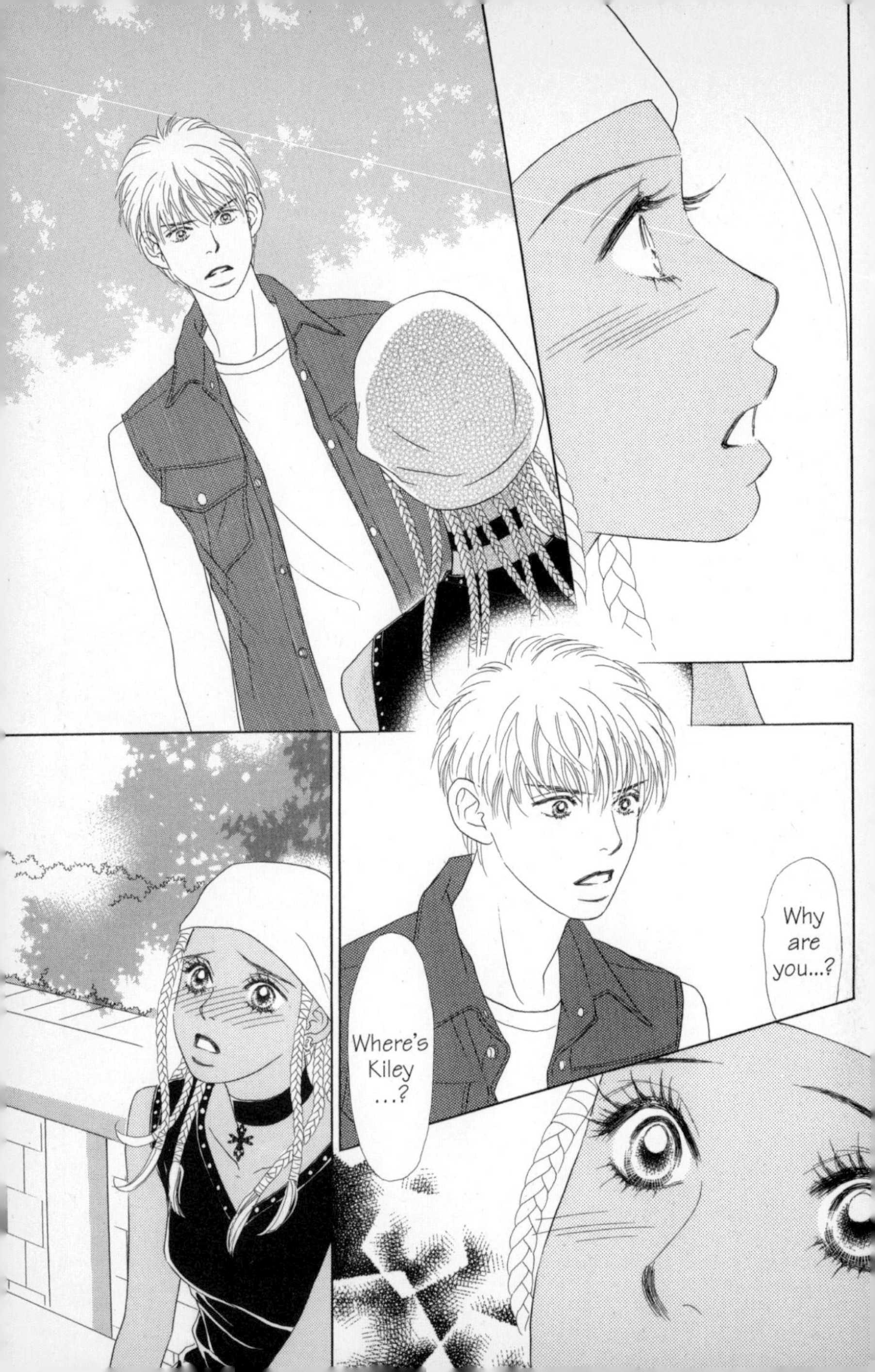
Why are you...?
Where's Kiley ...?

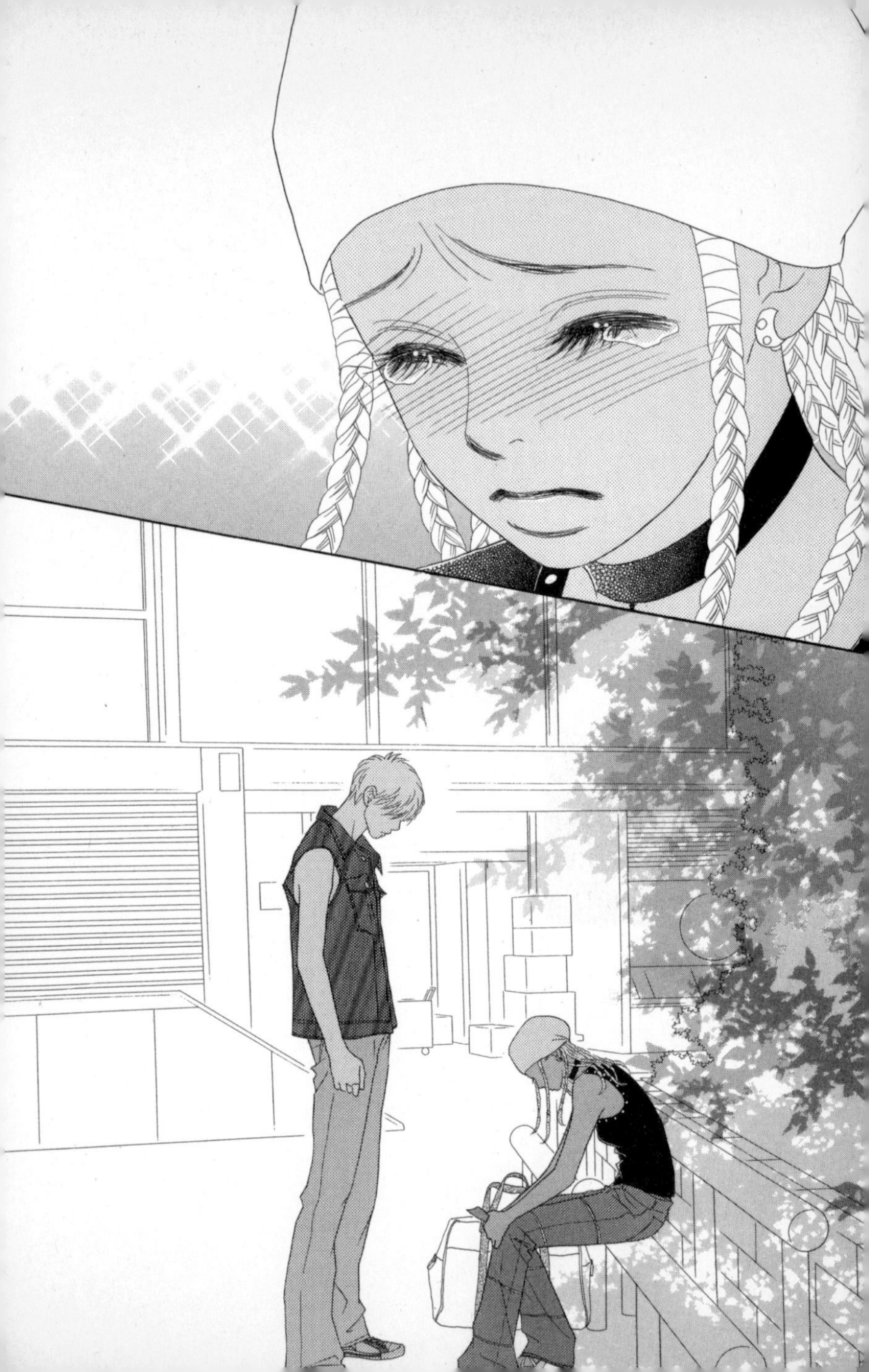

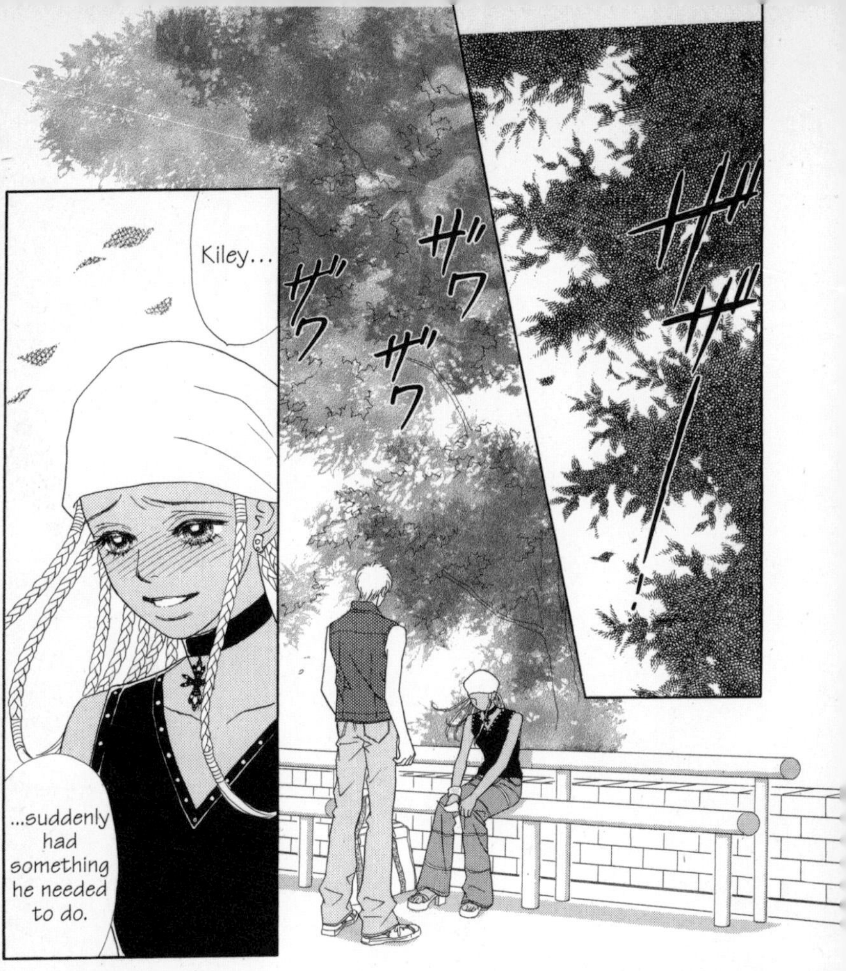
ザザー!
ザワ
ザワ
ザワ
ザワ
Kiley...
...suddenly had something he needed to do.

PEACH CLUB

Hello! Welcome to Peach Girl 15. Since 1997, this series is in its fifth year (as of November 2002). Through the years, we've experienced several staffing changes, and even won some awards. But only a year and a half has elapsed within the story. Momo and her friends are now in their second year of high school, and it remains to be seen how things will turn out. I haven't really thought much about life after high school for them, so it could be that the story might end while they're still in their second year. By the way, lately I've been suffering from hip pains, and it's been difficult to sit at a desk for a long period of time. As a result, I don't spend much time on the Internet, and I've let my home page kind of sit. Not good... But I can't overexert myself. These days, I get plenty of sleep, and I get to work on my base drawings and inking at a relaxed pace. I've realized that when you get enough sleep, your body and mind recover and everything is easier, which means I have to work a lot more days now!

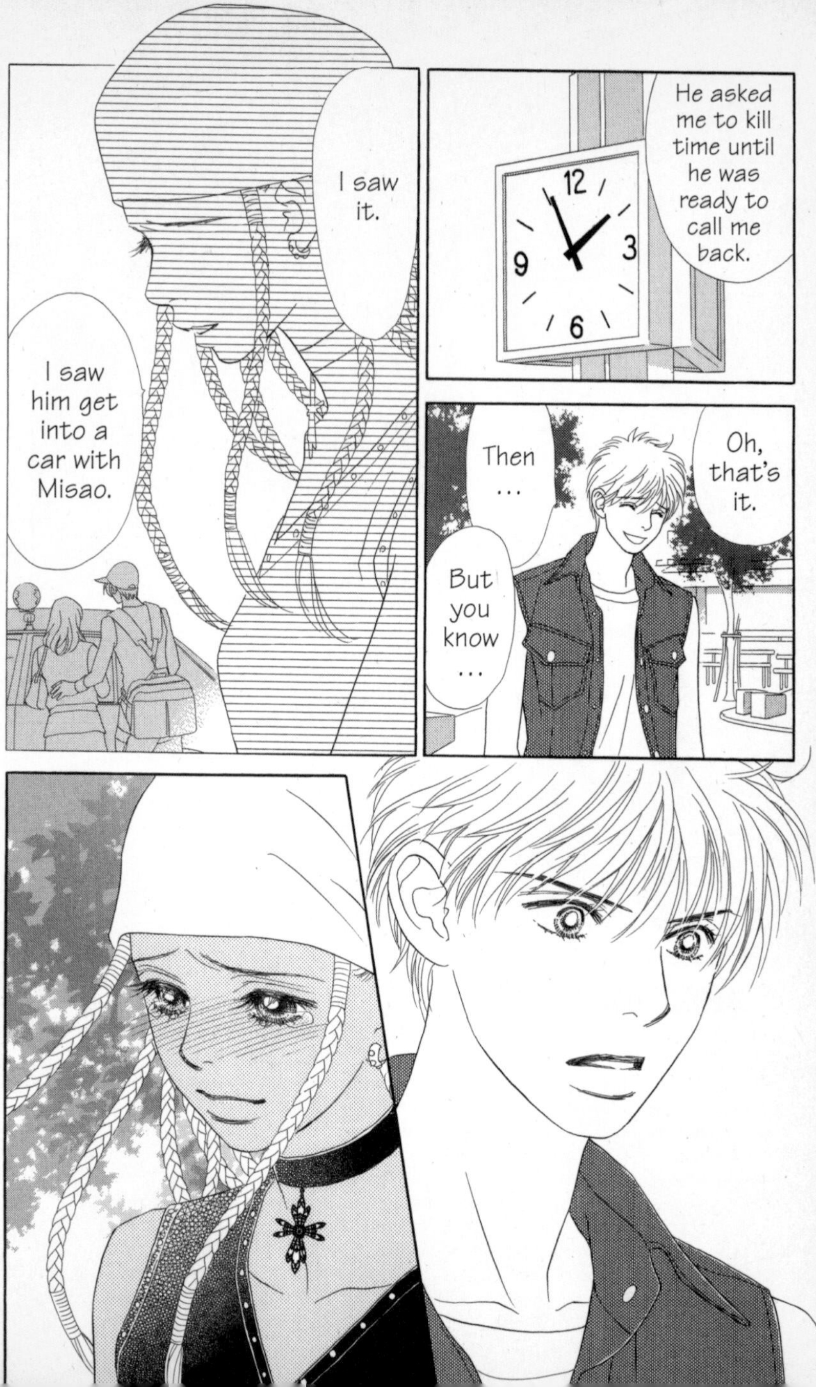
He asked me to kill time until he was ready to call me back.
Oh, that's it.
Then ...
But you know ...
I saw it.
I saw him get into a car with Misao.

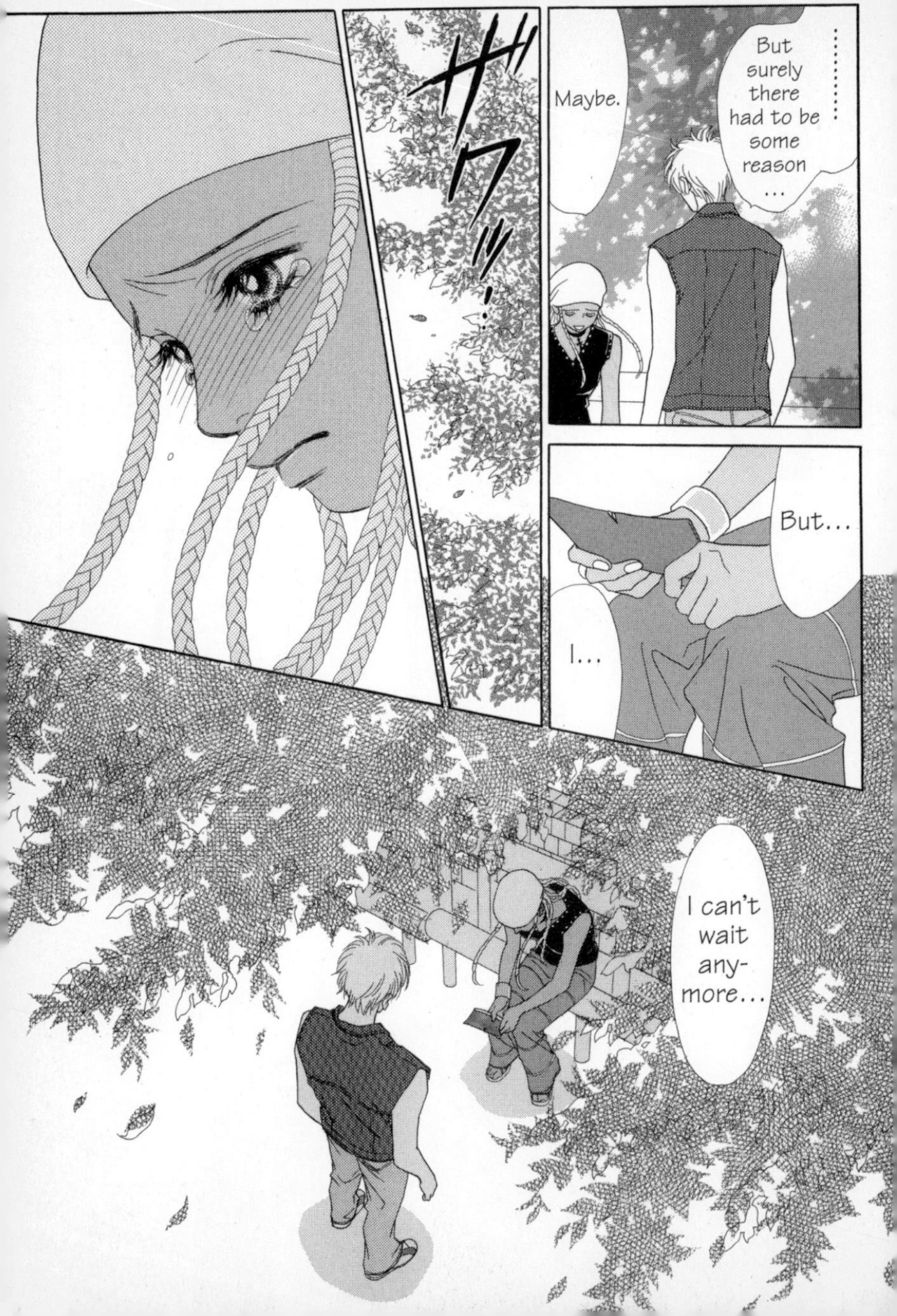

But surely there had to be some reason …
Maybe.
ザワッ!!…
But…
I…
I can't wait any-more…

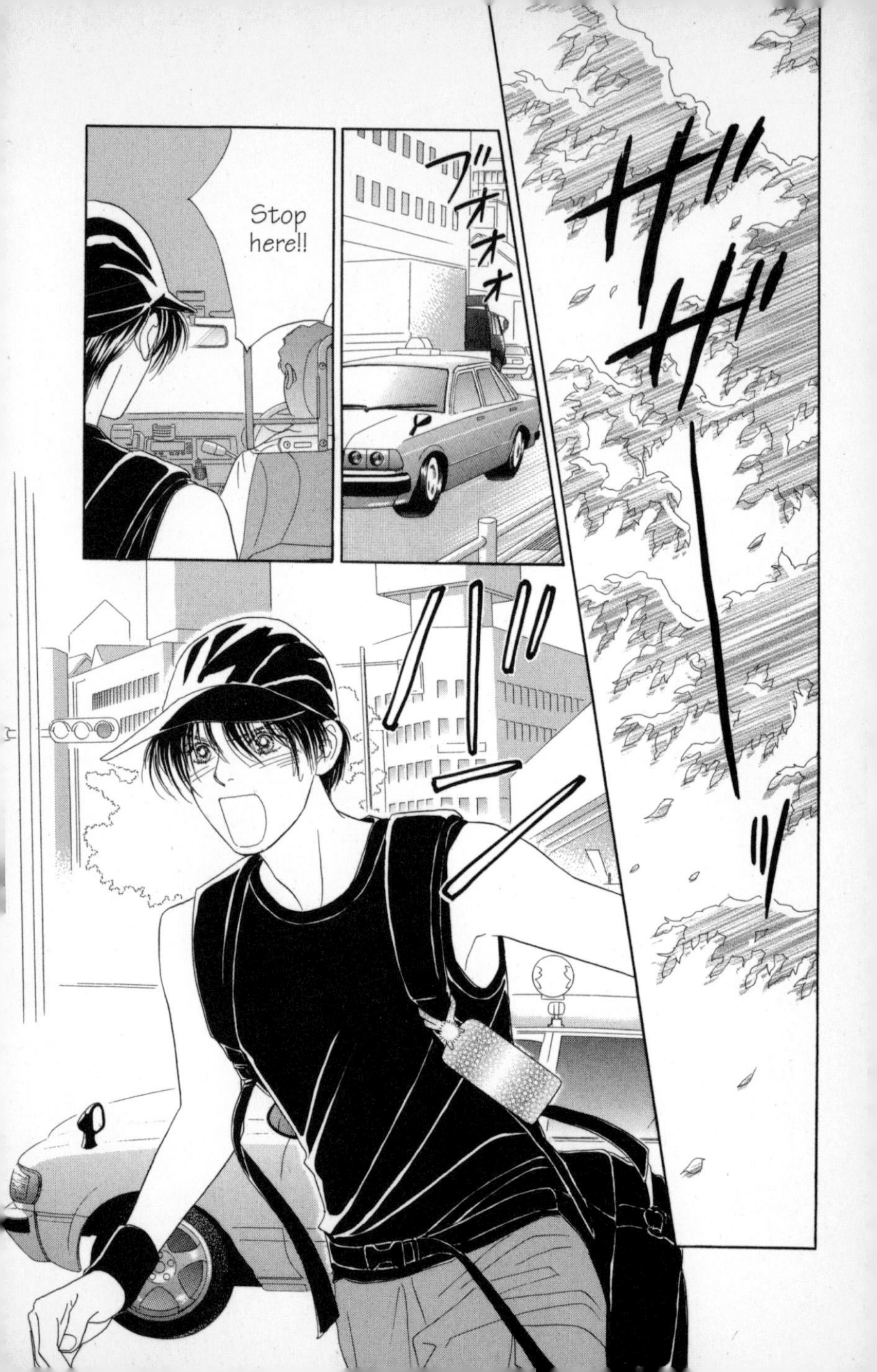
ザザーッ
ブオオオ
Stop here!!
バン

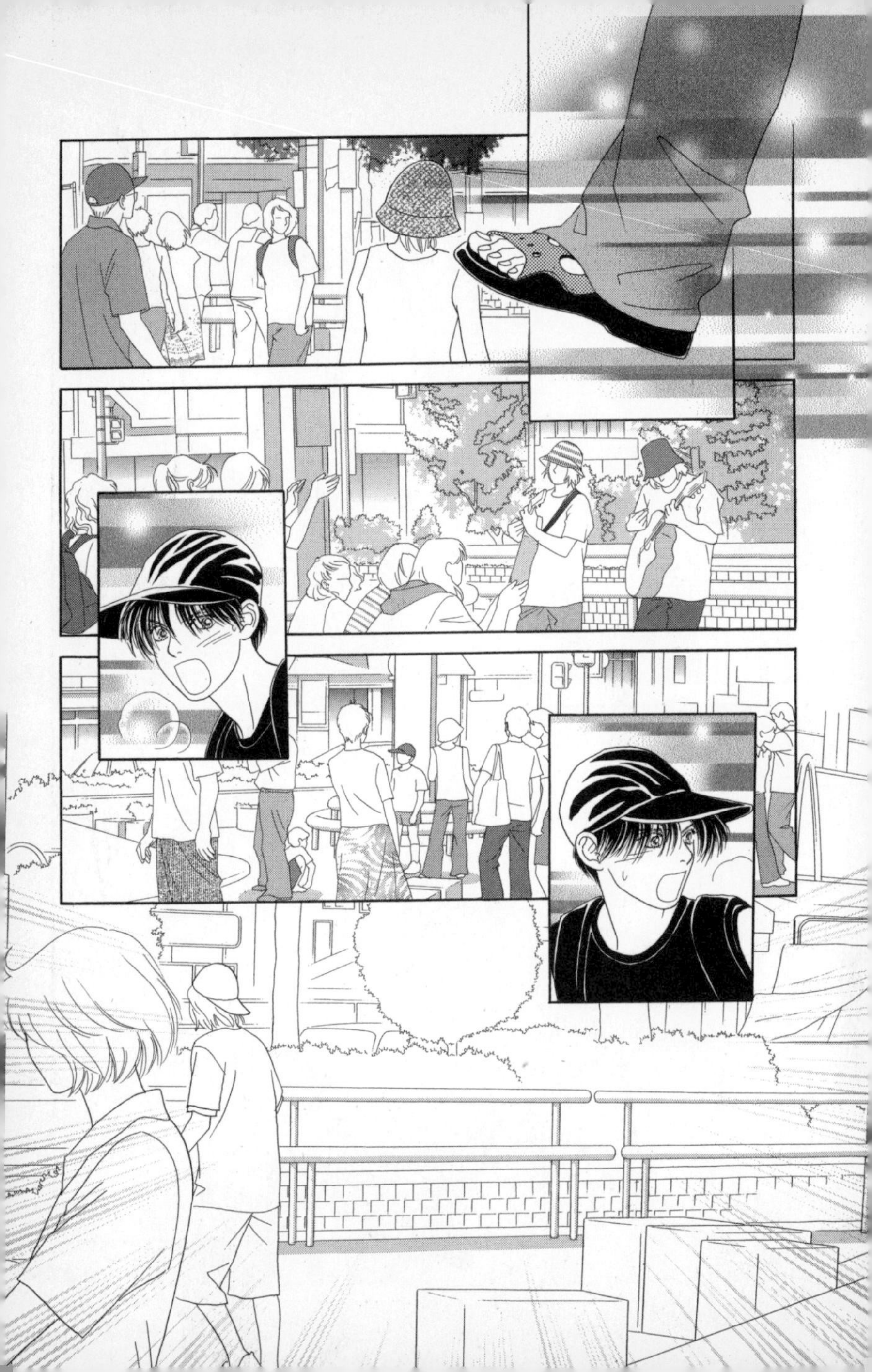

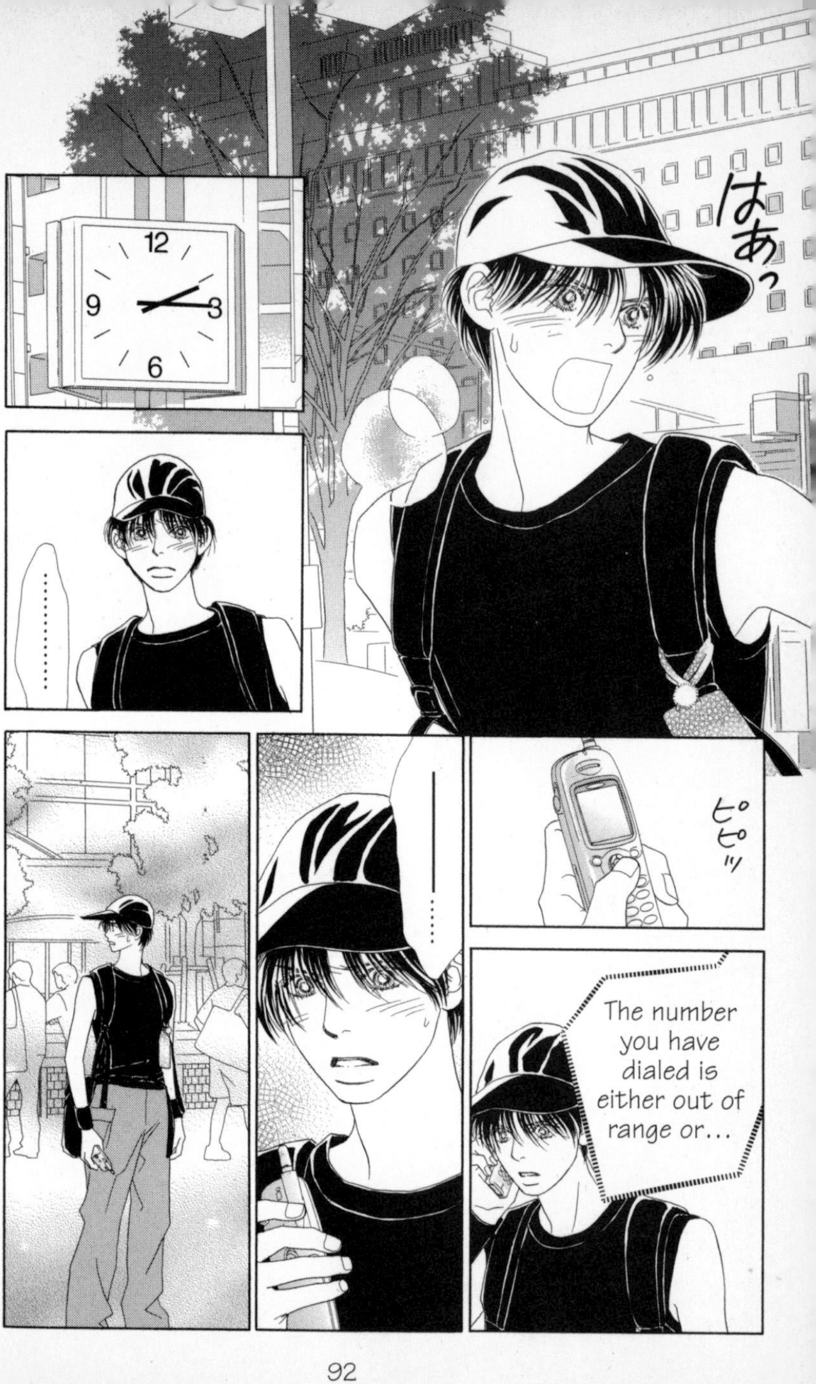
はあっ
……
ピピッ
The number you have dialed is either out of range or…
……

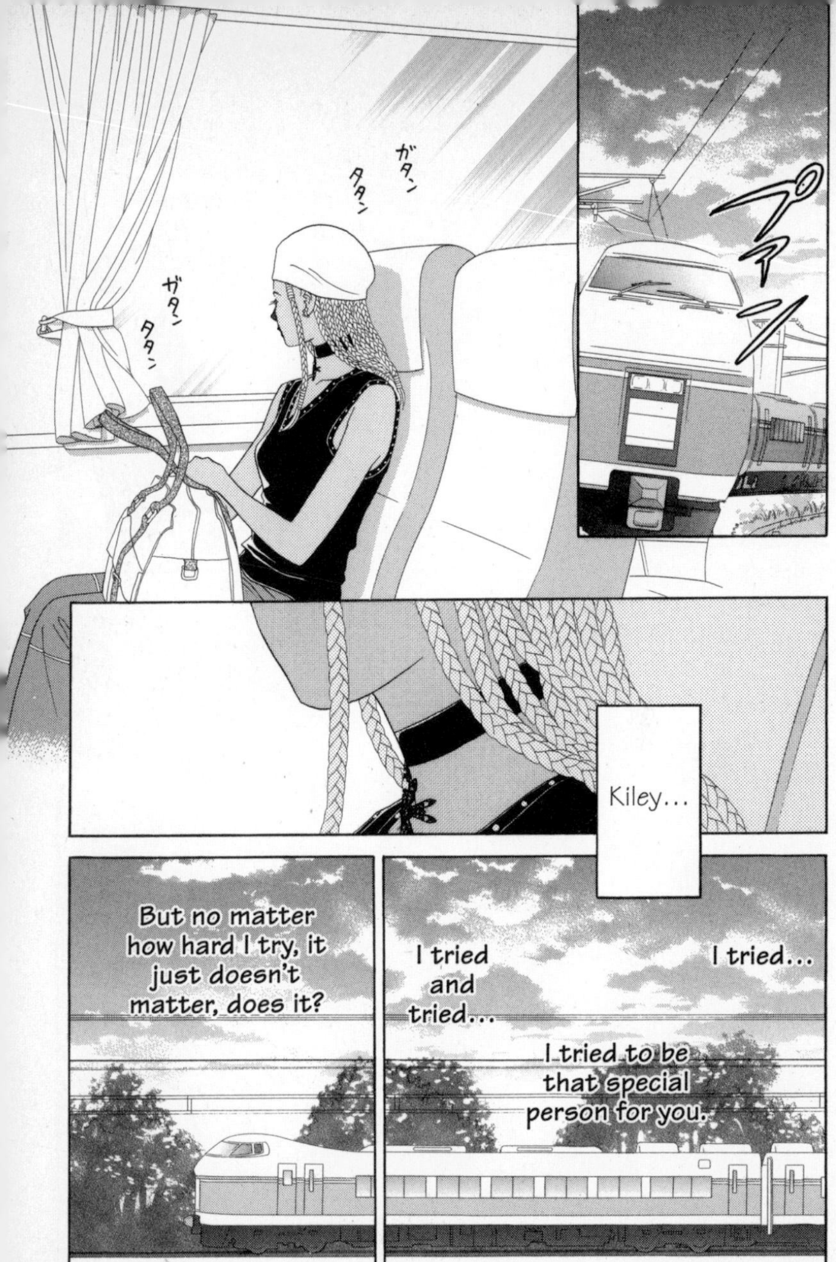
プァン
ガタン
タタン
ガタン
タタン
Kiley...
I tried...
I tried and tried...
I tried to be that special person for you.
But no matter how hard I try, it just doesn't matter, does it?

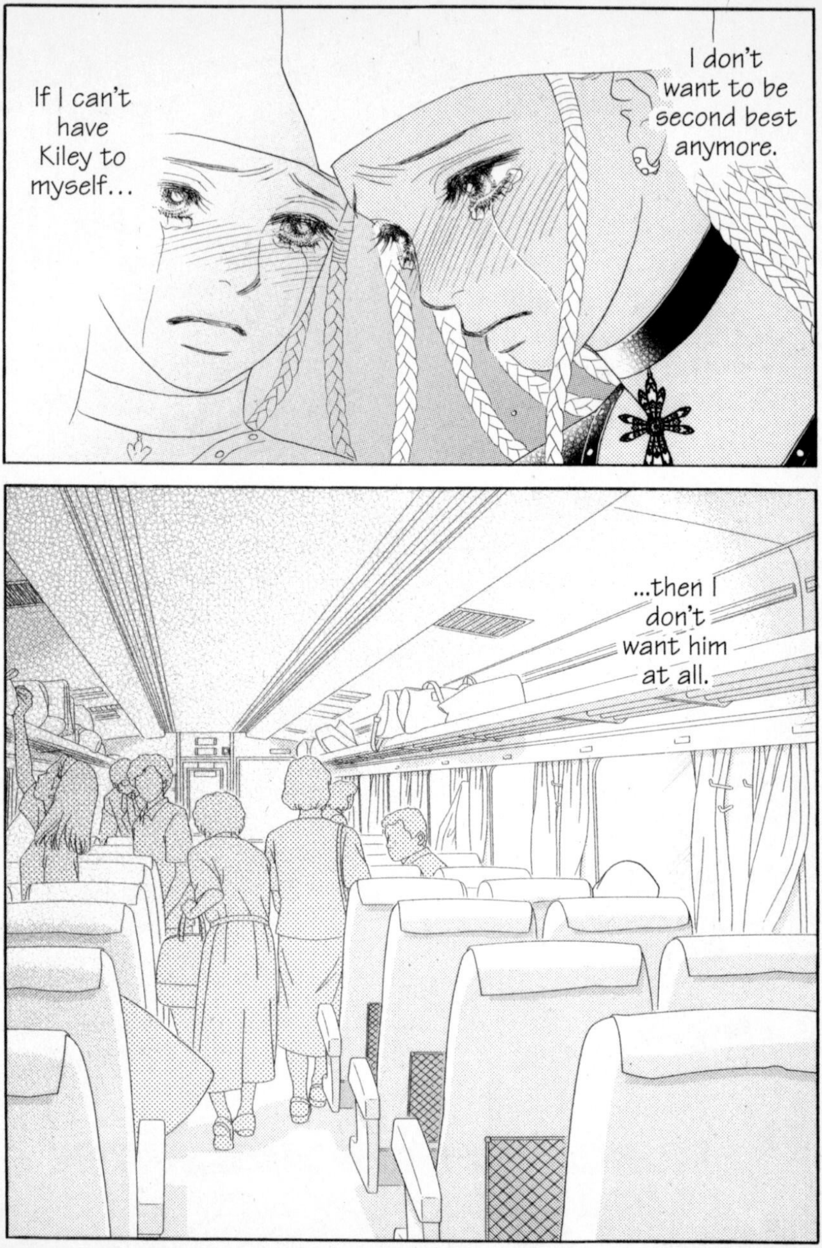
I don't want to be second best anymore.
If I can't have Kiley to myself...
...then I don't want him at all.

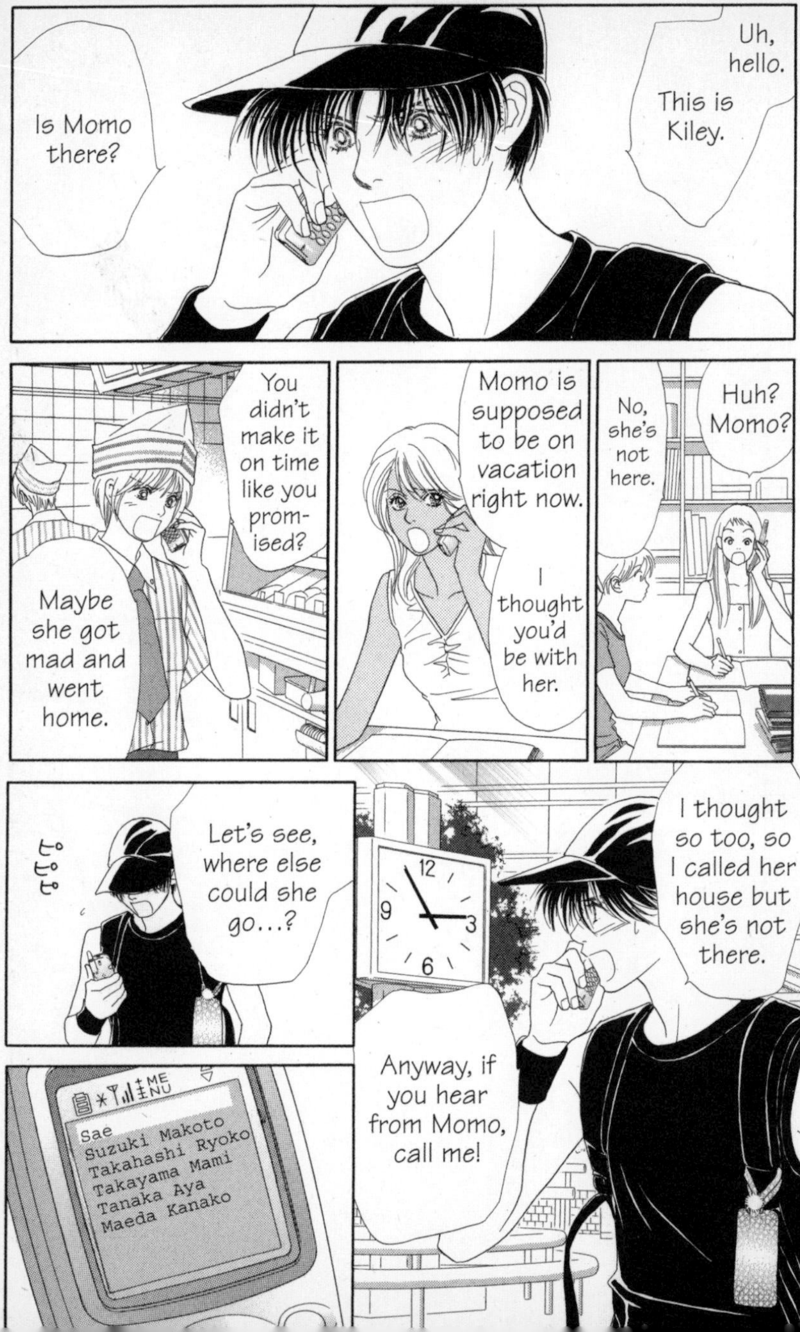
Uh, hello.
This is Kiley.
Is Momo there?
Huh? Momo?
No, she's not here.
Momo is supposed to be on vacation right now.
I thought you'd be with her.
You didn't make it on time like you promised?
Maybe she got mad and went home.
I thought so too, so I called her house but she's not there.
Anyway, if you hear from Momo, call me!
Let's see, where else could she go...?
ピピピ
MENU
Sae
Suzuki Makoto
Takahashi Ryoko
Takayama Mami
Tanaka Aya
Maeda Kanako

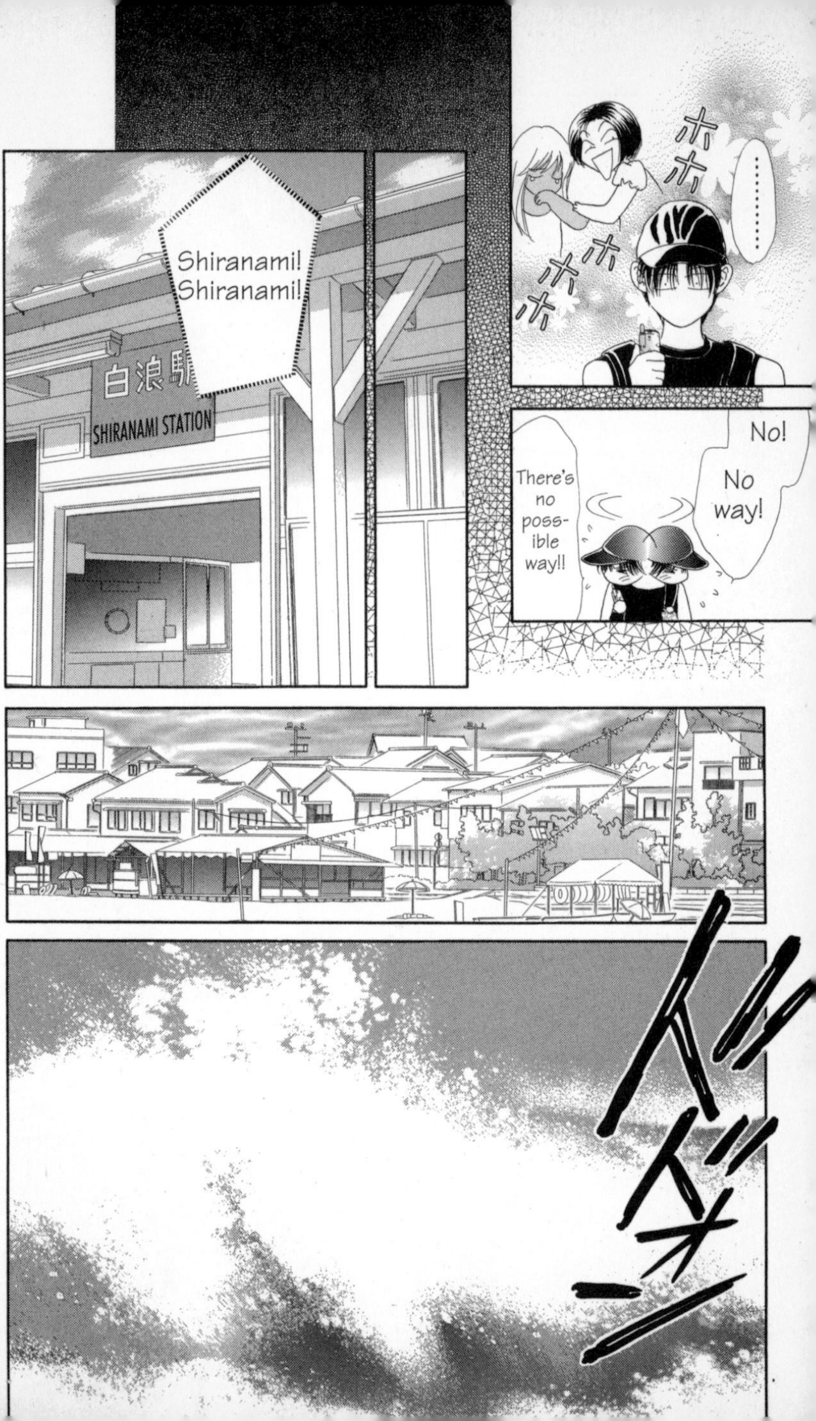
ホホ
ホホホ
......
No!
No way!
There's no possible way!!
Shiranami! Shiranami!
白浪駅
SHIRANAMI STATION
ドドオーン

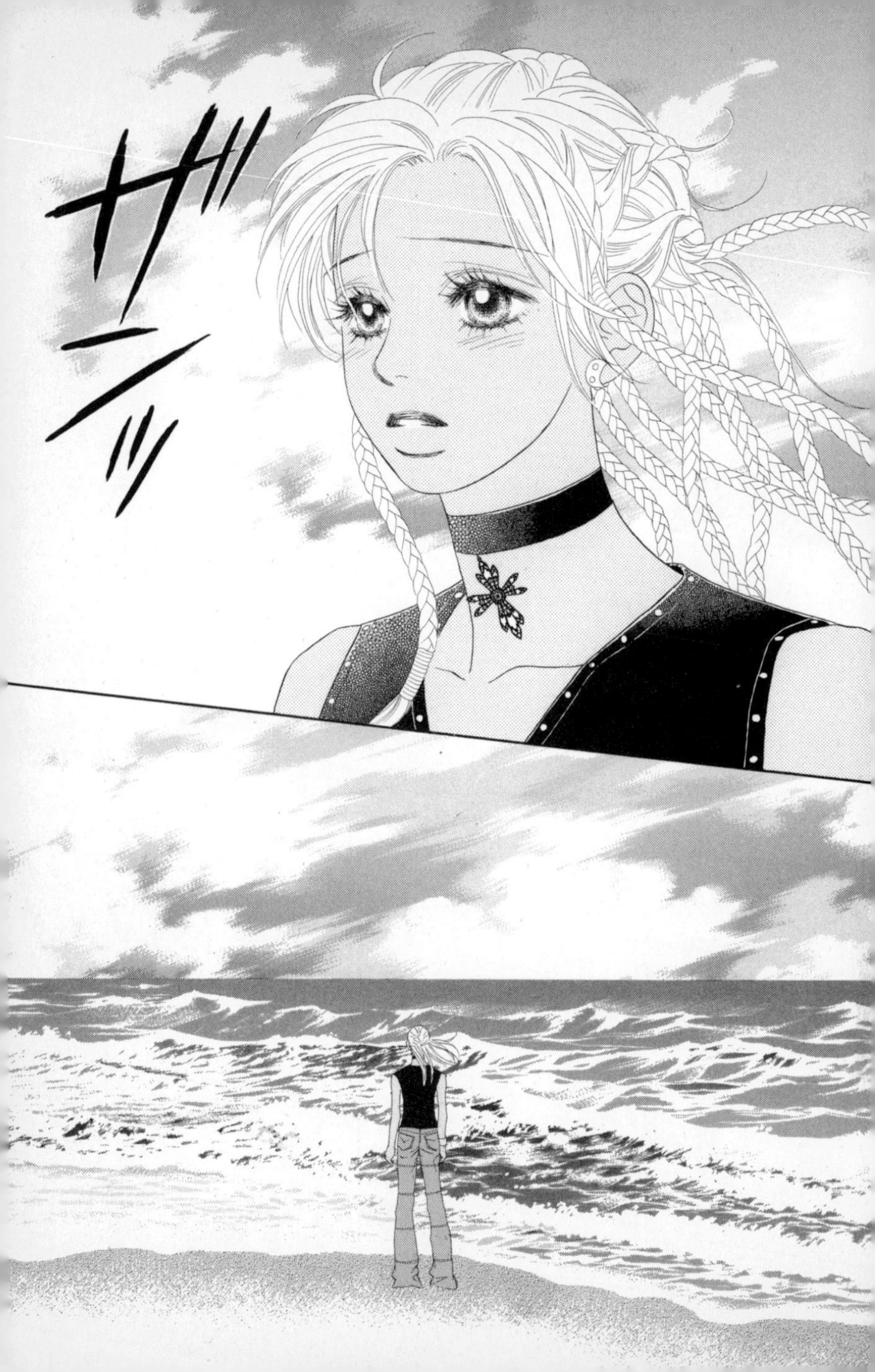
ザンッ

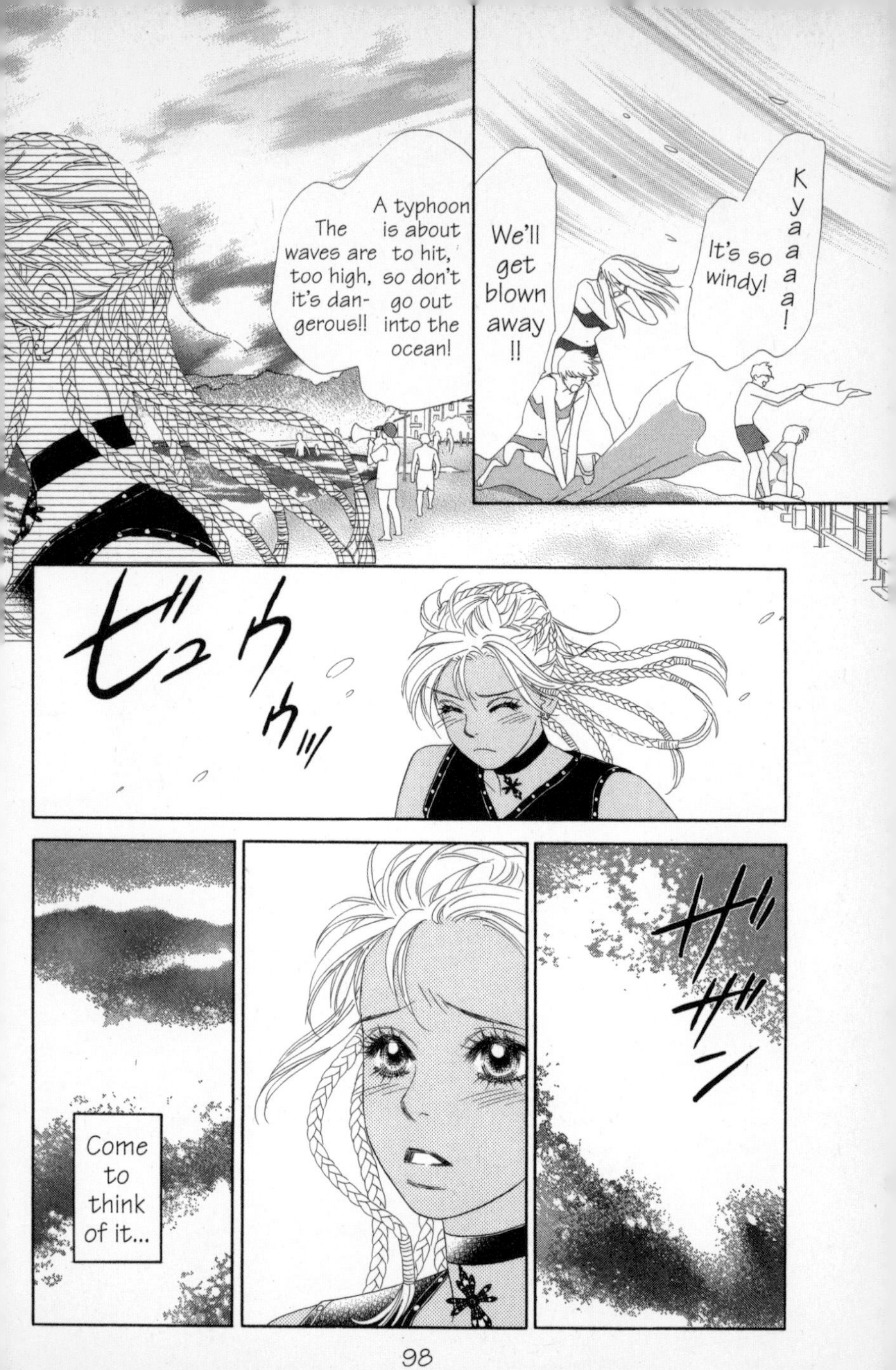
Kyaaaa!
It's so windy!
We'll get blown away!!
A typhoon is about to hit, so don't go out into the ocean!
The waves are too high, it's dangerous!!
ビュウウッ
ザザン
Come to think of it...

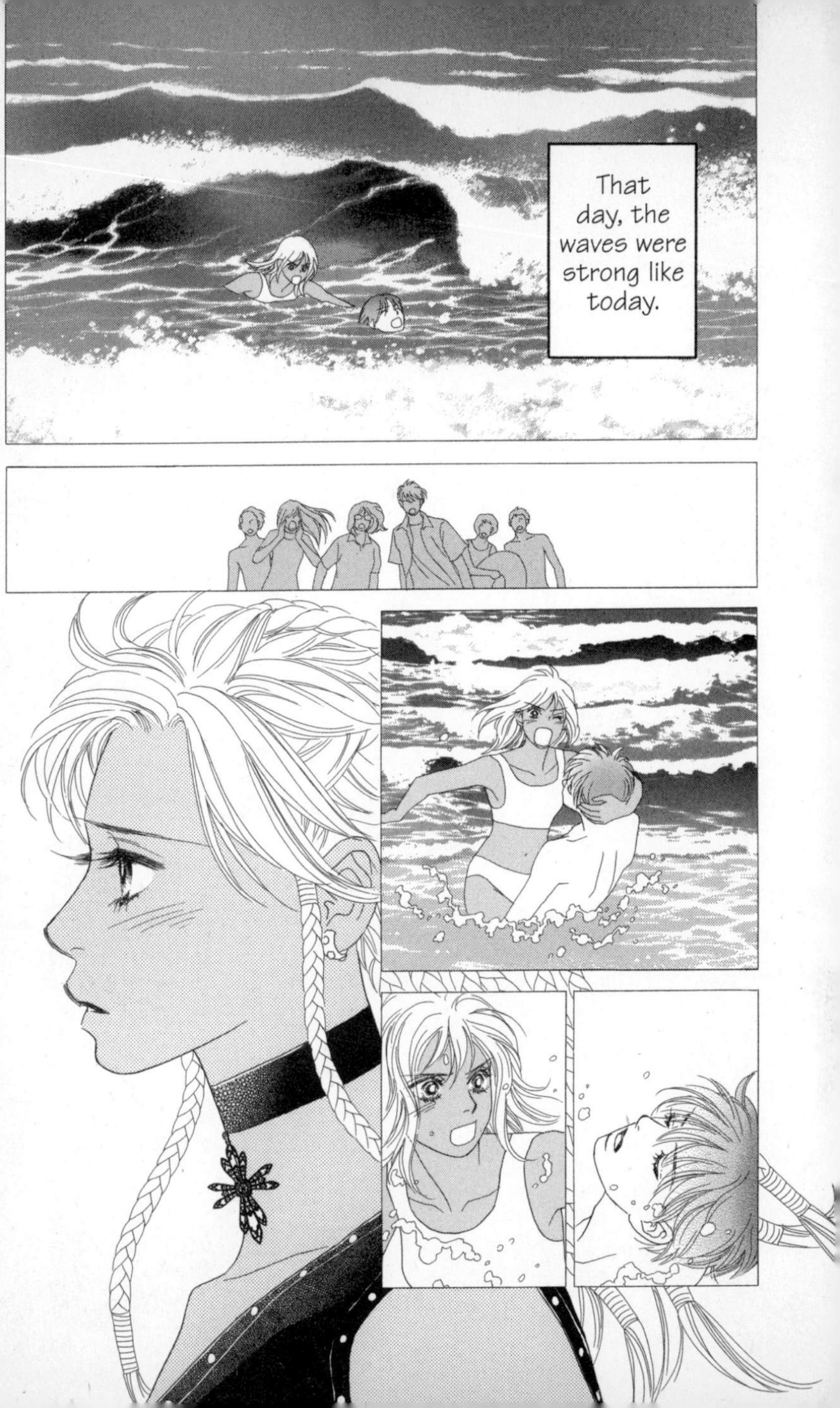
That day, the waves were strong like today.

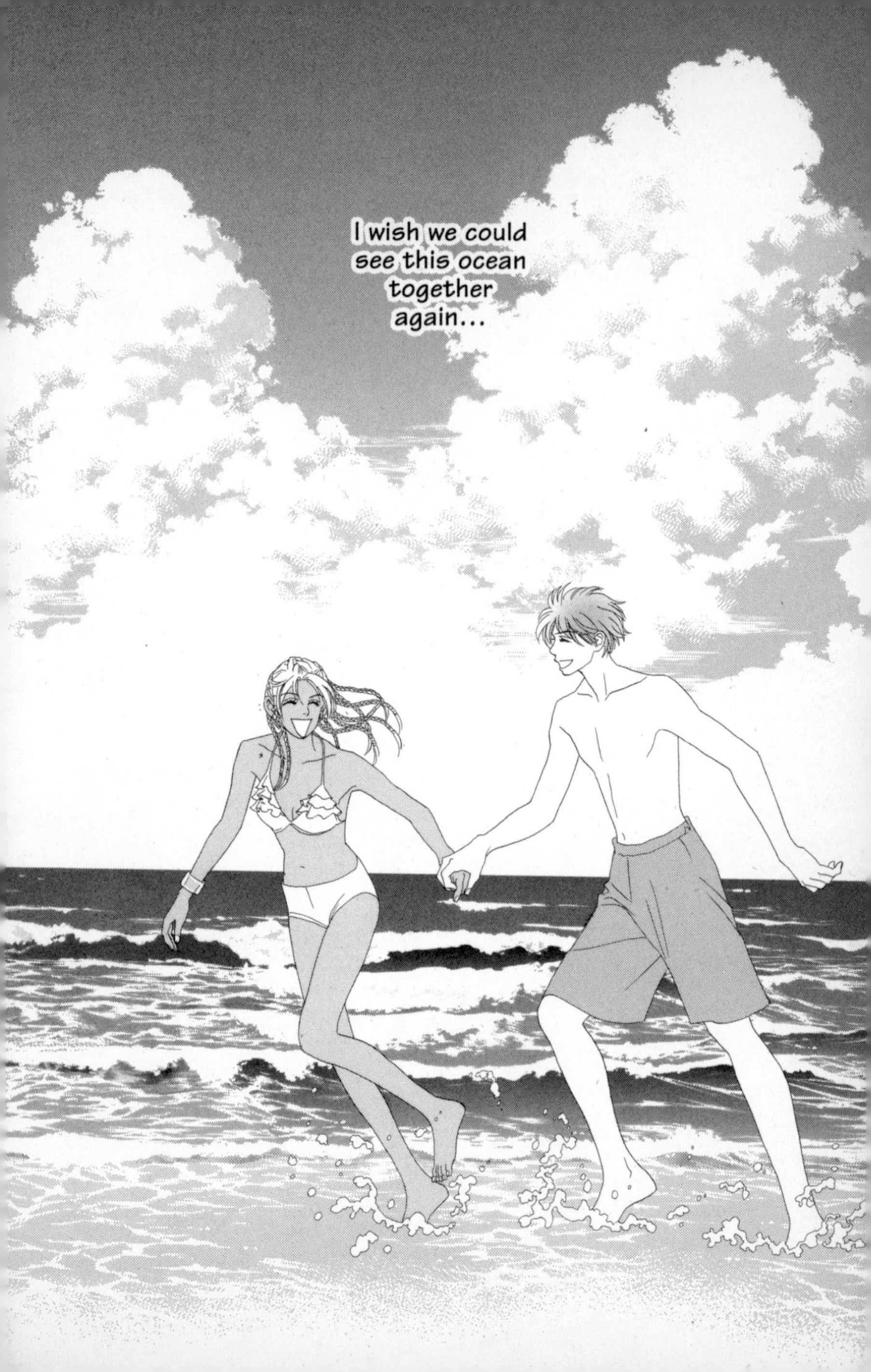
I wish we could see this ocean together again...

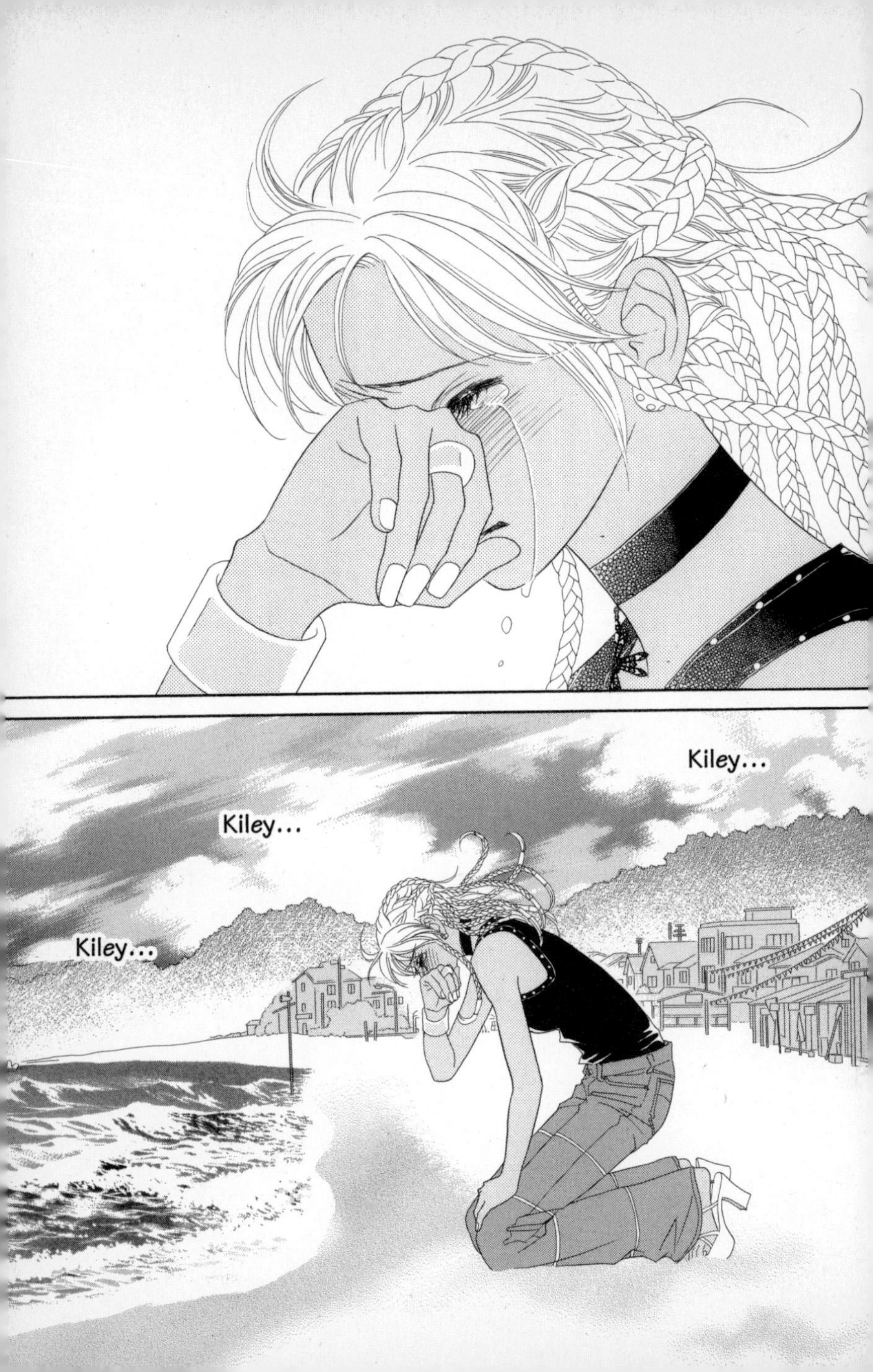
Kiley...
Kiley...
Kiley...

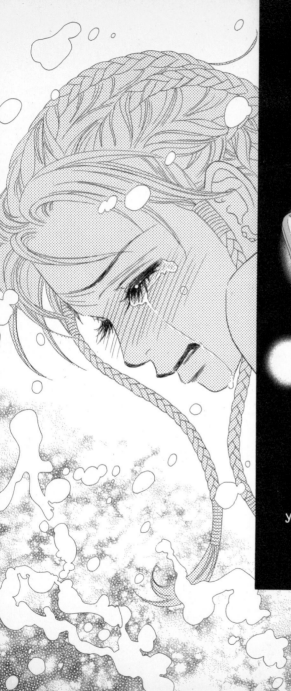

I was
waiting
for you.

I can't
wait to
see you.

DIGITAL

I believed
you. I waited
for you.

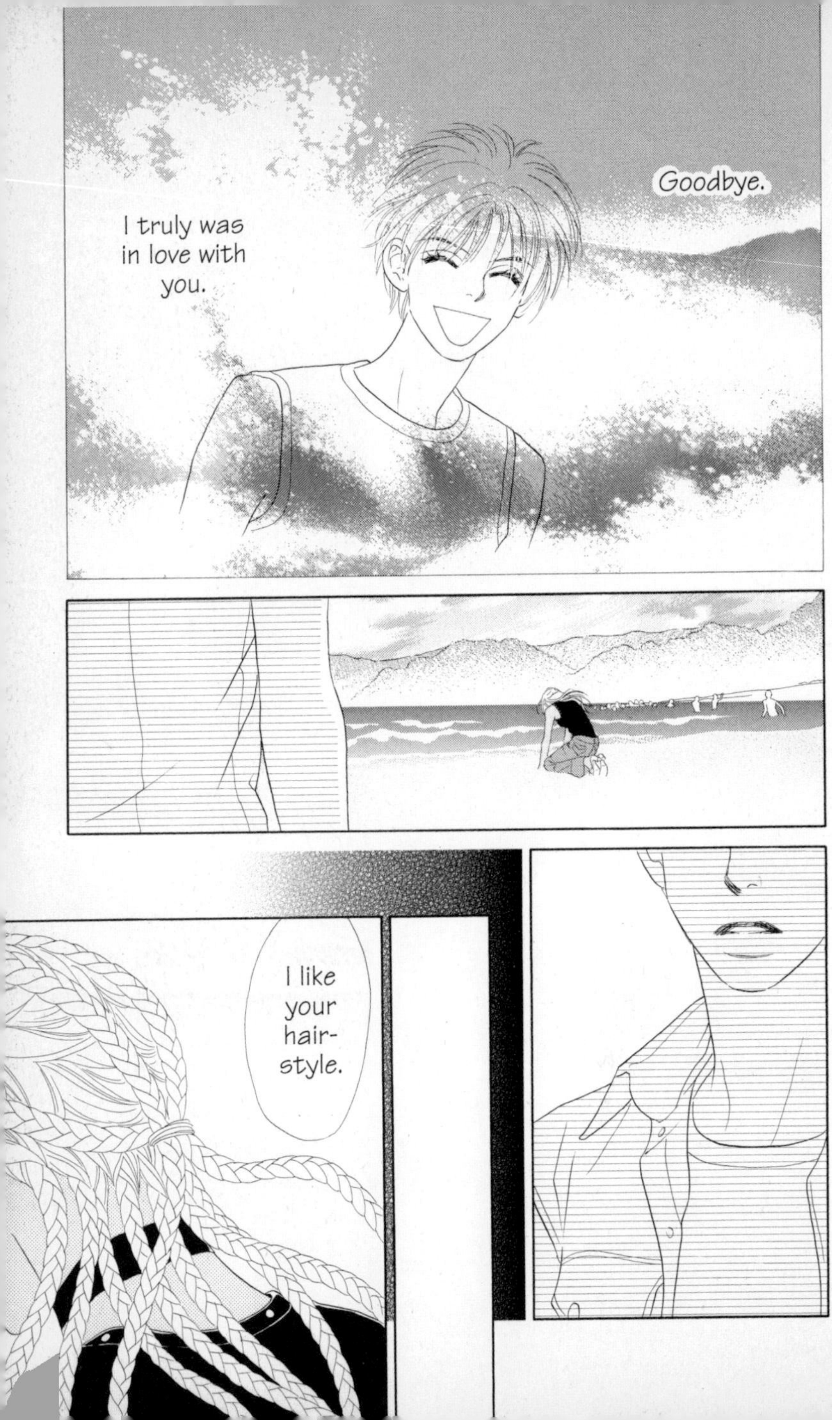
Goodbye.
I truly was in love with you.
I like your hair-style.

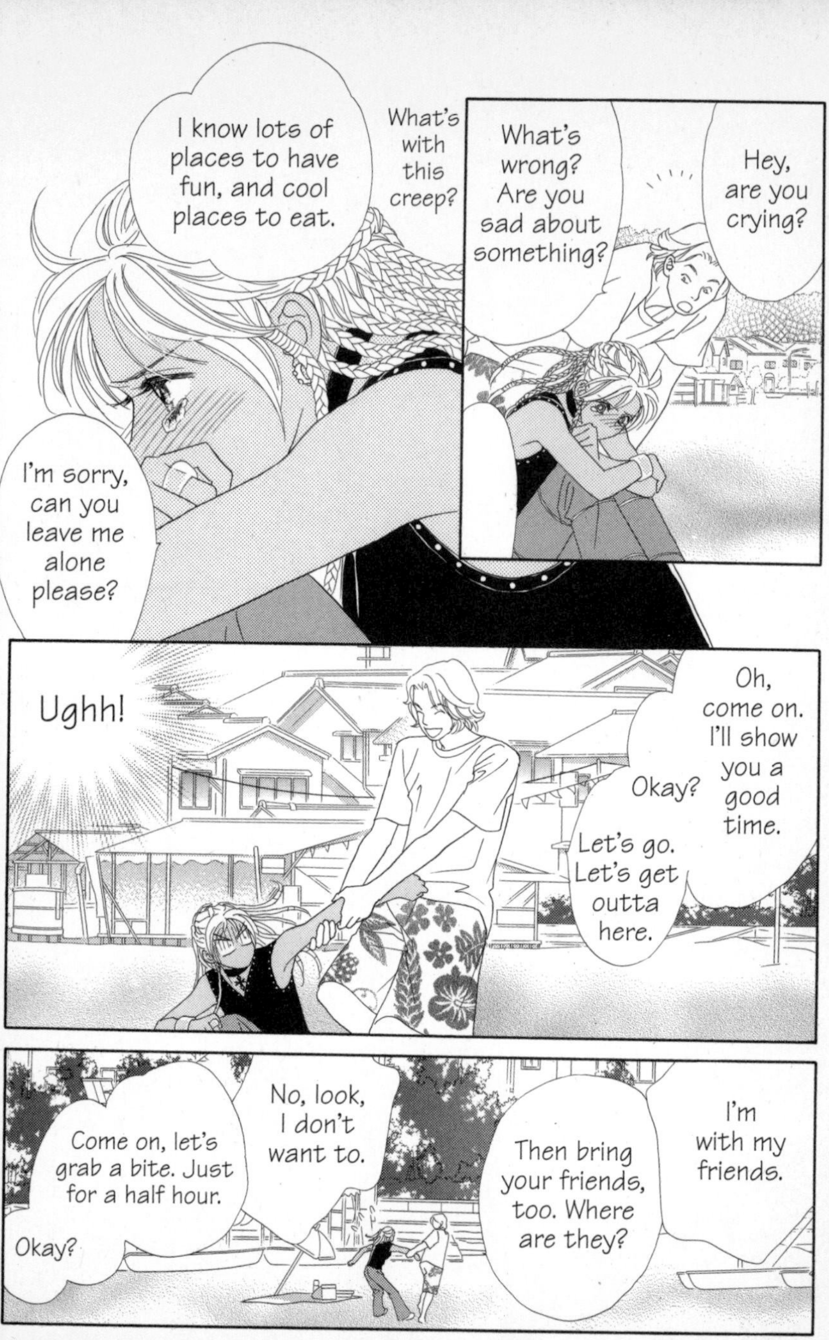
Hey, are you crying?
What's wrong? Are you sad about something?
What's with this creep?
I know lots of places to have fun, and cool places to eat.
I'm sorry, can you leave me alone please?
Oh, come on. I'll show you a good time.
Okay?
Let's go. Let's get outta here.
Ughh!
I'm with my friends.
Then bring your friends, too. Where are they?
No, look, I don't want to.
Come on, let's grab a bite. Just for a half hour.
Okay?

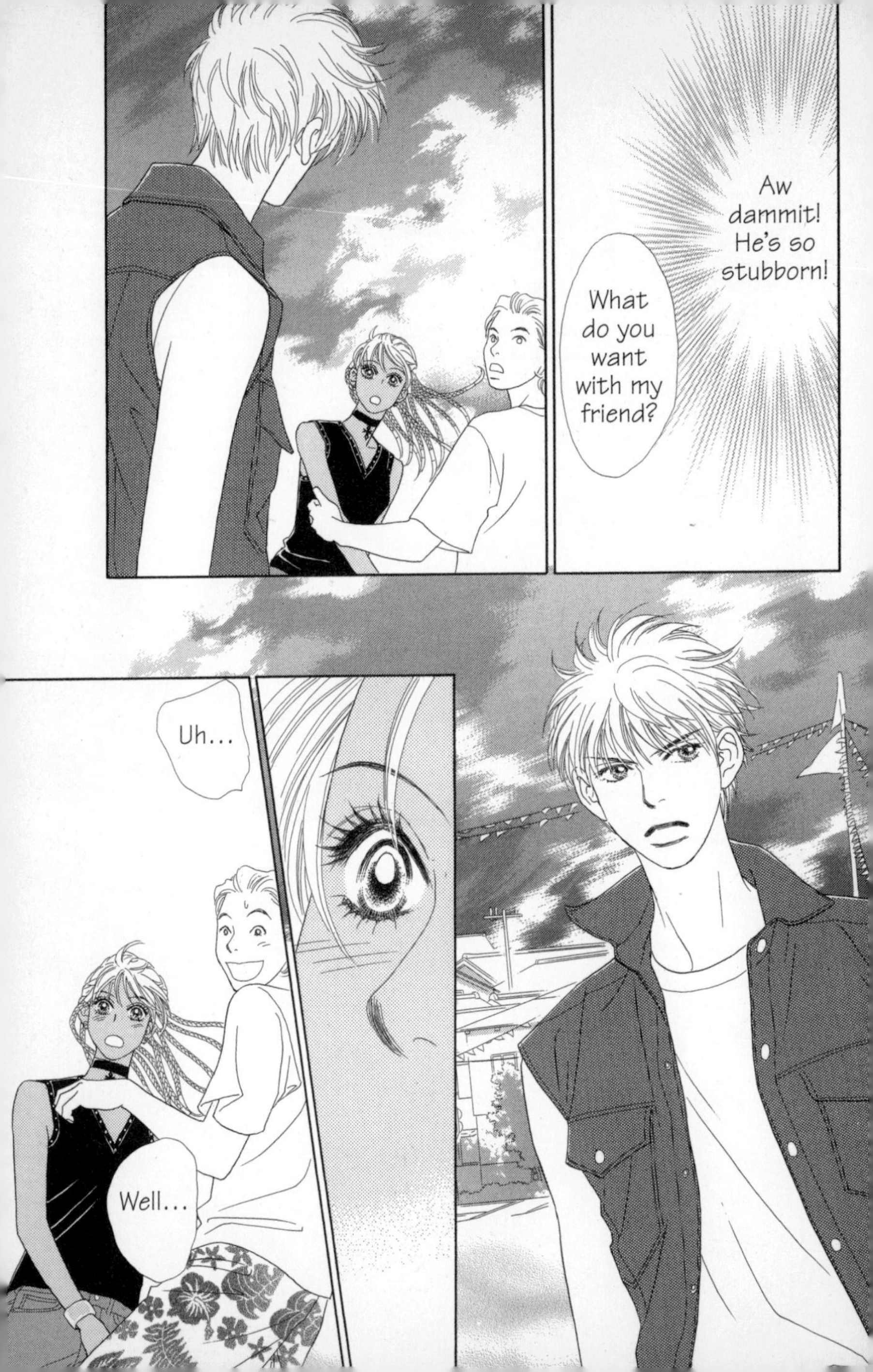
Aw dammit! He's so stubborn!
What do you want with my friend?
Uh...
Well...

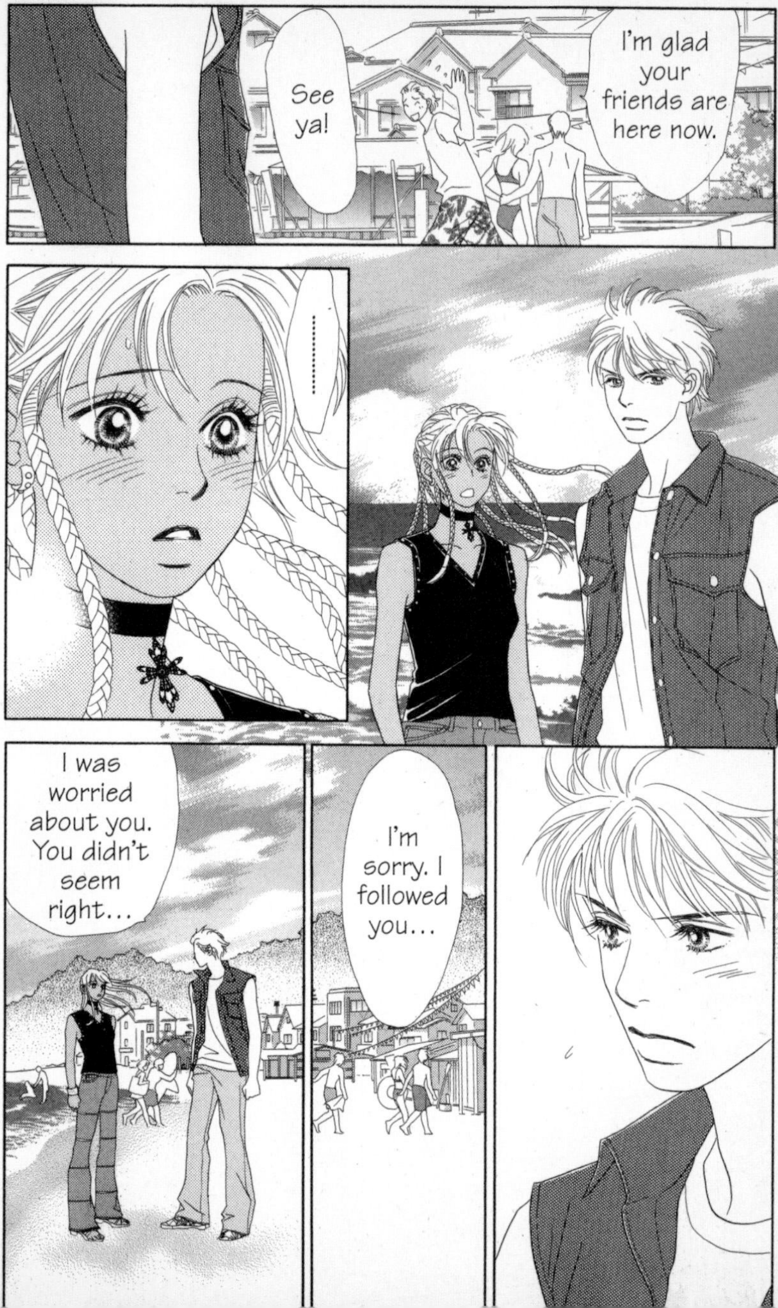
I'm glad your friends are here now.
See ya!
……
I'm sorry. I followed you…
I was worried about you. You didn't seem right…

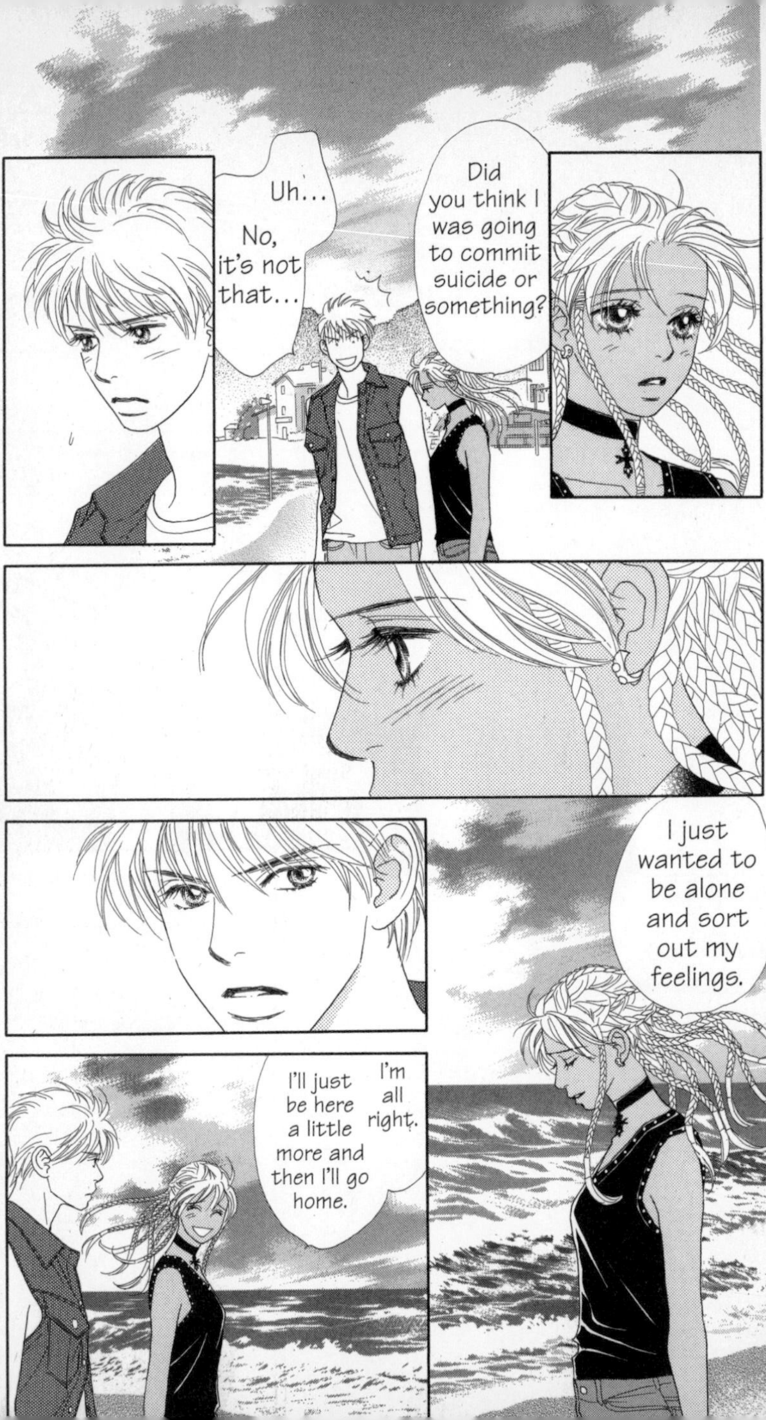
Did you think I was going to commit suicide or something?
Uh...
No, it's not that...
I just wanted to be alone and sort out my feelings.
I'm all right.
I'll just be here a little more and then I'll go home.

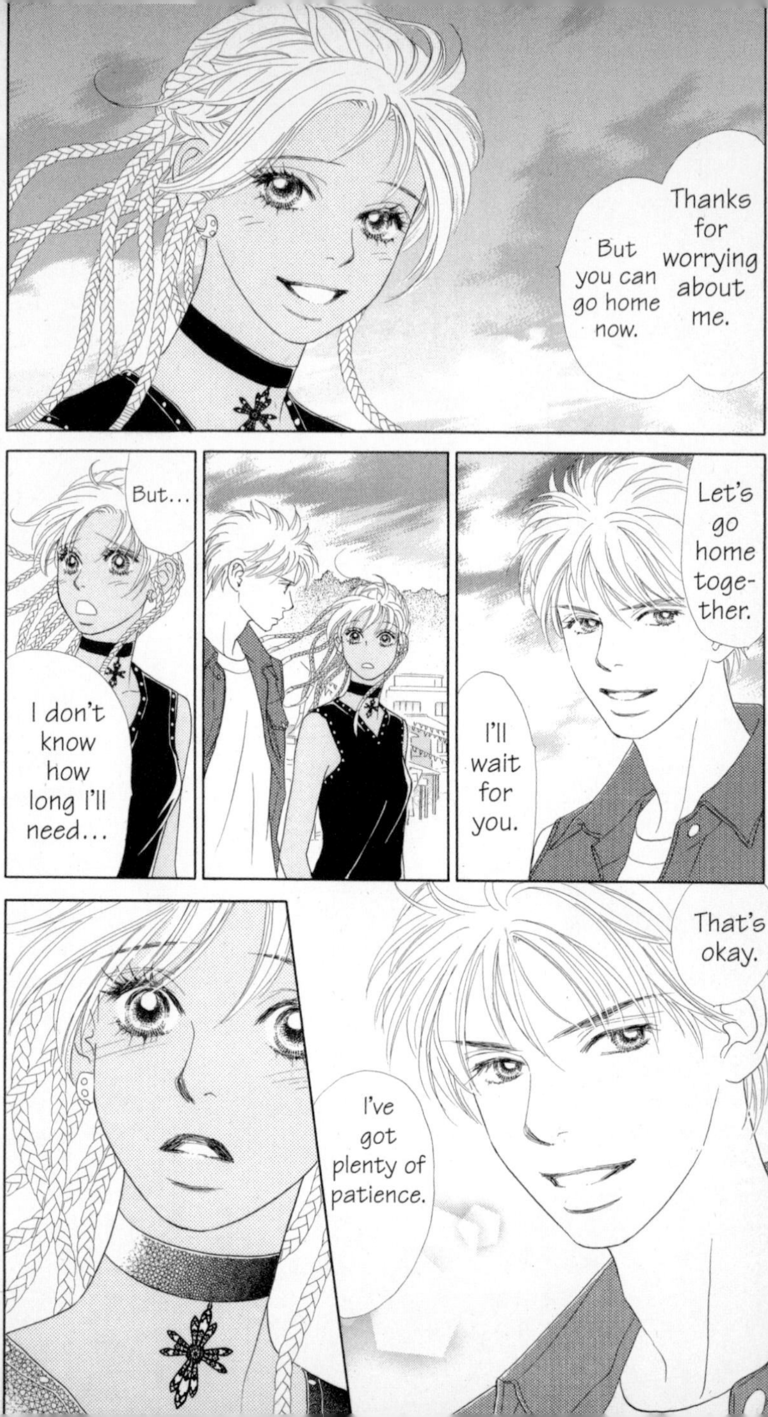
Thanks for worrying about me.
But you can go home now.
Let's go home together.
I'll wait for you.
But…
I don't know how long I'll need…
That's okay.
I've got plenty of patience.

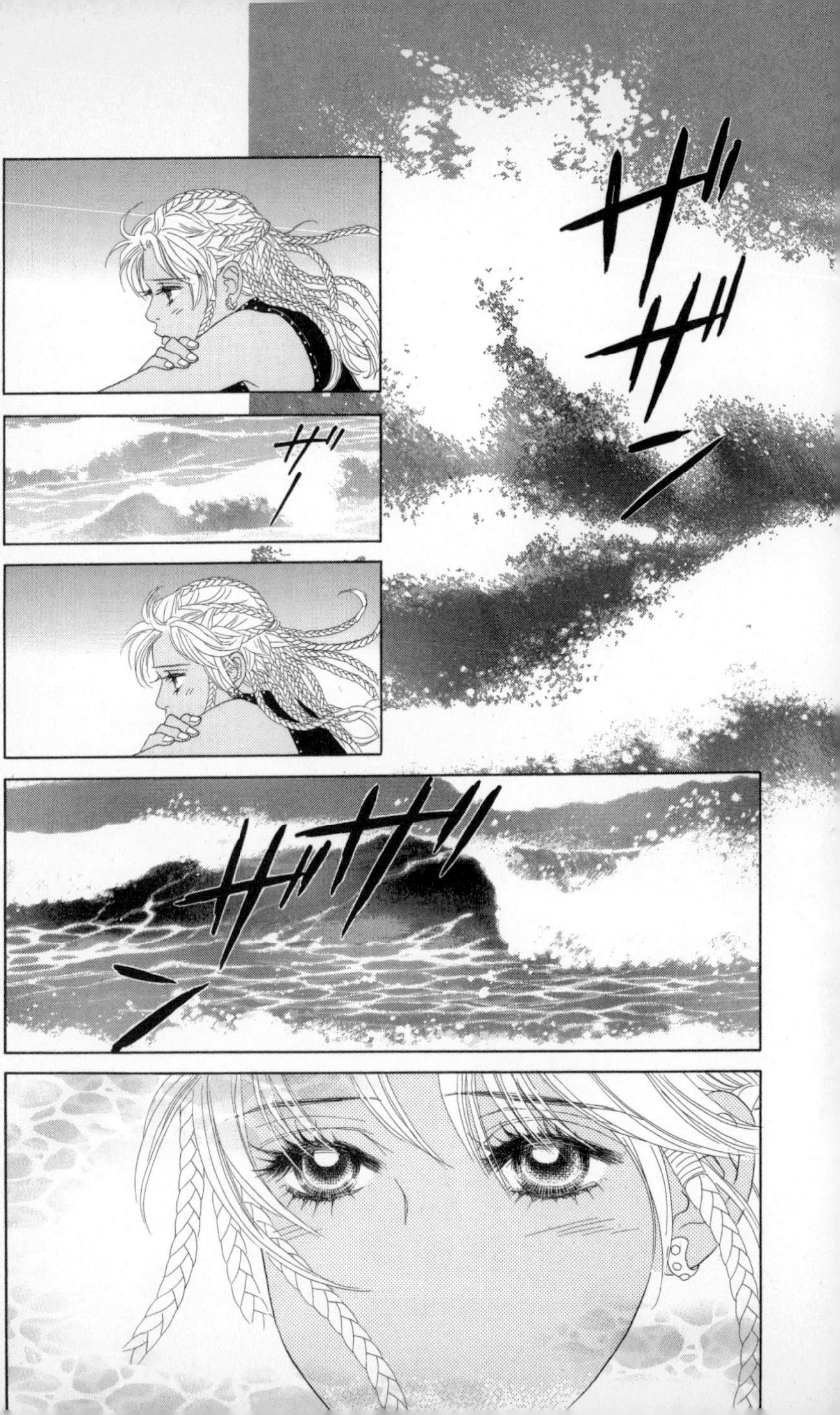
ザザーン

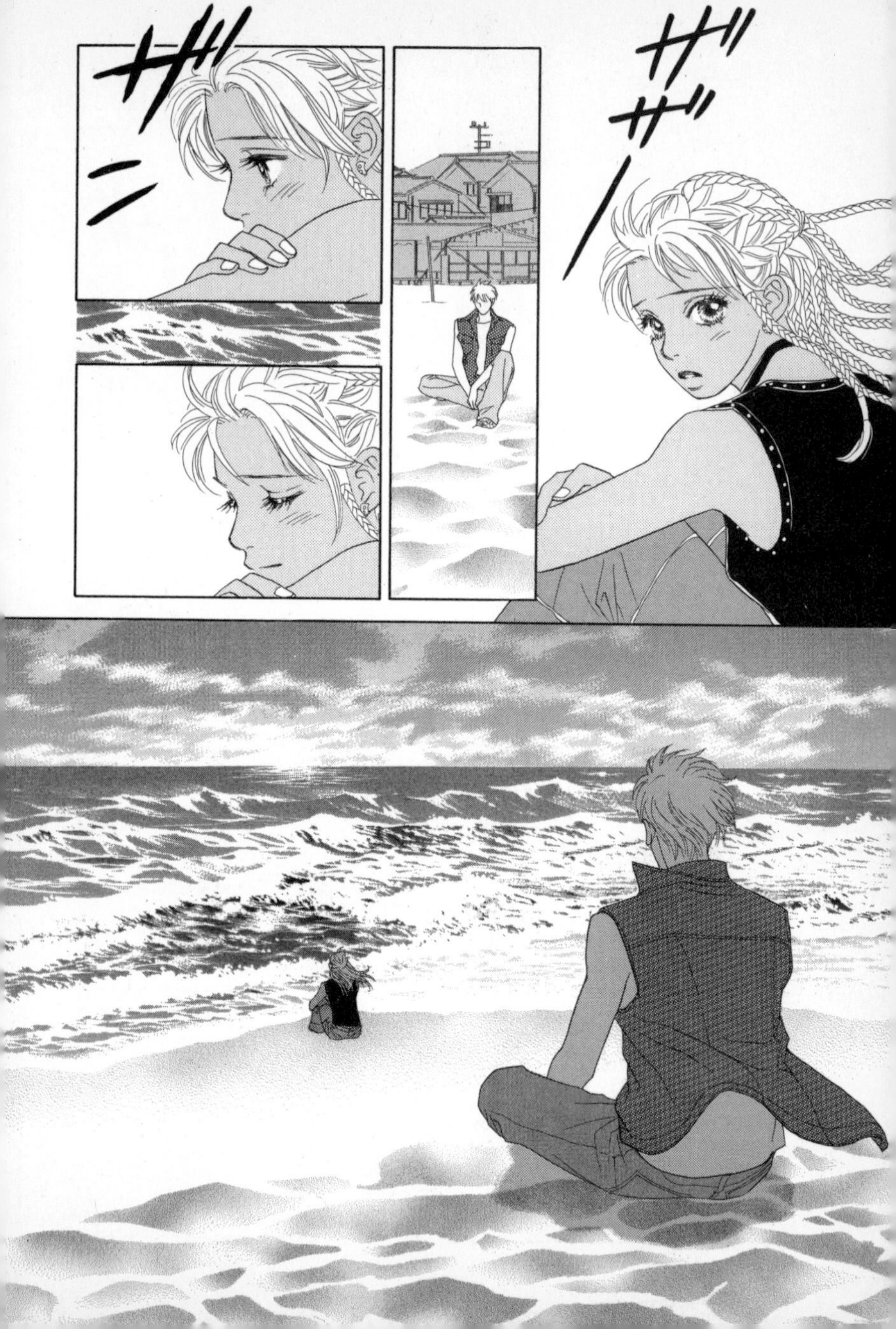
ザザー
ザン

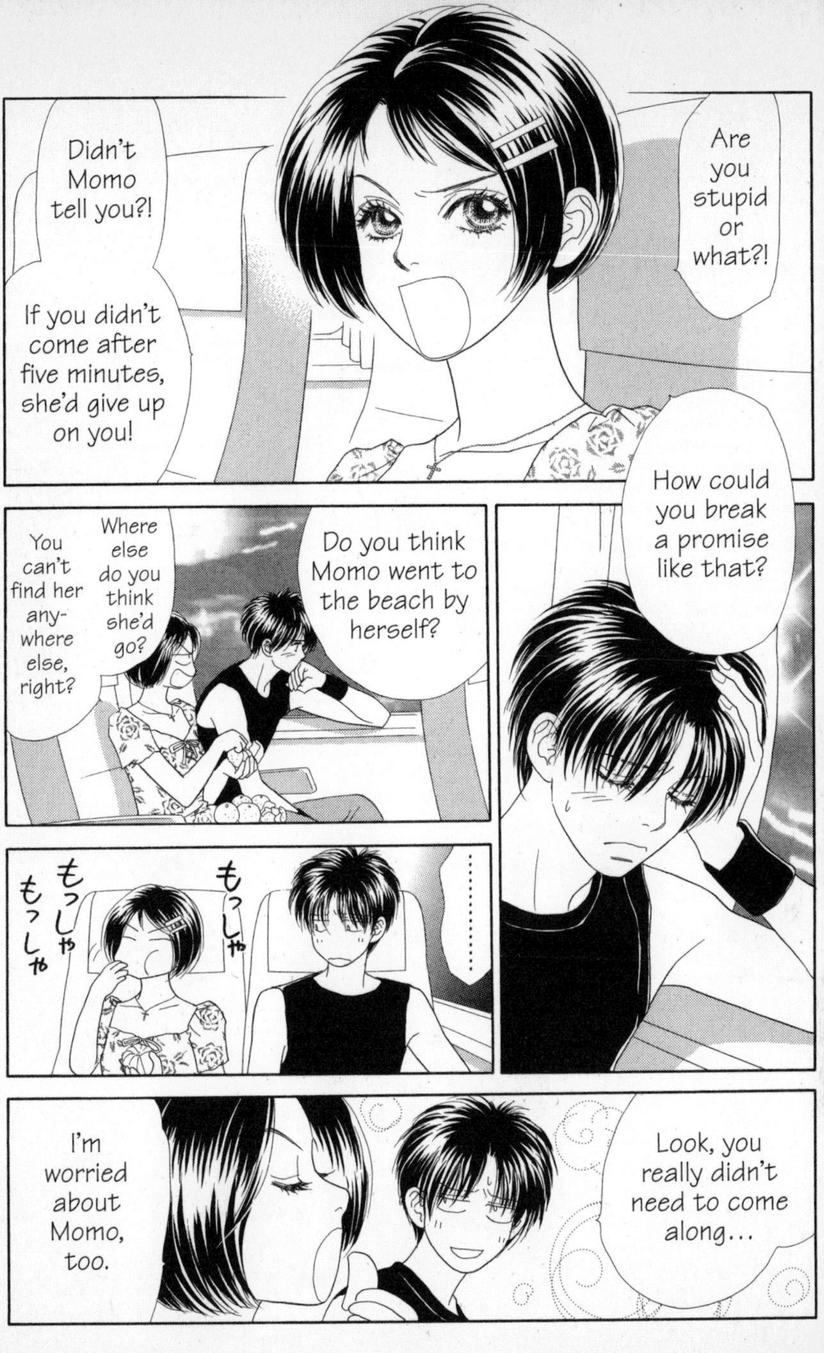
Are you stupid or what?!
Didn't Momo tell you?!
If you didn't come after five minutes, she'd give up on you!
How could you break a promise like that?
Do you think Momo went to the beach by herself?
Where else do you think she'd go?
You can't find her anywhere else, right?
......
もっしゃ
もっしゃ もっしゃ
Look, you really didn't need to come along…
I'm worried about Momo, too.

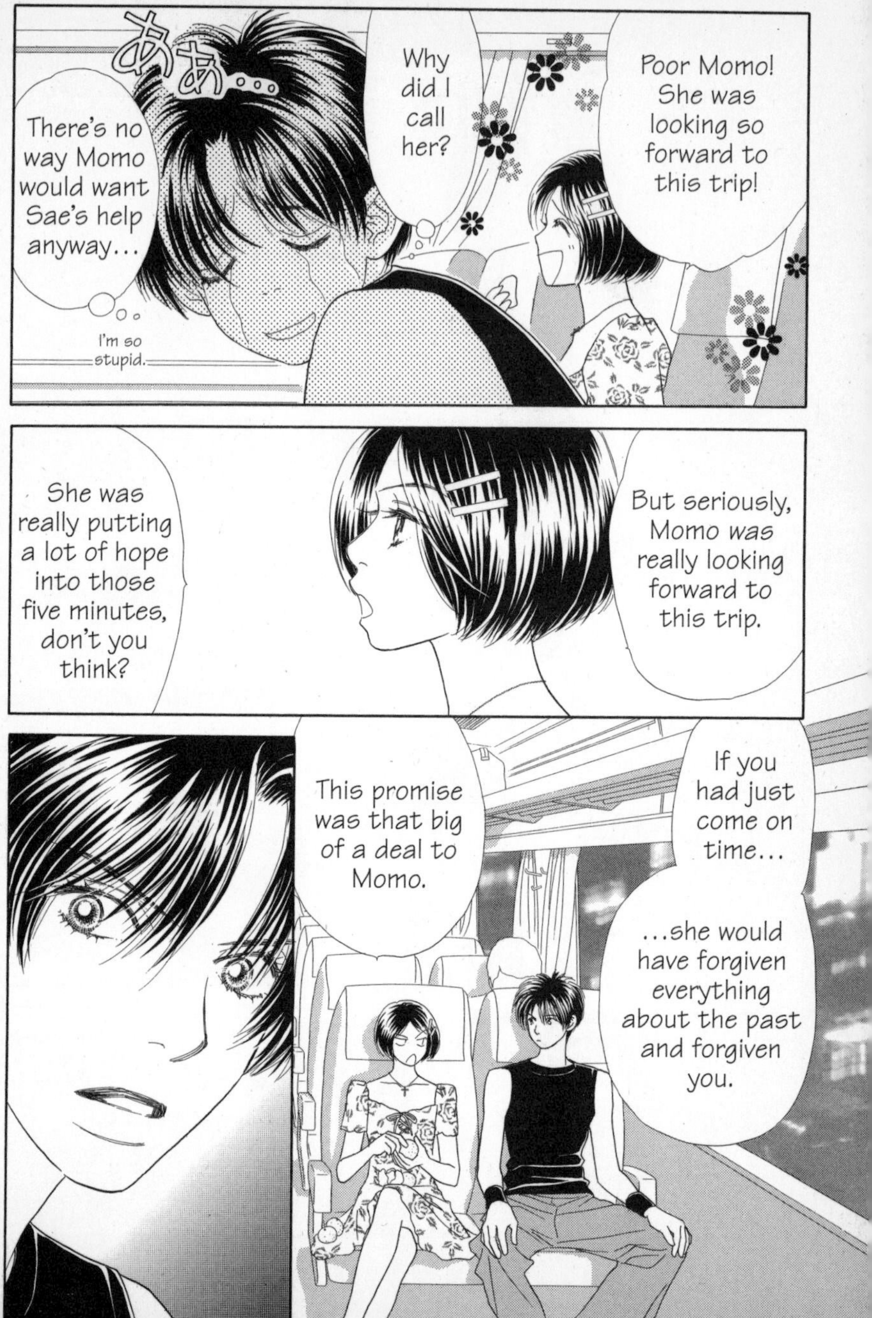
Poor Momo! She was looking so forward to this trip!
Why did I call her?
ああ...
There's no way Momo would want Sae's help anyway...
I'm so stupid.
But seriously, Momo was really looking forward to this trip.
She was really putting a lot of hope into those five minutes, don't you think?
If you had just come on time...
...she would have forgiven everything about the past and forgiven you.
This promise was that big of a deal to Momo.

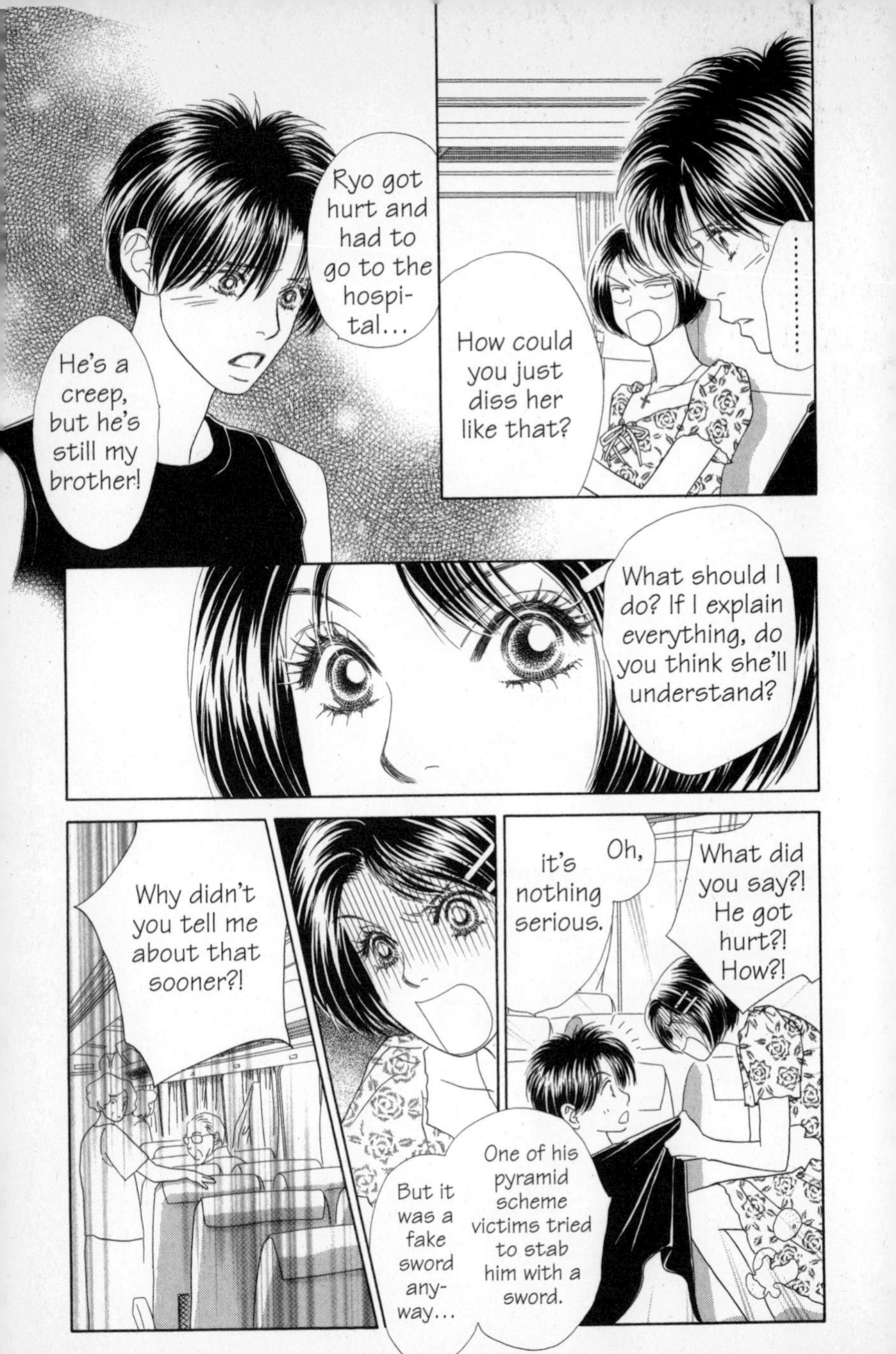
......
How could you just diss her like that?
Ryo got hurt and had to go to the hospital…
He's a creep, but he's still my brother!
What should I do? If I explain everything, do you think she'll understand?
What did you say?! He got hurt?! How?!
Oh,
it's nothing serious.
One of his pyramid scheme victims tried to stab him with a sword.
But it was a fake sword anyway…
Why didn't you tell me about that sooner?!

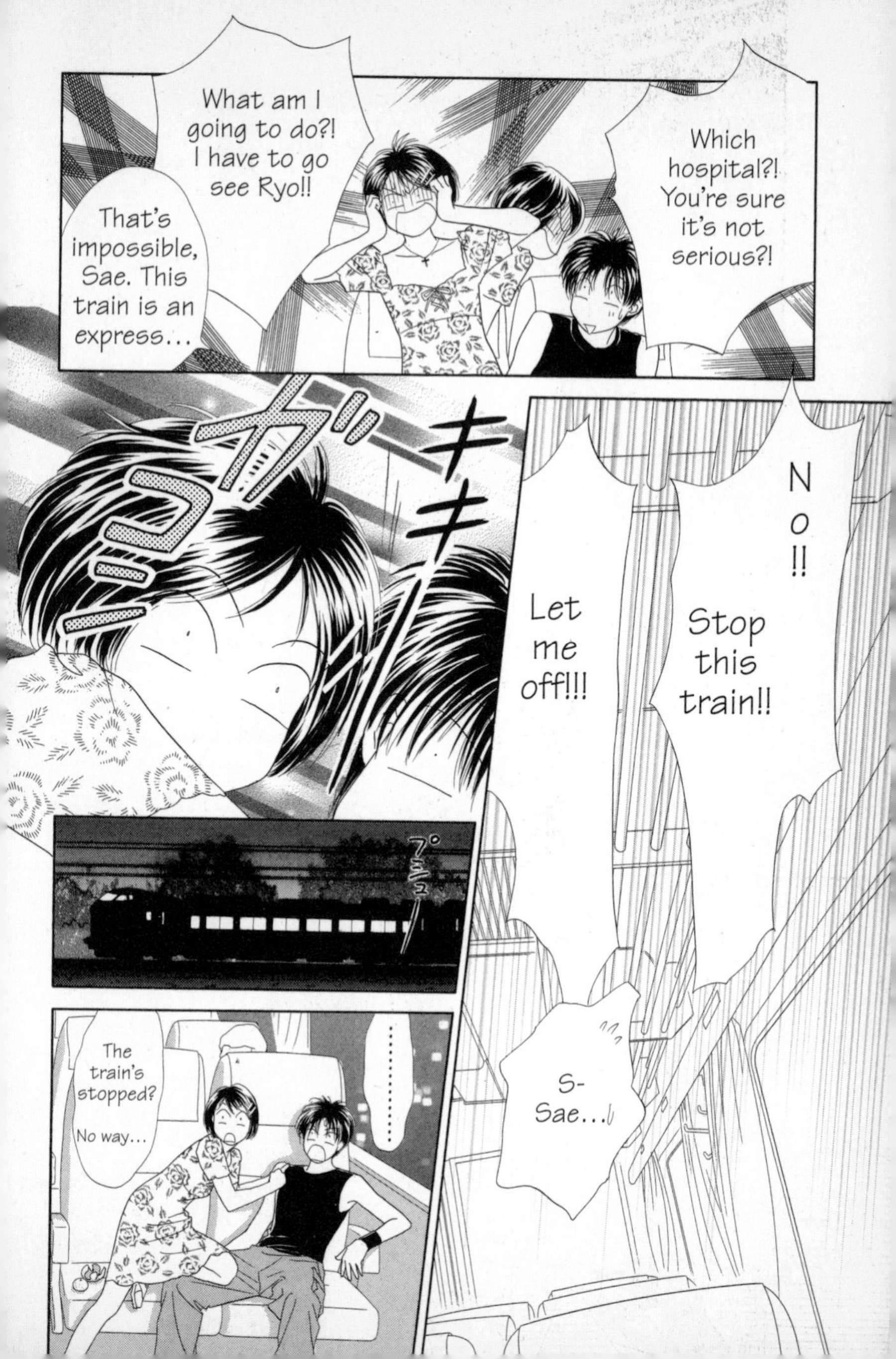
Which hospital?! You're sure it's not serious?!
What am I going to do?! I have to go see Ryo!!
That's impossible, Sae. This train is an express...
No!!
Stop this train!!
Let me off!!!
S- Sae...
....
The train's stopped?
No way...

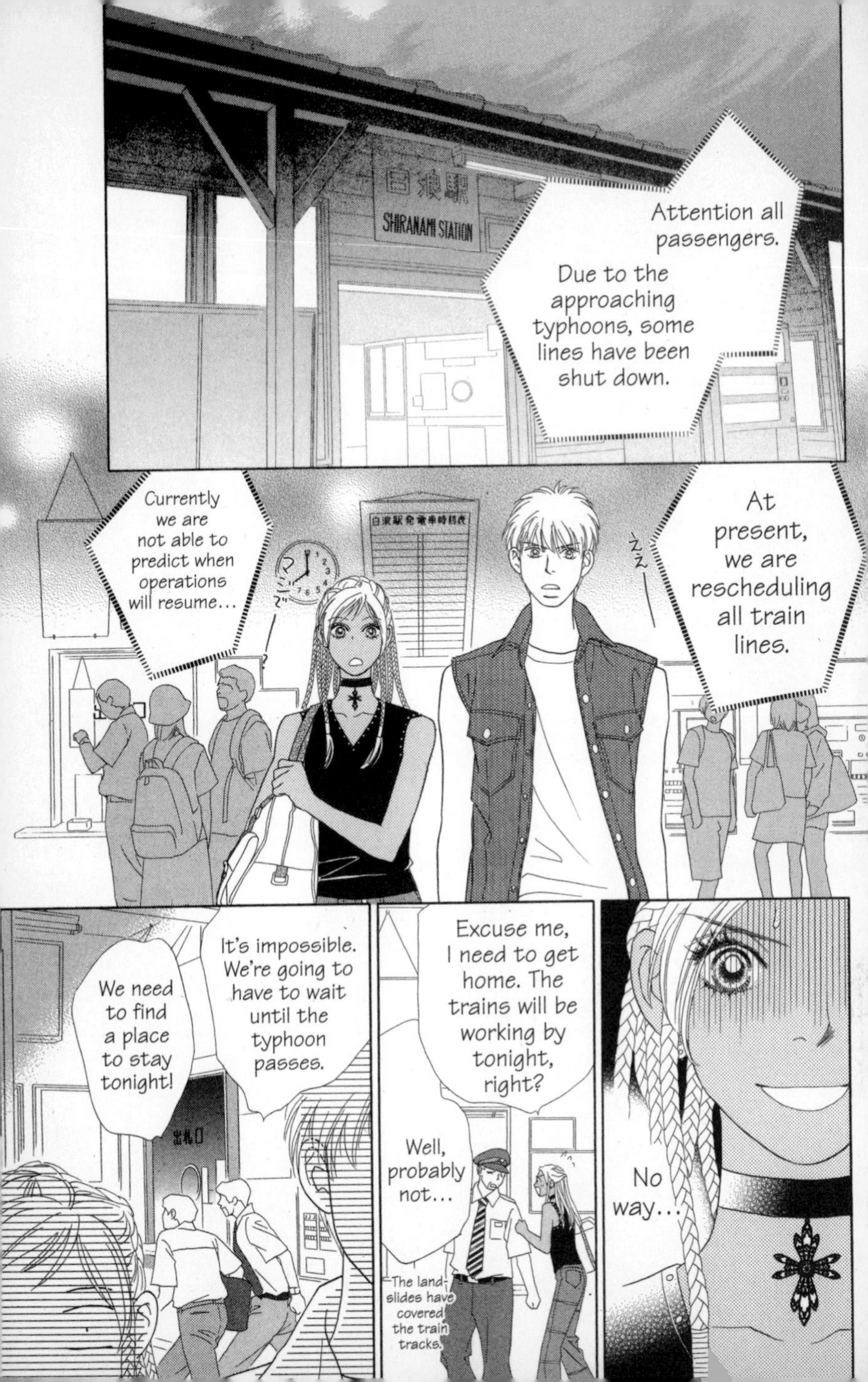
白浪駅
SHIRANAMI STATION
Attention all passengers.
Due to the approaching typhoons, some lines have been shut down.
At present, we are rescheduling all train lines.
Currently we are not able to predict when operations will resume…
No way…
Excuse me, I need to get home. The trains will be working by tonight, right?
Well, probably not…
The land-slides have covered the train tracks.
It's impossible. We're going to have to wait until the typhoon passes.
We need to find a place to stay tonight!

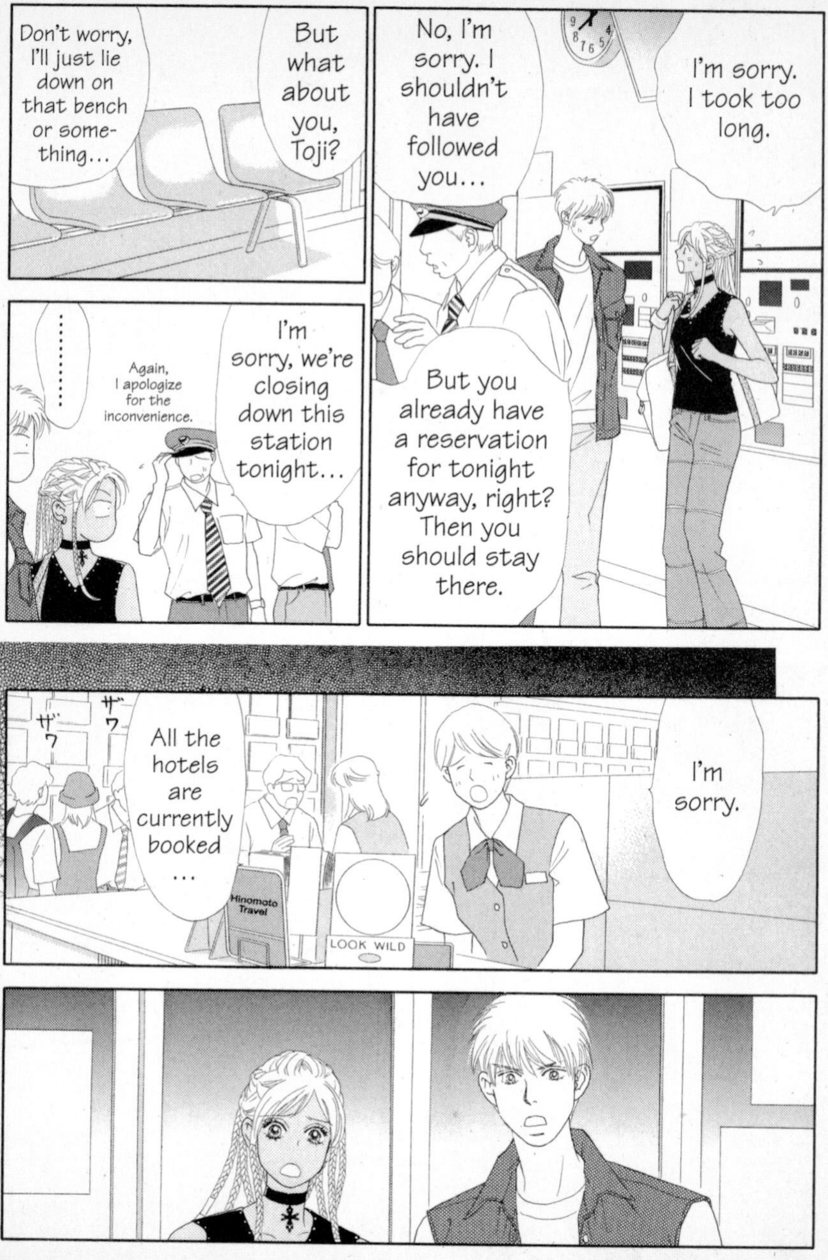
I'm sorry. I took too long.
No, I'm sorry. I shouldn't have followed you...
But you already have a reservation for tonight anyway, right? Then you should stay there.
But what about you, Toji?
Don't worry, I'll just lie down on that bench or something...
I'm sorry, we're closing down this station tonight...
Again, I apologize for the inconvenience.
....
I'm sorry.
All the hotels are currently booked ...
ザワ
ザワ
Hinomoto Travel
LOOK WILD

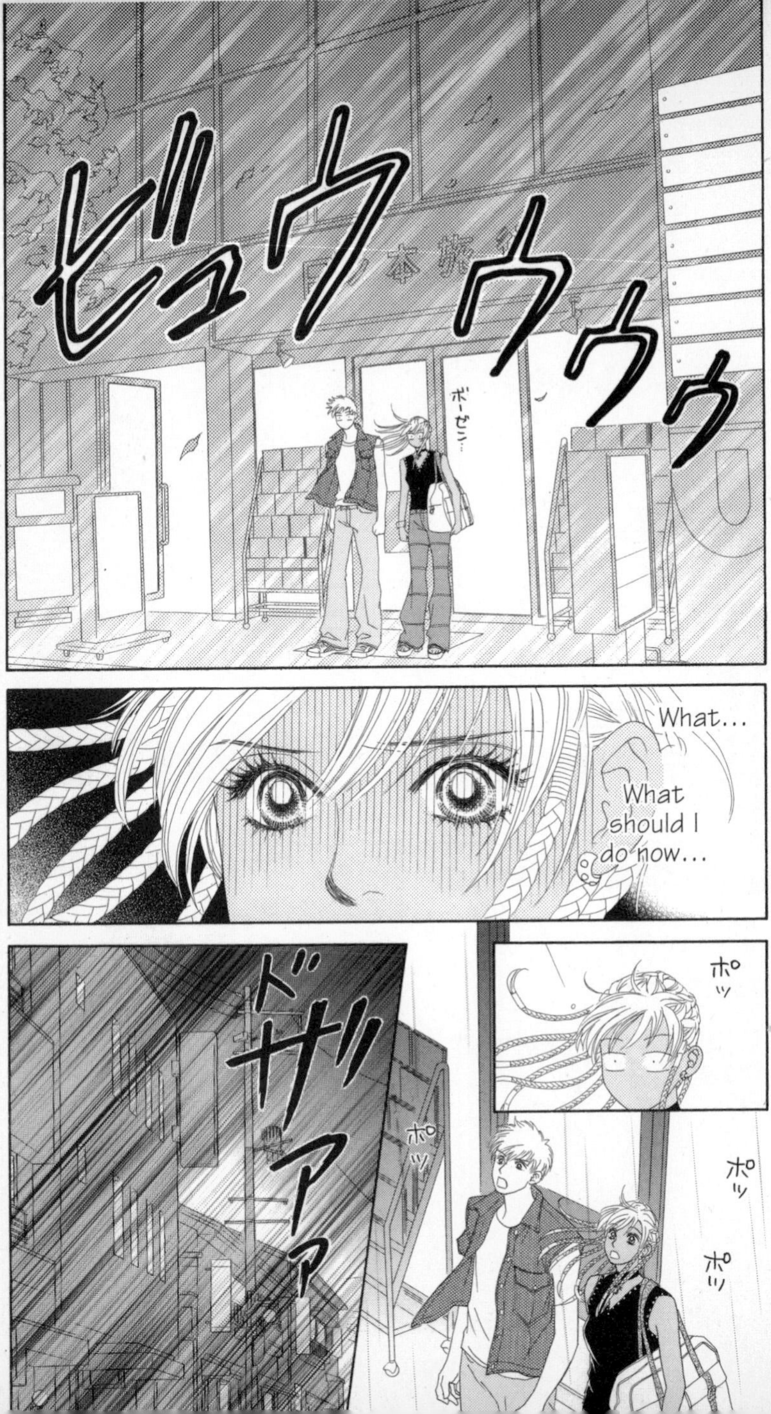
ビュウウウウ
ボーゼン…
What...
What should I do now...
ポッ
ポツ
ポツ
ポツ
ドザァァ

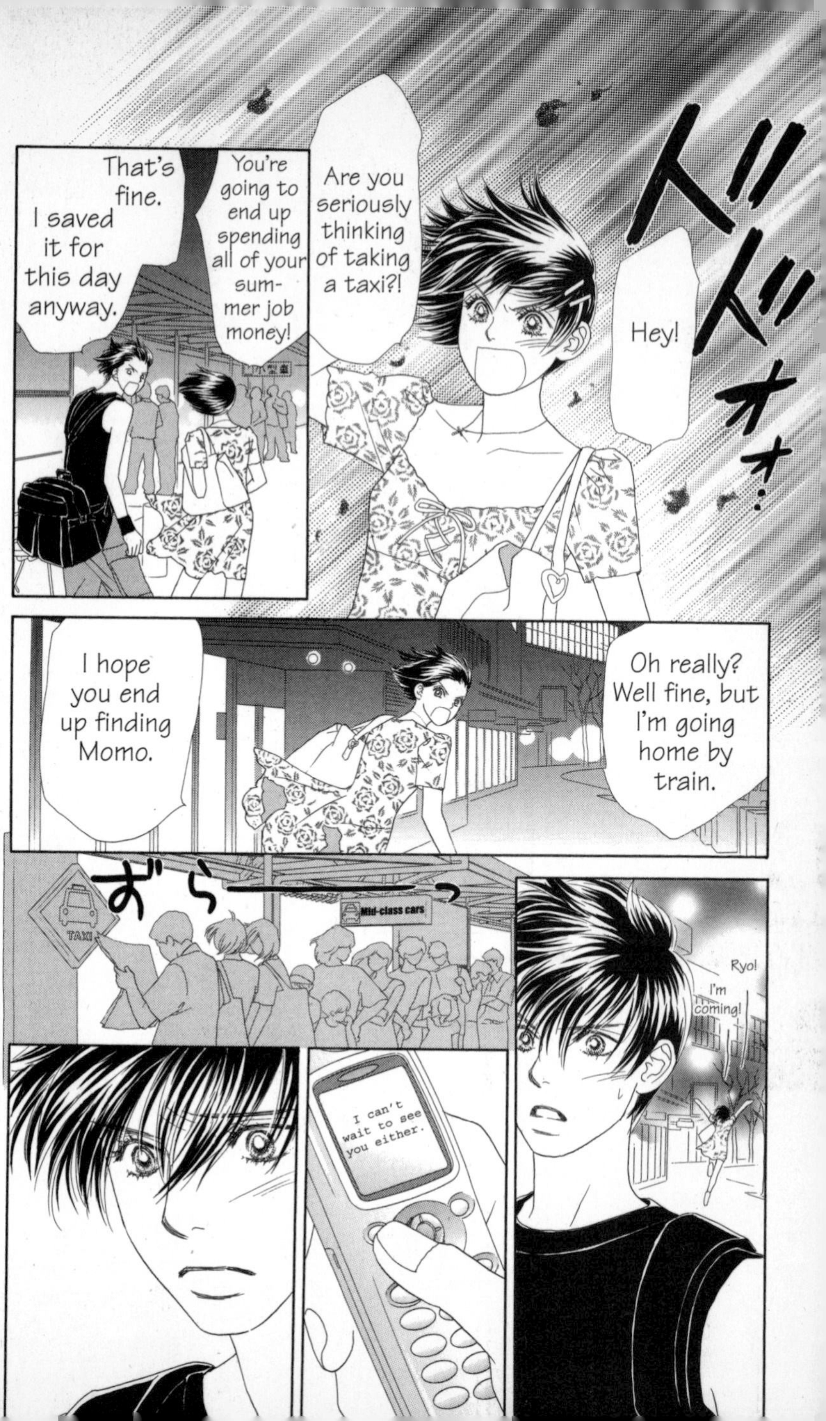
ドドドォォ…
Hey!
Are you seriously thinking of taking a taxi?!
You're going to end up spending all of your summer job money!
That's fine. I saved it for this day anyway.
Oh really? Well fine, but I'm going home by train.
I hope you end up finding Momo.
Ryo!
I'm coming!
おら——っ
TAXI
Mid-class cars
I can't wait to see you either.

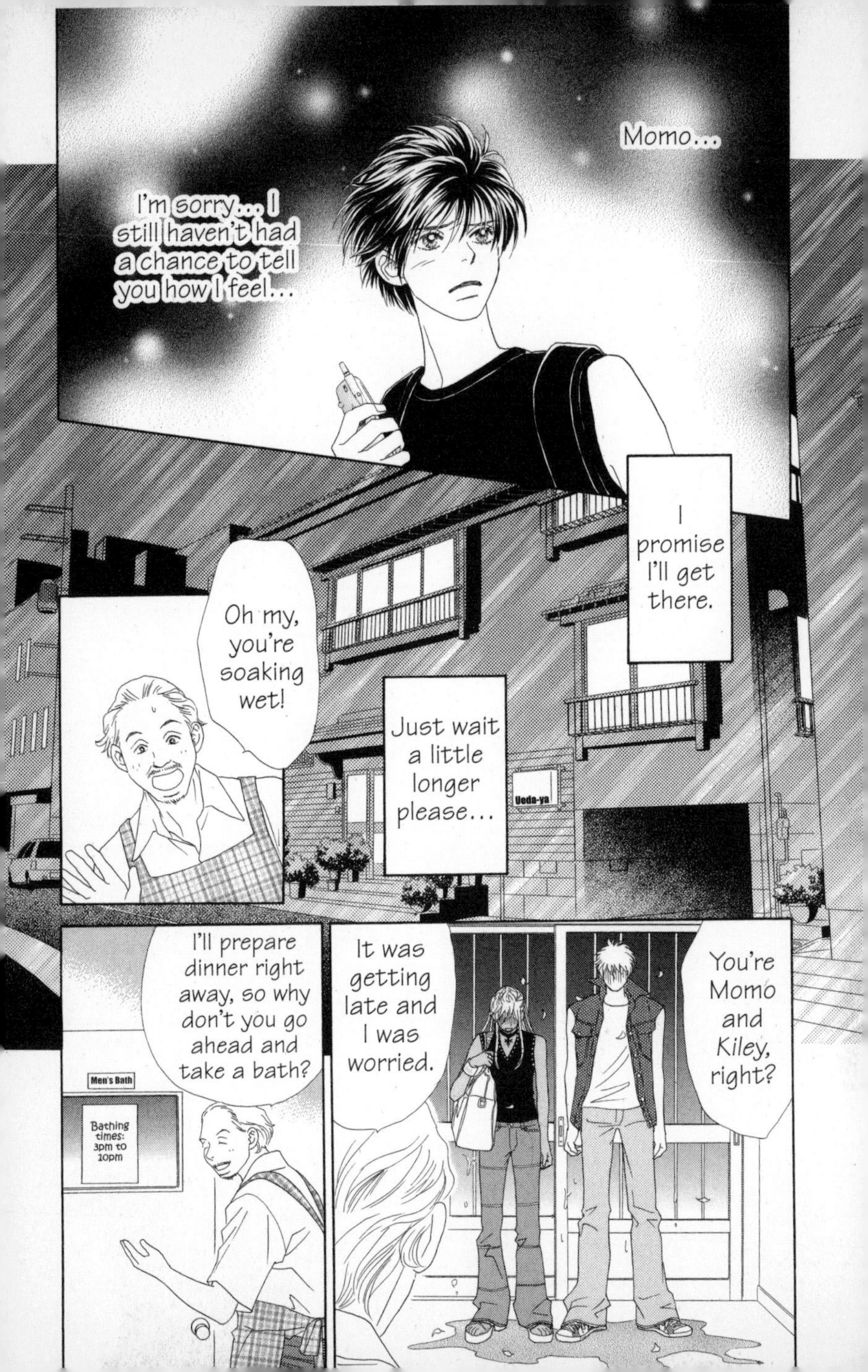
Momo...
I'm sorry... I still haven't had a chance to tell you how I feel...
I promise I'll get there.
Just wait a little longer please...
Ueda-ya
Oh my, you're soaking wet!
You're Momo and Kiley, right?
It was getting late and I was worried.
I'll prepare dinner right away, so why don't you go ahead and take a bath?
Men's Bath
Bathing times: 3pm to 10pm

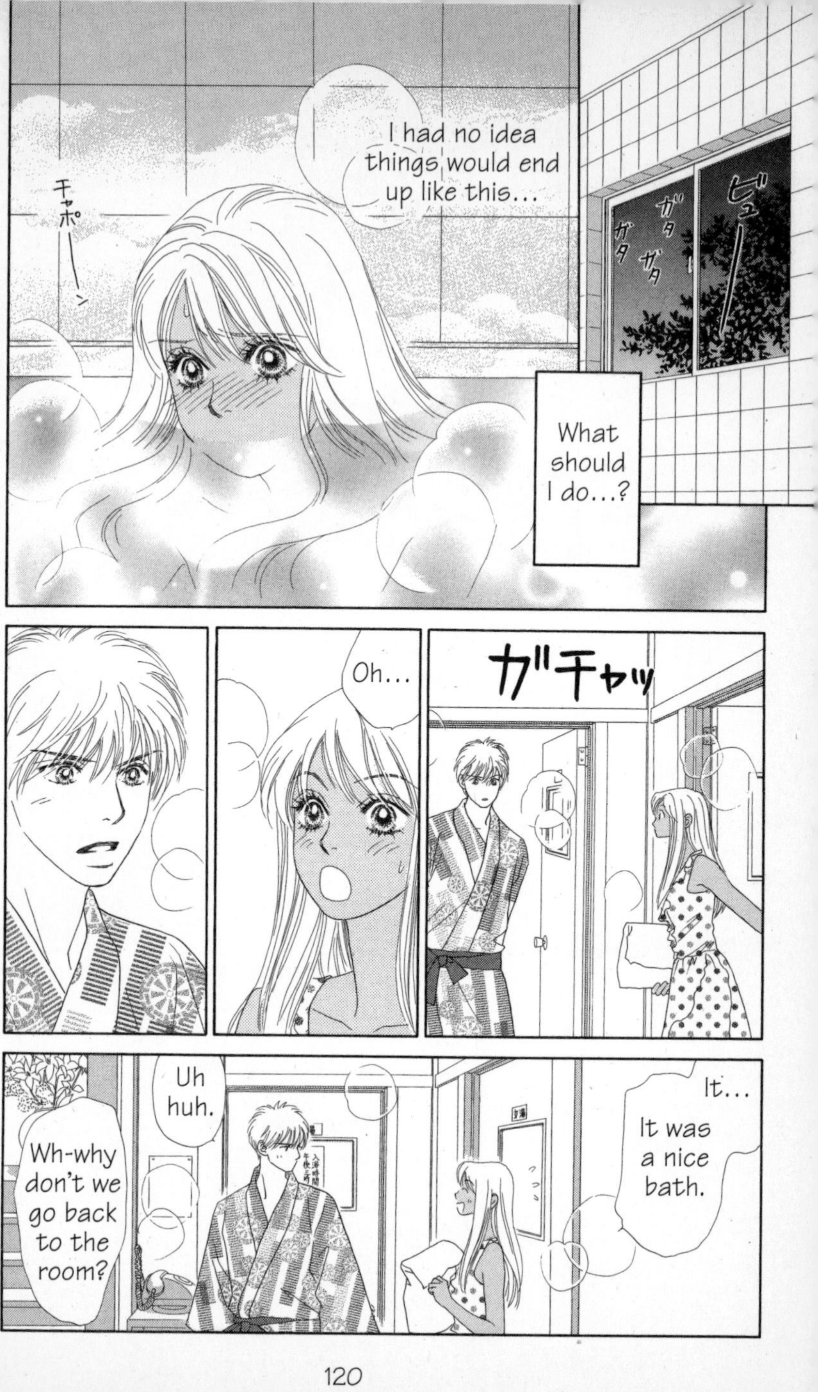
ビュー
ガタガタ
ガタガタ
I had no idea things would end up like this...
チャポーン
What should I do...?
ガチャッ
Oh...
It...
It was a nice bath.
Uh huh.
Wh-why don't we go back to the room?

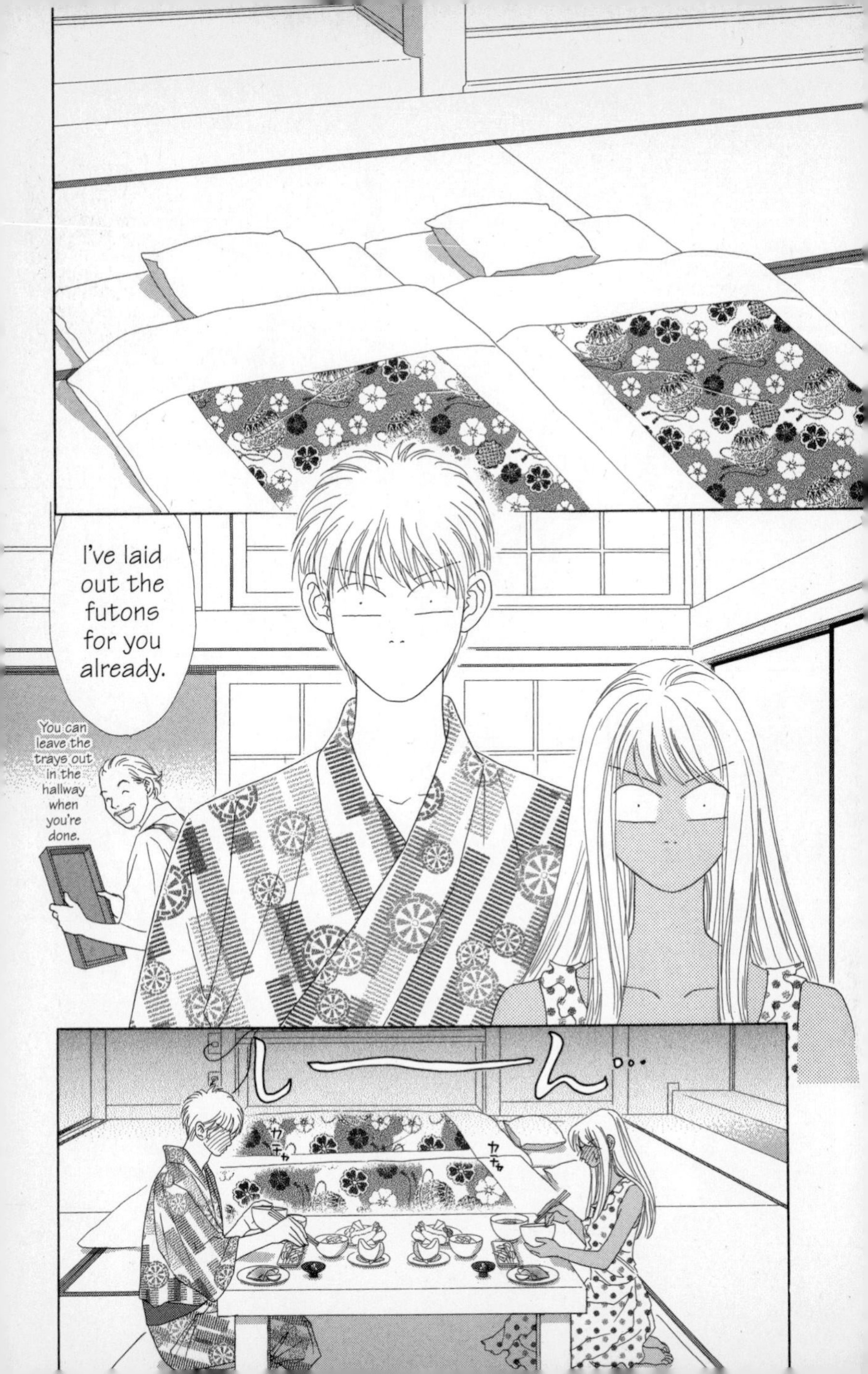
I've laid out the futons for you already.
You can leave the trays out in the hallway when you're done.
しーーん
Do•
カチャ
カチャ

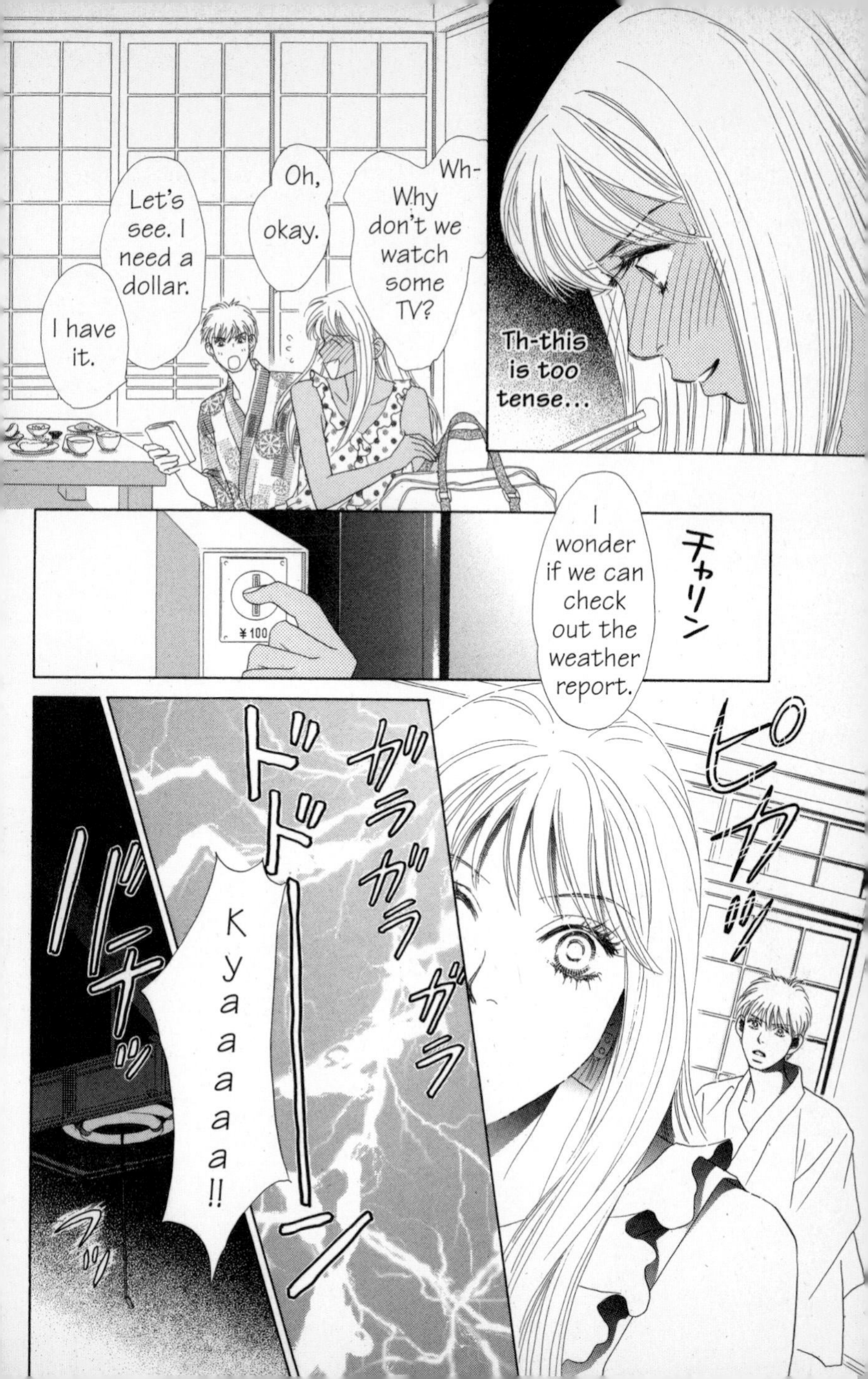
Th-this is too tense...
Wh- Why don't we watch some TV?
Oh, okay.
Let's see. I need a dollar.
I have it.
¥100
チャリン
I wonder if we can check out the weather report.
ピカッ
ガラガラガラ
ドドーン
Kyaaaaaa!!
バチッ
フッ

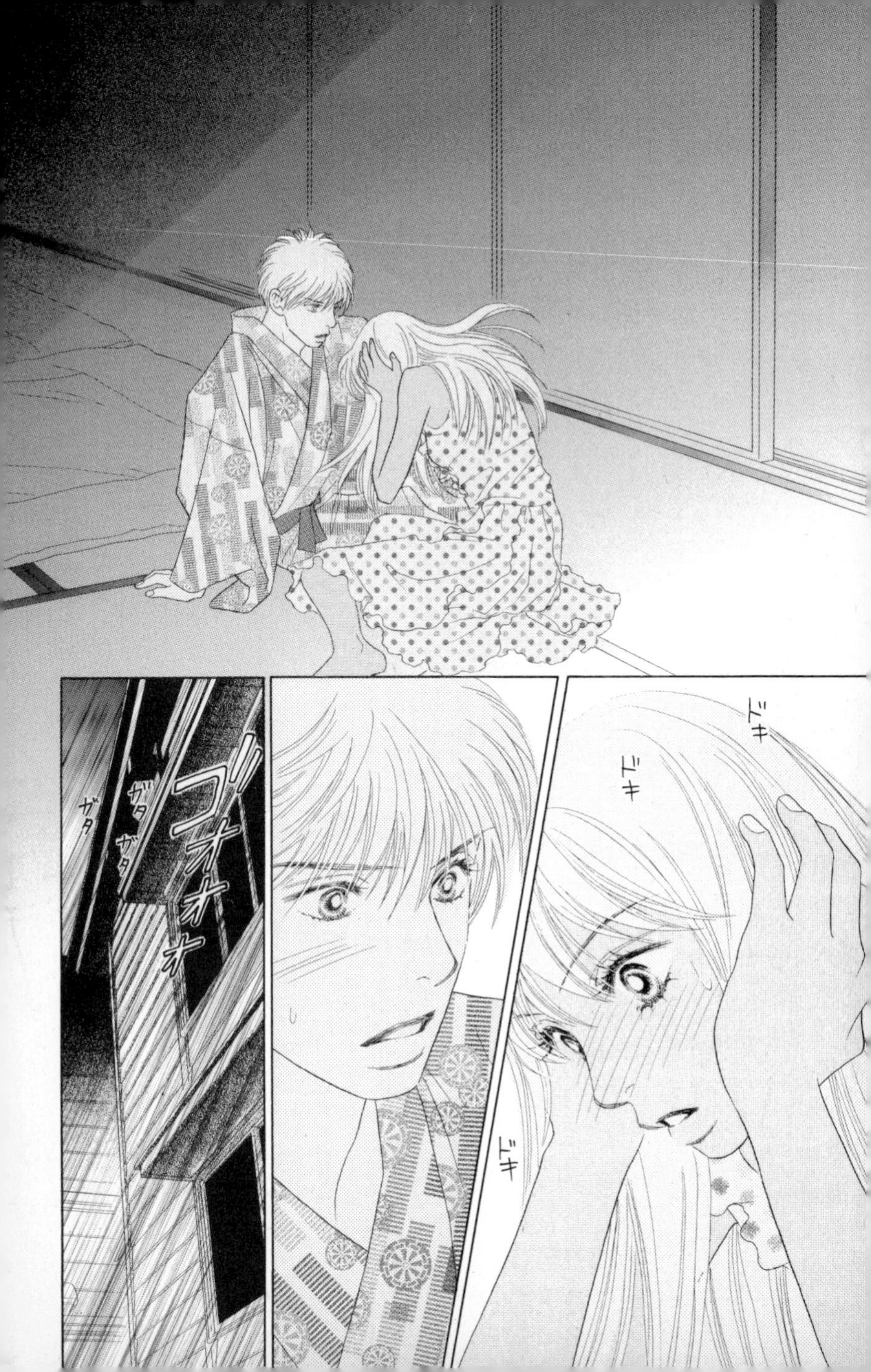
ドキ
ドキ
ドキ
ゴオオオ
ガタ ガタ
ガタ

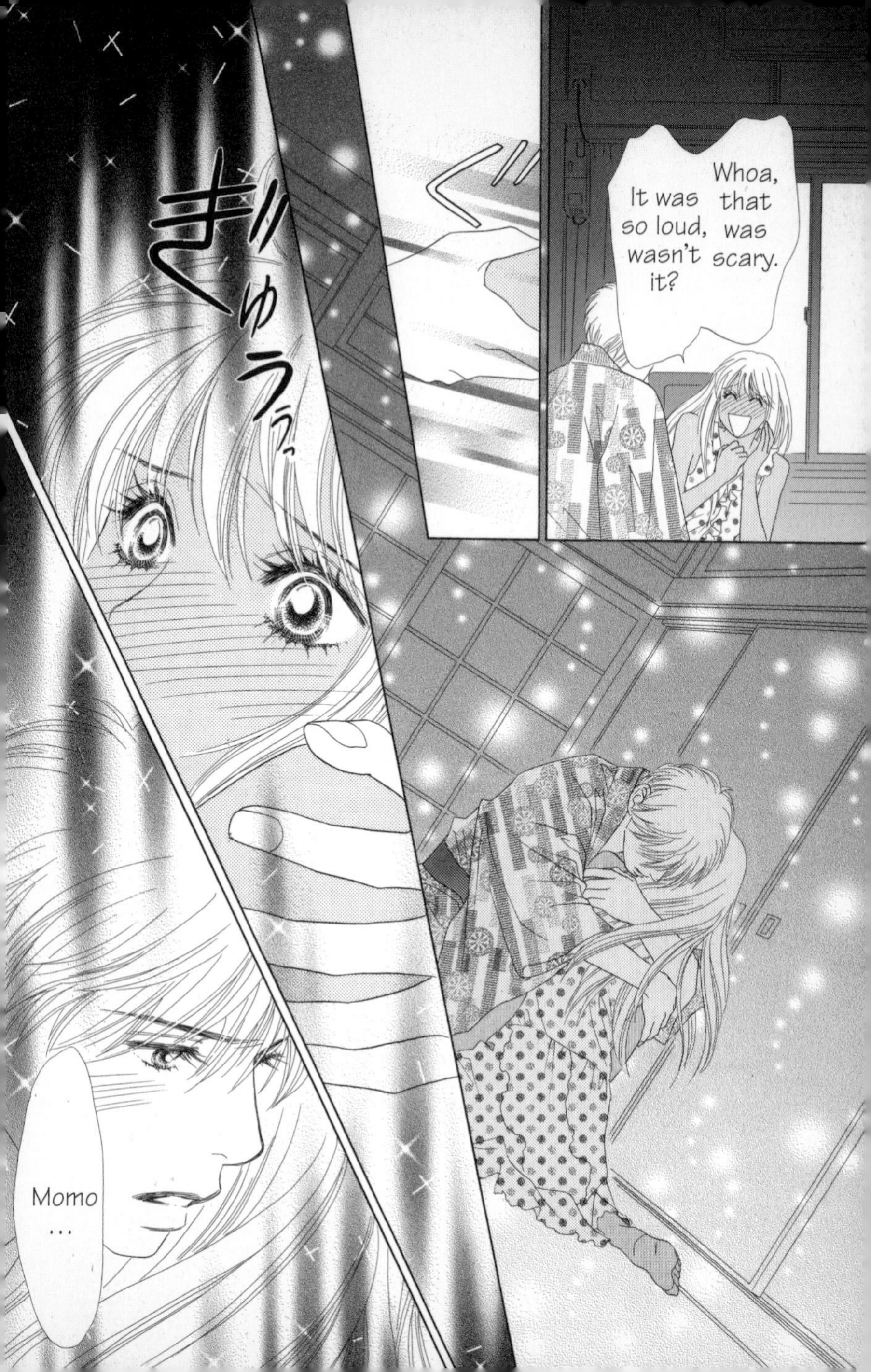
Whoa, that was scary.
It was so loud, wasn't it?
ぐ
ぎゅうぅっ
Momo ...

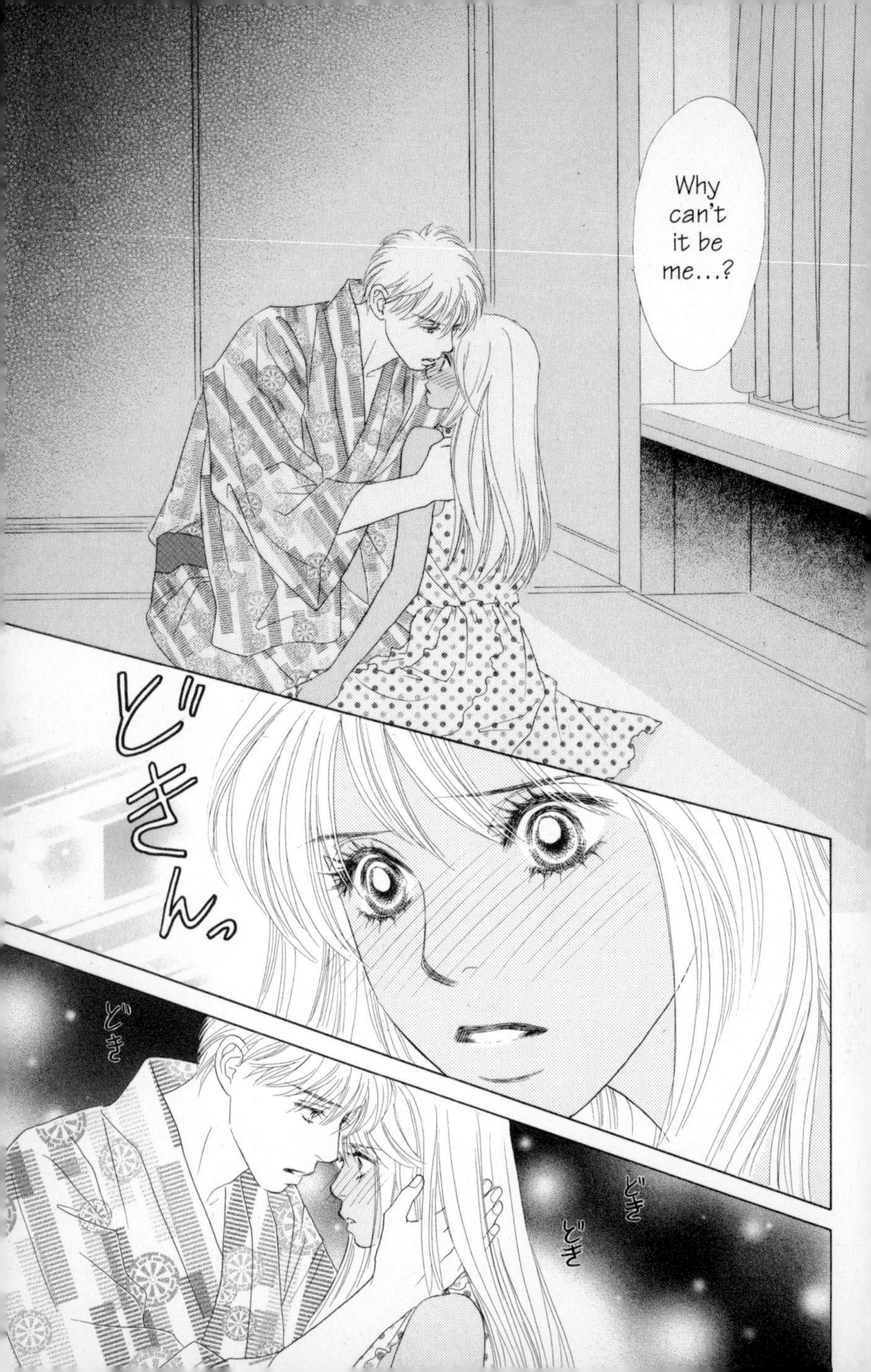
Why can't it be me...?
どきん
どき
どき
どき

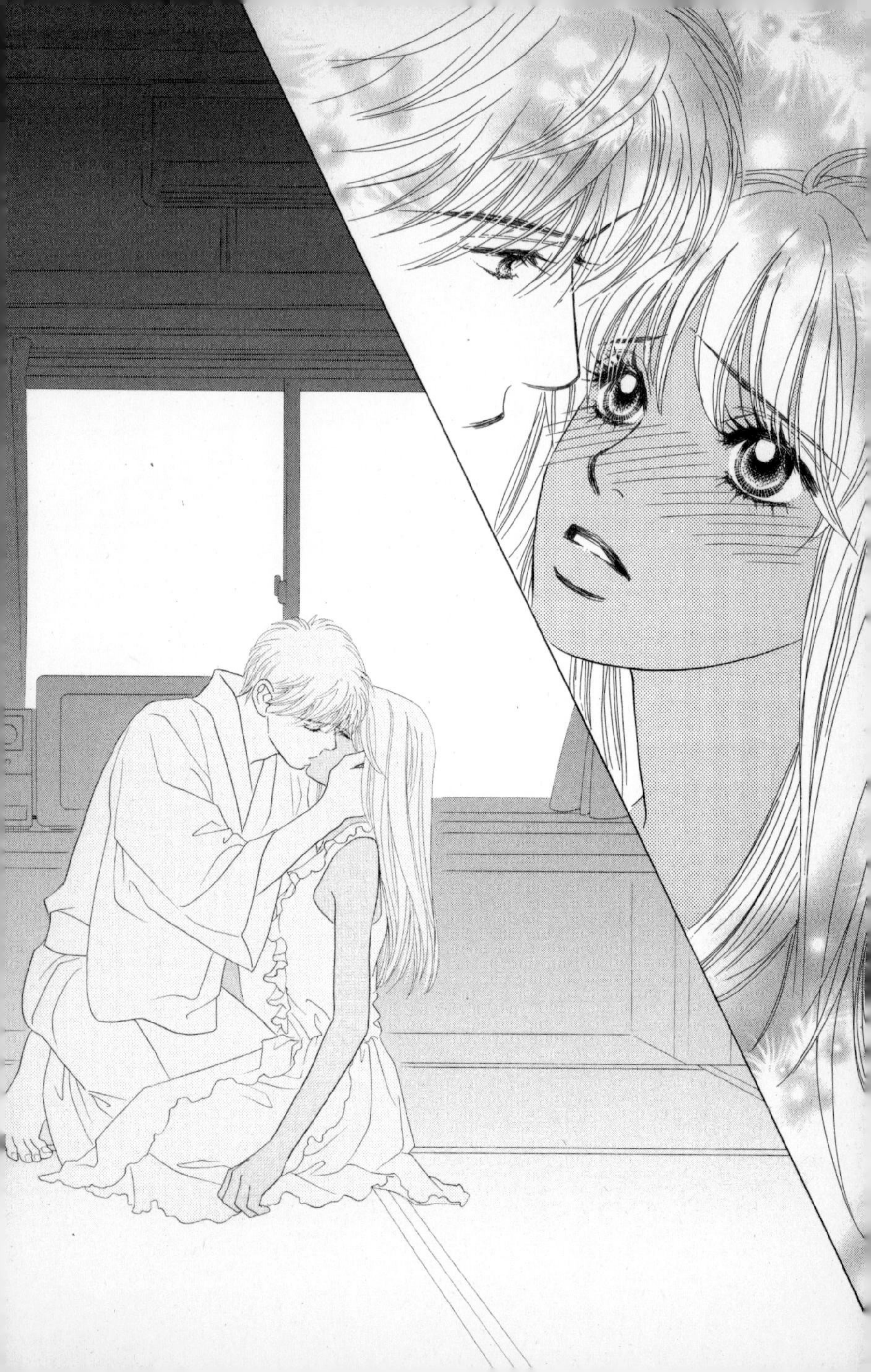

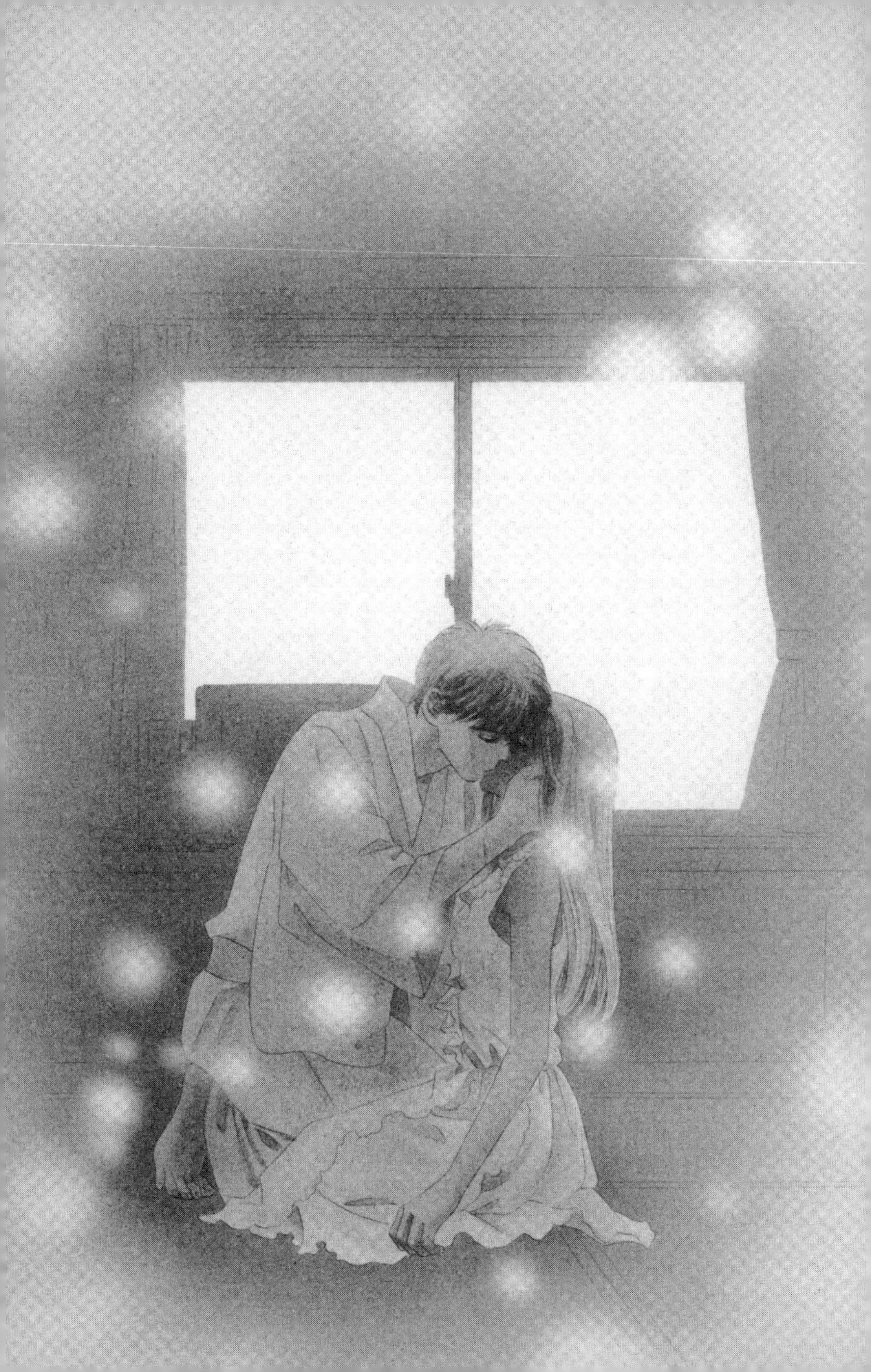

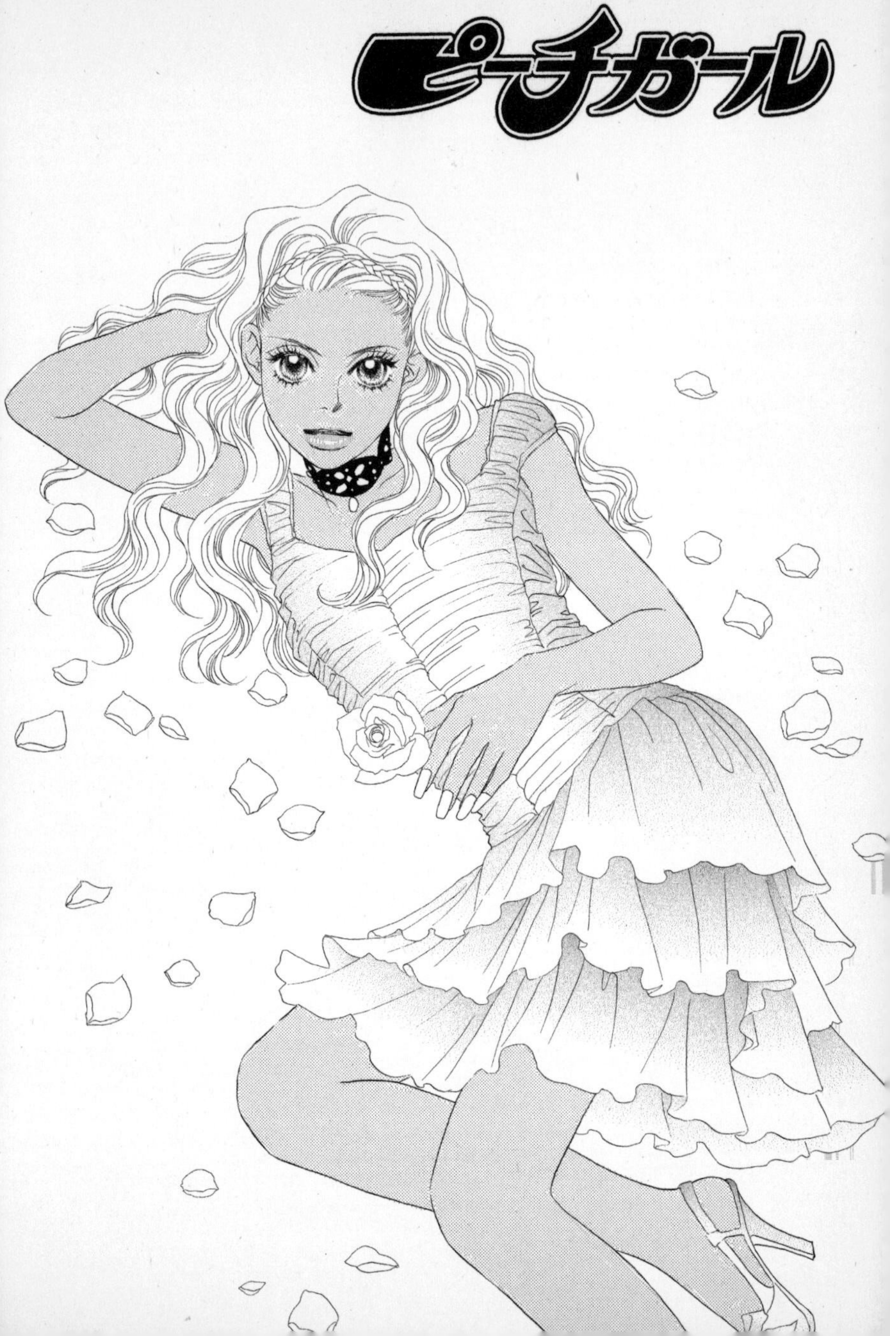
ピーチガール

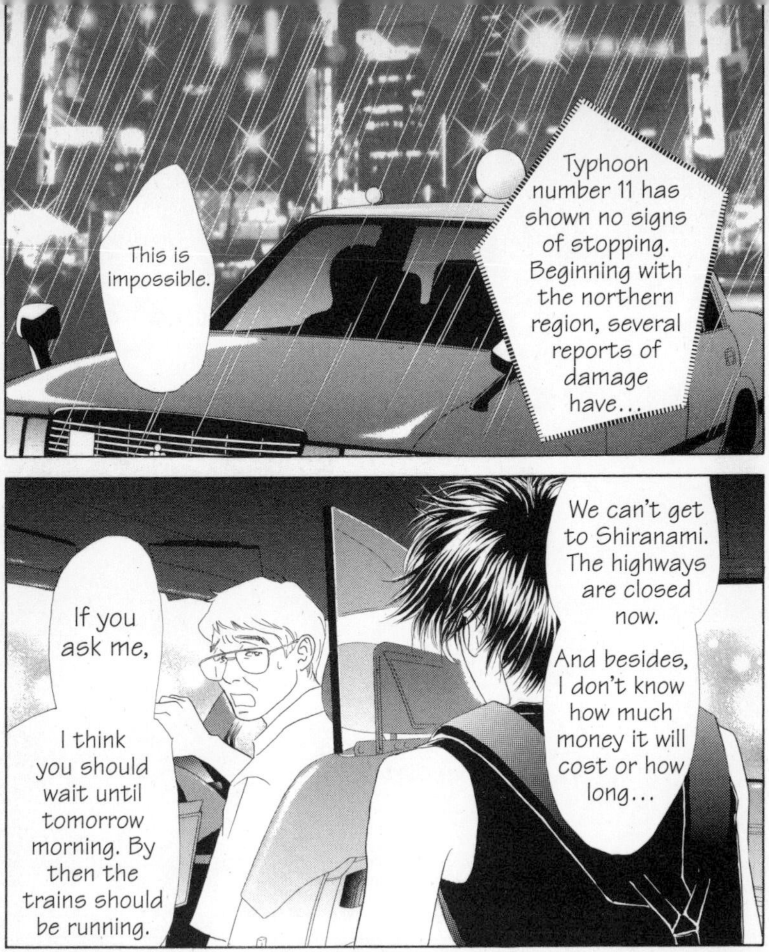
Typhoon number 11 has shown no signs of stopping. Beginning with the northern region, several reports of damage have...
This is impossible.
We can't get to Shiranami. The highways are closed now.
And besides, I don't know how much money it will cost or how long...
If you ask me,
I think you should wait until tomorrow morning. By then the trains should be running.

PEACH CLUB

So anyway, back to my hip problems. It hurts when I sit at my desk for long periods of time. But now it hurts when I sleep too. When I'm working, sleep is the thing I look forward to the most, so this is a bad situation... I can feel it when I cough or sneeze, and when it's really bad, I can't even bend over in the mornings to wash my face. Sometimes it's even hard to just walk. It seems that I have collapsed disks in my back, so I might have to live with the pain for the rest of my life. The doctors told me that I should work out my abdominal and back muscles to relieve the stress on my spine. Come to think of it, when I work out my abs, it does feel better. But when I'm busy, I just kind of let things slide... So these days, instead of playing on the Internet, I'm getting into cooking. It's easier to keep standing, and it's a nice break from work. And besides, I can get a nice walk when I go shopping for ingredients. Of course, I can't do it when I'm on deadline. But it's fun just checking out cook books. I also like reading about sewing and flowers.

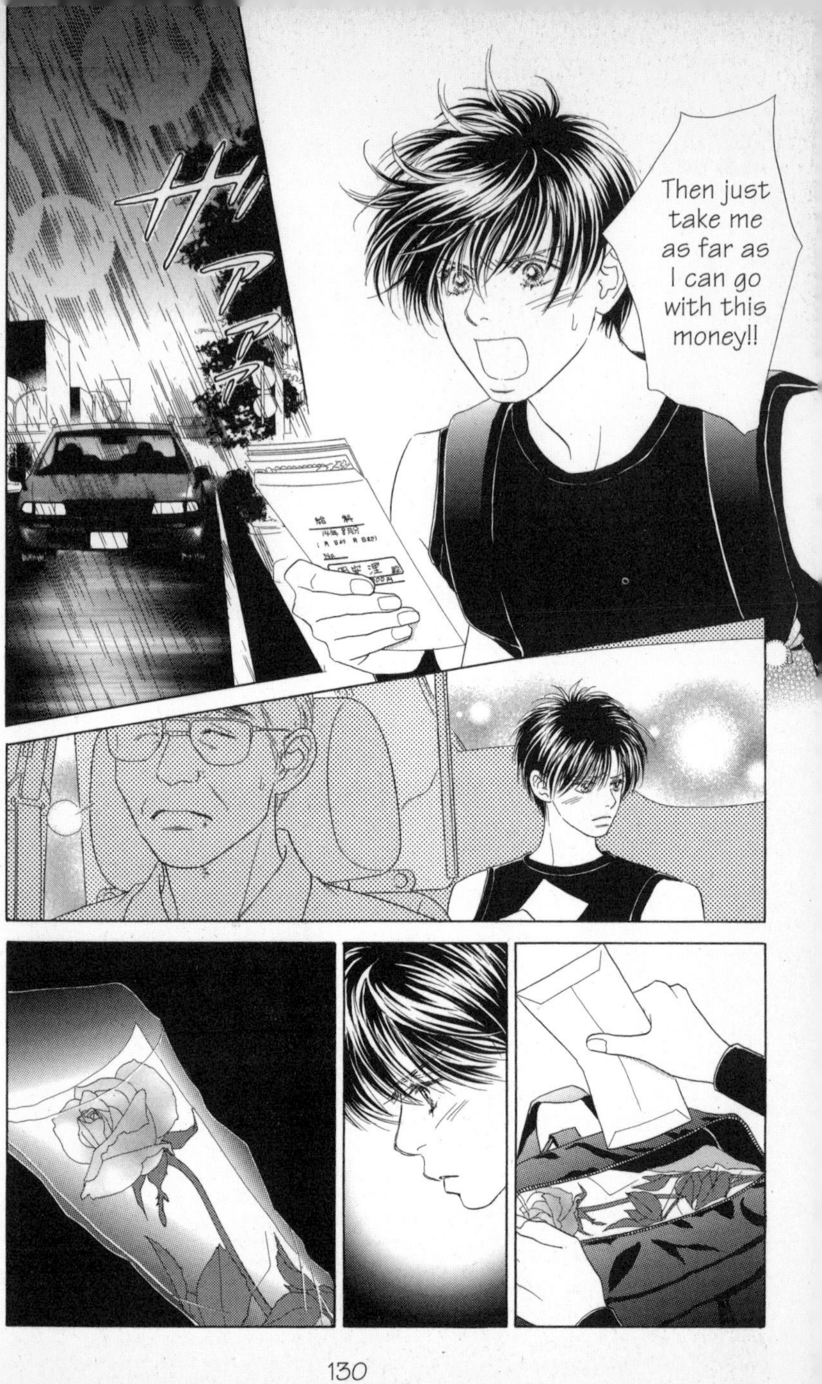
Then just take me as far as I can go with this money!!

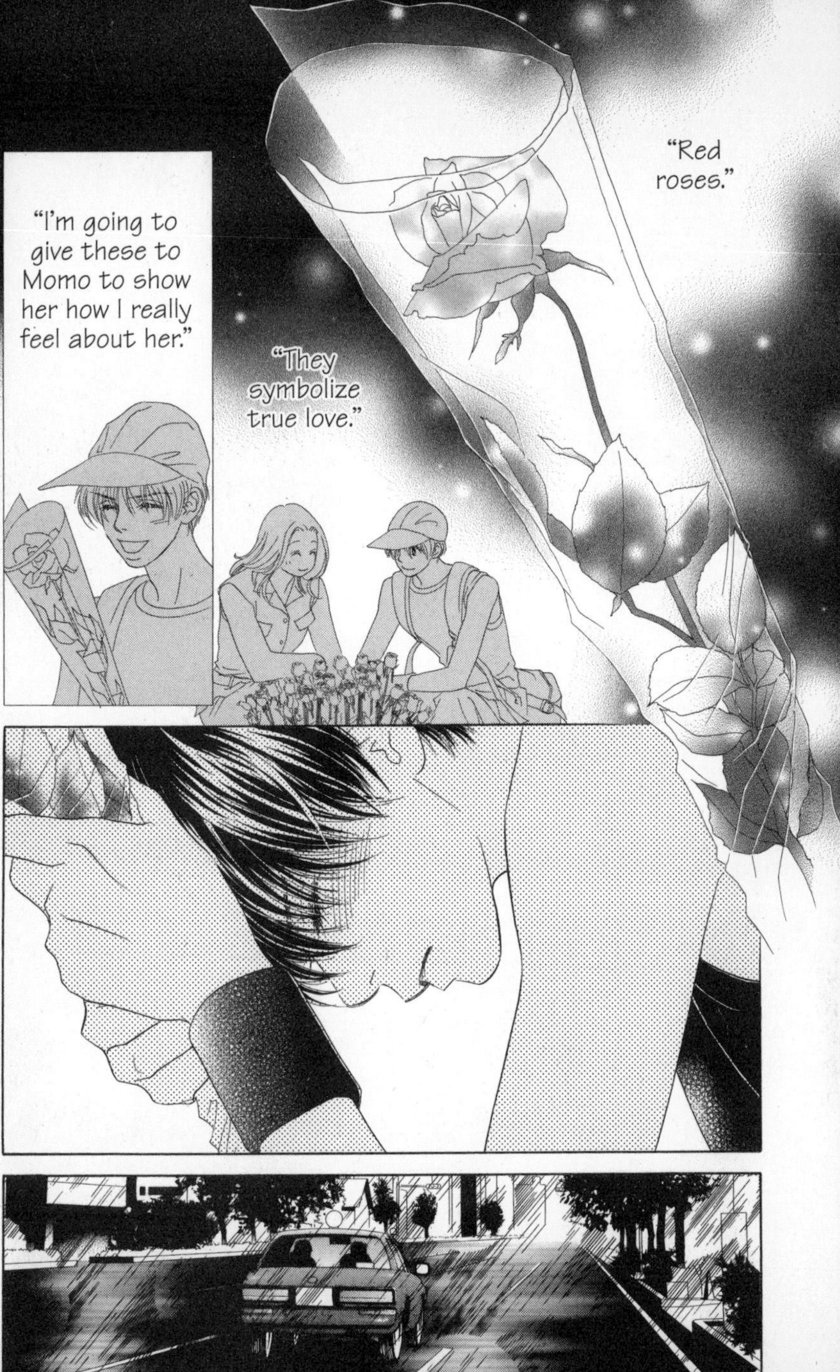
"Red roses."
"They symbolize true love."
"I'm going to give these to Momo to show her how I really feel about her."

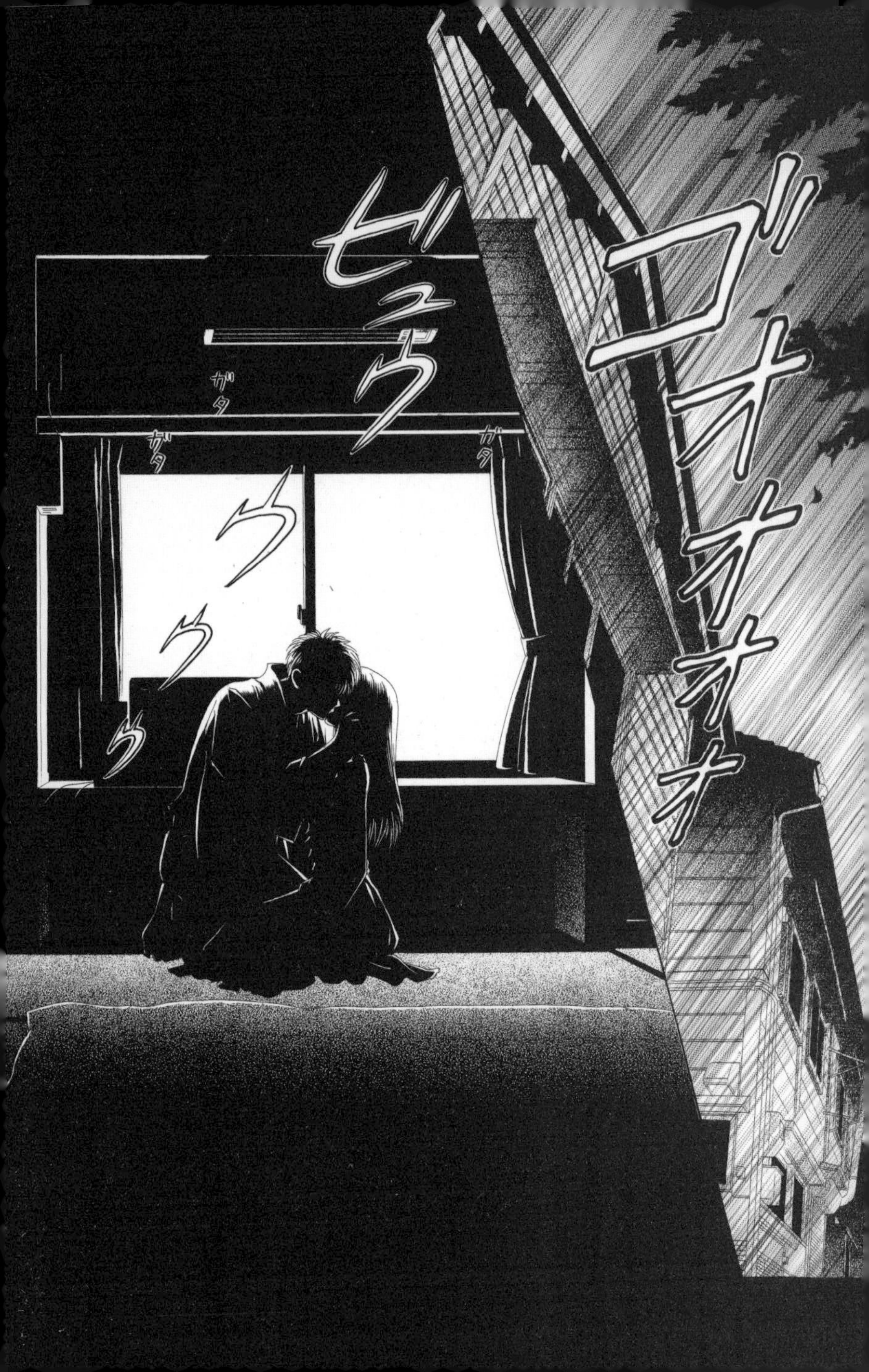
ゴオオオオ
ビュウウウウ
ガタ
ガタ
ガタ

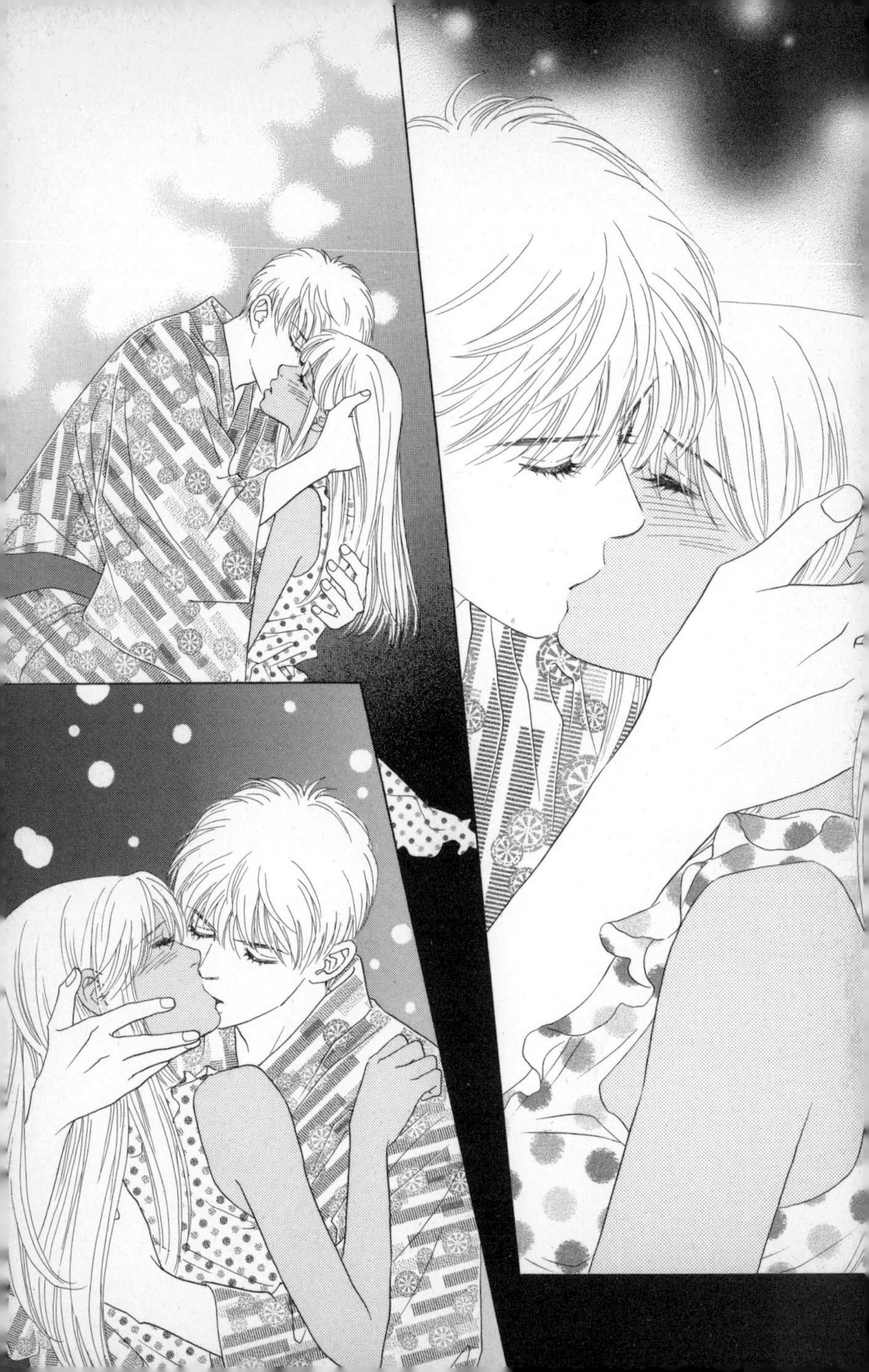

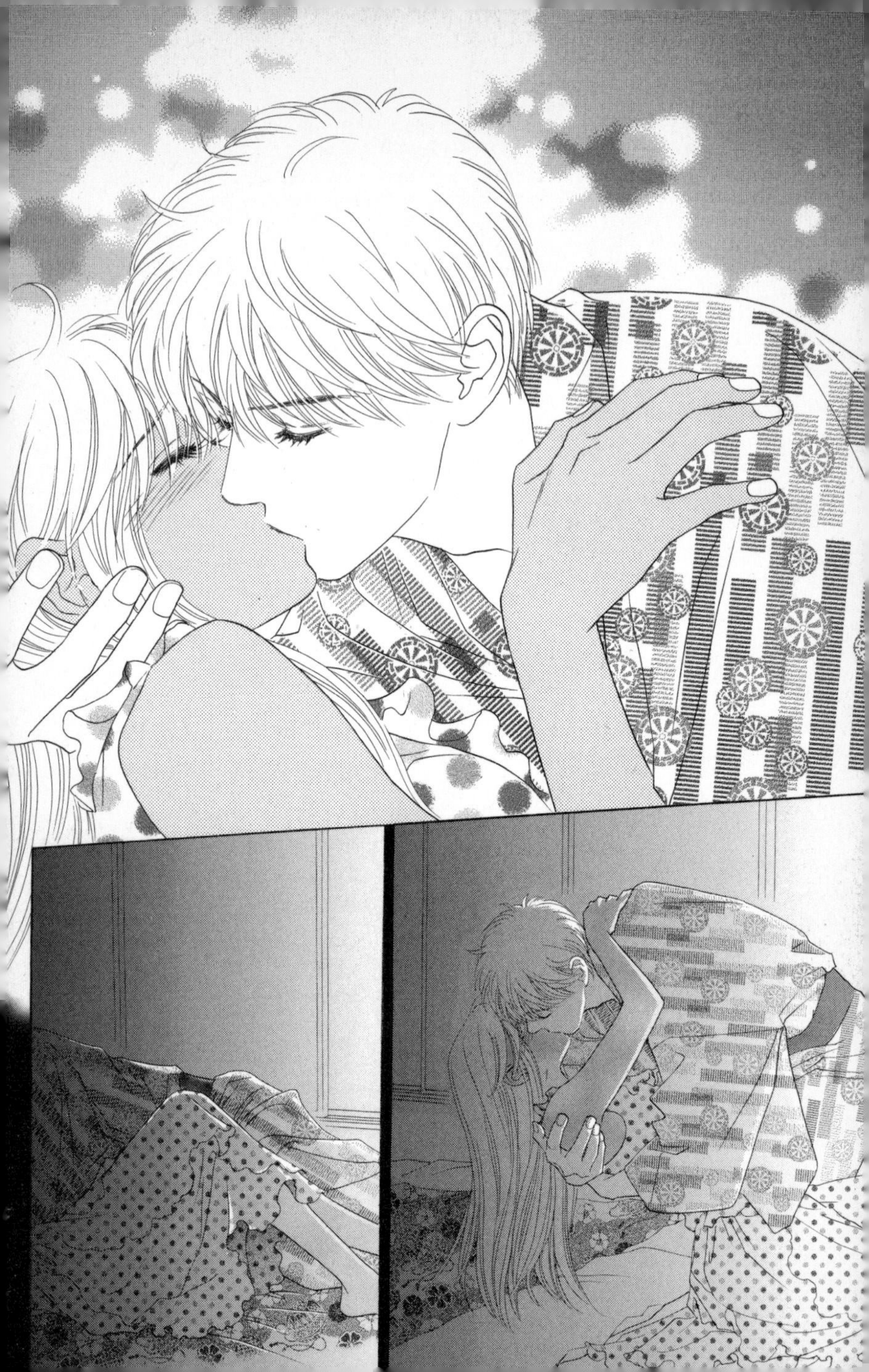

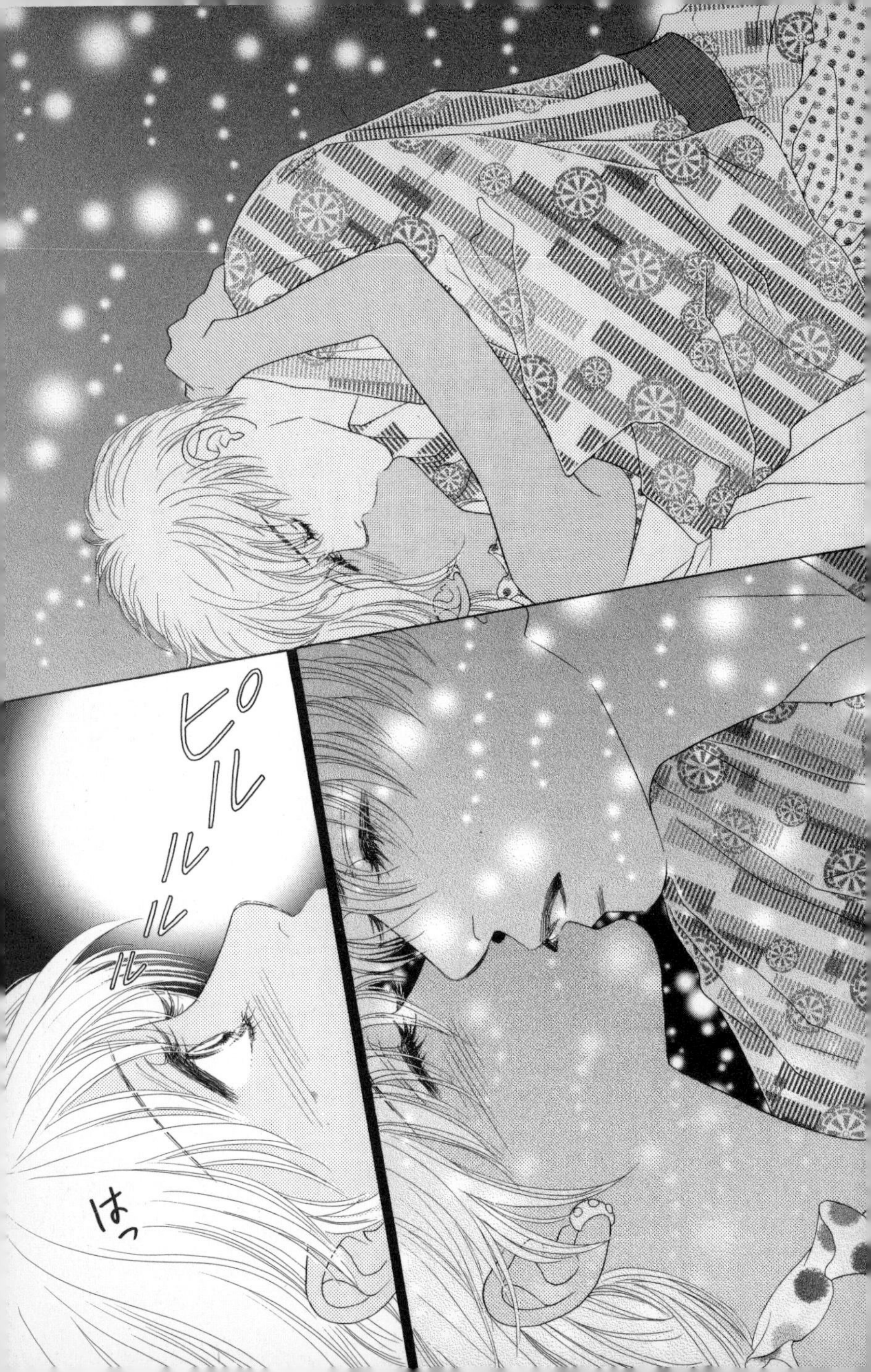

ピルルルル
はっ

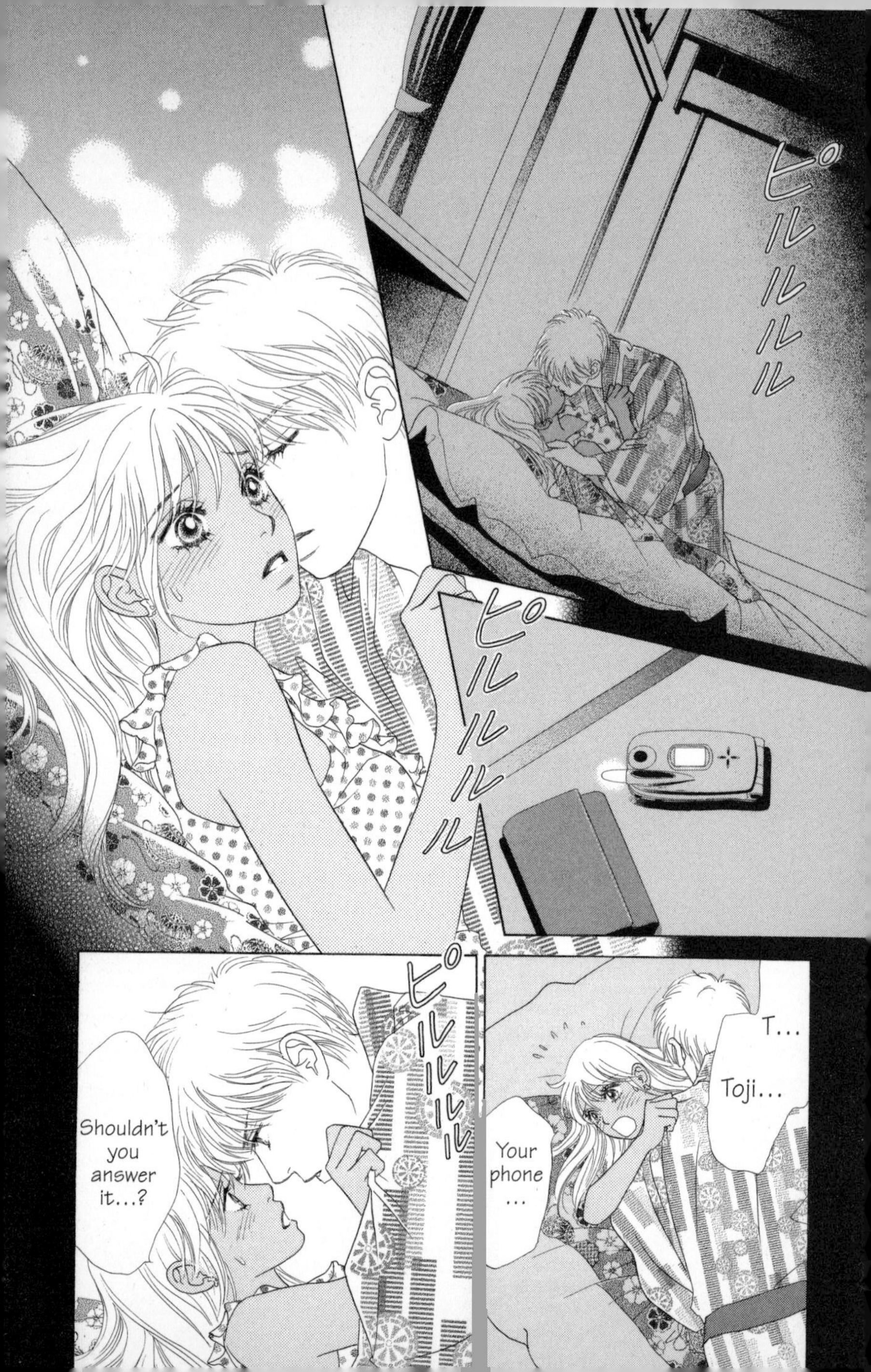
ピルルルル
ピルルルル
T…
Toji…
Your phone …
ピルルルル
Shouldn't you answer it…?

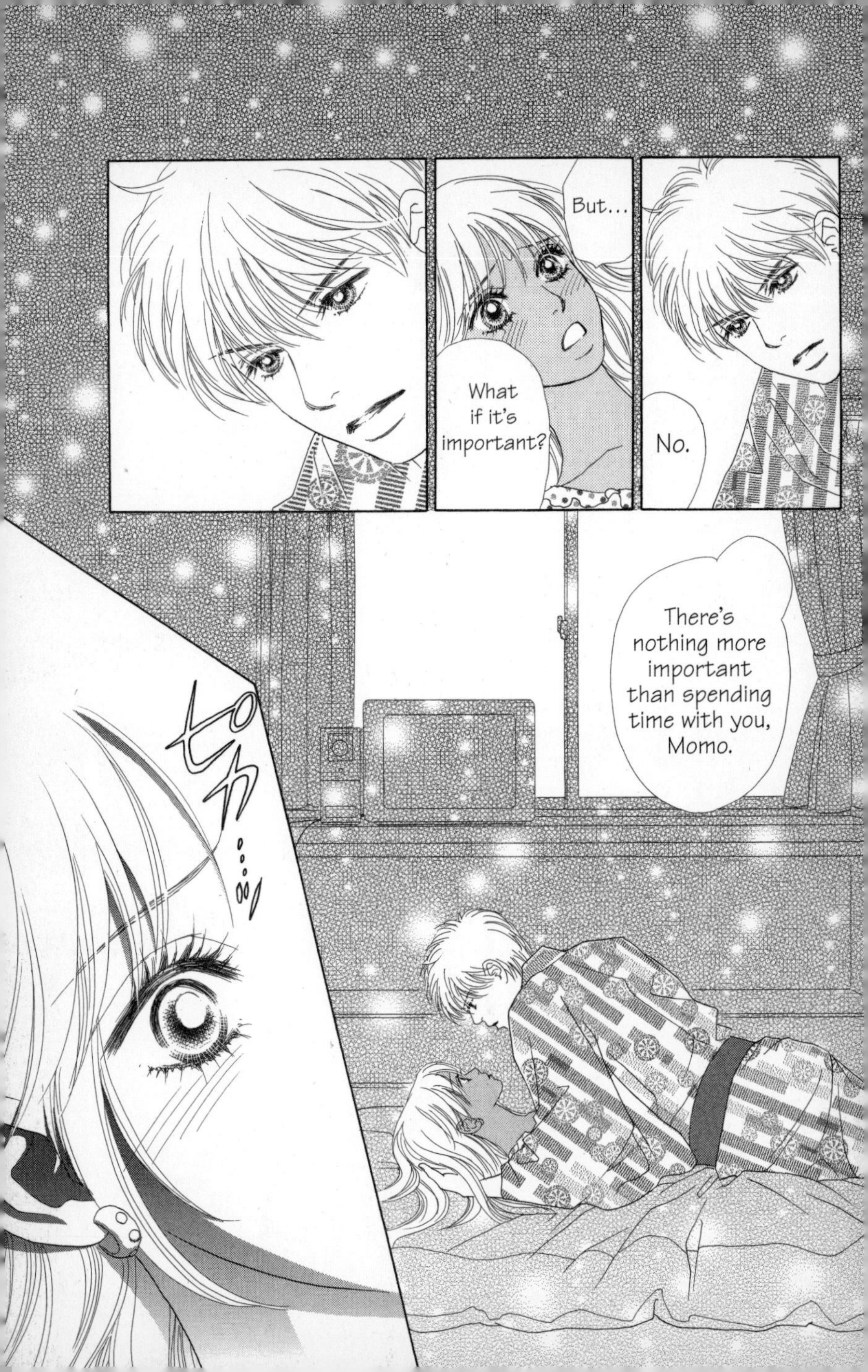
But…
What if it's important?
No.
There's nothing more important than spending time with you, Momo.
ピク…!

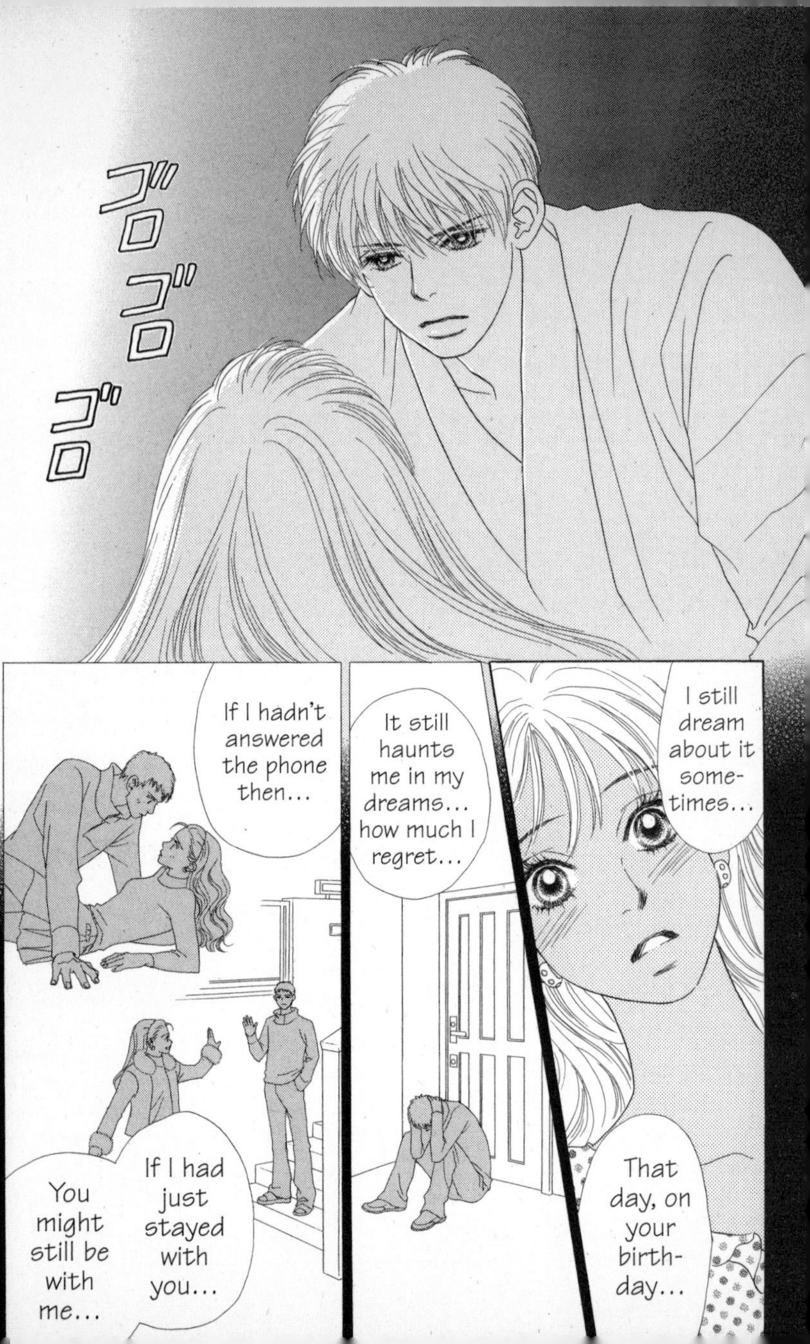
ゴロゴロ
ゴロ
I still dream about it some-times…
That day, on your birth-day…
It still haunts me in my dreams… how much I regret…
If I hadn't answered the phone then…
If I had just stayed with you…
You might still be with me…

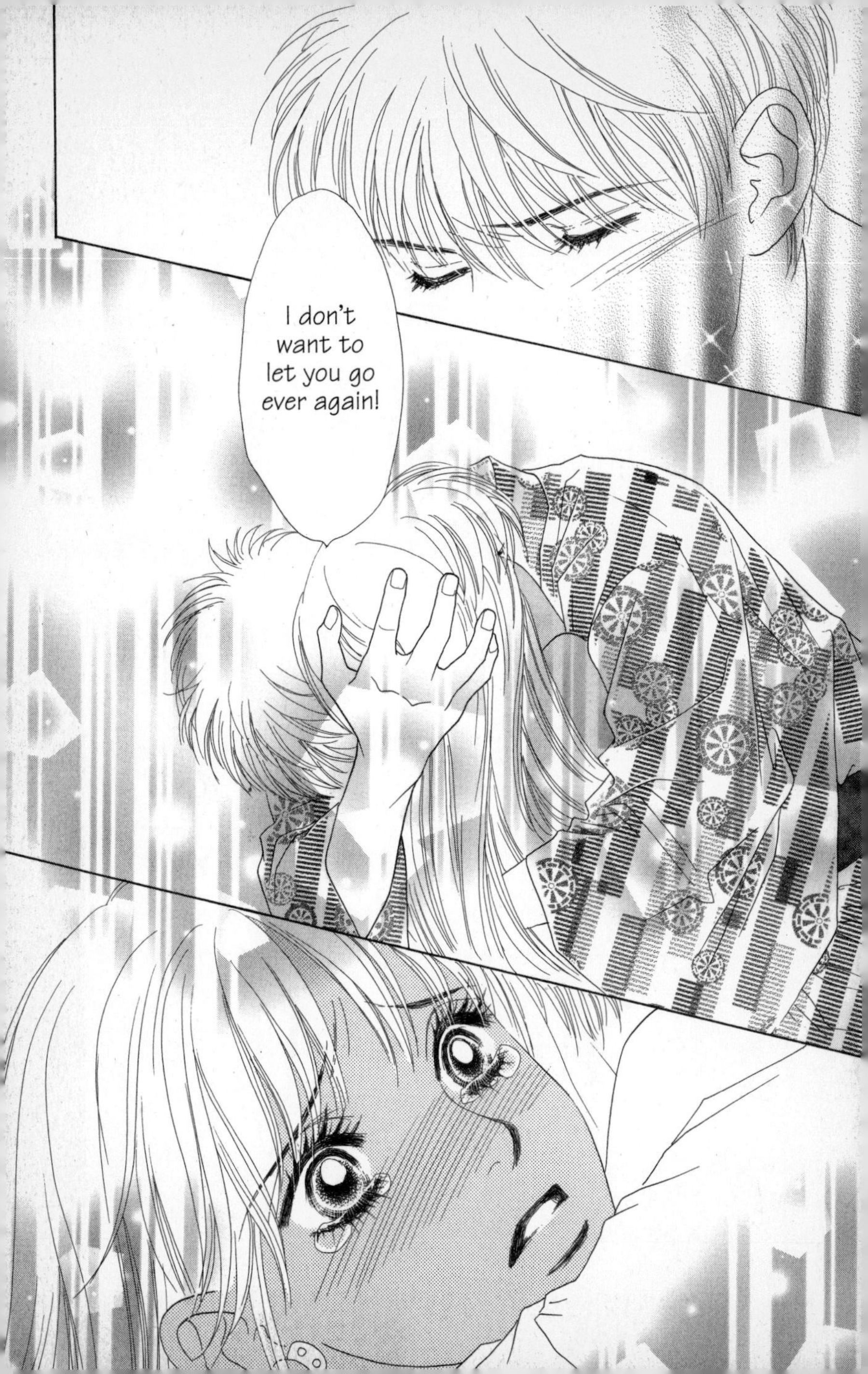
I don't want to let you go ever again!

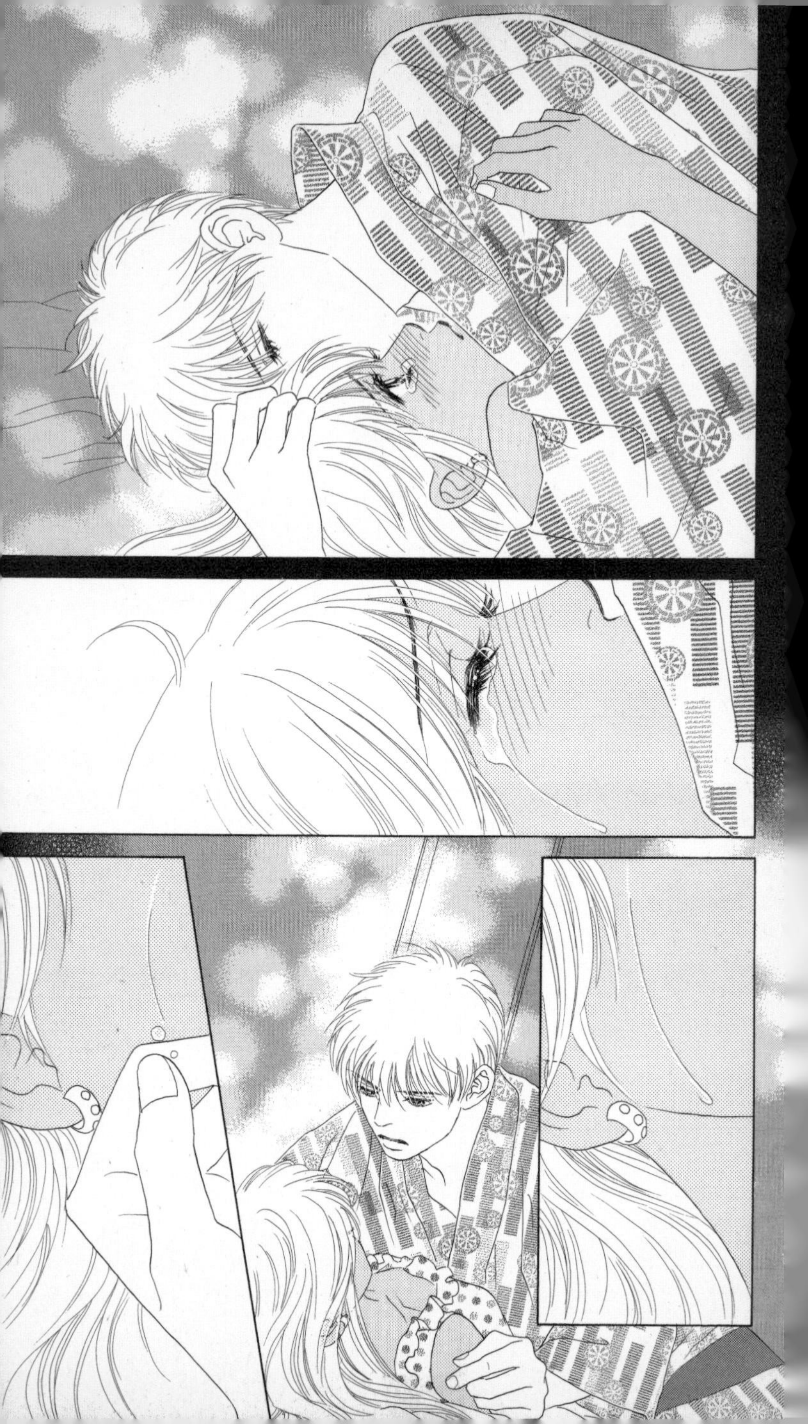

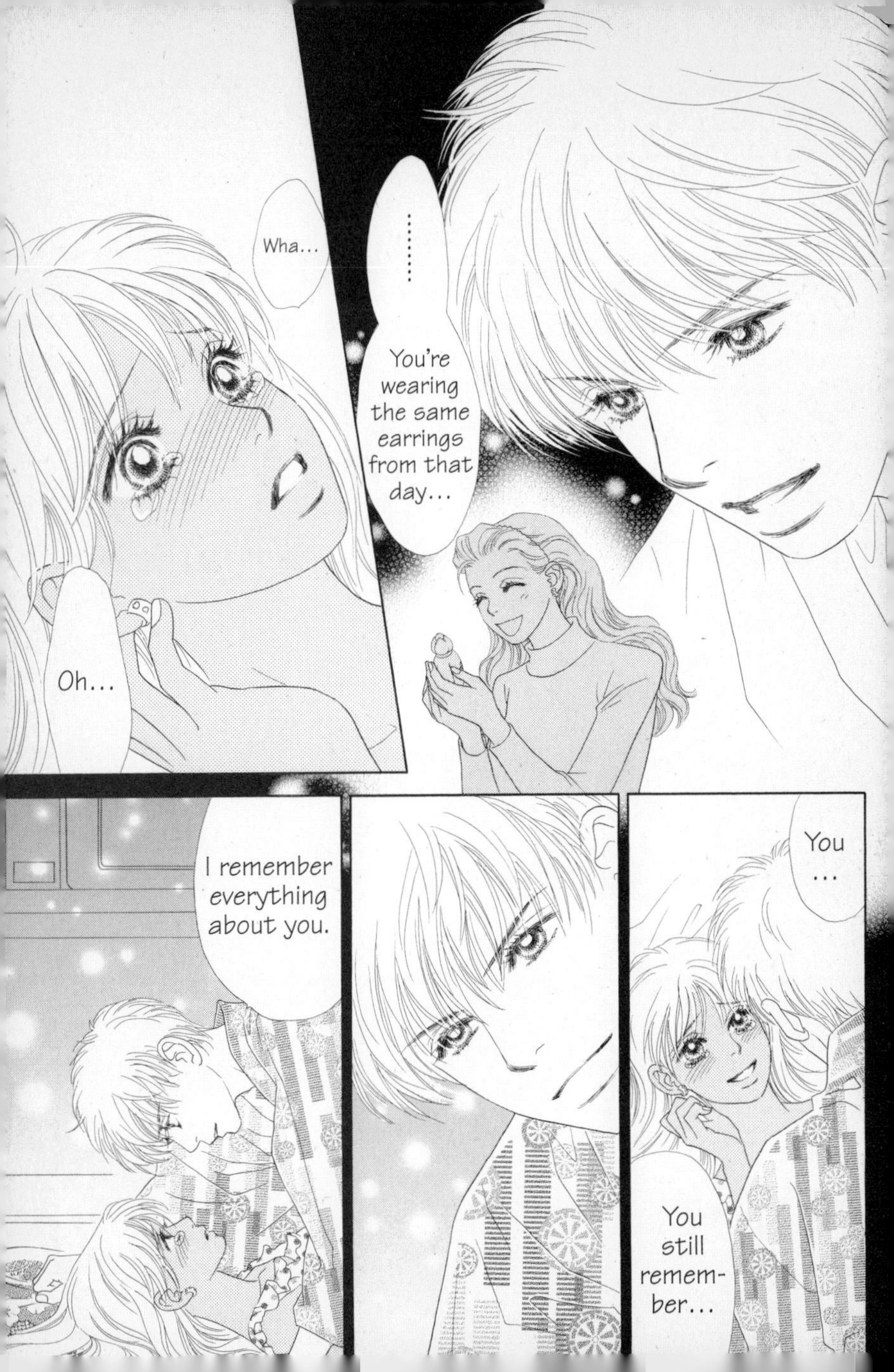
......
You're wearing the same earrings from that day...
Wha...
Oh...
You ...
You still remember...
I remember everything about you.

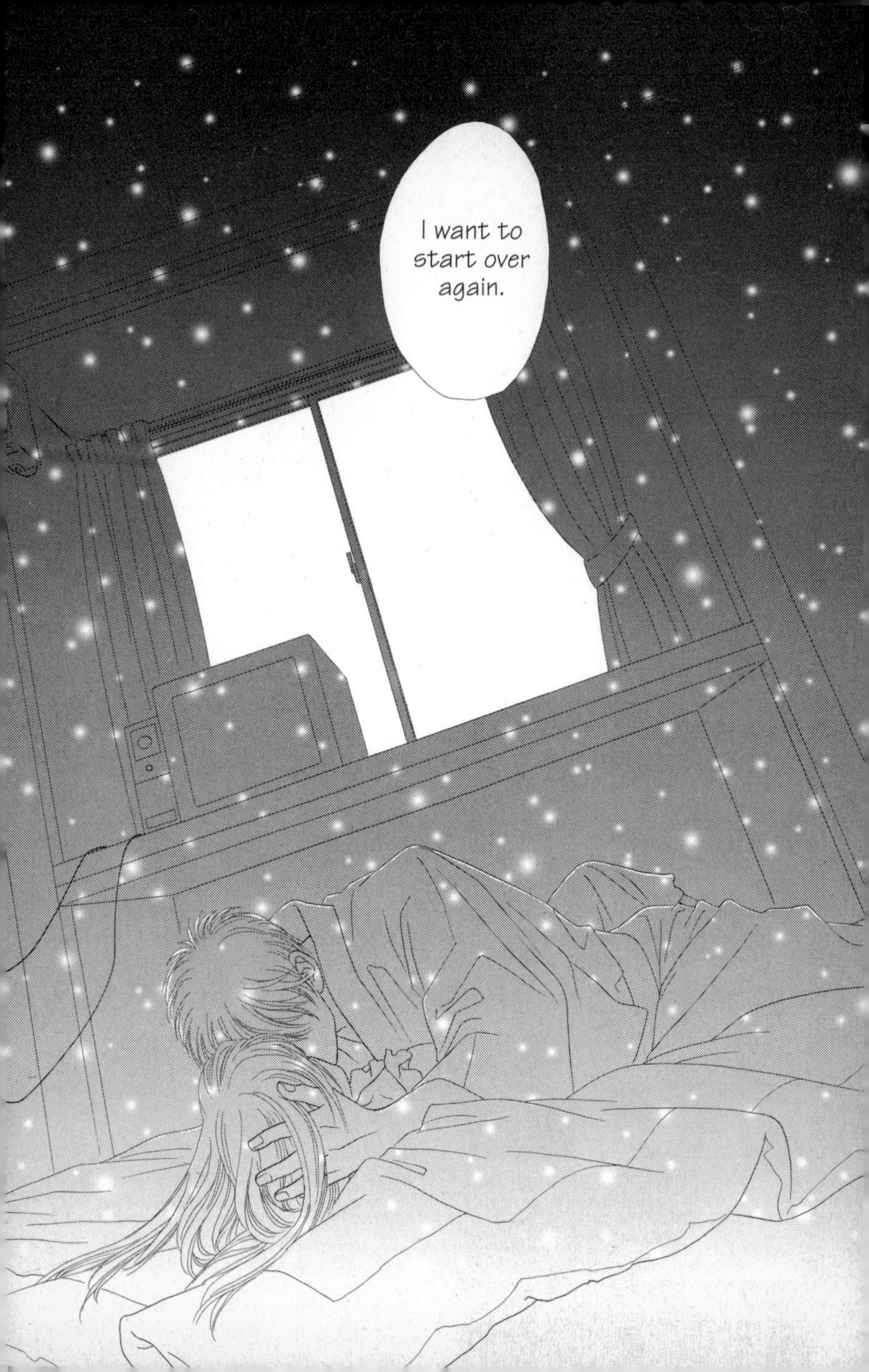
I want to start over again.

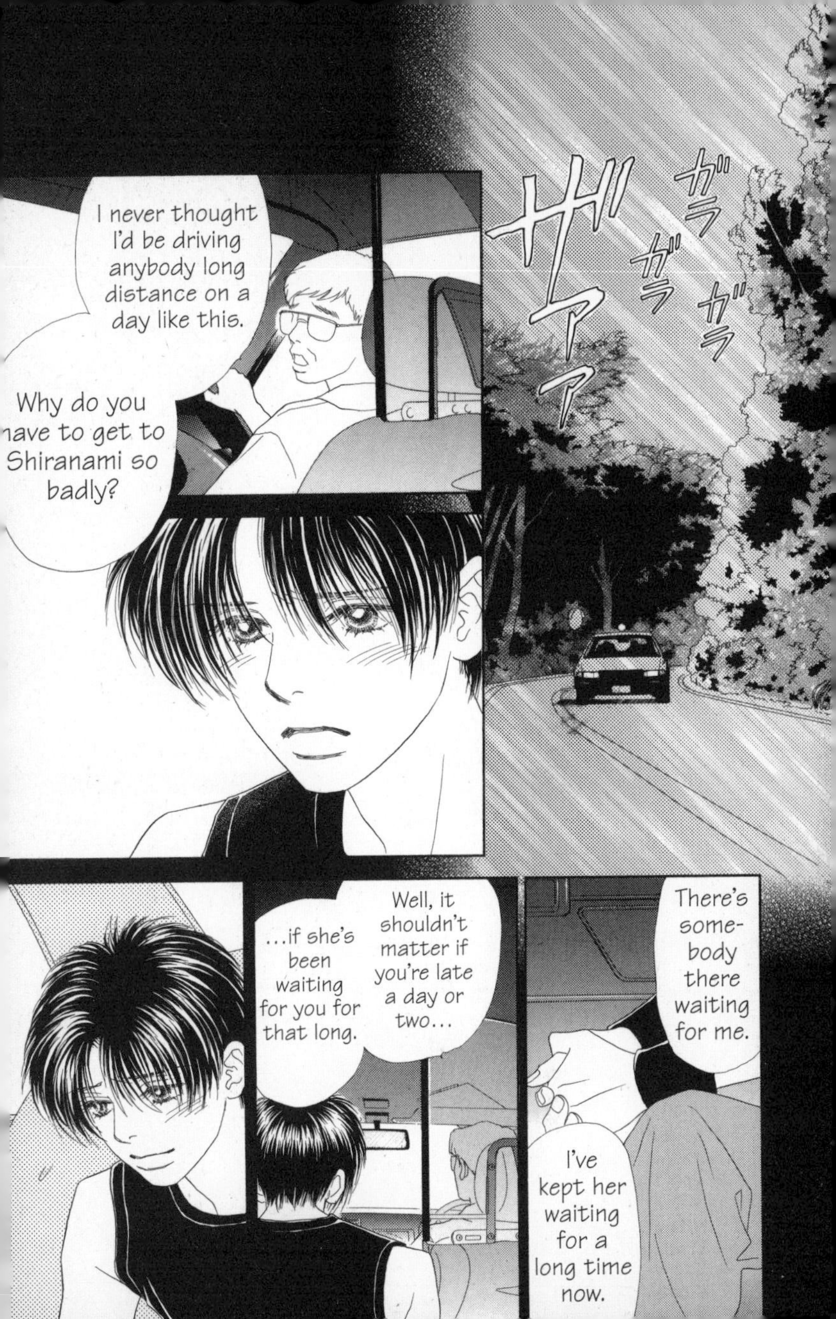
ガラガラ
ザァァ
I never thought I'd be driving anybody long distance on a day like this.
Why do you have to get to Shiranami so badly?
There's somebody there waiting for me.
I've kept her waiting for a long time now.
Well, it shouldn't matter if you're late a day or two…
…if she's been waiting for you for that long.

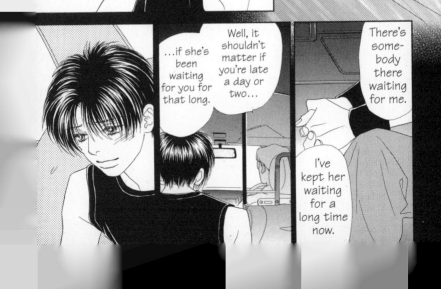

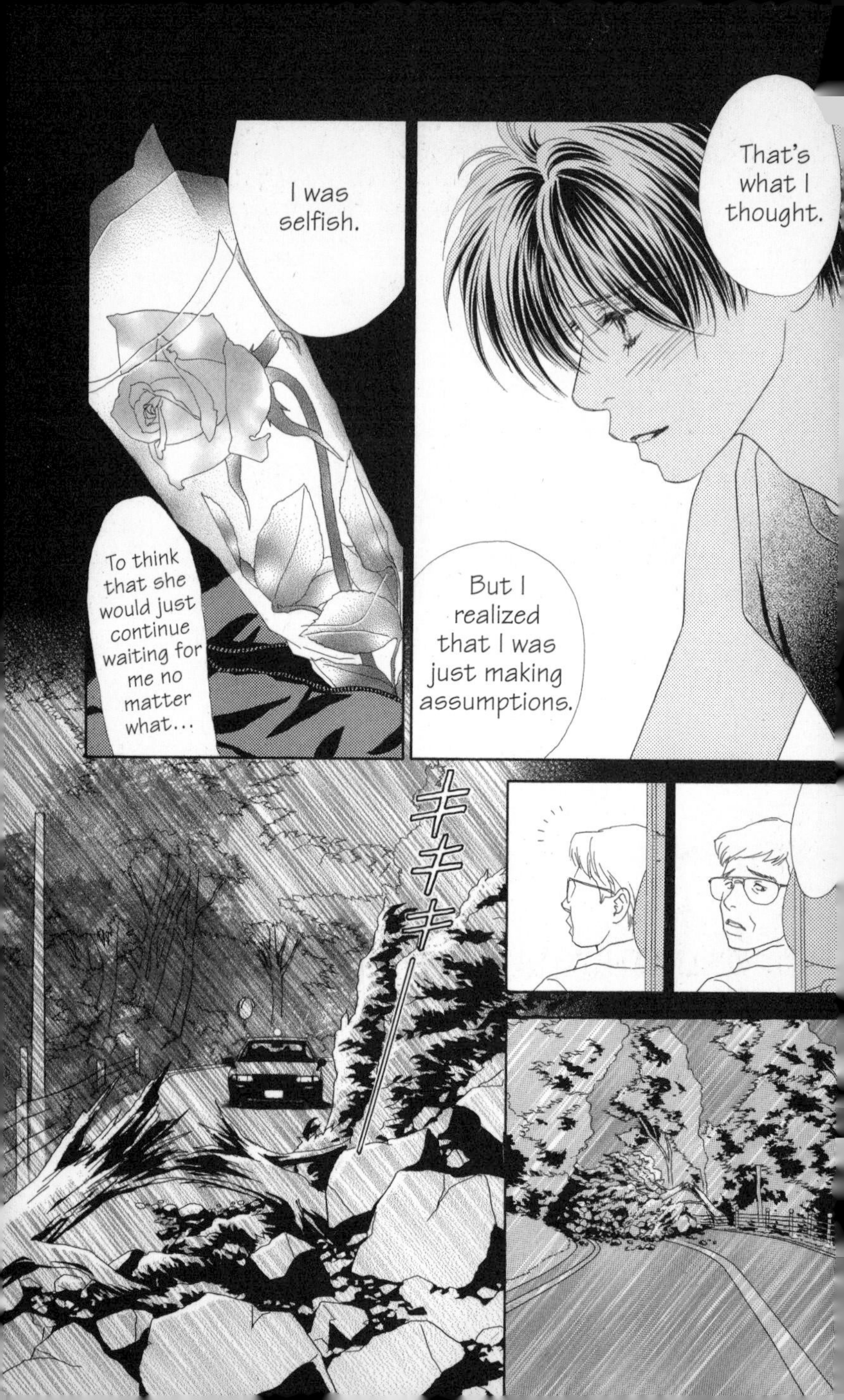
That's what I thought.
But I realized that I was just making assumptions.
I was selfish.
To think that she would just continue waiting for me no matter what...
キキキ

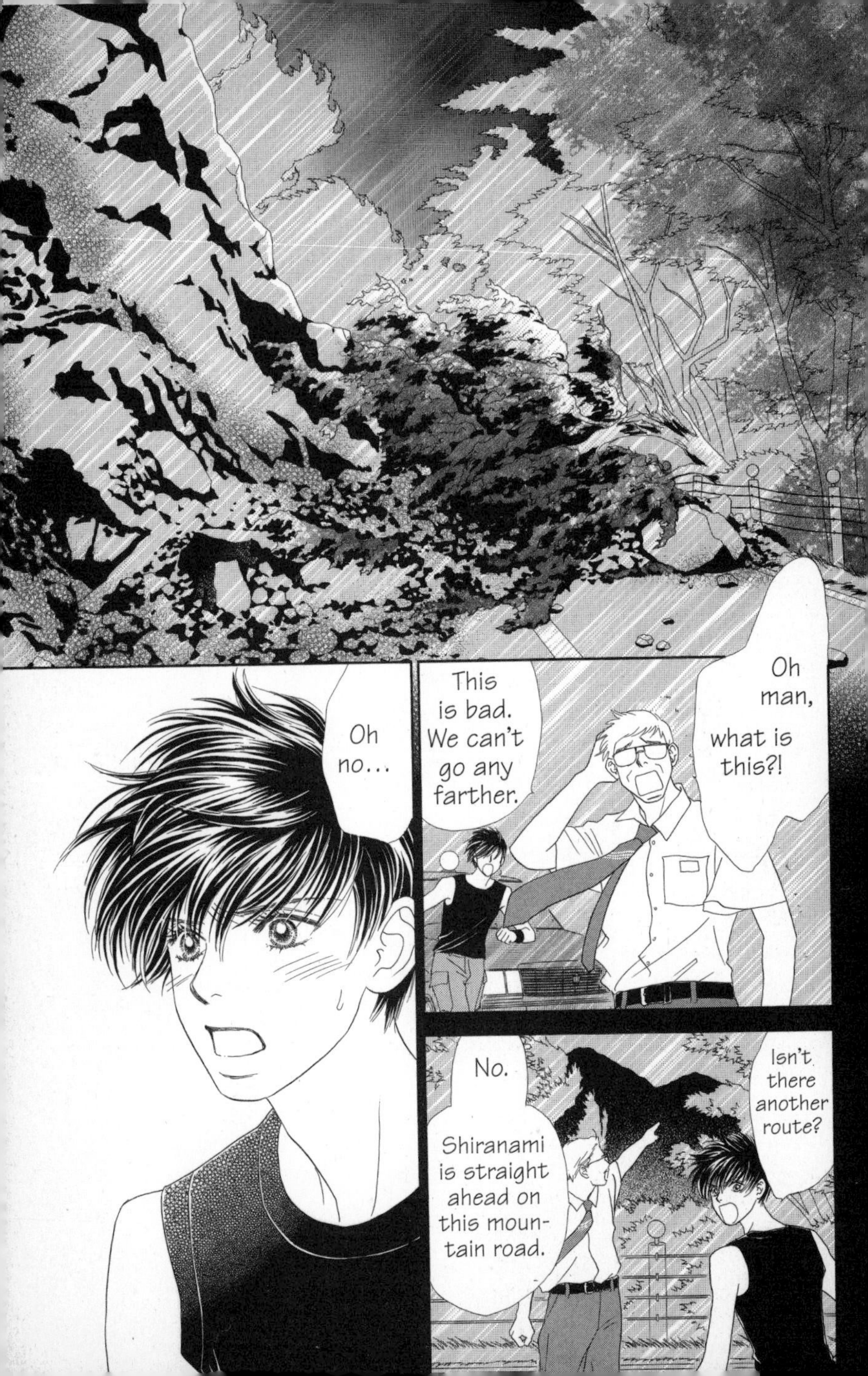
Oh man, what is this?!
This is bad. We can't go any farther.
Isn't there another route?
No.
Shiranami is straight ahead on this mountain road.
Oh no...

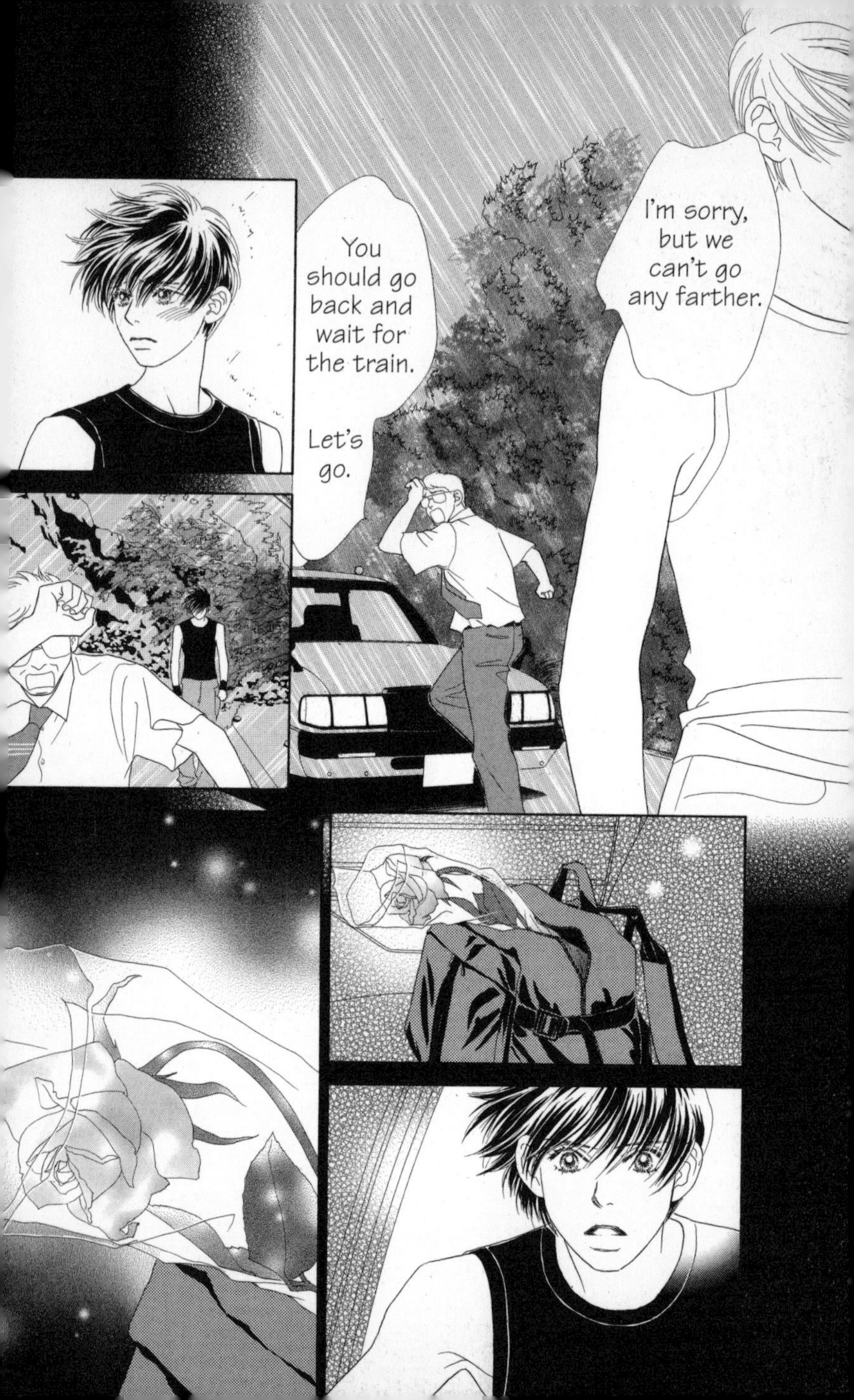
I'm sorry, but we can't go any farther.
You should go back and wait for the train.
Let's go.

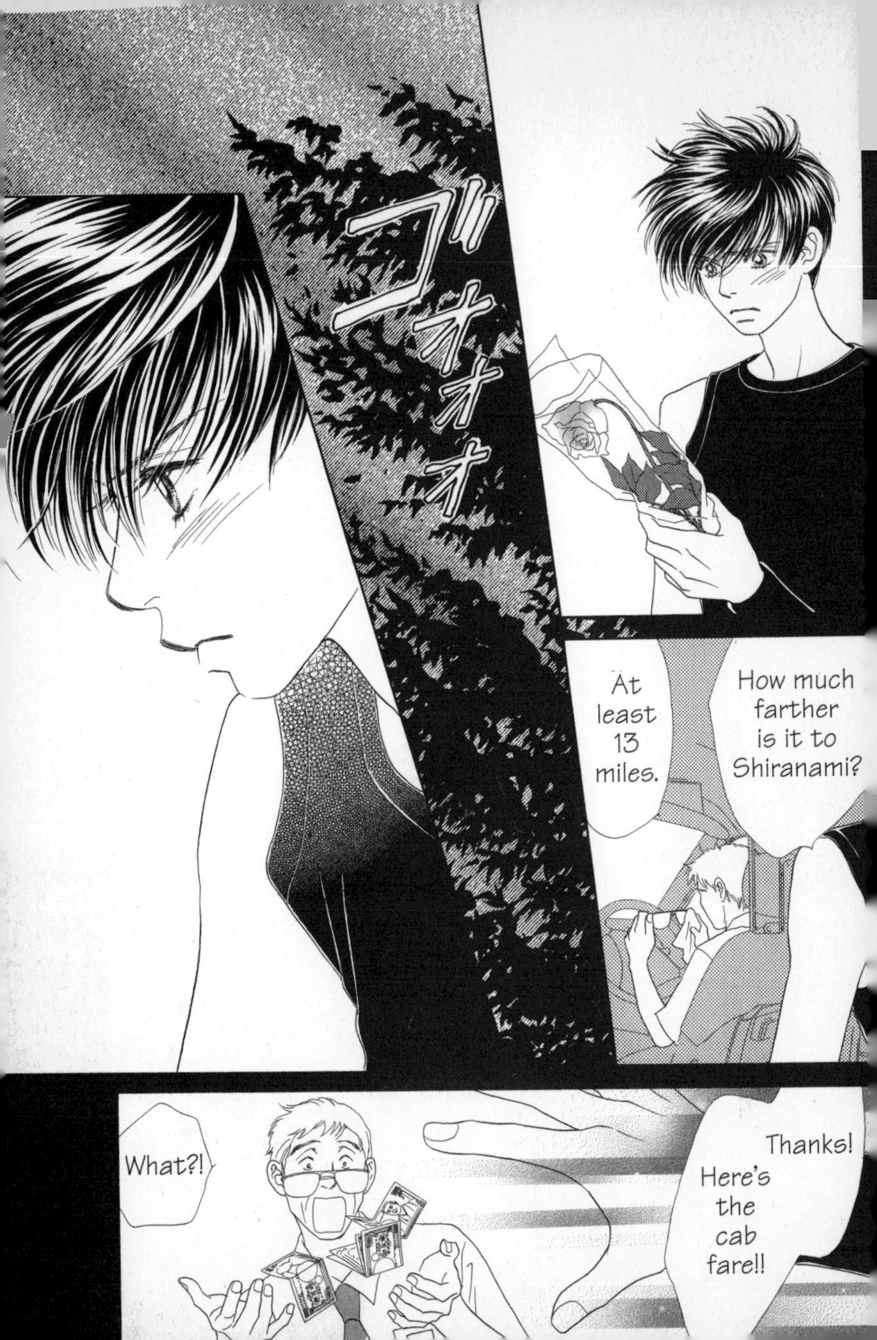
How much farther is it to Shiranami?
At least 13 miles.
ゴオオオ
Thanks! Here's the cab fare!!
What?!

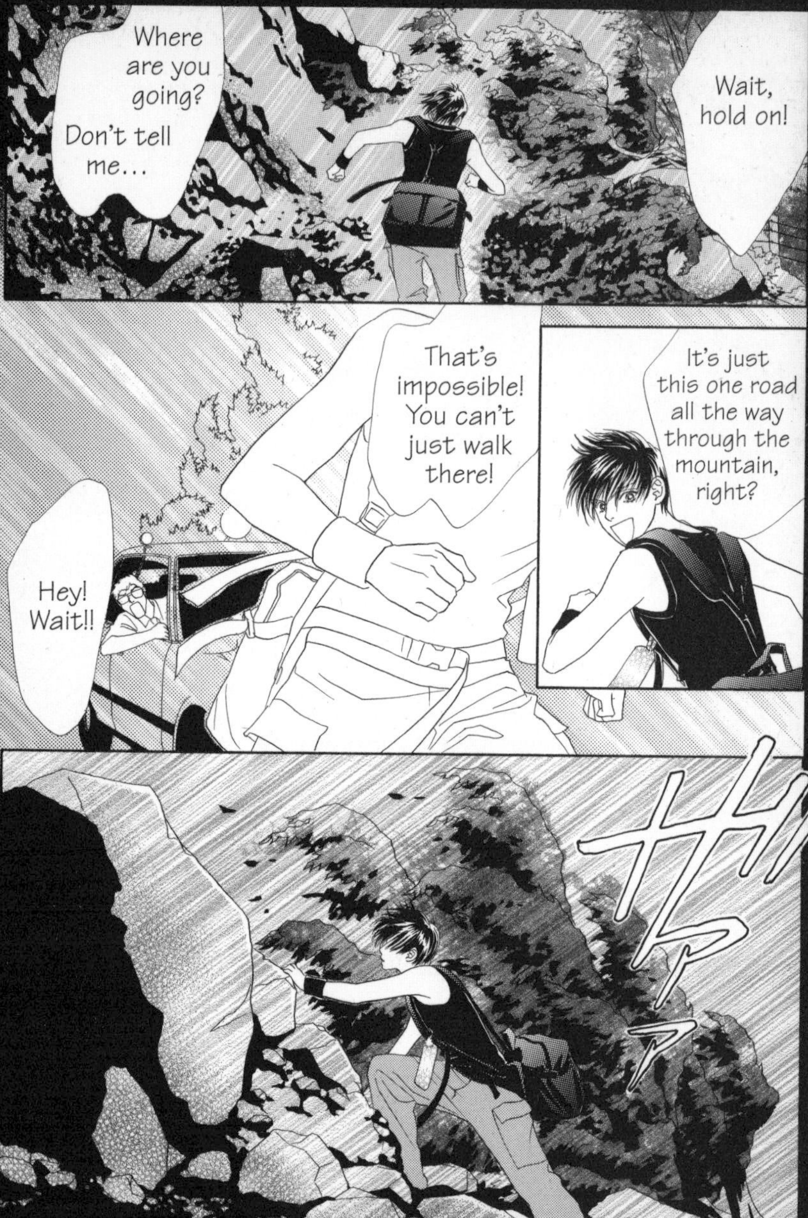
Wait, hold on!
Where are you going?
Don't tell me…
It's just this one road all the way through the mountain, right?
That's impossible! You can't just walk there!
Hey! Wait!!

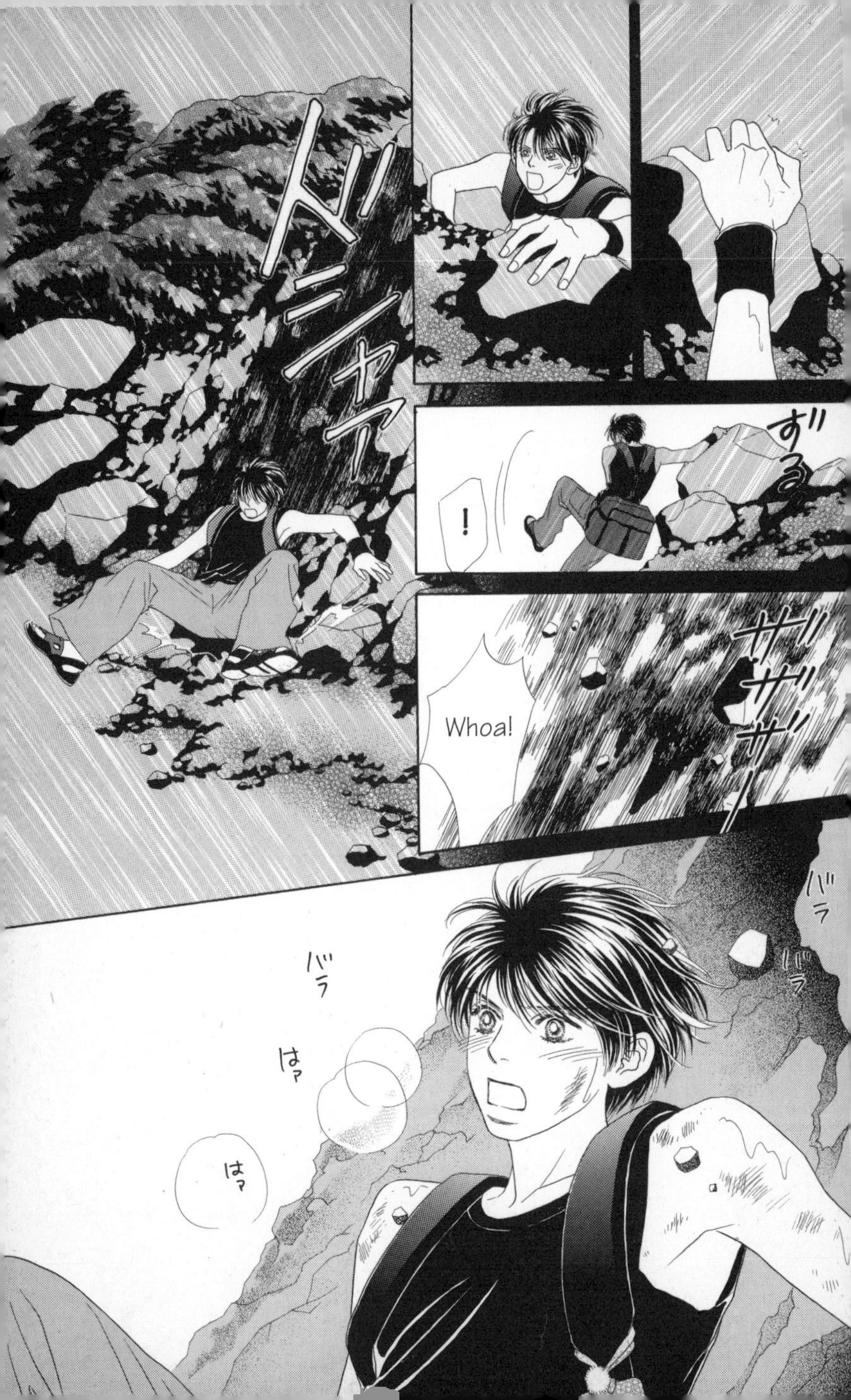

ずる
!
ザザザー
Whoa!
ドシャア
バラ
バラ
バラ
はァ
はァ

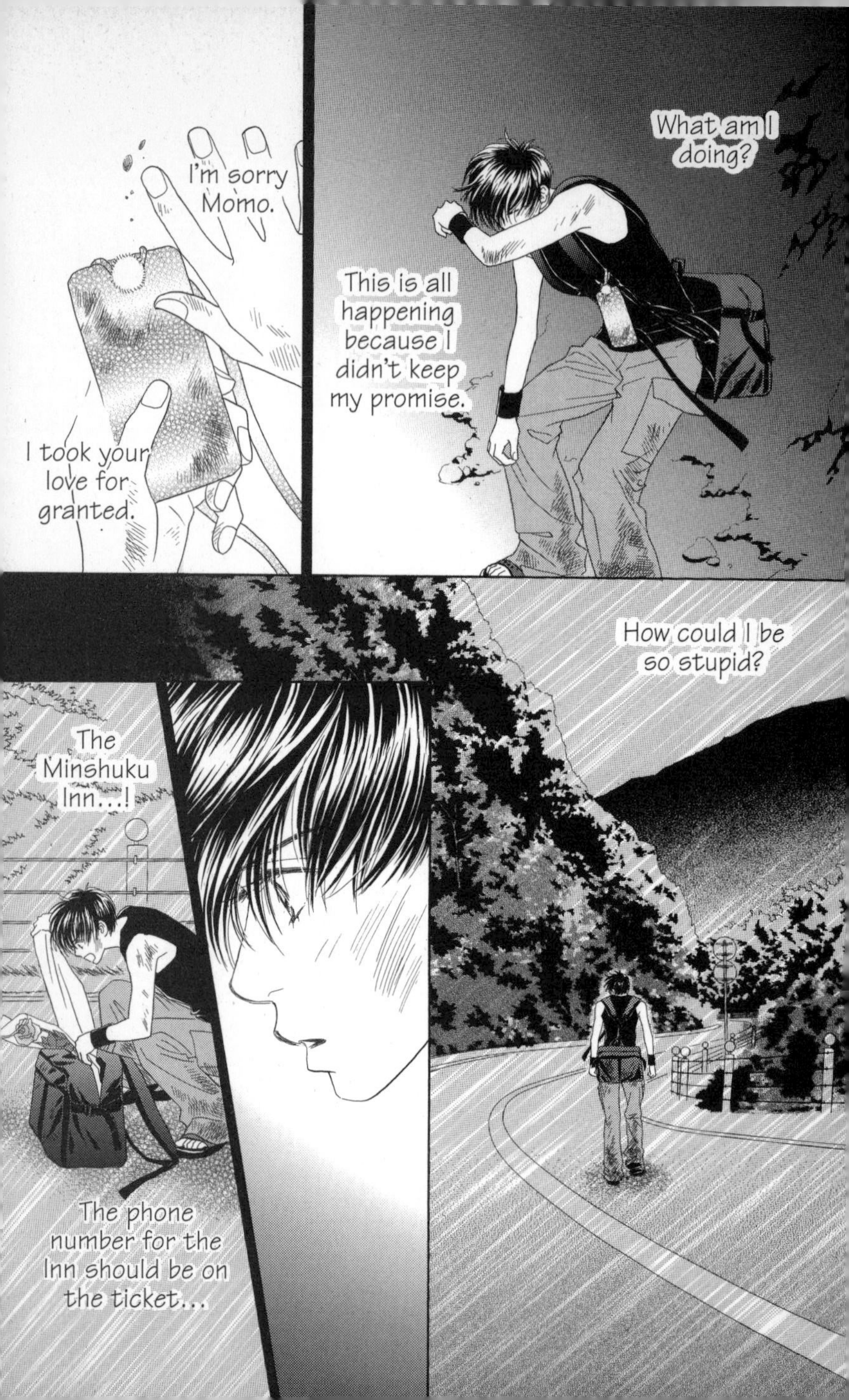
What am I doing?
This is all happening because I didn't keep my promise.
I'm sorry Momo.
I took your love for granted.
How could I be so stupid?
The Minshuku Inn...!
The phone number for the Inn should be on the ticket...

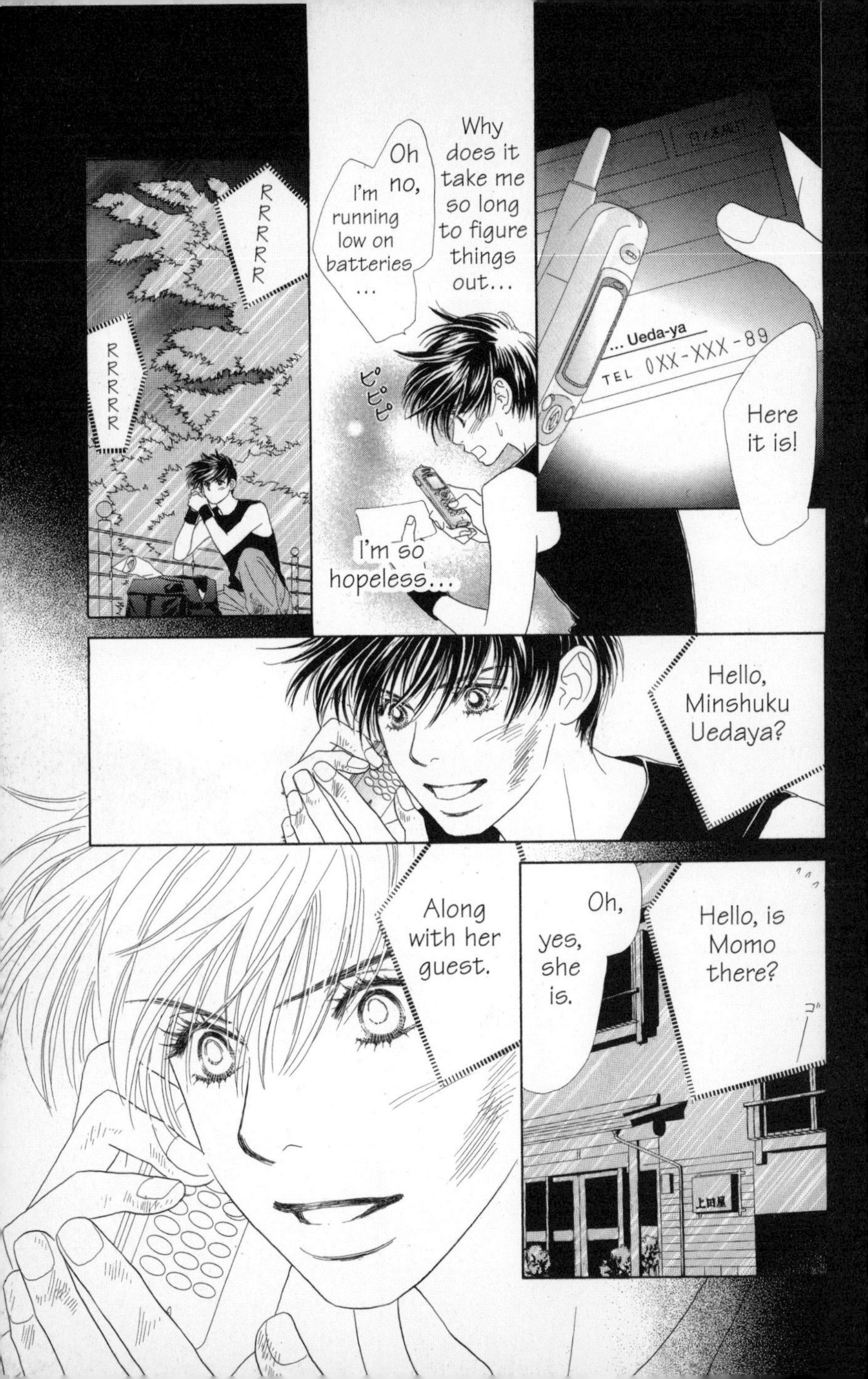
... Ueda-ya
TEL 0XX-XXX-89
Here it is!
Why does it take me so long to figure things out...
Oh no, I'm running low on batteries...
ピピピ
I'm so hopeless...
RRRRR
RRRRR
Hello, Minshuku Uedaya?
Hello, is Momo there?
Oh, yes, she is.
Along with her guest.

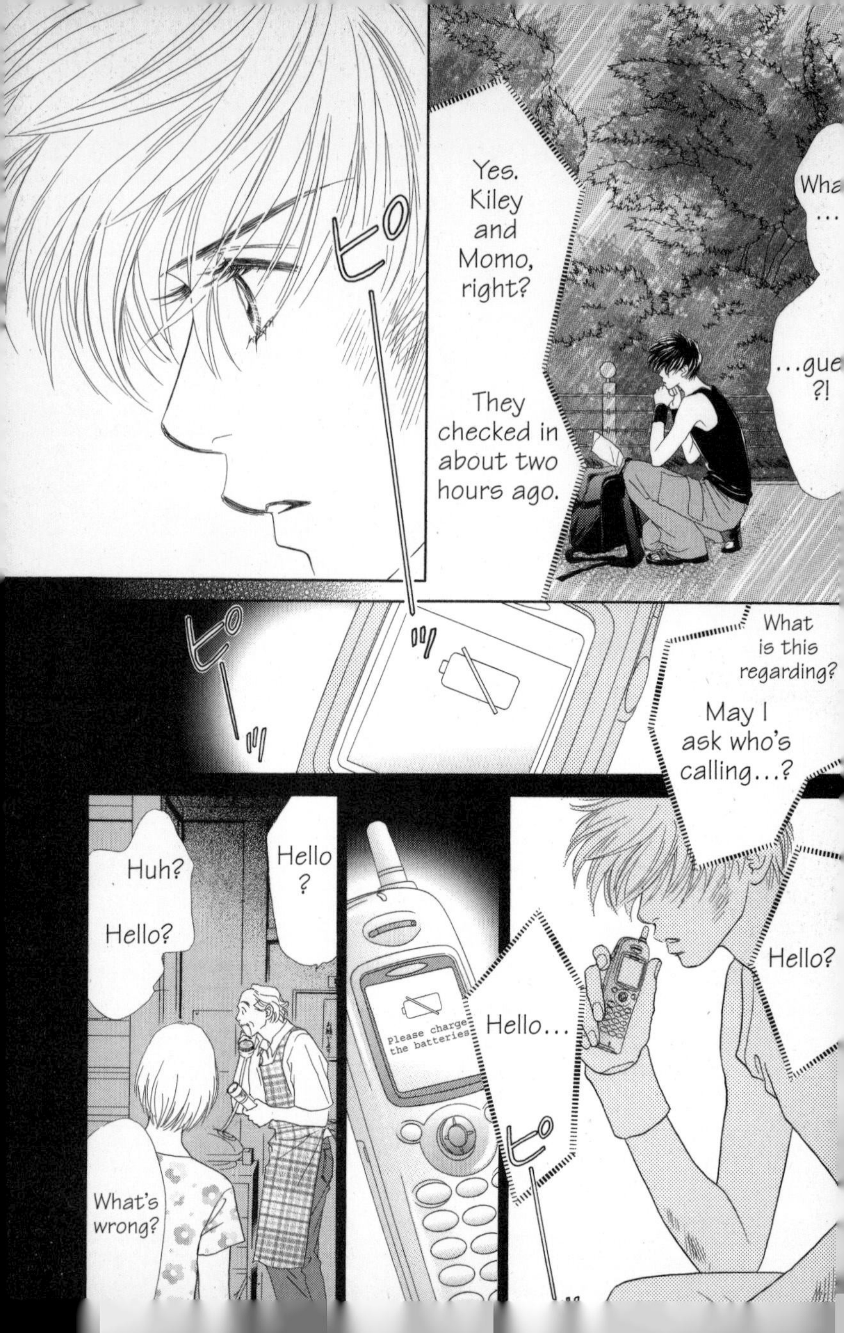
Wha...
...gue ?!
Yes. Kiley and Momo, right?
They checked in about two hours ago.
ピ
What is this regarding?
May I ask who's calling...?
ピーッ
Hello?
Hello...
ピ
Please charge the batteries
Hello?
Huh?
Hello?
What's wrong?

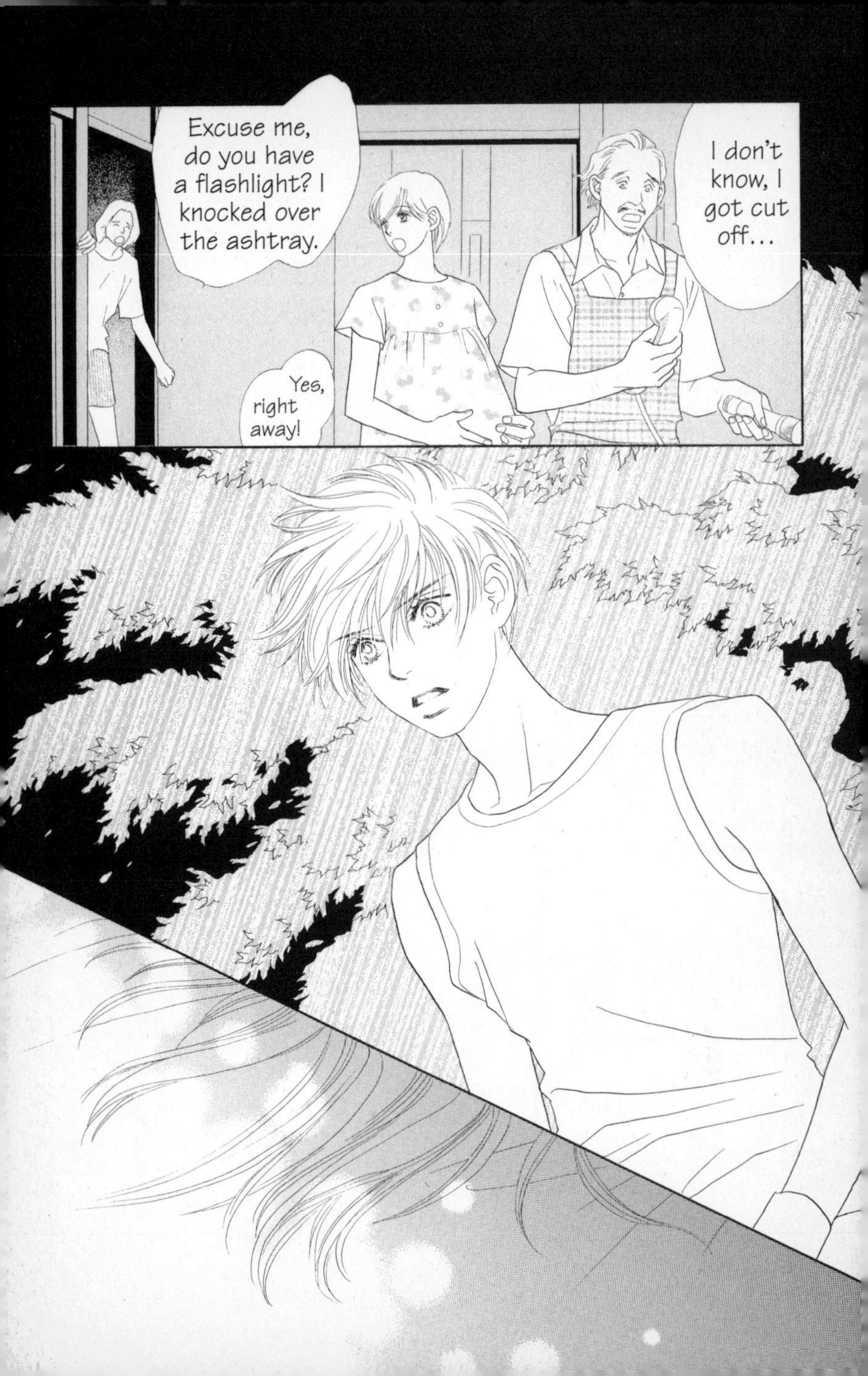
I don't know, I got cut off…
Excuse me, do you have a flashlight? I knocked over the ashtray.
Yes, right away!

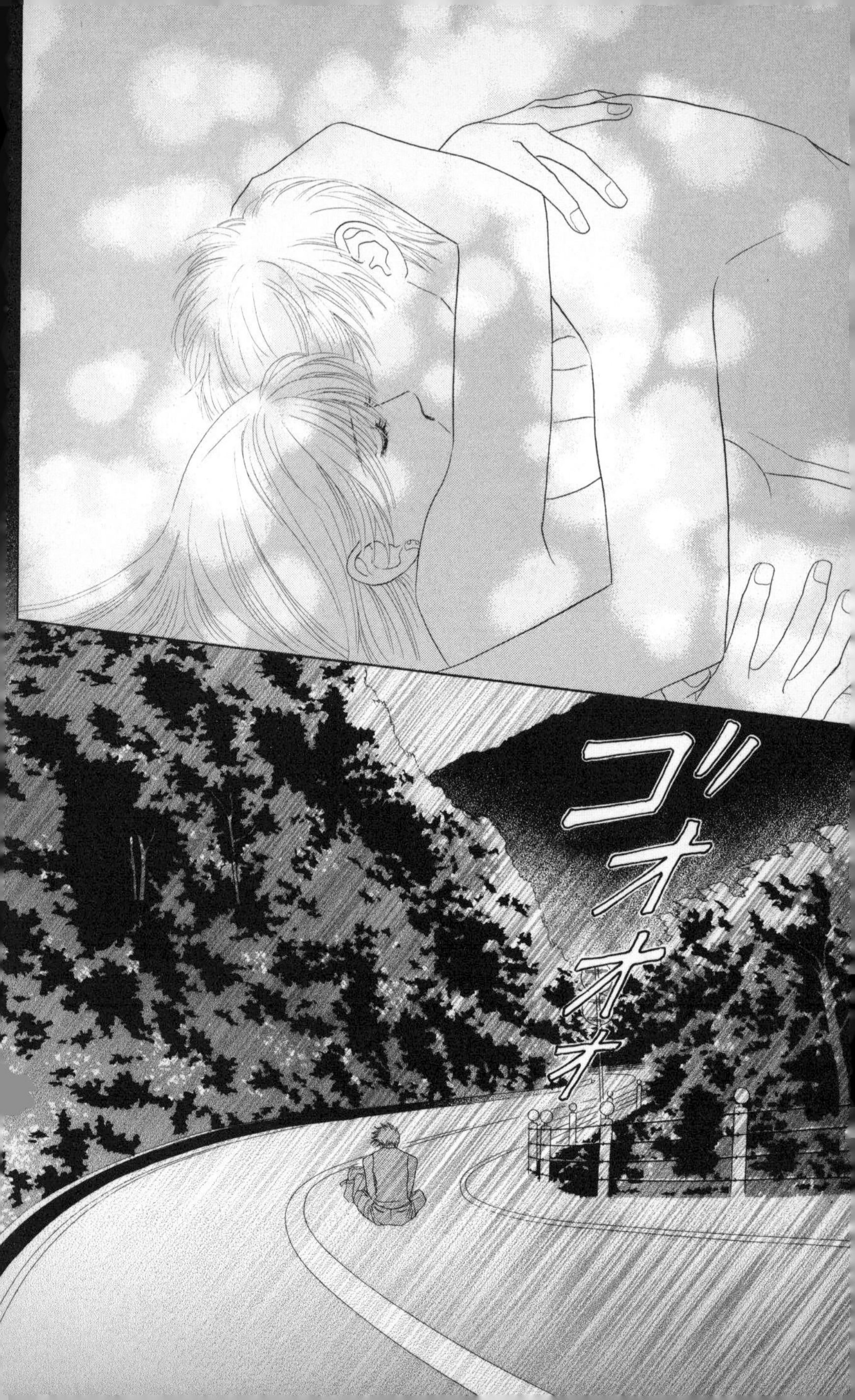
ゴオオオ

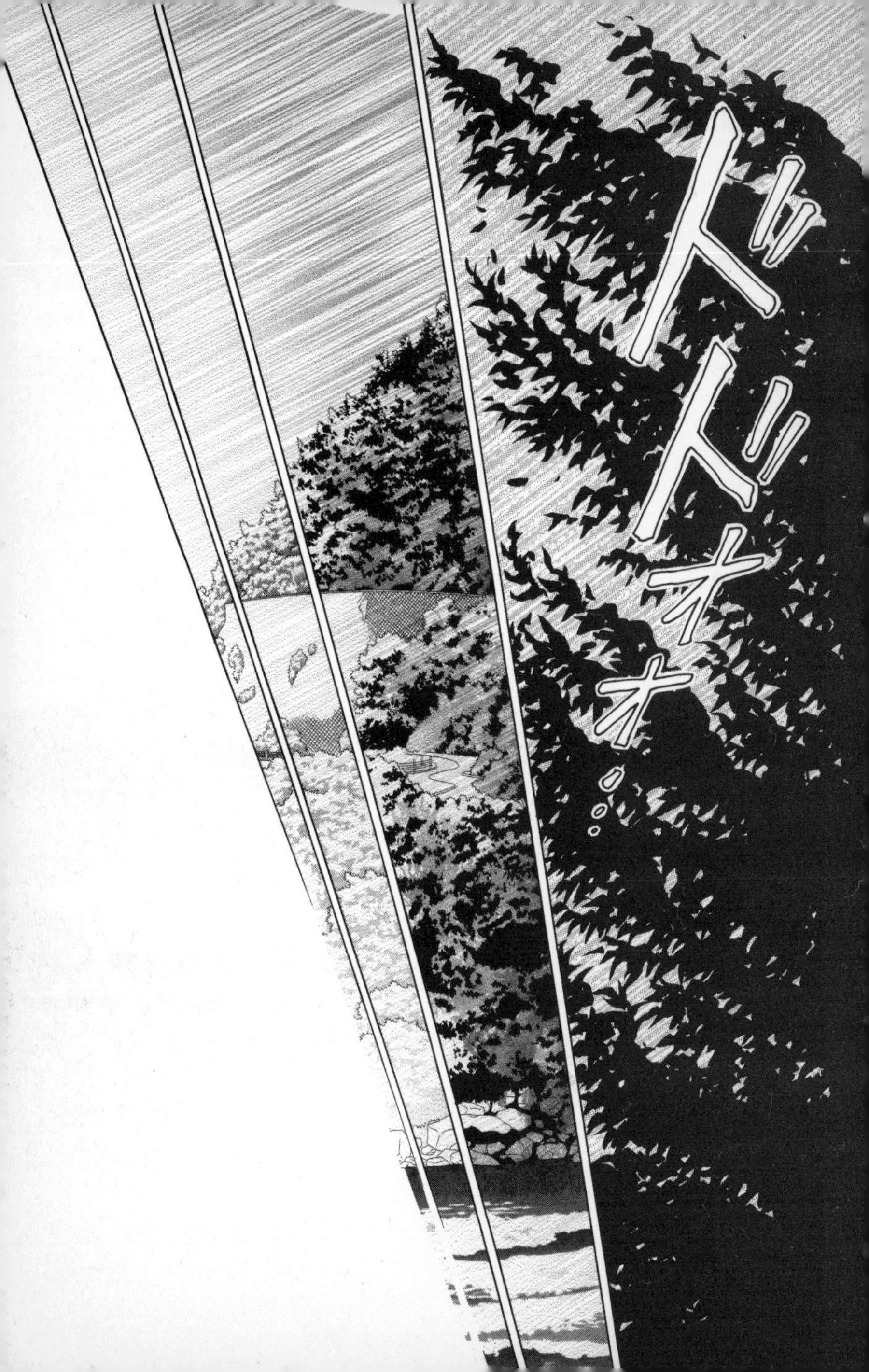
ドドオオ…

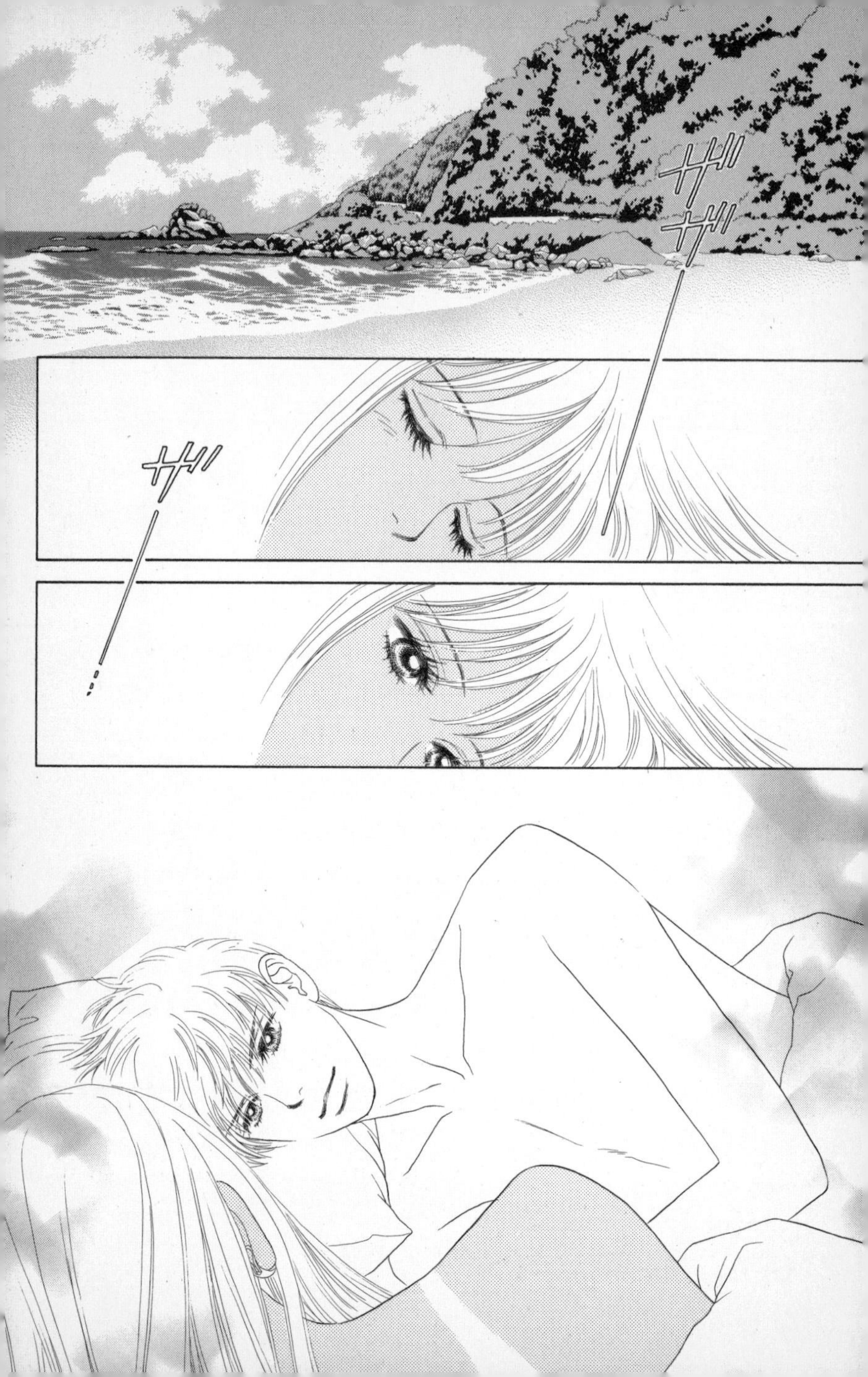
ザザ
ザザ
ザザ…

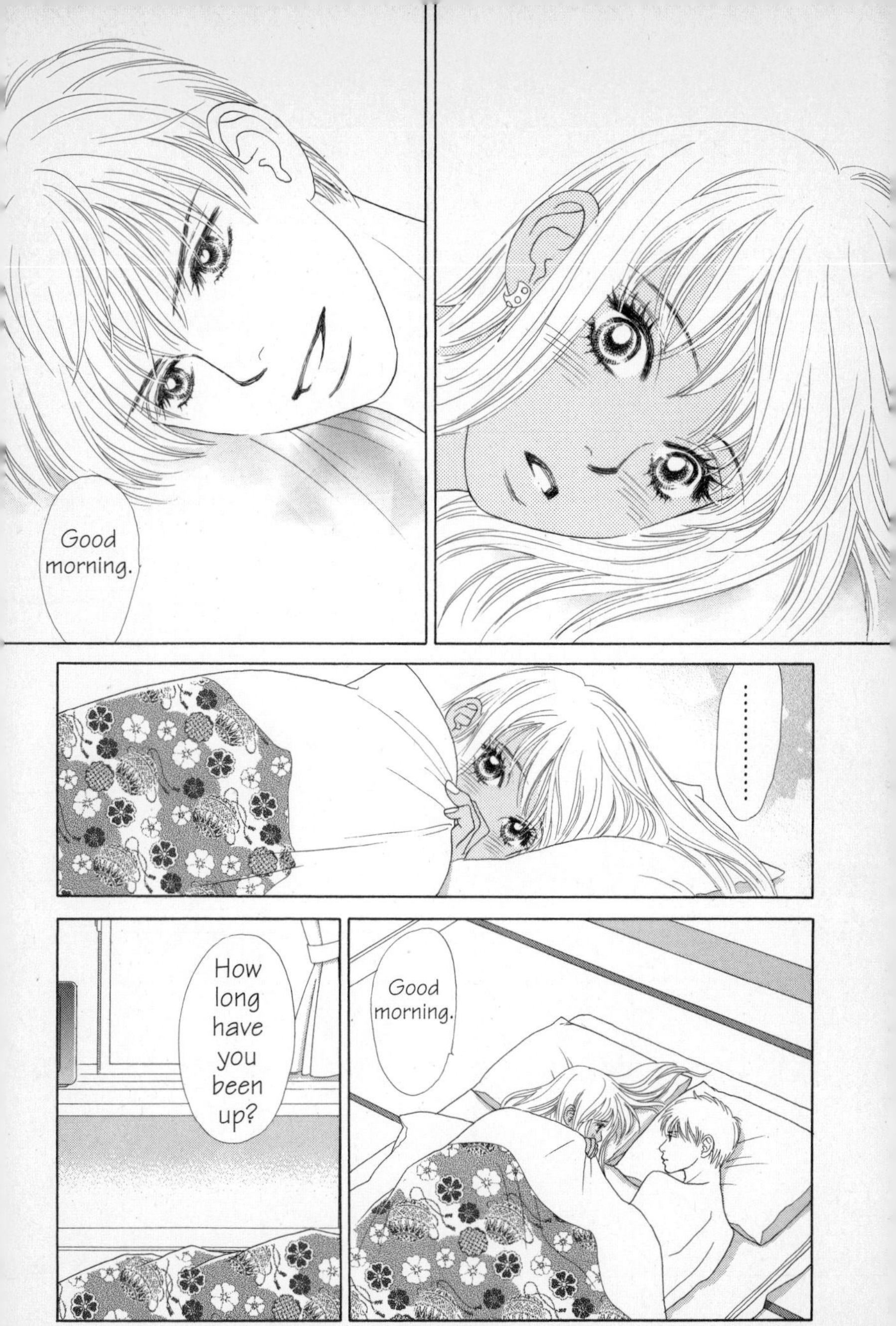
Good morning.
......
Good morning.
How long have you been up?

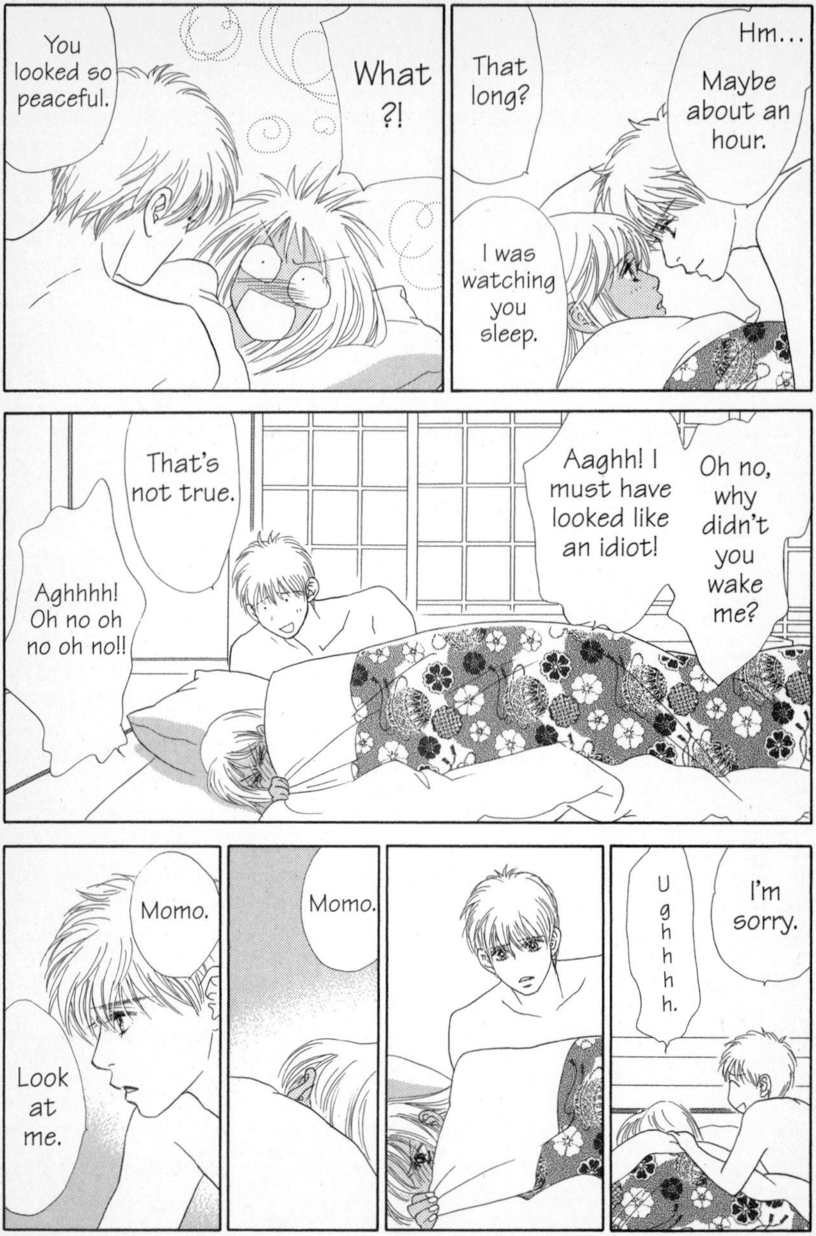
Hm…
Maybe about an hour.
That long?
I was watching you sleep.
What ?!
You looked so peaceful.
Oh no, why didn't you wake me?
Aaghh! I must have looked like an idiot!
That's not true.
Aghhhh! Oh no oh no oh no!!
I'm sorry.
Ughhhh.
Momo.
Momo.
Look at me.

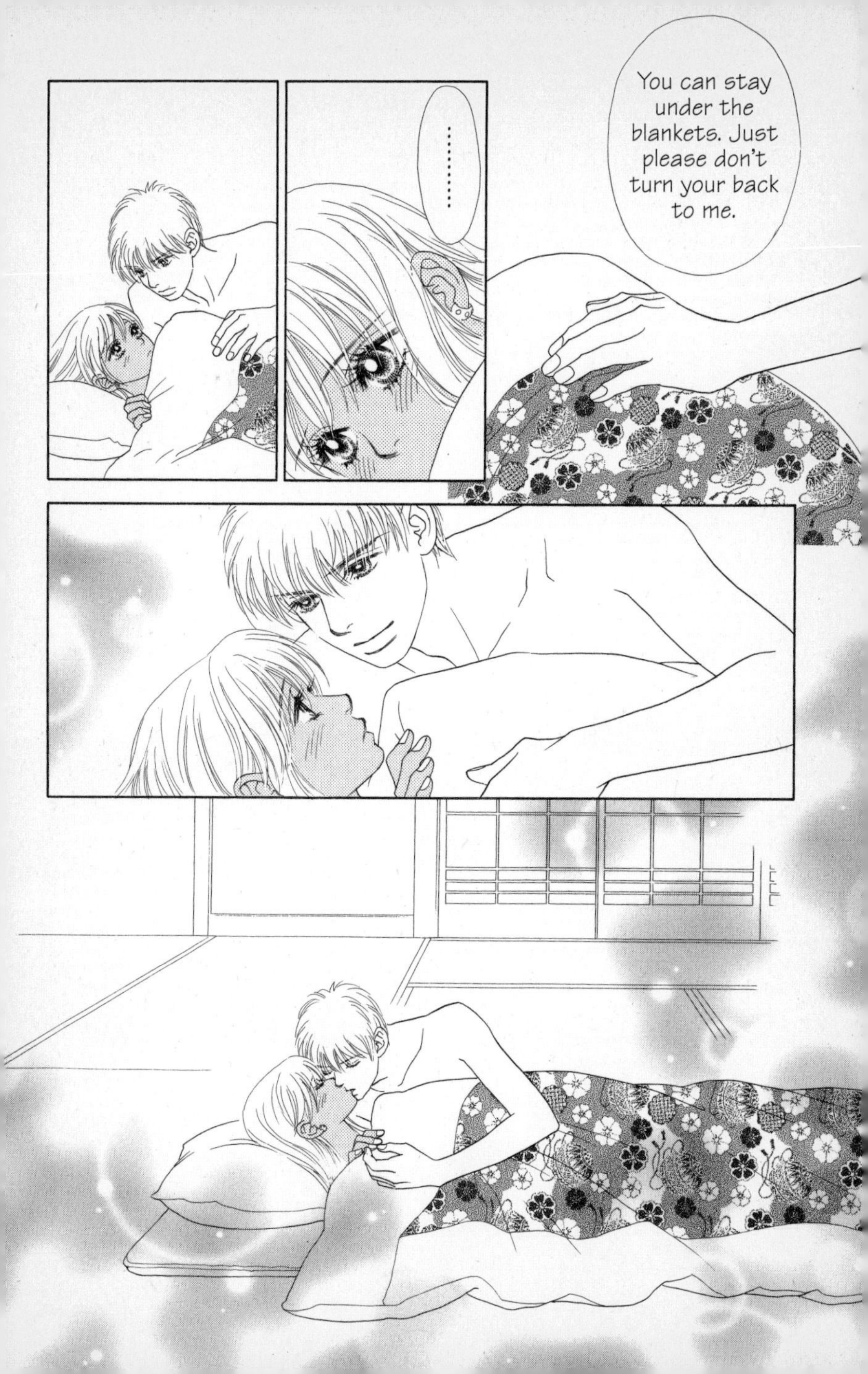
You can stay under the blankets. Just please don't turn your back to me.
......

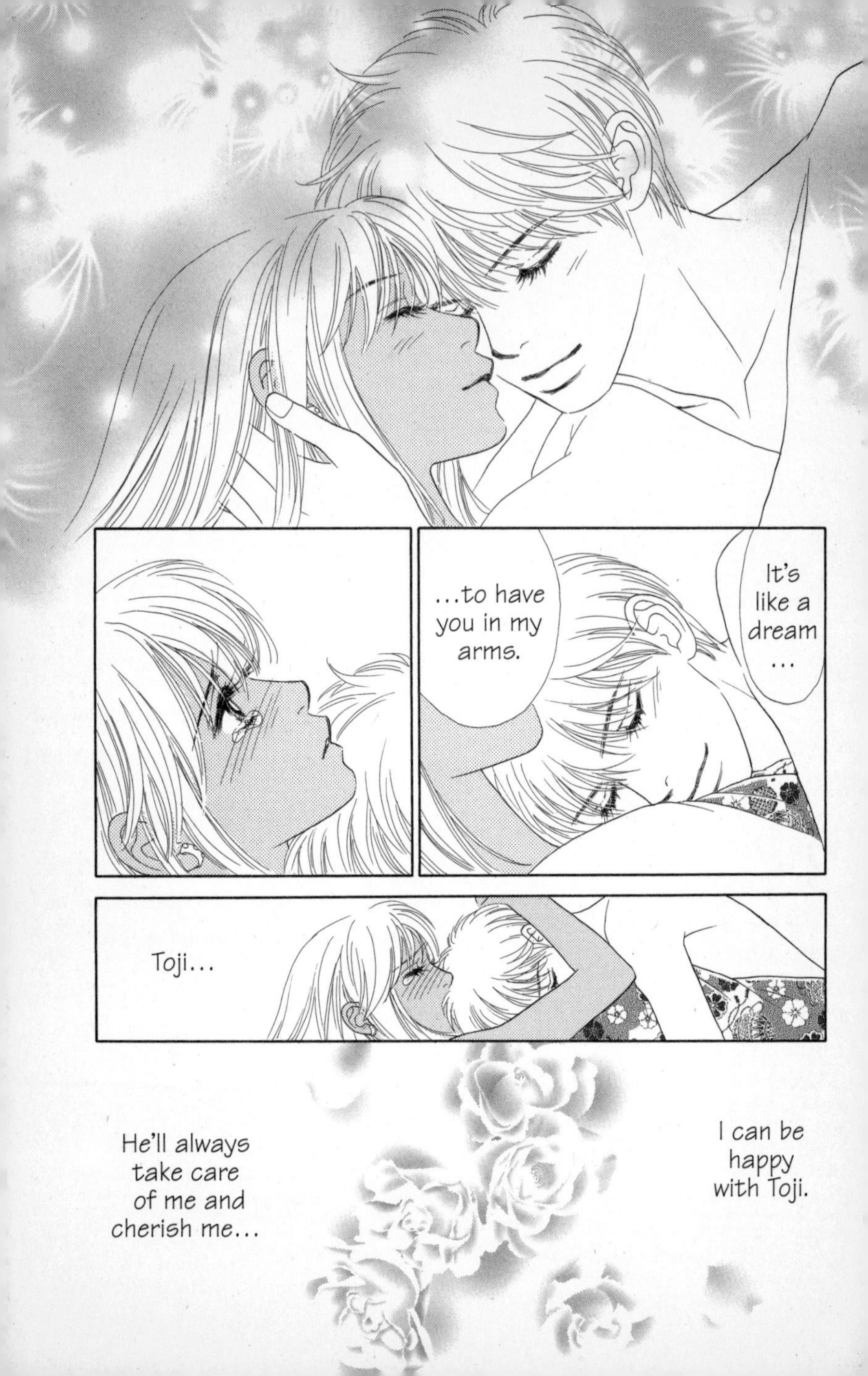
It's like a dream...
...to have you in my arms.
Toji...
I can be happy with Toji.
He'll always take care of me and cherish me...

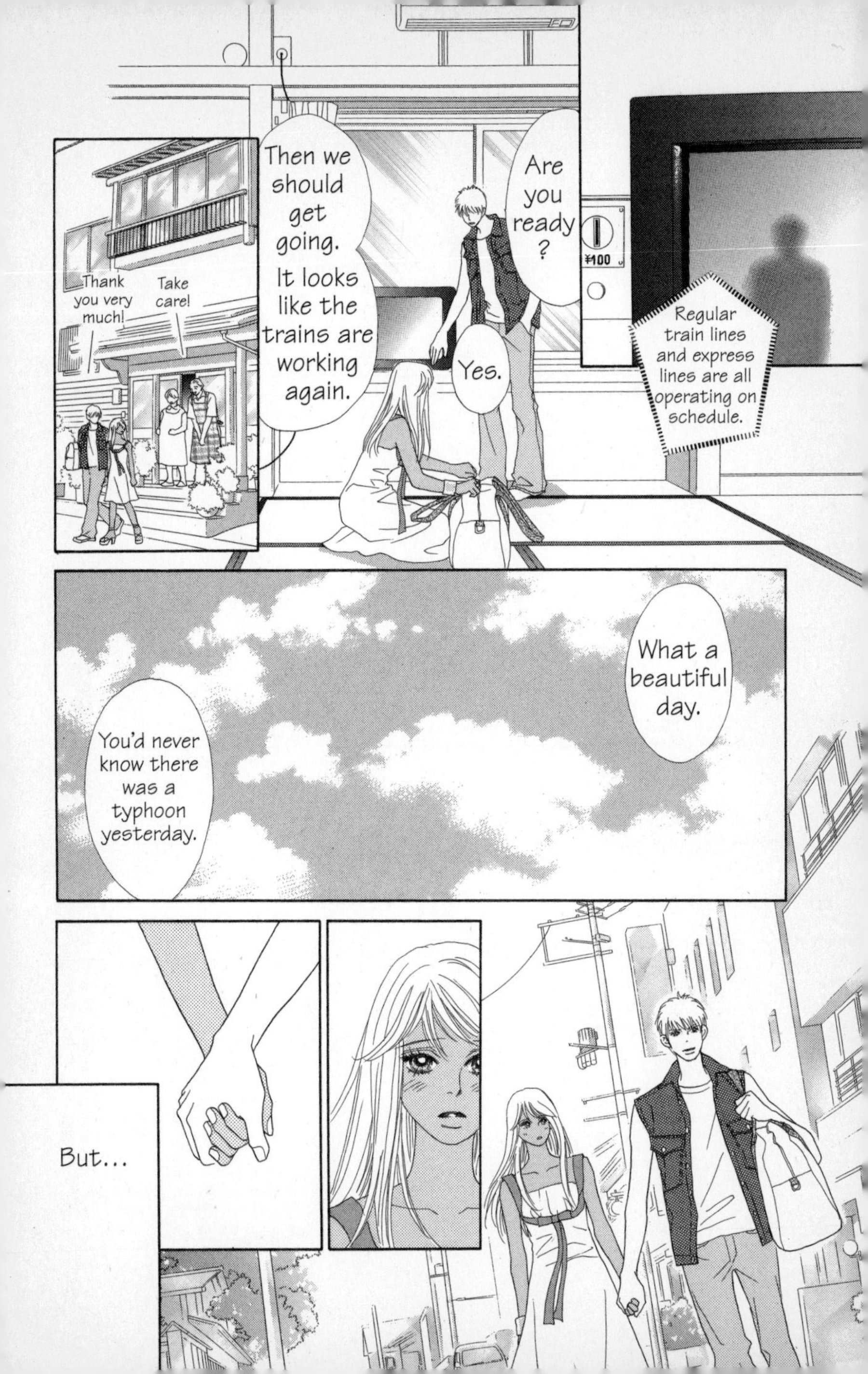
Regular train lines and express lines are all operating on schedule.
Are you ready?
Yes.
Then we should get going. It looks like the trains are working again.
Take care!
Thank you very much!
What a beautiful day.
You'd never know there was a typhoon yesterday.
But...

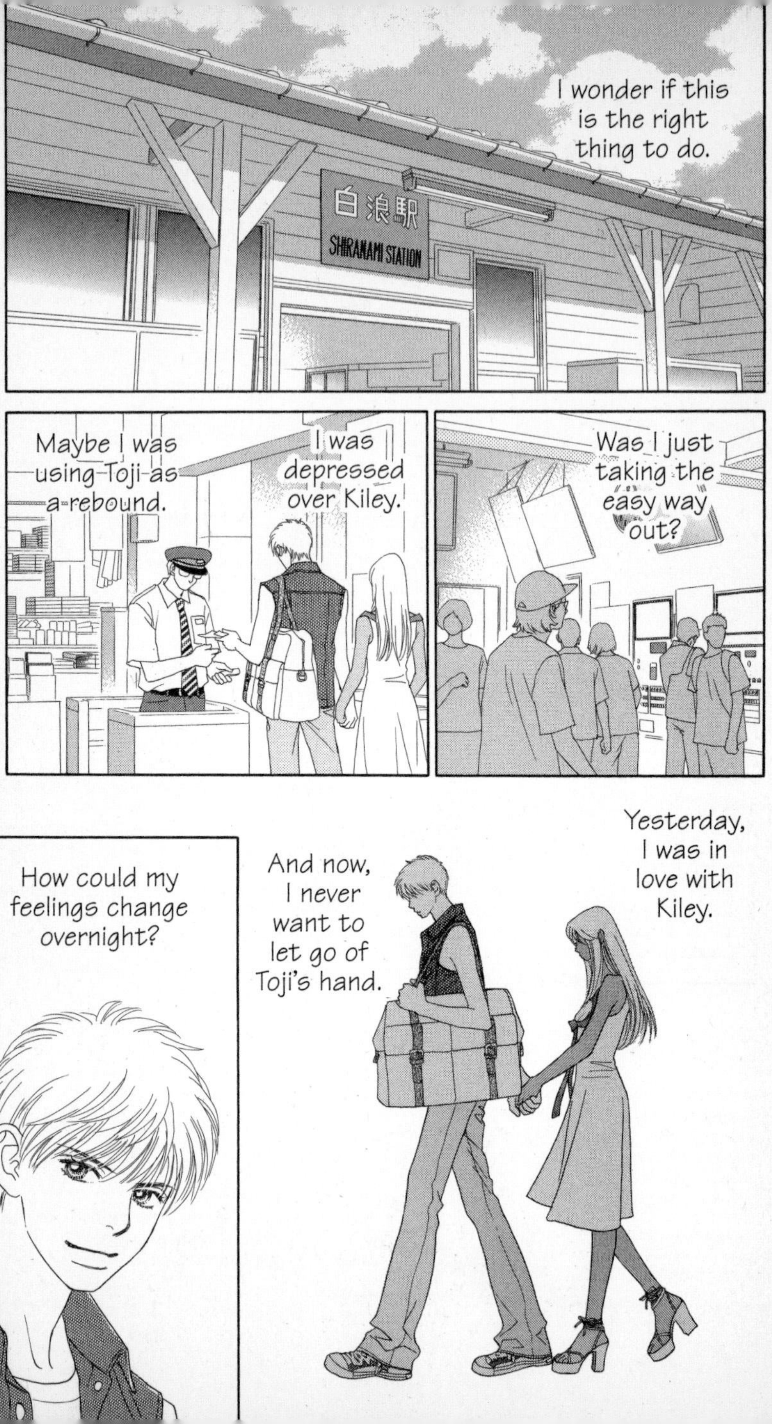
白浪駅
SHIRANAMI STATION
I wonder if this is the right thing to do.
Was I just taking the easy way out?
I was depressed over Kiley.
Maybe I was using Toji as a rebound.
Yesterday, I was in love with Kiley.
And now, I never want to let go of Toji's hand.
How could my feelings change overnight?

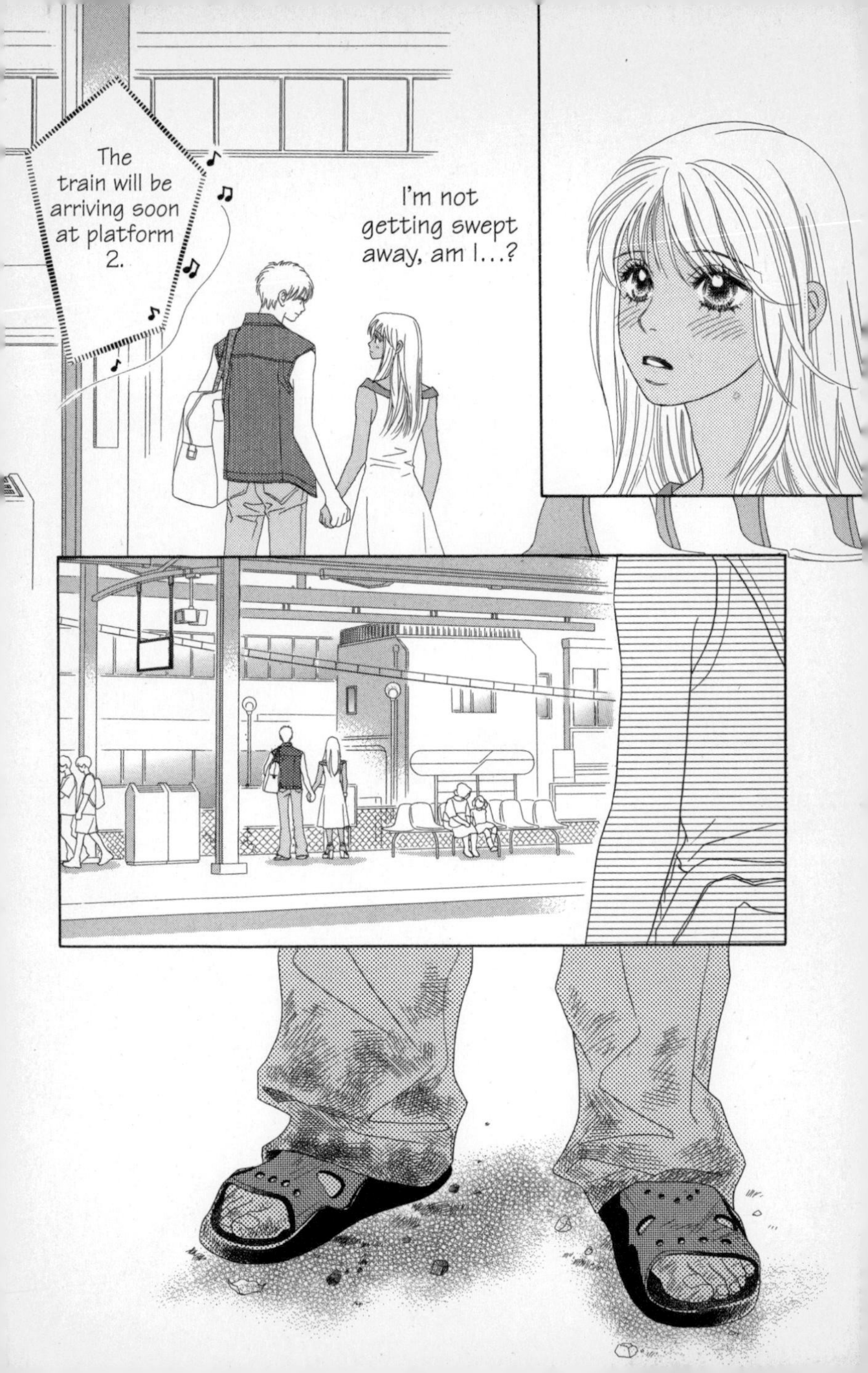
I'm not getting swept away, am I...?
The train will be arriving soon at platform 2.

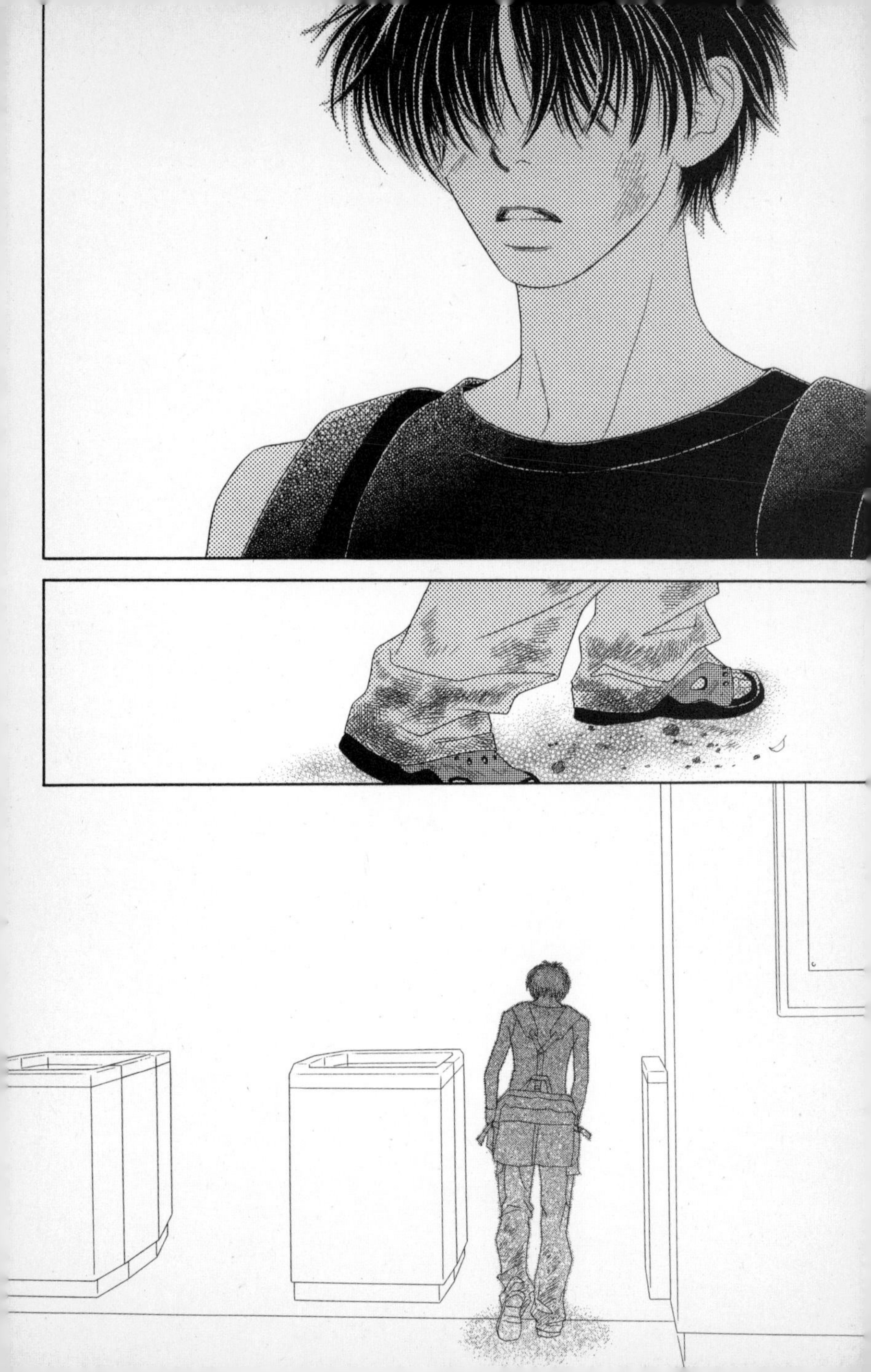

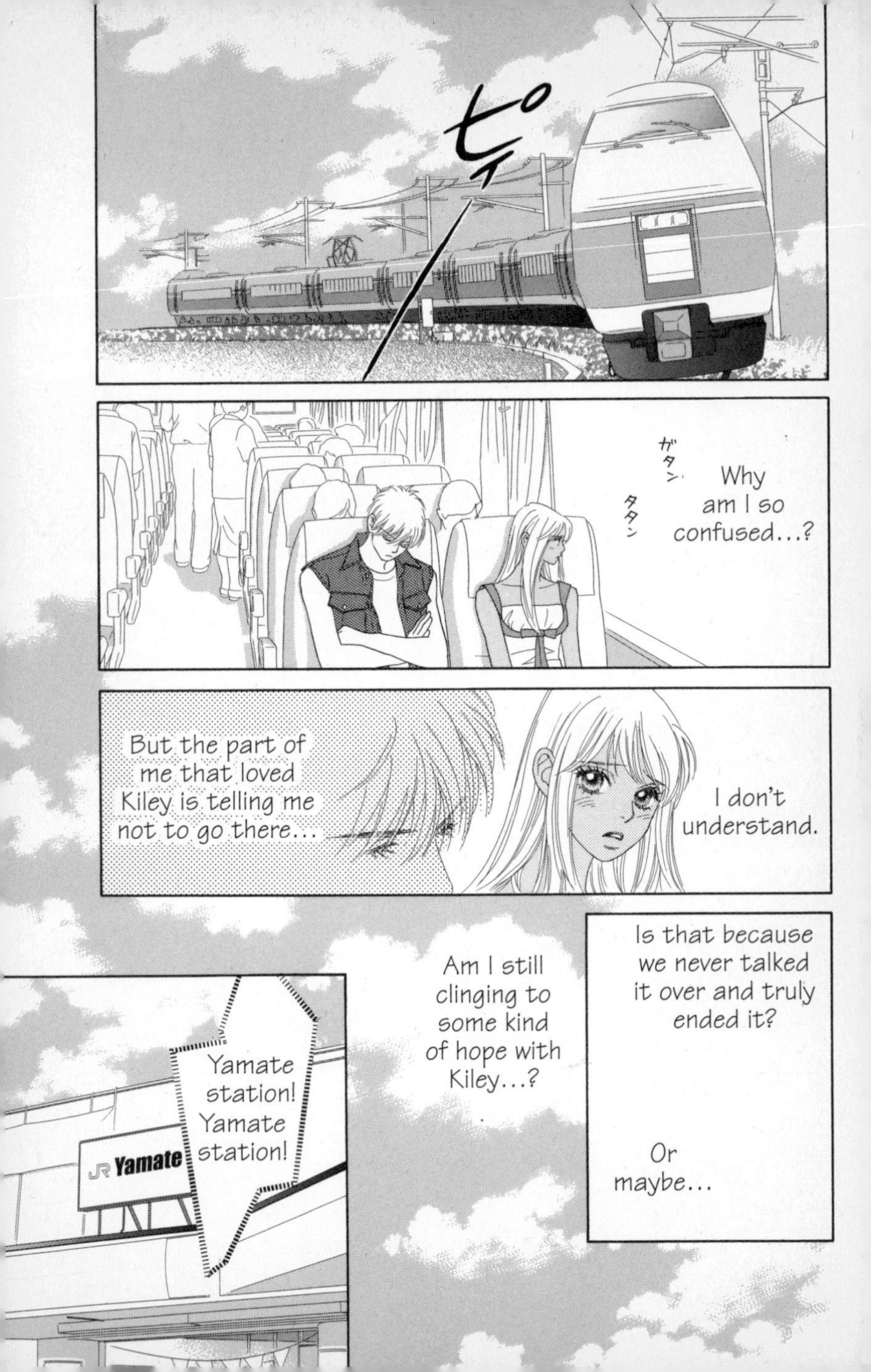
ピィ
ガタン
タタン
Why am I so confused…?
I don't understand.
But the part of me that loved Kiley is telling me not to go there…
Is that because we never talked it over and truly ended it?
Or maybe…
Am I still clinging to some kind of hope with Kiley…?
Yamate station! Yamate station!
JR Yamate

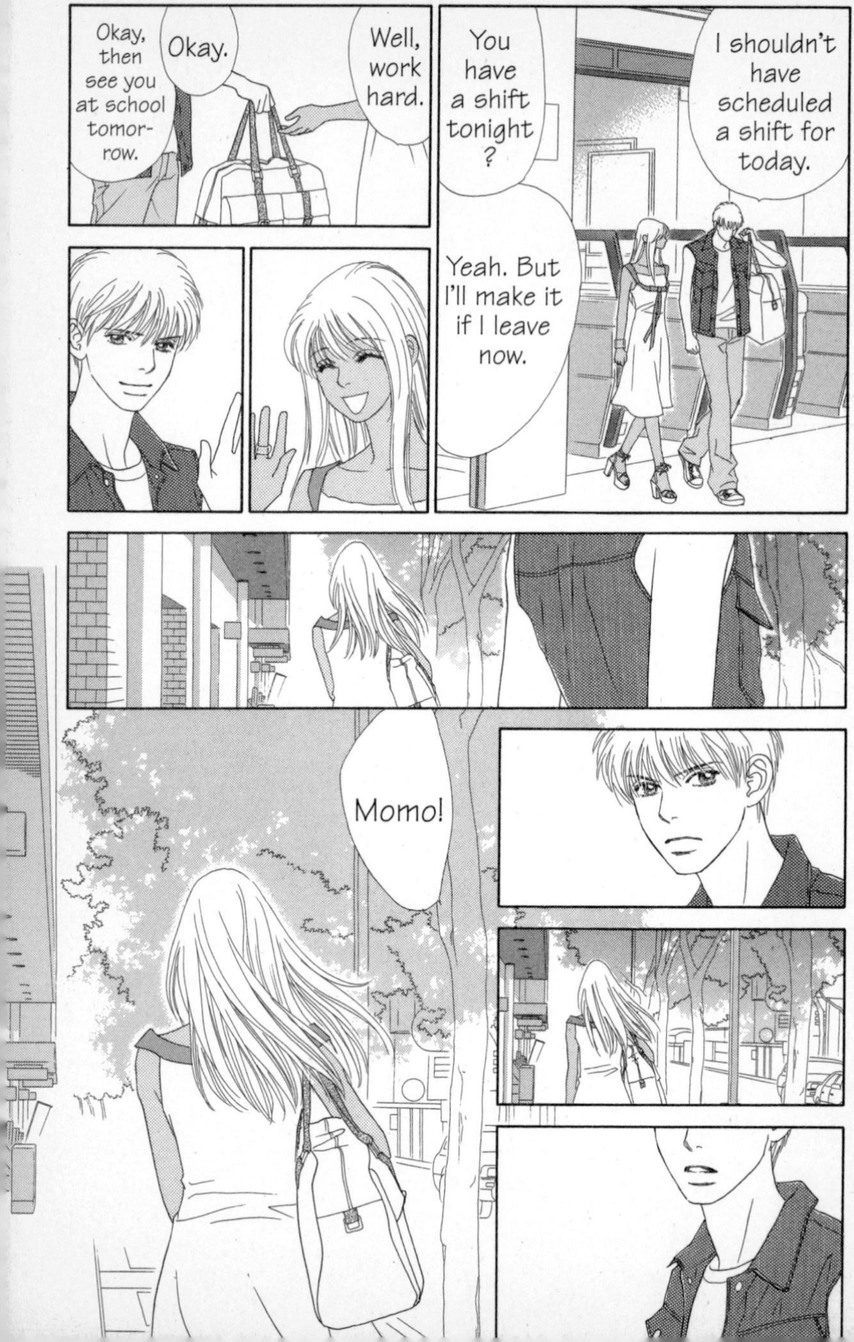
I shouldn't have scheduled a shift for today.
You have a shift tonight?
Yeah. But I'll make it if I leave now.
Well, work hard.
Okay.
Okay, then see you at school tomor-row.
Momo!

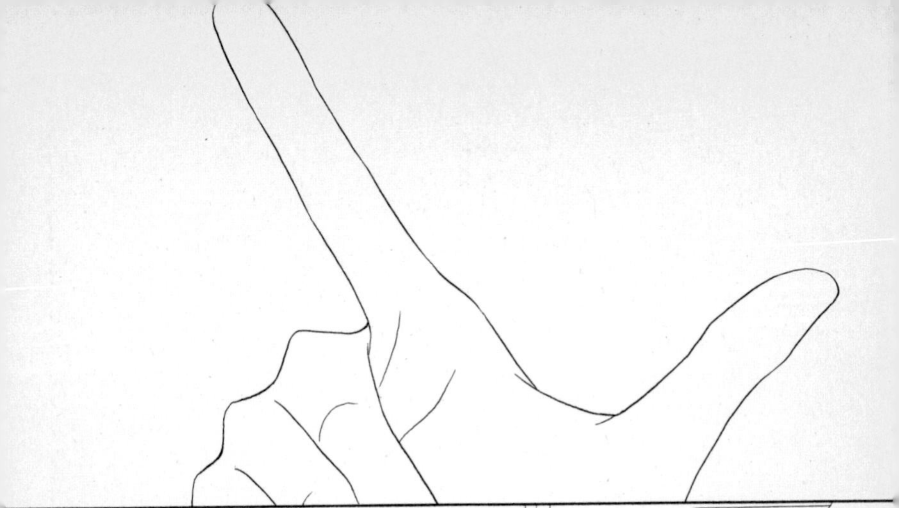

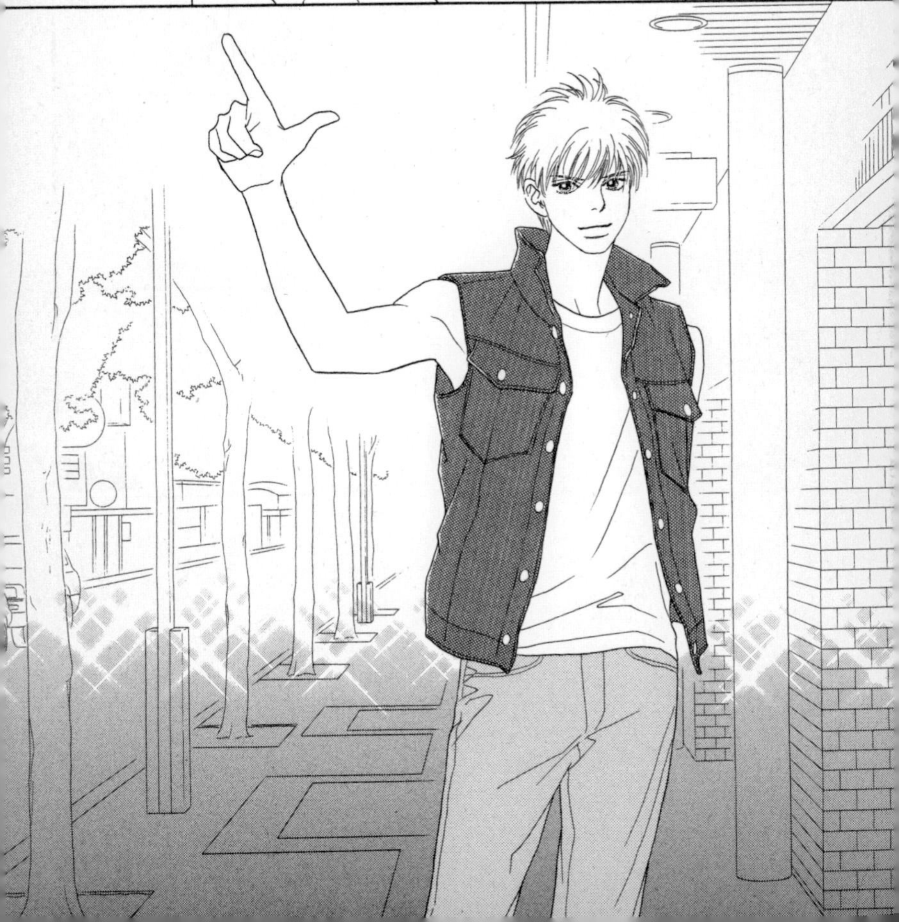

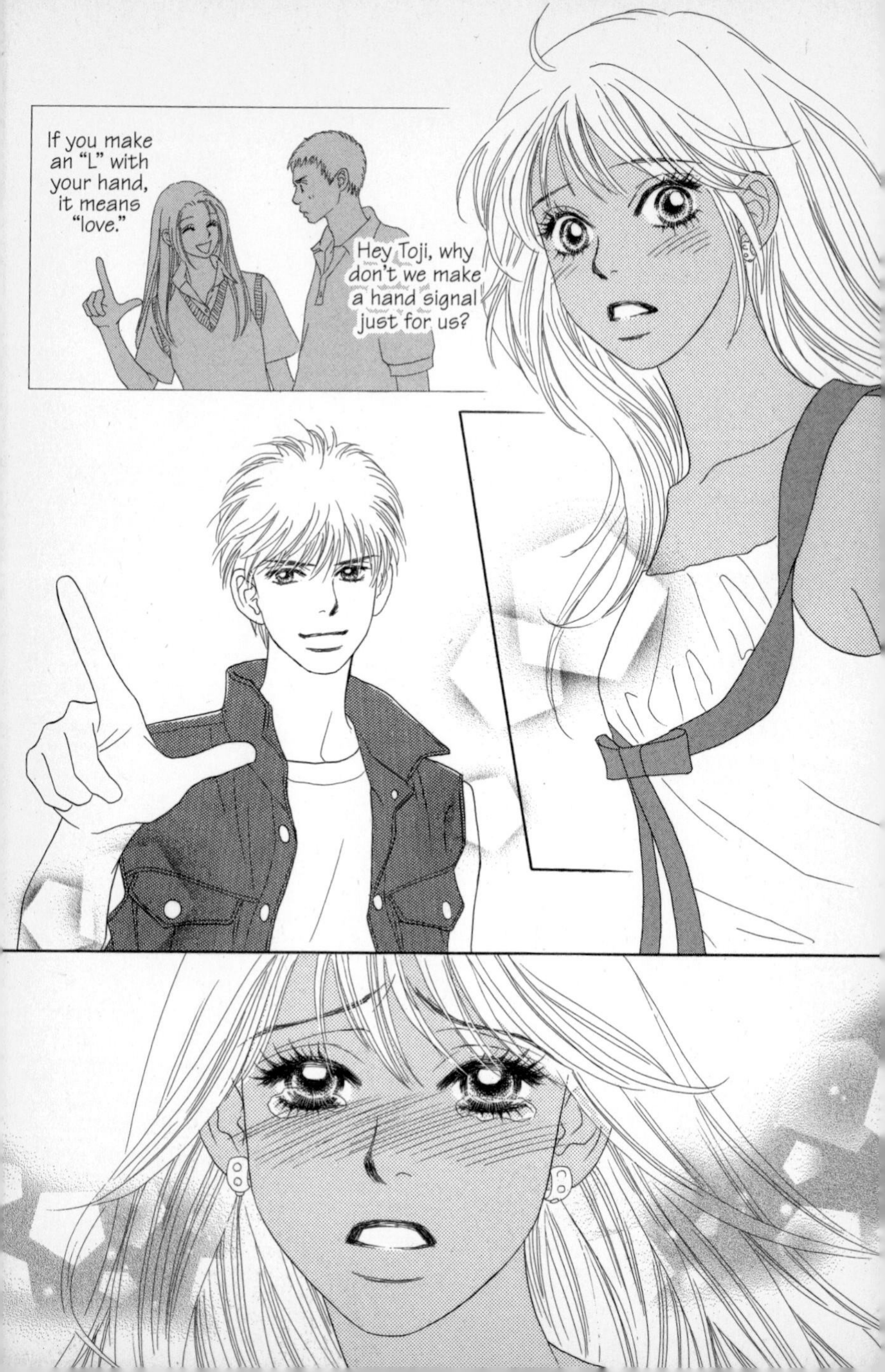
Hey Toji, why don't we make a hand signal just for us?
If you make an "L" with your hand, it means "love."

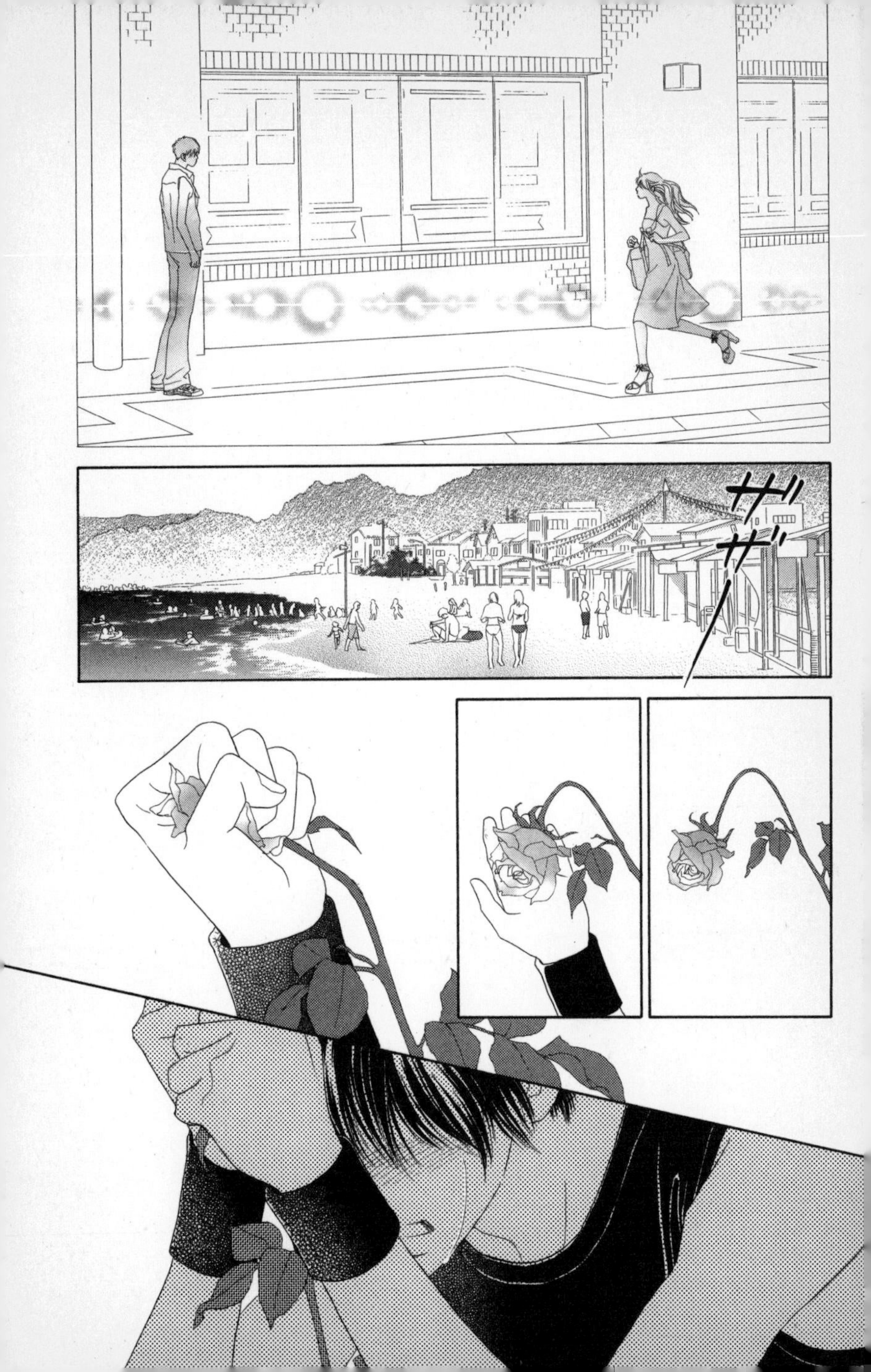
ザザー

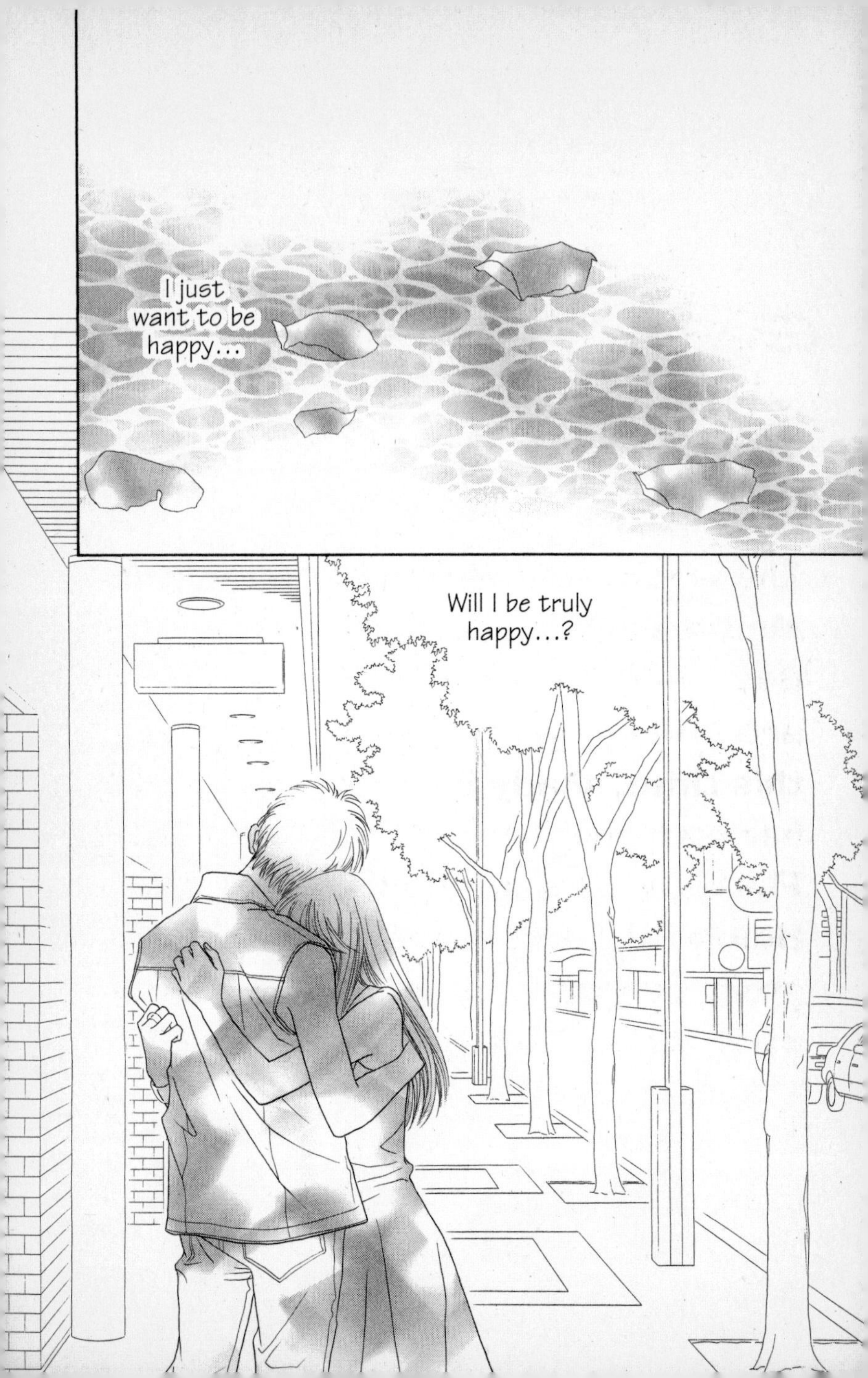
I just want to be happy...
Will I be truly happy...?

COMING SOON IN

Peach Girl
Change of Heart

The whole school can't believe who Momo shows up with on their first day...is it Toji or Kiley? Both hotties are still vying for Momo's heart but this time, shady Sae's too busy with her own problems to get in the way! Find out in Peach Girl: Change of Heart volume 8 what karma has in store for Sae and Ryo as they confront a life-changing decision!

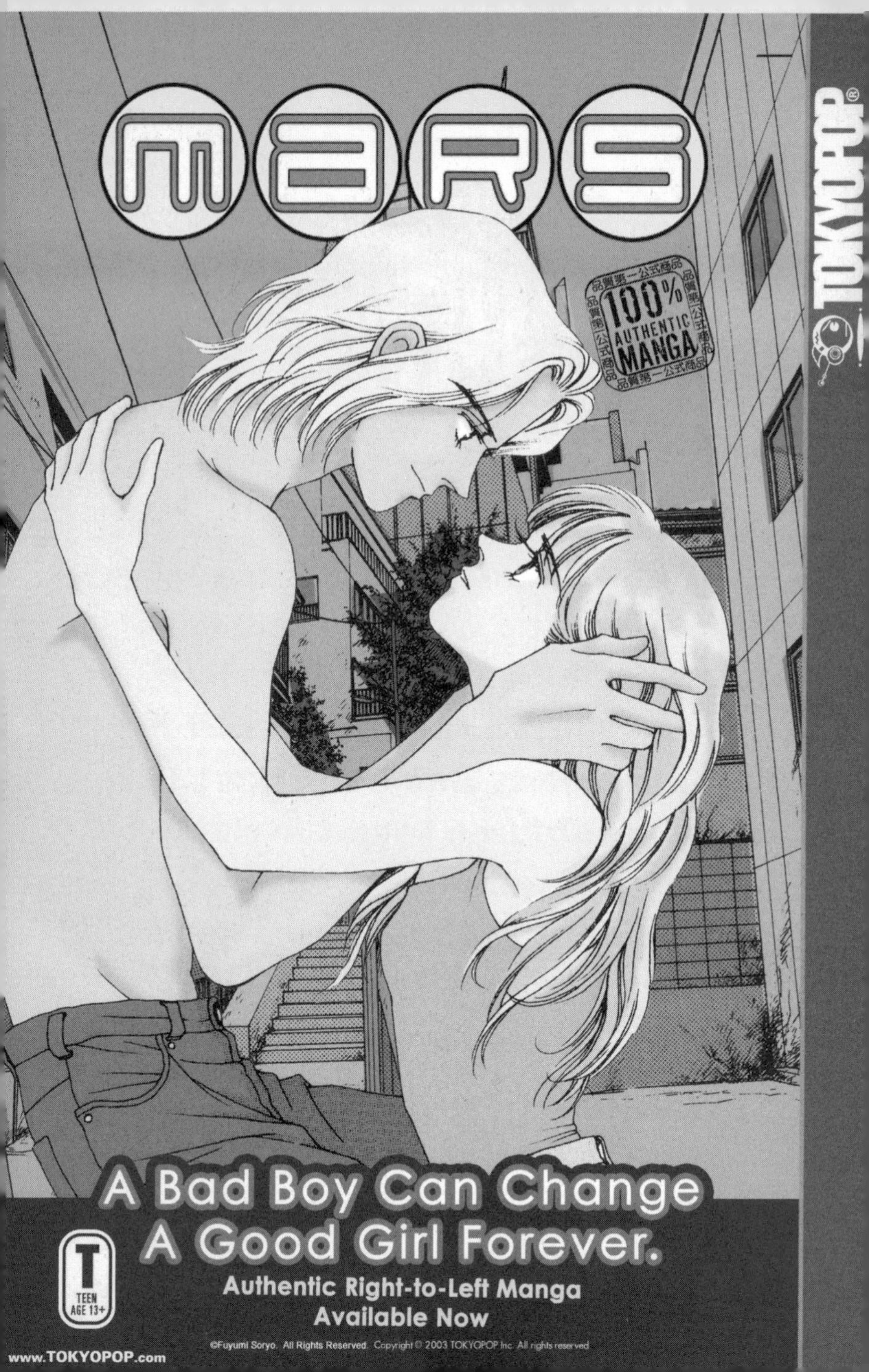
MARS
100% AUTHENTIC MANGA
品質第一公式商品
TOKYOPOP
A Bad Boy Can Change
A Good Girl Forever.
Authentic Right-to-Left Manga
Available Now
T
TEEN
AGE 13+
©Fuyumi Soryo. All Rights Reserved. Copyright © 2003 TOKYOPOP Inc. All rights reserved.
www.TOKYOPOP.com

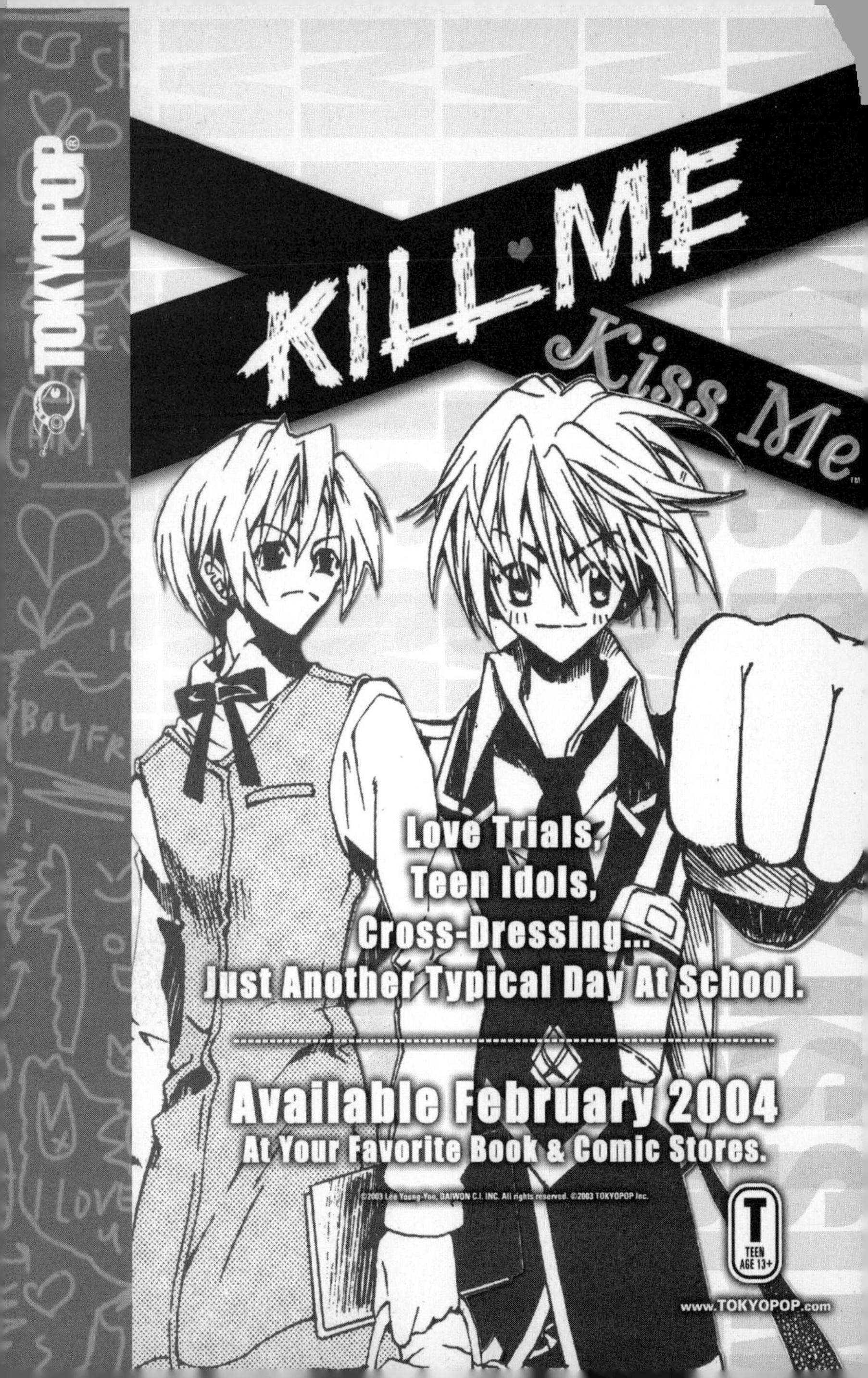
TOKYOPOP
KILL ME
Kiss Me
Love Trials,
Teen Idols,
Cross-Dressing...
Just Another Typical Day At School.
Available February 2004
At Your Favorite Book & Comic Stores.
©2003 Lee Young-Yoo, DAIWON C.I. INC. All rights reserved. ©2003 TOKYOPOP Inc.
T
TEEN AGE 13+
www.TOKYOPOP.com

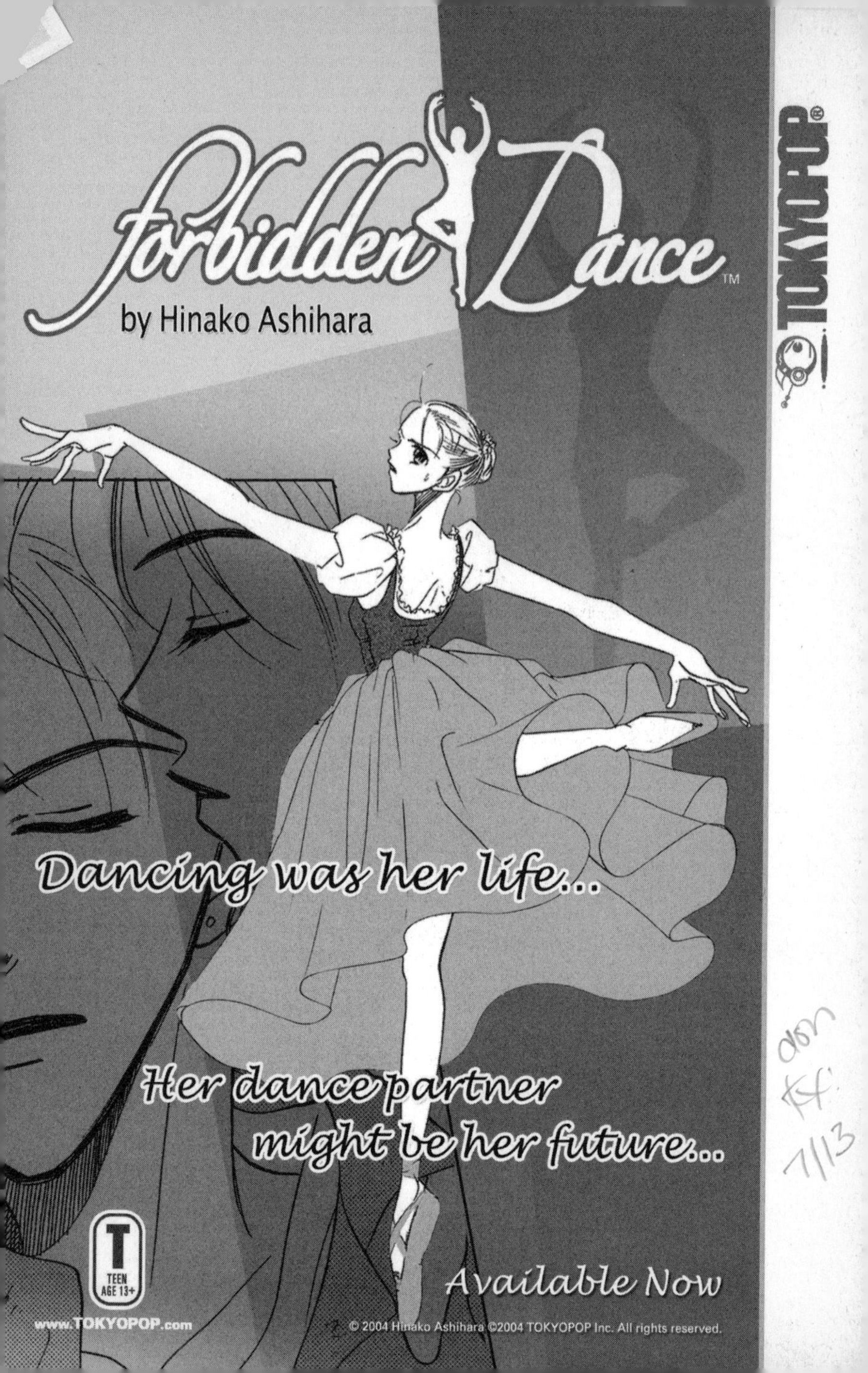

Forbidden Dance™
by Hinako Ashihara
TOKYOPOP®
Dancing was her life...
Her dance partner
might be her future...
T
TEEN
AGE 13+
Available Now
www.TOKYOPOP.com
© 2004 Hinako Ashihara ©2004 TOKYOPOP Inc. All rights reserved.